Christian Materialism

Robert J. Cormier

Theological Press, Inc.
New York

Christian Materialism
copyright © 1987 by Robert J. Cormier

ISBN 0-9618442-0-5

Published by Theological Press, Inc.
286 Fifth Avenue
New York, New York 10001
Printed in the USA

Table of Contents

Preface

Christian Materialism is a response to the crisis of faith which has gripped the West. It explains this crisis in terms of a divergence of "world" and religious thought having its origins during the Renaissance. It aims to cure this crisis in a reconciliation of world and religious thought—a theological leap forward like those for which we remember Augustine and Thomas Aquinas, but greater than both combined.

I apologize for this outrageous claim; but you rarely make your point unless you point it out. In any case, the facts now follow and they will speak for themselves.

I have but one more apology. *Christian Materialism* is the product of much reflection and many drafts. It could have been rewritten many more times—and not without profit. Yet, there comes a time when one must acknowledge that good is good enough, accept the essential imperfection in anything of this world, and present his work for the judgment of his fellows.

The rest I leave to God's providence.

Robert J. Cormier

April, 1987
Rutherford, New Jersey

Introduction

An Introduction to the Idea

In 1859, Charles Darwin published *The Origin of Species.* The work was his explanation of "evolution," any idea that the species were produced by the gradual development of more primitive forms of life. According to Darwin, evolution was propelled by what he called "natural selection," the supposed fact that the struggle for survival will always be won by the "fittest" of every litter. Steadily, Darwin argued, this saw to the structural improvement of primitive species. With time, it saw to the development of whole new structures. Where the demands of survival favored different improvements, different species eventually emerged. With more time, these evolved into the various species that now exist.

To be sure, the idea of evolution had not originated with Darwin. Indeed, Anaximander had spoken of evolution as early as the 7th century B.C. Though it was soon to be forgotten, evolution had begun to reappear in the writings of a number of 19th century scientists trying to answer the newly perplexing question of the origin of the species. Darwin is remembered because it was he who amassed a body of evidence to support the idea of evolution so great it could not be ignored. It was he who advanced the then most plausible way to account for this evidence, the process of natural selection. And finally, it was he whose book brought the entire matter to public attention.

Although *The Origin of Species* did not state that the origin of man could be attributed to the same processes to which it attributed the origin of all other species, the implication was no less clear. Moreover, this implication was immediately recognized by nearly everyone who came to hear of Darwin's work. It was only partly for this reason that both the theory and its author were condemned by Christians of all kinds.

To most Christians, the theory of evolution was the first attack their faith had ever faced. The theory held that the various species were the product of evolution, a natural process requiring millions upon millions of years. This was not the teaching of the Bible. Genesis said that the heavens, the earth, and everything in it had been created by God in six days. It told of man's creation out of clay. To the minds of most Christians, if Darwin was right, the Bible was wrong. If so, it could not be the inspired, inerrant word of God upon which Christian doctrine depends. Furthermore, inasmuch as evolution explained the origin of species by a *natural* process, it appeared to deny the necessity of a Creator

— God Himself. If this were not enough, in its implicit explanation of the origin of man, the theory considered him the descendant of primitive primates. In any case, any attribution of man to the ancestry of lower forms of life seemed to all but explicitly deny him his human, and immortal, soul.

To most churchmen, and here specific reference is being made to Catholic churchmen, Darwin's theory was hardly a first attack upon their faith. As they saw it, the Church had never been without its enemies; Darwin was simply the latest. Always the Church had prevailed; always it would. Yet, as they were also aware, the Church was currently in the midst of what had already been three centuries of a decline that had begun with the defection of Martin Luther. As yet, little had successfully been done to stop this decline and now the theory of evolution would only make things worse. Despite this, they were still sure that the Church would eventually prevail. They could not doubt that its teachings were true.

Institutionally speaking, the Church could not have thought otherwise. It considered itself the one true Church instituted by Jesus Christ in order to continue His work — principally to preach, and therefore to teach, the saving revelation of God to man. Therefore, it was sure to have expected and perceived His heavenly guidance and protection. Obviously, this included the divine guarantee that the Church would not teach error.

To be clear, this guarantee (or "infallibility") was taught to be no substitute for believing the Sacred Scriptures. The Church taught that the Scriptures were the inspired, inerrant word of God. It taught that they were written in order to preserve revelation. But, since any scriptural passage can be interpreted in a host of different if not contradictory ways, the good use of Scripture obviously depended upon the divine guidance to interpret it correctly. Furthermore, even though the Scriptures preserved all that man needed to know, they were not believed to spell out all that God wanted him to know. Certain truths were preserved in the form of an unwritten but still Sacred Tradition that the Church had faithfully passed down from the apostles. Though these truths were implicitly taught in Scripture, they might not have been noticed had they not been taught by Tradition. Thus, the actual guarantee of their truth was the fact that the Church transmitted them, especially if they were accepted by a formal act of Church teaching — an act of the "magisterium" — the ultimate *earthly* source of what is true.

It was the issue of Sacred Tradition and, specifically, its citation in support of the doctrine of Indulgences, that led to Luther's successful break with the Church of his Baptism. Though his dispute with the Church also involved the more fundamental notions of grace and faith, it soon became a dispute over the authority of the Church *per se.* The result was the Protestant Reformation and its rejection of that authority in favor of an insistence upon the supreme authority of the Bible.

But soon after the Reformation, Catholics and Protestants began to encounter a rejection of even those beliefs they held in common. With the intellectual "Renaissance," and later "Enlightenment," of Western Europe had come an increasing hostility to almost any mention of the supernatural, the invisible, or anything else that could not be proved scientifically. In increasing numbers, members of the educated sector of society began to support an almost complete attribution of the Scriptures to fable or fabrication with little or no historical basis. Though this did not always involve a denial of some sort of God, for a growing number, it did. Of late, the still increasing hostility to anything that could not be seen had even come to include a denial that man is comprised of body and soul. To most churchmen, Catholic or not, the theory of evolution appeared to support these developments across the board.

Therefore, it should not be surprising that evolution was condemned by almost every churchman. To most, the issue could not have been more clear; it was *The Origin of Species* or the Bible, evolution or creation, Darwin or God. Though some sought to challenge Darwin's theory on the basis of criticisms offered by his colleagues in the scientific community, most made clear that they did not understand his theory and, unwittingly or not, misrepresented it, subjecting it to the most ridiculous of critique and caricature.

It was all to no avail. Although the ensuing decades of scientific debate did identify serious problems with the theory of natural selection — especially with respect to its inability to account for many of the more complex structures that creatures possess — a number of complementary processes came to be suggested. Theories of evolution were even offered to explain the way the most primitive life-forms might have emerged out of non-living matter. Meanwhile, the evidence to support the idea of evolution *per se* continued to mount. Though scientists were by no means convinced that they had discovered all of the dynamisms by which to explain it, they were all but universally agreed that evolution had taken place. It was fast becoming impossible for an educated, intellectually honest person to disagree.

For a time, churchmen found themselves upon the horns of a serious dilemma. It was becoming impossible to deny the evidence. Yet, it seemed that to accept the evidence would be to admit that the Scriptures and the magisterium had been wrong. This neither could they do.

In the face of this dilemma, certain religious thinkers (or "theologians," those who do "theology") began to consider the possibility that evolution did not require them to abandon their religious beliefs. They began to consider the idea that evolution and creation were not so mutually exclusive as first had been feared. Perhaps it was not evolution *or* creation, but creation *by means* of evolution. After all, evolution might explain the origin of the species but it could never explain itself; it could never explain the existence of a universe in which evolution was not only possible but led to the development of man. Surely the Christian could safely claim that this had been the work of God. The discoveries that had discredited the six-day model of creation in no way required or even implied a denial that God is responsible for all that is. Was this not the "essence" of the Genesis account of creation? Had not the Genesis account expressed the essential truth long before man had discovered the means by which God had chosen to create? Could it not be said that Genesis inerrantly expresses, or contains, a truth that will always evade our complete understanding?

Actually, as must be acknowledged, when the new ideas of creation and truth were first articulated, they were condemned by most Christian leaders, including various organs of the magisterium. After all, creation had always been pictured as a six-day miracle; the Bible had always been taken literally. The new view was too new. Nonetheless, under the still increasing weight of the evidence for evolution, resistance began to soften. Church leaders began to become accustomed to the idea of creation by means of evolution. Indeed, before long, many actually began to insist that the complexity of the process gave profound testimony to God's creative genius. Likewise, as they became accustomed to the distinction between the essence of the truth and its expression, they learned to accept the fact that the truth can be expressed in statements which are not themselves true in a factual sense — a story. In this light, Genesis was now said to be the story in which God had chosen to reveal the simple fact of creation.

In what proved a remarkably short time, reflection upon the distinction between the truth and its expression gave rise to the realization that the Genesis story was not just an expression of a simple fact but a simplified version of this fact. It was a story tailored to the simplicity of the nomadic Hebrews to whom God had first spoken, a people who could never have understood the complex idea of creation of which man eventually became capable. It was, by all rightful definitions, a "myth." Moreover, since myth was common to primitive peoples, not to mention the fact that the Genesis account of creation clearly resembled the myths of any number of peoples, theologians were now led to a new appreciation for the mediatory role of the human writer in the creation of the sacred texts. God might well be their author but it had become clear that the human writers had contributed much to their content. In doing so, they surely brought to the task the limitations of the people of their time. For this reason, it also became clear that not only must the essence of the truth be distinguished from its expression, it must also be distinguished from its understanding.

Armed with these distinctions, theologians were now freed to study the Scriptures with the aid of the methods by which one would attempt to discover the true religious meaning and historical basis of any ancient text. The scholars were soon confident that not since their writing had Christians been so aware of the true richness of these texts, and the historical facts behind them. Thus, even though "modern biblical criticism" did concede much of what certain biblical critics had been saying for centuries, it also proved to provide new religious insights and scientifically respectable evidence that the historical basis of Christianity was indeed sound. It was ironic that the theory of evolution had done so much to force the faith along the intellectual path which led to these developments.

Evolution likewise contributed to the new conception of Church teaching which became necessary when the Church finally formally accepted the new view of Scripture. Over the course of history, Church teachings had come to include a number of references to the literal, historical truth of all of the Scriptures and all of their parts. As well, when the theory of evolution was first made public, both the theory and attempts to reconcile it with creation were condemned. Again a dilemma, the Church could not declare that it had taught error, and yet, if it were to maintain certain now untenable positions, necessary theological progress would not take place. Faced with this dilemma, the Church saw fit to apply the distinctions between the essence, expression and understanding of the truth to its own doctrinal declarations. In this light, troublesome statements about scriptural inerrancy were now said to assert the essential truth that the Scriptures unerringly teach the truth "necessary for our salvation." Statements condemning evolution were now said to have condemned the idea that a "totally" natural explanation of the world could ever be possible.

This was only the beginning. Theologians were now convinced that the truth must constantly be re-expressed, or even "reformulated," in order to keep pace with the times, in particular, the intellectual fruit of general human progress. They had become convinced that, like everything else, doctrine must develop. The result was a veritable avalanche of theological progress. Modern versions of nearly all of the Church's teachings were rendered. In some cases, especially with regard to the salvation of non-Catholics, and even non-Christians, the versions differed quite dramatically from the historical teachings on these topics. What is more, the reform of certain concepts, particularly grace and faith, actually succeeded in reducing the doctrinal disagreement that still separates the Church from most Protestant denominations. Eventually, evolution began to be mentioned by name in certain theological theses. Not surprisingly, it became the basis of theologies of progress and it was a major cause of an increasing, if not novel, theological awareness of the fact and importance of the unity of the human race.

Of course, none of this took place quite so easily as retrospect can sometimes suggest. Indeed, as history will readily attest, new ideas are always resisted. Nonetheless, by 1965, much of what "post-evolution" theology had done was either explicitly or by implication incorporated into the documents of the Second Vatican Council, that great assembly of Catholic leaders that sought to renew — and to modernize — many aspects of Church life. Among its many accomplishments, the once "evil" idea of evolution had been defused of all its sting. The council had rendered a Christian interpretation of the idea. At the same time, it was also to be acknowledged that evolution had contributed significantly to the contemporary expression and understanding of Christianity. In other words, the two ideas had interpreted each other. It could well be said that a "Christian Evolutionism" or even an "Evolutionistic Christianity" had been struck.

A Christian Evolutionism may have been struck, but as was revealed by historical studies now guided by the modern understanding of truth, this was not the first result of Christianity's successful enounter with "outside" ideas. Scriptural studies clearly showed that Christianity was at first a sect, an interpretation — Jesus' interpretation — of the Judaism of His day. Judaism was itself a religion at home within the philosophically simple view of the world common to the "semitic" peoples of the ancient Near East. To them, a rock was a rock, a tree was a tree, a man was a man and there was little more that needed to or could be said. Naturally, Judaism and, by implication, "semitism" had been the source of what Jesus and the first Christians took for granted with regard to the world, God, and a host of other notions. In other words, Christianity was at first "Christian Judaism" or, perhaps more accurately, "Christian Semitism."

After a time, as the new faith spread beyond the borders of Palestine, it began to encounter people who did not see things as the semites did. It began to encounter "hellenics" — people who saw the world through the ideas of the Greek philospher Plato. Hellenic thought was more sophisticated than semitism; in particular, it involved a distinction between the material world of the body and the immaterial, or spiritual, world of the soul. At first, Christianity was not at home in the company of such ideas; it did not involve the sophisticated explanations demanded by the rigor of Greek thought. Indeed, this was the making of a crisis that had already begun to cause division. As a matter of fact, Christianity would not have been able to survive in the Greek world if it had not learned to explain itself according to the hellenic understanding of reality. Fortunately for Christianity, this is precisely what happened. Under the influence of men like Paul, Christianity began to distinguish itself from its Judaic, semitic origins. This was the beginning of centuries of struggle which saw the so-called "Fathers of the Church" — in unknowing collaboration with those less "orthodox" — strive to make sense of their faith in the world of their day. At the same time, as the Fathers attempted to clarify their faith and explain it, and to respond to questions that had never been answered — or even asked — they made use of a number of concepts, such as "person" and "nature," which semitism could never have supplied. Culminating in the work of Augustine, the result was the christianization of a once foreign world-view. A "Christian Hellenism" had been created and if it had not, Christianity would not have survived to spread as it did.

Several centuries later, as the medieval period of Western history was just beginning, the thought of Plato's pupil, Aristotle, swept through the intellectual circles of what was now Christian Europe. Aristotle's philosophy was more sophisticated and, as we would now say, more scientific than that of Plato. It featured the mutual dependence of matter and spirit. This idea was a response to the problems Aristotle had perceived in Plato's complete distinction of the two. Indeed, this distinction had become the source of problems concerning the proper Christian attitude toward anything "worldly" which were created and never resolved when Christianity and hellenism had interpreted each other. Aristotelian philosophy appeared to offer a solution to these problems. Furthermore, it appeared to describe reality so insightfully that its precepts could not be ignored. Once again Christianity had to interpret a new world-view. Culminating in the work of Thomas Aquinas, a Christian interpretation of Aristotle's philosophy, or "scholasticism," was effected. In the process, scholasticism affected Christianity. Moreover, thanks to the rigor of scholastic thinking, Christian doctrine was never more completely explained; ancient problems were resolved and a deeper understanding of the inexhaustible truth of revelation was apparently reached. A "Christian Scholasticism" had been created. The Church had again succeeded in an explanation of Christian beliefs which would see to their survival in the light of a new world-view which thinking men knew they had no choice but to accept.

To the minds of most of the members of the Second Vatican Council, the Church had again made sense of a new world-view. Though they never referred to their work as the creation of a Christian Evolutionism, they were undoubtedly confident that their work had satisfied the demands of evolutionary thinking. Though they might have acknowledged that their work had produced a somewhat more dramatic step forward than had ever before been taken — after all, it did involve the abandonment of nearly nineteen hundred years of biblical literalism —they would still have insisted that the apostolic faith had been preserved. Indeed, they would have insisted that the Church's understanding of this faith had improved. They were surely confident that they had articulated an understanding of the faith that would keep it intelligible, credible and attractive to the world of their day and, thereby, in such ways as to halt and even reverse the distinctly un-Christian, and un-Catholic, direction in which the Western world had been steadily moving for what was now over four hundred years.

Despite such optimism, the increasing disregard for Christian belief has shown no signs of abatement. Instead, the years following Vatican II have seen both a deepening entrenchment of this disregard and its spread among an ever larger sector of the general population. To this fact churchmen will normally respond by saying something to the effect that the current crisis cannot so simply be attributed to an intellectual dissatisfaction with scholastic, or "classical," or even contemporary understandings of basic beliefs. Instead, as is always insisted, the actual antecedents of the present crisis include the profound economic, political and social changes which most fully describe Western civilization's passage from its medieval to modern period. Theological reforms do not easily address circumstances such as these. Nonetheless, the Church has faced crises before, it will face them again. With dedication and patience, Vatican II's reforms will have their effect. In God's good time, these reforms will turn things around.

It is the conviction of this author that patience will not be enough. First, however, let it be stated that the decline of Christianity in the West *has* been due to a complex coalition of causes which include the impact of several inter-related societal changes. Neither can it be denied that the reforms collectively dubbed Christian Evolutionism have spoken to the theological element of this decline and significantly contributed to the credibility of Christianity in this century. Indeed, it is not to be imagined that Christian beliefs would have retained the esteem they still enjoy if these innovations had not been adopted. Nonetheless, important and impressive though they have been, they will not be sufficient to secure Christianity's resurgence within an ever more modern society.

Christian belief last enjoyed a unified and nearly universal acceptance, even among the educated wherever it was indigenous, during the period of Christian Scholasticism. During the period of Christian Scholasticism, the truths of faith and reason supported each other. Scholasticism not only had room for the supernatural, it required God. According to its precepts, the Christian understandings of God and man made philosophical sense. It systemized everything from angels to anatomy and everything fit. The decline of scholasticism has coincided with the decline of Christian belief everywhere. This decline will never be reversed until Christianity successfully interprets and is interpreted by the world-view that has replaced scholasticism. This has not been evolutionism. Evolutionism is simply an element of a far more comprehensive system of ideas.

Evolution has precious little to tell us about reality as it is as such. It does not propose to describe what it is for something to "be"; nor does it explain what it is that makes things what they are, or what it is that makes them different; these are the tasks of a "metaphysic." Evolution offers no "epistemology," an understanding of the nature and origins of human knowledge offering principles by which truth can be determined with confidence. Evolution, providing as it does a natural explanation of the origin and development of life, only makes sense within the framework of a comprehensive world-view in which the emergence of the living from non-living matter can happen. This is provided by "materialism," the implicit basis of the "seeing is believing" approach to truth that led to the demise of its predecessor and has caused the decline of Christianity, belief in God and, ultimately, the belief that man is something special.

By materialism, reference is *not* made to the attitude of people who appear to live for the pursuit of material goods alone — "consumerism." Neither is intended the judgment that nothing but matter exists, an idea which denies the existence of God by definition, as in the "Dialectical Materialism" of Karl Marx. By materialism is meant the idea that all the world and everything of it, including man, can be attributed to the

interaction of the most elementary units of matter whatever they are
—those unintelligent realities, uncomposed of smaller units, which move
in space and time, are described by physical laws, and are oft-imagined as
little billiard balls colliding in the dark. Christianity will never regain the
credibility which it has lost until it has confronted, interpreted, and been
interpreted by this understanding of the world at large. In other words, a
"Christian Materialism" must be created.

It might seem madness to contend that Christian belief could ever find
a home in a materialistic world-view. Materialism asserts that everything
can be explained in terms of matter. It specifically involves the denial that
the so-called "spiritual" aspect of man's existence demonstrates his
possession of a uniquely spiritual part, element or principle — a soul. The
soul has always been considered the seat of man's immortality. It has
always been considered the source of man's ability to conduct a spiritual
relationship with his God, particularly the most important aspect of that
relationship, the free will with which man culpably accepts or rejects
God's offer of salvation. A free will would scarcely seem possible within
the framework of a materialistic conception of man's mind.

For many reasons, the suggestion that there could ever be a synthesis
of Christianity and materialism must appear at least as implausible as the
idea that Christianity could similarly interpret and be interpreted by
evolution. Indeed, even though the many results of that synthesis are
largely taken for granted — today — it was not so long ago that the
possibility of a reconciliation of science and the Scriptures could hardly
have been imagined except by a very few. Nonetheless, a synthesis was
achieved. Though biblical literalism had to be abandoned, a new and
more profound understanding of Scripture took its place. In the process,
solutions to age-old problems were advanced while important new
insights were acquired. Theology took a great step forward.

Theology must continue to move forward. It must complete the
christianization of modernity begun by its successful encounter with
evolution. It must successfully confront the world-view which evolution
insinuated from the very beginning. It must interpret and be interpreted
by the world-view whose mostly inarticulate embrace has coincided with
a decline of Christianity that will not stop until this is done. Although this
will require new understandings of basic Christian beliefs far more
dramatic than have hitherto been necessary, the result will be an
explanation of these beliefs which is not only credible but will be believed.
Actually, as the completion of the christianization of modernity,
Christian Materialism will concretize much of what modern theology has

already begun to suspect, and lead it past its present problems to remarkably new and systematic solutions to the crucial questions with which any belief system must deal if it would hope to enjoy the confidence of the modern world. This will begin a Renaissance of faith that did not take place when modernity was born.

* * *

At this point, "An Introduction to the Idea" should profit from a word about the phrase "Christian Materialism." After all, this phrase would seem to emphasize the effect of Christianity upon materialism without suggesting an equally profound effect of materialism upon Christianity. Yet, when one considers the *prima facie* antipathy of the current understandings of both ideas, it is likely obvious that a very two-way exchange is indeed ahead. In this light, would not this work have better been entitled "Materialistic Christianity?"

Actually, the work is better entitled "Christian Materialism" because the form of the phrase accentuates the fact that materialism involves assertions that are logically prior to those of Christianity. Materialism is a description of the world at large; it attempts to describe *what* the world is. Christianity is an explanation of the world; it attempts to explain *why* the world is. (Notably, materialism claims to account for the mental processes by which this explanation can take place.) Nonetheless, it is by no means clear that the implications of a materialistic world-view are to be taken as the supreme source of truth before which Christianity must stand or fall. Presently, the supremacy of a hypothetically "proved" materialism can remain an open question which will in due course be addressed.

Catholic Materialism?

Although a lengthy explanation of the title of a work is rarely appropriate, mention should be made of the full scope of what *Christian Materialism* hopes to accomplish.

The principal goal of the work will be a rendering of Christianity which is credible to the modern, materialistic world.

But, as the almost immediate references to Catholic churchmen and the demands of the Catholic magisterium have likely made clear, this work proceeds from, or at least *to,* a definite Catholic interest. This is explained as follows:

Materialism will demand rather dramatic reforms of *basic* Christian beliefs — beliefs which are commonly held by virtually all Christians.

Where it does concern beliefs which currently divide the denominations, it will frequently appear to indicate compromise views of these beliefs. Nonetheless, the discussion must start somewhere. Catholic was the Christianity that last knew universal agreement. It still involves an official position which can be attributed to the largest number of individual Christians. And, finally, in its idea of a magisterium, it provides a means by which dramatic departures from perennial beliefs can still be taught with authority. Though this presumes that the Church is of uniquely divine origin, this idea will hardly go untested. Nonetheless, despite a rigorous critique, and a careful clarification of what it properly involves, we shall see that certain aspects of Christian Materialism lend it significant support. This and the doctrinal upheaval that materialism demands will open the door to a Christian unity that is presently impossible. This will be a second goal of the work.

A third goal concerns Christianity's proper approach to the other world religions. Since *Christian Materialism* aims at a reconciliation of Christianity and modern thinking, it will necessarily attempt to ground its teachings in sufficient evidence. If this is achieved, the Christian participation in the so-called "inter-religious dialogue" will recognizably proceed from a position of strength.

The General Plan of the Work

In order to accomplish its stated aims, *Christian Materialism* will proceed according to the following general plan:

Excluding the "Introduction," which is almost complete, and a "Conclusion" which will be a reflection upon the practical aspects of the theological reforms that will have been suggested, *Christian Materialism* will be a work of four parts.

Part I will be a presentation of the "Christianity" from which its reform will proceed.

Part II will be a presentation of a "Materialism" which does not involve the ideological baggage which would normally render its Christian interpretation impossible.

Part III will examine "The Conflict" between Christianity and materialism which results regardless of how either is explained.

Part IV will attempt "The Synthesis" of the two for which so much has already been claimed.

* * *

The attempt to create a Christian Materialism will involve certain procedural problems of which mention must be made. First of all, a work of its kind, a global reform of Christian beliefs, is necessarily limited to no more than a sketch of each of the topics with which it must deal. Volumes could have been written about the most particular aspects of any one of them. Their thorough treatment would have required a lifetime of research; even then it would not have been complete.

Fortunately, the work will not require such a project; its sketches will prove sufficient. Materialism will challenge and demand a reform of the most basic Christian beliefs. The bases of these beliefs can be stated quite simply; they involve the broadest of scriptural and traditional themes and they rely upon the most straightforward of philosophical assertions. All of these lend themselves to concise presentation. In like manner, since the most basic elements of a materialistic world-view, regardless of how they are explained, confront classical Christian presumptions so clearly, an equally concise presentation of materialism will also be possible. Thereafter, highly streamlined accounts of their conflict and synthesis will follow. The new perspectives forced upon us by materialism will free us from having to deal with most of the argumentation that is normally mustered in order to build a case for any theological position. Just as the new perspectives possessed by the first Christians freed them from having to deal with the complex rabbinical casuistry that had once been the only way to deal with the myriad and often contradictory or otherwise impossible demands of the Law, and just as modern biblical criticism has freed scholars from all sorts of scriptural problems, materialism will save us from endless quibbling over many of the questions with which the history of theology has previously been preoccupied. Along the way, it will sweep into irrelevance most of the issues which currently divide the experts of all denominations and proceed to what will clearly be the only position the facts allow.

Actually, were the concise treatment of topics not of logistical necessity, it would still be of value. Since the adoption of a materialistic world-view will affect the way in which almost everything is understood, its effect on Christianity will obviously involve an inter-related re-interpretation of almost everything that Christians believe. These re-interpretations must be viewed as parts of a whole. In isolation, a given implication of materialism will not make Christian sense. Just as many of the specific results of modern biblical criticism, especially denials of the historical character of certain biblical events, would still seem "heretical" if seen apart from their place in the modern theology of Scripture, so it is that most of the specific implications of materialism, seen apart from the holistic reform of the faith to follow, cannot but confuse and disturb. It is for this reason that a fast moving treatment of individual issues would have been essential even were it not required by the problems of length.

Of course, even were it not necessary to view the specifics as parts of the whole, there would still be good reason to recommend that this work be read with patience. The process of synthesis seldom takes place in a smoothly systematic manner. The inter-relation of ideas is such that a direct transition from one to another cannot be expected. A given idea will have any number of simultaneous implications. The pursuit of any one will require the temporary suspension of an investigation of the rest. Possibilities will often suggest themselves "out of the blue." Conclusions will often be provisional, the final determination of their truth dependent upon the data of several sources, only one of which can be examined at one time. This work will be especially subject to these and related problems. Nonetheless, patience will provide its rewards. With this in mind, let us now proceed to Part I.

Part I: Christianity

Introduction to Part I

As an attempt to present the Christianity which is to engage in the mutual interpretation of materialism, Part I faces a formidable challenge. It must not only do justice to the diversity of opinion as to the meaning of Christianity, but it must also do justice to the diversity of opinion as to its truth. In the process, it must also make clear the principles which legitimately govern the project of synthesis. To this end, Part I will trace the shift from the *nearly* universal acceptance of the same faith to the present state of religious affairs.

Chapter I will establish our starting point, "The Faith of 1500." In 1500, Christian Scholasticism had been the status quo for two hundred years. Never before and never again was there to be such agreement as to the content and credibility of Christianity. Nonetheless, the progressive decline of this faith was to begin within decades.

In order to take advantage of the clarity made possible by a streamlined display of this faith and, also, so not to present unexplained doctrines in the explanation of others, the faith of 1500 will be presented without the immediate corroboration of the theological evidence which was thought to justify each and every doctrine.

This will be the topic of Chapter II; it will take the form of "A Defense of the Faith of 1500" from the point of view of an informed and orthodox churchman of that period. As such, it will also be a rich source of the scriptural, traditional and philosophical data upon which this discussion will later draw.

Chapter III will describe the several stages of "The Decline of the Faith of 1500." It will describe the many problems with Catholic, and Christian, and religious belief which modernity has already raised and to which any attempt to re-establish the credibility of Christianity must respond.

Chapter IV will examine "The Impact of Evolution." It will largely be an elaboration of the "Introduction to the Idea" of Christian Materialism. It will describe the origin and results of the modern theologies of Scripture and doctrinal development.

Chapter V will bring Part I to a close with a careful examination of the principles that would properly govern "The Future of Doctrinal Development" in order to demonstrate the dramatic degree to which reform can still be called legitimate.

* * *

Part I involves problems unique to its purposes. First of all, it will involve a highly generalized account of what was true and why. There surely was not a single late-medieval theologian who would have agreed with all of the arguments which will be posited as the typical opinion. Thomas Aquinas notwithstanding, this opinion will largely be an abstraction. To make matters worse, by 1500, not all of the Church's teachings had required a "defense." For this reason, the project will occasionally infer theological argument from a general look at the state of the late-medieval mind. Worst of all, the selection of available material for the defense was determined by the author's knowledge of what information would best serve the foreseen needs of eventual argument; indeed, the very structure of this presentation was determined with this expediency in mind.

Despite these problems, it remains the considered opinion of this author that the benefits to be gained by such a project well outweigh them. He also insists that none of them constitute an excessive scholarly liberality. The fact that there might not have been a single late-medieval theologian, or 18th century scientist, who would have unequivocally ascribed to all that will be said of them is simply the nature of generalization. Generalization is necessary if one chooses to write about "man," and not just about "men." The inferral of arguments in support of positions that were not in dispute by 1500 will always be identified and care will be taken to demonstrate that these arguments are consistent with the mind of that period. Finally, with regard to the liberality of a "selective" history of the kind described, may it be clear that such a study need not and will not be a misrepresentation of what was indeed thought. The justification of the project rests with the fact that it allowed an uncumbersome provision of data which could not have been provided otherwise. This, it is hoped, will be seen.

There remains one more problem that must be pointed out. An historically exact description of the faith of 1500, its defense, and its decline would require the use of the technical terminology employed during the periods in question. For example, the defense would employ scriptural references taken only from the "Vulgate," the translation of the Scriptures into Latin by Jerome (c.342-420) which was pre-eminent for centuries and believed by many to have been an inspired translation. The use of the Vulgate, however, or historically exact terminology generally, would be a cumbersome and unnecessary impediment to the clear and concise provision of data for which Part I was conceived. Therefore, to the extent that accuracy permits, its arguments will be translated into familiar, hopefully more helpful language. For both practical and scholarly reasons, scriptural references will be taken from *The Revised Standard Version of the Bible, Catholic Edition.*

Chapter I: The Faith of 1500

Section I: A Late-Medieval History of the Faith

No description of the faith of 1500 could but profit from a description of the late-medieval memory of how this faith had come to be — a late-medieval history of the faith. This would also be a late-medieval history of the Church. After all, to the late-medieval churchman, the history of Christianity and the Church were synonymous. The Europe of 1500 was almost universally Catholic and the Church was the apparent product of fifteen centuries of steady growth.

To the late-medieval churchman, this was only as it should be. Instituted by Christ, the Church — which was founded upon the apostles with Peter as their head — was sure to enjoy divine help. This was apparent from the beginning. Thousands of Jesus' fellow Jews were converted during Christianity's very first days. With the conversion of Paul, and at his instigation, the faith was brought to the "Gentiles" (or non-Jews). Almost overnight, he and the other apostles had spread Christianity throughout the Roman Empire, founding churches wherever they went. Peter went to Rome, the capital of the Empire, to become the head of the church there. For this reason Peter's successors as head of the Church of Rome rightfully assumed his position as head of the "universal" Church.

As the Church grew in numbers, it incurred the fear and so the wrath of what was clearly perceived to be an "evil" Empire. Thus, the Church had to endure the persecutions of the Roman emperors Nero (c.64), Domitian (81-96), Marcus Aurelius (c.177) and Diocletian (303-4). Nonetheless, aided by God, it not only endured, it spread. By 313, the emperor Constantine was inspired to grant Christians the right to worship as they chose. This allowed the Church to assume a public place in Roman society. As it did, the empire began to display the serious symptoms of an internal decline which was the result of centuries of Roman decadence. Among these symptoms was the loss of an ability to defend itself. This enabled the Visogoths to sack Rome in 410. Since the Church was the only institution to retain the people's confidence, it had no choice but to assume the burdens of civil government. When, in 476, the rest of the Empire — of the West[1] — fell to the simultaneous assaults

---

1. For purposes of administration, the Empire had been divided into East and West approximately two centuries prior.

of several "barbarian" tribes, the Church had to fill the institutional vacuum that had been created. It had been providentially assured to play a major role in the formation of a new order.

It was not remembered to have taken long. No sooner were the conquerors settled than holy missionaries walked into their camps. Like the apostles, they too were armed with the power to do miracles and, almost overnight, they converted whole barbarian tribes.[2] Many souls were saved. Moreover, the Church grew not only in spiritual but "temporal" (or social, economic and political) power. Although this did not prevent the 8th century fall of Christian North Africa to the followers of Mohammed, the Church still dominated the European society. Indeed, the Church *was* society. Naturally, its teachings were wholeheartedly believed by almost everyone who knew of them.

To late-medieval churchmen, the almost universal credence of Church teachings could not have appeared more appropriate. Not only was the Church to be believed, but its teachings were the product of almost fifteen centuries of inspired reflection upon all that God revealed. The result was an articulation of the faith that had never spelled things out so clearly, so free from the possibility of misinterpretation, or so rich in its exposition of the truth.

It had not come cheaply. Fifteen hundred years of reflection had also been fifteen hundred years of struggle. Indeed, the apostolic faith had often been in danger of being lost to the errors of those who did not understand it and would not submit to Church teaching. Had it not been for the heroic efforts of the Fathers of the Church and popes, the truths entrusted to the Church might well have been lost. Instead, thanks to their efforts, the true content of the faith was ever more clearly exposed. This fed simultaneous efforts to explore its inexhaustible richness. By the year of the Lord 1500, the result was a magnificent system which left little to doubt and less unsaid.

Section II: God

If its principal tenets are to be presented in the order of their logical priority, any accounting of the faith of 1500 must begin with some statement of the belief that "there is one God, the 'supreme' being (and implicitly 'person') upon whom the existence of all else depends."

Although God was also considered "ineffable," i.e. so overwhelmingly

2. According to various "Lives of the Saints," Patrick gained the confidence of the Irish by ridding their island of snakes while men like Boniface, Stanislaus, and Cyril and Methodius used similar methods to convince the Germans, Poles and Russians.

superior to His creatures that they cannot know Him as He is, it was still believed that certain things could be known "about" Him. The Scriptures were the principal source of this information. Information was also available from a reflection upon creation, God's handiwork. Though this was mostly a source of information about what God is *not* (the *via negativa*), it also made possible a reflection upon the infinite which was informed by the various degrees of finite qualities of which creation consists (the "analogy of being"). Together, these sources made possible a knowledge of God which always began with an inventory of His "general attributes":

God is uncreated; He has not been brought into existence by any other being.

He is self-sufficient; His existence in no way depends upon anything other than Himself.

He is eternal; He has had no beginning.

He is immortal; He will always be.

He is a spirit. He is immaterial; He is not made of the stuff of the material, visible world.

He is simple; He is in no way the product of smaller, more elementary parts or elements. He is not made out of anything that can be distinguished from His existence as a whole. He is His "substance" (the "what-it-is-that-makes-it-what-it-is").

He is perfect; He bears no flaw or incompleteness. He is and has all that there can be.

He is all-good; He is the best, most beautiful, most desirable being that there can be. Moreover, since He is all-good, He cannot tolerate evil — at least not forever.

He is infinite; there is no end to all He is or has. He cannot be exhausted.

He is immense, and therefore omnipresent. He is boundless. He is everywhere at once.

The inventory of God's general attributes always concluded with the insistence that He is immutable, not subject to corruption, alteration, internal development or external growth.

Of course, it should not be imagined that the general attributes were believed to describe *all* that God is. Indeed, they were not even thought to say all that could be said. God was also to be described in terms of "particular perfections." Though infinite in number, two were always singled out for special mention:

God is omniscient; He knows everything that can be known with certainty. He knows the past, the present and the future at a single glance. No detail, however trivial, can escape His attention; He never forgets. Moreover, He has a perfect intellect; no aspect of reality or Himself, however complex, exceeds His ability to understand it. No problem could ever be too perplexing for Him to solve.

God is also omnipotent; He can do anything that can be done, and He can do it instantly and without strain. He also has a perfect will; He does nothing that He does not want to. In deciding, He experiences no conflict or hesitancy.

Two perfections were also considered "special characteristics of God's goodness":

God is all-loving; He loves unselfishly and unconditionally. He loves with infinite fervor; He gives of Himself unreservedly. His love is unfailing and untiring. If offended, He forgives completely — no matter how serious the offence. He forgives time and time again.

Nonetheless, God remains uncompromisingly just. Having informed His creatures of the demands of His goodness, He will not fail to judge their response and He will reward or punish them accordingly, and impartially.

Section III: The Trinity

Awesome though each of His attributes was imagined, none was thought to bespeak God's greatness better than His existence as the "Blessed Trinity," the one God existing from all eternity as a community of three divine and equal persons — the Father, the Son, and the Holy Spirit. Though a "mystery" always evading exact description, the Trinity was typically explained as follows:

From all eternity, the Father expressed Himself in the loving generation of a Son equal to Him in all things but being the Father. This "generation" consisted of the Father's supremely unselfish giving of His very substance. He did not create the Son out of any other stuff; neither did He bring Him into existence at any particular moment in time.

Co-eternal with the Father's generation of the Son was their mutual "spiration" of the Holy Spirit. In this equally loving act, the Spirit received all that was possessed by the Father and the Son with the single exception of being either. Thus, neither was the Spirit created.

Though a community of three absolutely[3] distinct persons, the Trinity remains absolutely one God. Since each possesses all that the others are and have, they actually dwell within each other and this "mutual

---

3 An "absolute" cannot be qualified with respect to what it really is in any way.

indwelling" is so complete that they exist and act as one. Nonetheless, they remain distinctly three persons because each retains the uniqueness of His relation to the others.

Section IV: Angels and Demons

God's existence as the Trinity surely satisfied any need that He might have felt for either community or creativity. But, it was also clear that He desired to demonstrate His greatness, or "glory," and needing someone to demonstrate it to, and wanting to satisfy a loving desire to share His life with others other than Himself, He created the angels. They were spirits like Himself but finite in their attributes. Finite though they were, these attributes were still precious gifts; they included rationality, free will and immortality. The angels were also given the ability to see God (the "beatific vision"). This required the Holy Spirit to dwell within them, bringing with Him the "sanctifying grace" that made them both worthy and able to share God's life — to "participate" in the life of the Trinity. This grace also gave them the knowledge and strength to live in accord with the demands of holiness, especially obedience. All He asked was that they acknowledge His glory in the deference due the fact that He was indeed their God and they were His creatures.

As happy a situation as this was imagined, some of the angels refused God the deference that was due Him. Instead, they deemed themselves His equals and refused to obey Him. This was the first sin. It caused these angels to become repugnant to God and the Holy Spirit immediately ceased to dwell within them. Not only did they lose the beatific vision but, cut off from the assistance of sanctifying grace, they soon became totally ungodly, evil beings. They could never have a place in God's presence. Furthermore, having rejected God's infinite goodness, they had committed a sin of infinite seriousness; thus, the demands of justice required a punishment of equal measure. Therefore, God banished the evil angels, now called "demons," to a place of terrible and eternal punishment called "hell."

Section V: The Creation of the World and Man

It was obvious that God's motives for creating had not been exhausted by His creation of the angels. Clearly, it was also His will and pleasure to create another kind of being with whom to share His life — man. Like the angels, man would be given rationality, free will and a participation in the life of the Trinity. But, for reasons known to God alone, man would be the participant of both the spiritual world and a material world of His own careful design. To this end, He determined that humankind would consist of a spiritual soul and a material body. Human souls would naturally be endowed with rationality, free will and immortality while their bodies would enable them to dwell in the material world over which they would be given dominion.

His plan conceived as such, God created the heavens and the earth. Then He filled the earth with living things. Then He created the body of Adam, the first man. Into this He placed his soul.

God gave Adam many wonderful gifts which were in no way essential to his human nature. These "preter-natural" gifts built upon his nature, freeing him from ignorance, other fallibilities, uncontrollable emotions, other frailties, suffering and bodily death. He also gave him the supernatural gift of the indwelling of the Holy Spirit and with it the sanctifying grace which made possible the beatific vision. Finally, God gave Adam a companion, Eve, the first woman. Once again, He asked nothing but their recognition that He was their God and Creator.

Section VI: The Original Sin and Its Consequences

It was the lament of history that, despite the idyllic life that He had given them, Adam and Eve rejected God. Like the evil angels — and at the temptation of one of them — they too deemed themselves God's equals and chose to disobey the one commandment He had given them. This was the original human sin. Immediately, Adam and Eve became repugnant to God's sight and the Holy Spirit left them. The attendant loss of sanctifying grace naturally cost them both the beatific vision and God's help to live good, holy lives. What was worse, the original sin caused a disordering of their wills (called "concupiscence") which left them powerless but to sin again and again.

Since Adam and Eve had sinned against God's infinite goodness, they like the evil angels were liable to a punishment of equal severity. They had already forfeited the indwelling of the Holy Spirit and suffered the disordering of their wills. To this God added the loss of the preter-natural gifts by which He had protected them from every fallibility, frailty, suffering and bodily death. Even nature was cursed; now it would work against them. This would condemn them to miserable lives of struggle just to survive. Then, when their bodies finally did die, they would be consigned to the terrible and eternal punishment of hell. Most tragically, since Adam was to be the father of all mankind, all his descendants would inherit the "stain" of original sin. Man had "fallen."

Section VII: The Divine Plan for Salvation

Obviously, God did abandon man to his perfectly just punishment.

Mercifully, He decided to give him another chance. But, since He remained just, He did not deem it right to re-establish a rapport with him until he had paid an appropriate restitution for his sin. Having "fallen," however, man had neither the means nor the ability to offer restitution for his now rapidly accumulating offences, much less the infinite restitution due sins of infinite seriousness. Nonetheless, unwilling to be prevented from restoring humanity to a share in divine life, God devised a plan. Needing a man to pay man's debt but, at the same time, a man whose offering would be equal to the debt, the Father would bid the Son to become man and offer up His life as a sacrifice of infinite value (or "merit") by which to "atone" for the original and all subsequent sins. Once He did so, man could be forgiven and made fit to receive the gift of divine life.

It was clear that God had not thought it just to restore man to divine life either *en masse* or in a moment. Instead, He decided to offer salvation to men as individuals. Remaining subject to the trials and tribulations of fallen life, each would be asked to respond to this offer according to requirements that the Son would also make known.

Before His sacrificial death, the Son would announce the Father's loving offer of salvation. He would reveal His own identity and role in God's plan for salvation. In response, He would urge man to a repentance for sin consisting of faith, in Him and in His teaching, and obedience to commandments that He would teach by word and deed. If a person had faith and did obey, he would be saved.

Required to retain his fallen nature, however, man would not be capable of either faith or obedience on his own. Therefore, on account of the infinite merit of the Son's sacrifice, the Father would send him supernatural help (or "actual grace") by which both would become possible. Communicated by the Holy Spirit, this grace would correct what was fallen in human nature and more. All that men must do is accept grace by striving to co-operate with it.

Though invisible, grace would be at work before, during and after any act of Christian faith or obedience. The grace of illumination would give faith. It might even give a vivid mystical experience. It would at least involve the stirrings of "conscience." In any case, it would inform a person of God's will. Thereupon, the grace of strength would enable him to do God's will. It would enable him to overcome concupiscence and resist temptations of all kinds. In the extreme, it would empower acts of Christian heroism that would never have been imaginable otherwise. Nonetheless, were actual grace not at work, men could do nothing by which they could merit the sanctifying grace which would make them worthy and capable of the beatific vision. If sanctifying grace were already present, it would increase.

Section VIII: The Early History of Salvation

It was clear that God's plan for salvation had actually involved much more than the sending of His Son. It was the Father's wisdom to prepare the world to receive His Son. He would choose a people as His own and gradually He would reveal Himself to them, teaching them to expect the Son. When at last He came, they would acclaim the Son and announce His offer of salvation to all the world.

With this in mind, God began to fill the world with many people. Using human parentage, He created their bodies. He reserved to Himself the direct creation of their souls.

Despite God's most generous plans, man only became more sinful. Eventually, God became angry; He sent a great flood to wipe out the world. He spared only Noah whom He told to build an ark in which to bring his family and two of every kind of creature. It was their task to repopulate the world.

Once the world was repopulated, God revealed Himself to Abraham, a Hebrew. He told Abraham that He had chosen the Hebrews to be His own. He promised that He would make them a great nation with a land of their own. He then gave Abraham a son, Isaac, who became the father of the twelve tribes of His people.

Though they were forced into slavery in Egypt, God did not abandon His people. He called upon Moses to lead them out of slavery to their promised land. *En route,* He revealed what He expected in return for all He had promised. They were to obey the "Law" He now explained to Moses. These were the terms of a "covenant" that He would never break.

Arriving at the promised land, God's people found it occupied. God therefore led them in its conquest. In time, as He promised, He made them a great nation with David as their king. Soon thereafter, forgetting all that God had done for them, the people ceased to obey the Law. Patiently, God raised up prophets to call them back to its obedience. When they refused, He punished them. At one point, He drove them from their land. But He did not forget them and, in time, He restored them to their land though not their former greatness. For this — and more — He taught them to expect a "messiah," a savior.

When finally the time had come, God chose Mary, a virgin, to become the mother of His Son. Anticipating the merit of her Son — and to spare

Him the stain of original sin — the Father enabled her to be conceived without it — "immaculately." Remaining a virgin, she conceived by the power of the Holy Spirit. When He (the Son) was born, she and her husband Joseph, the foster father of the child, named Him "Jesus." He was eventually to be called "Christ" (Greek for "messiah").

Though she was legally married to Joseph, Mary remained a virgin throughout her life. This even involved the miraculous maintenance of her virginity during childbirth.

Section IX: The Incarnation

The incarnation was admittedly a mystery. Jesus Christ was true God and true man. He was the Second Person of the Trinity and a man like us in all things but sin. He is still the complete, the "hypostatic" union of two natures, one divine and one human, forever united in one person.

Though one person, Jesus' divine and human natures remain distinct and unmixed, each retaining its own characteristics. While on earth, His divine intellect provided him the beatific vision and super-human knowledge of anything He needed to know. His human intellect contributed the knowledge of things He learned from experience. His divine will was incapable of sin while His human will did not sin. He actually possessed a perfect humanity.

Section X: The Life and Mission of Jesus Christ

The Church did not claim to possess a great deal of information about the early life of Jesus. About His so-called "public" life, however, there was much to be told.

When He was ready to begin His public life, the Father sent John the Baptist to be His herald. Thereupon, Jesus began to announce the Father's offer of salvation, his "good news," the "gospel." He proclaimed the coming of God's kingdom. He called for repentance and faith, not only in His teachings but also His divinity. And He called for obedience to God's law; this He summed up in the command to love God above all else, and to love your neighbor as yourself.

In order to make clear that He was who He said that He was, Jesus worked many miracles and made many prophecies that later came true.

Despite these wonders, Jesus was rejected by God's chosen people. Now called the "Jews," their leaders were jealous of their once supreme earthly authority. On account of His claim to divinity, they accused Him of blasphemy and saw to it that He was crucified. This He accepted as His Father's will.

With His death, Jesus atoned for the original and subsequent sins of mankind. Man was forgiven; the punishment of hell could now be lifted. Grace was won; salvation became possible. To announce this to those who had done their best to keep the Law prior to His death, Jesus descended to hell. To make this known on earth, and as the supreme sign of His divinity, Jesus rose from the dead and appeared to the disciples that He had previously chosen to be witnesses to this event.

Section XI: The Church

The risen Christ was not long to be seen upon the earth. But, this did not mean that He left it without some visible means by which He could continue to offer man salvation. It was knowing that the Jews would reject this role that Jesus instituted the Church.

Jesus had actually been preparing His institution of the Church throughout His public life. Early on He had called together the twelve apostles, the inner circle of His disciples who were to be the spiritual fathers of God's new people. He taught them all that God wanted man to know. He named Peter their leader. Then, just before He was to return to His Father, Jesus commissioned them to preach His message to all the world. In this way, they would be the visible conduit of the actual grace in which He would actually be at work. He also gave them authority to govern His people, the Church.

Actually, Christ would remain the head of the Church. Since He had given the Church His mission, He promised to send it the Holy Spirit. Through the Spirit, Jesus would guide His Church. The Spirit would also inspire its preaching and guarantee that it spoke the truth. To this end, the Spirit would inspire the writing of a "New Testament." The books of this New Testament would be treasured together with the sacred books of the Hebrews, the "Old Testament," which He had also inspired.

Through Moses, God had written the "Pentateuch": the books of Genesis (hereafter Gen.), Exodus (Ex.), Leviticus (Lev.), Numbers (Num.) and Deuteronomy (Deut.). Through various others He had written Joshua (Josh.), Judges (Judg.), Ruth (Ruth), and four books of Kings (Kings),[4] the two of Chronicles (Chron.), the four books of Esdras,[5] Tobit (Tob.), Judith (Jud.), Esther (Esther) and Job (Job). Through King David, He wrote the Psalms (Ps.) and through David's son Solomon, He wrote the Proverbs (Prov.), Ecclesiastes (Eccles.), the Song of Songs,[6] Wisdom (Wis.) and Ecclesiasticus.[7] He then inspired the

---

4. The first two books of Kings would later be known as the two books of Samuel (Sam.).
5. The first two books of Esdras would later be known as Ezra (Ezra) and Nehemiah (Neh.).
6. The Song of Songs would later be known as the Song of Solomon (Song.).
7. Ecclesiasticus would later be known as Sirach (Sir.).

prophets Isaiah (Is.), Jeremiah (Jer.), Ezekiel (Ez.), Daniel (Dan.), Hosea (Hos.), Joel (Joel), Amos (Amos), Obadiah (Obad.), Jonah (Jon.), Micah (Mic.), Nahum (Nah.), Habakkuk (Hab.), Zephaniah (Zeph.), Haggai (Hag.), Zechariah (Zech.) and Malachi (Mal.) to write the books that bear their names.[8] Finally, He inspired the two books of Maccabees (Mac.).

In order to record the life and mission of Jesus, God employed Matthew (Mt.), Mark (Mk.), Luke (Lk.) and John (Jn.) to write the "gospels" by whose names they are known. Through Luke, He added a history of the early Church known as the Acts of the Apostles (Acts). Through Paul, He explained the gospel in fourteen letters: one to the Romans (Rom.), two to the Corinthians (Cor.), one each to the Galatians (Gal.), Ephesians (Eph.), Philippians (Phil.) and Colossians (Col.), two to the Thessalonians (Thess.), two to his friend Timothy (Tim.), one each to Titus (Tit.), Philemon (Philem.), and the Hebrews (Heb.). Through Peter (Pet.), He added two more letters; through John (Jn.), three; and through James (Jas.) and Jude (Jude), one each. Finally, He gave John a vision of the future which was recorded as the Apocalypse.[9]

We have already seen that belief in the inspiration, and therefore inerrancy, of the Bible was in no way thought to compromise belief in a sacred unwritten Tradition. It was simply that not everything revealed was written down. Should there arise any doubt about the true content of Tradition — or the correct interpretation of the Scriptures — the successors of the apostles, the bishops, received divine guidance in deciding the question. It was further taught that should there arise some doubt as to the true teaching of the bishops, the truth could be known with certainty if the teaching were proclaimed by either the pope or an "ecumenical" council, i.e. a meeting which at least represented the bishops throughout the world. It was from these organs that the Church taught infallibly. But, let there be no mistake, actions of the magisterium were not believed to reveal new truth; they were simply considered to clarify the teachings that Jesus entrusted to the apostles, the so-called "deposit of faith" which closed with the death of the last apostle.

Since the bishops spoke for God, the people were obviously required to have faith in their teachings — and to obey them. Refusal was a serious sin. It could even put a person outside the "communion" (or "spiritual unity") of the Church. "Excommunication" was especially feared because outside the Church there was no salvation.

---

8. The latter twelve were called the "minor" prophets.
9. The Apocalypse would later be known as Revelation (Rev.).

* * *

When the time came for Jesus to leave the earth — visibly — He ascended
to the right hand of His Father. Shortly thereafter, just as He had
promised, the Holy Spirit descended upon the apostles. Inspired, they
were remembered to have taken up His mission with the success which we
have already mentioned.

Section XII: The Sacraments

In order to enable the Church to *completely* fulfill His mission — visibly
— Jesus personally instituted seven "sacraments": efficacious outward
signs through which He had instructed His apostles to communicate even
the *sanctifying* grace that He had won for mankind.

If a person repented and professed faith, he must receive a "Baptism"
of water and the invocation of the Trinity. This would remove the stain of
original sin and forgive his personal sins. The Holy Spirit would come to
live within Him, bringing the sanctifying grace that would make him
holy. This grace would free him from slavery to sin and bring him love,
peace and joy. The Spirit would also impart to his soul a permanent
"character" — a change in its very being, an "ontological" change —
which would give the person a share in the mission of Christ, including
the power to baptize. Of course, this would incorporate him into the
Church, spiritually uniting him to all its other members. It was on
account of this unity that the infant children of its members could be
baptized as a precaution against a premature death.

If the hands of an apostle were imposed upon the head of an already
baptized believer, the Holy Spirit would come to him in a personal way in
order to assist him to persevere in his faith and to proclaim it with
particular courage. This "Confirmation" of the gifts given at Baptism
also imparted a permanent character; it made the person a "soldier" of
Jesus Christ.

Knowing that sanctifying grace would not so recreate man's fallen
nature as to free him from the possibility, or even likelihood that he
would fall back into sin — whether it be a minor (or "venial") sin which
resulted in the loss of some sanctifying grace, or a major (or "mortal") sin,
which cost the person all the grace that made him holy — Jesus gave the
apostles the power to forgive sins and restore the grace which had been
lost. Naturally, He also gave them the power to determine the appropriate
"Penance" which the sinner must pay in order to satisfy the rightful
demands of justice. If there was just cause, however, the apostles were
also empowered to release a person from its rightful demands, supplying
for him the necessary restitution by drawing upon the infinite merits of

Jesus' sacrificial death.

Desiring to give *Himself* to His Church — continually — Jesus instituted the "Eucharist." On the night before His death, at His last supper with His apostles, He changed ordinary bread and wine into His body and blood for their consumption. Thereafter, when the apostles repeated His words over bread and wine, His "real presence" would be re-evoked; retaining their natural appearance and taste, their substance would be completely changed into His body, blood, soul and divinity. Thus, this change was rightly called "transubstantiation." Reception of the Eucharist would create an especially intimate "communion" between a person and Christ. Naturally, this was an extremely potent source of grace. Furthermore, each time the Eucharist was effected, Jesus' sacrifice on the cross, the merit of the original sacrifice was re-obtained for the Church's benefit and, in a special way, for the good of any person or purpose which was intended by the person who offered it.

Choosing to raise "Matrimony" to the status of a sacrament that would make visible His love for the Church, Christ would impart to married people a special grace which would help them live their lifelong contract.

In order to enable the Church to continue to demonstrate His power to heal the sick, Jesus instructed the apostles to anoint their sick with oil. In this "Extreme Unction," He would send the sick a special grace by which they would be strengthened in both body and soul.

Finally, in order to accommodate the needs of a Church destined to spread throughout the world, and, not wanting the sacraments to cease with the deaths of the apostles, Christ empowered them to extend their sacramental powers to such representatives (the first priests) and successors, the bishops, by the laying on of hands and the invocation of the Holy Spirit. In both cases, a special character bearing these powers would be imparted to the souls of those who had been chosen. To the bishops, He gave the power to continue the succession in perpetuity. Of course, in all of their choices as to whom to give "Holy Orders," the bishops could depend upon the guidance of the Holy Spirit.

Nonetheless, the effectiveness (or "validity") of a sacrament does not depend upon the personal holiness of him who performs it. Sacraments work *ex opere operato* ("by the act having been done").[10] They work whenever they are performed for the benefit of someone who does not deny their effectiveness, putting an obstacle in the way of his reception of

---

10. It should also oe mentioned that "sacramental" action was also said to include the "blessings" by which God's favor could be invoked upon persons or objects.

their graces.

Section XIII: God's Working in the World

God's working in the world was hardly thought to have been limited to His working by means of the sacraments. After all, actual grace was already at work in the belief prior to Baptism. Moreover, God moved other things besides the human soul; He was frequently seen — and always expected — to intervene in human history, often in very dramatic ways.

He is responsive to prayers of petition. In the Trinitarian scheme of this response, it was already the Spirit who inspired the prayers and the Son who pled the cause. This the Son would be especially likely to do in response to the "intercession" of Mary or one of the "saints " who had followed Him most faithfully on earth and are surely near Him in heaven.

God works whether or not He is requested to. Often He sees to the just retribution for much of what takes place on the earth, rewarding the good and punishing sinners. Sometimes He works especially dramatic miracles just to demonstrate His power.

Through it all, God is involved in every moment that passes, providentially making sure that some good purpose is served by everything that happens. He is gradually preparing His kingdom. Once He is finished, the Son will return to judge the living and the dead.

Section XIV: Human and World Destiny

Although a "second coming" was definitely expected, and was expected to involve a judgment of the living and the dead, it was also believed that the dead have already received an indication of their eternal destiny.

When someone dies, his soul is released from his body and he goes to God for individual judgment.

The singular exception was that of Mary. Since she was immaculately conceived — and, as a matter of fact, did not sin during the course of her life — she did not need to die; this she did of her own accord in order to conclude her life like everyone else. Once she did, however, she was immediately assumed into heaven both soul and body.

If someone dies without the stain of original sin, or some personal sin, or the restitution of some personal sin unpaid, with a soul holy from sanctifying grace, he enters immediately into the heaven that God has prepared for all the saved. There he sees Him as He is and begins to enjoy the eternal happiness of life with Him.

If he dies without original sin but with the stain of some personal sin, or a debt to God unpaid, he goes to a "purgatory" where he suffers until he is purified of his sins and/or his debts are paid. But, terrible though this is, his punishment will eventually come to an end. Furthermore, prayers offered for his benefit can lessen the suffering that justice would otherwise demand. The sacrifice of the Mass (the Eucharist) is especially efficacious in this regard. As well, the Church can reduce the debt that a person had accumulated for his forgiven sins by means of an "Indulgence." Like the remission of earthly penance, these are even more valuable because the successful completion of one's earthly penance will not normally satisfy *all* the demands of divine justice.

If he dies with the stain of mortal sin, he is damned to the terrible and eternal torments of hell.

Finally, if he dies as an infant, before Baptism but without the stain of personal sins, he goes to a place of relative happiness called "limbo." Unworthy to receive the sight of God because he retains the stain of original sin and is therefore unworthy of sanctifying grace, he has not *personally* committed a sin for which punishment is due.

When Jesus finally returns in glory, all men will be reunited to their bodies. Each person will stand for public, final judgment. The damned will return to hell and the saved will be given a new, heavenly earth which Jesus will rule. And His kingdom will have no end.

* * *

This was the faith of 1500. To the extent that it was understood, it was the faith of almost everyone in Europe.

Chapter II: A Defense of the Faith of 1500

Section I: The Late-Medieval Idea of Apologetics

Having described the faith of 1500, it now can be defended. Of course, as must be stated, to the eyes of its most learned representatives, this faith did not need to be defended. After all, it was believed by almost everyone they knew. Furthermore, according to Church teaching, faith was a response to the experience in which God had made Himself known to all believers. It was the self-validating product of illuminating grace. Moreover, since grace was occasioned by the work of the Church, it confirmed everything the Church taught. Augustine (354-430) insisted that were it not for the authority of the Church, he would not have believed the gospel.[1]

Nonetheless, it was also Catholic tradition that Church teachings could also be confirmed by the so-called natural light of reason, i.e. a clearheaded examination of all the evidence properly explained (hence the classical term "apologetic," from "apology" or "explanation"). As Anselm (c.1033-1109) had explained, evidence was available because God wanted no conflict between realms of faith and reason.[2] What is more, as Abelard (1079-1142) had demonstrated, were reason *not* at work, the data of revelation could easily be misinterpreted.[3]

For a variety of reasons, Christians had been apologists from the very beginning. They accepted the scriptural mandate: "always be prepared to make a defense to anyone who calls you to account for the hope that is in you" (1 Pet.3:15). There were written "apologies" by Christianity's second century. Due to the necessities of that time, these were principally designed to 1) prove that Jesus was indeed the messiah promised the Jews, 2) win legal tolerance for Christians in the Roman Empire, and 3)

---

1. See his *Against the Letters of the Manicheans, 6.* Throughout this work, the titles of cited texts will be translated (or not) according to the author's judgement as to which rendering would be most useful to the reader of English.

2. See his *Monologian.* In this same work, Anselm made clear that he did not believe that reason could ever replace faith as the supreme source of knowledge about God. Indeed, he defined theology as "fides quaerens intellectum" ("faith seeking understanding"). In the dictum "credo ut intelligum" ("I believe in order to understand"), he insisted that true understanding is only possible after the surrender of faith.

3. For his understanding of the importance of apologetics in general, see his *Dialogue Between a Philosopher, a Jew and a Chrtistian;* for his demonstration of the difficulties in interpreting revelation — which featured his compilation of apparently contradictory scriptural passages — see his *Sic et Non.*

demonstrate that Christianity was superior to the "pagan" philosophy of the hellenic world. When external pressures finally lessened, however, there was time and leisure to provide apologetics for almost every element of Christian faith. By 1500, these efforts had resulted in a defense of Church teachings that left little unproved and less unsupported.

Section II: The Apologetic for the Existence of God

A) The Possibility of a Natural Knowledge of God

The starting point of every late-medieval apologetic of the truth of Church teachings was a proof for the existence of God. After all, God is the indispensable presupposition of all else that Christians believe. In 1500, this did not appear to be a problem. Though God was principally known through the grace of illumination, He also willed that "He the Creator can be known in the things that were made" (Rom.1:20, cf. Wis.13:1-9). Despite the fall, this was still possible because He did not want faith to be without reason. This was clear from the very fact that so many proofs were possible.

The proofs for the existence of God can helpfully be divided into two groups: 1) studies of the human soul, and 2) studies of nature at large. The "ontological" argument of Anselm[4] resists classification. Furthermore, this argument never enjoyed the confidence accorded to the others that we shall consider. For these reasons, we shall consider it separately, and first.

B) The Ontological Argument

Though much has been written about the ontological argument and its supposed subtlety, it is simple to state.

When we think of God, by definition, we are thinking of a being which is greater than any other that can be conceived. This being must exist because, if He does not, we could easily conceive of a being who is greater, namely a god who *does* exist. Certainly, it is greater to exist.

C) A Knowledge of God from a Study of the Soul,

The So-Called Augustinian Arguments

Christian argumentation for the existence of God based upon a study of the soul was indebted to Augustine, whose writings contained several. Of these, two enjoyed widespread popularity. For both, he was known to be indebted to Plato (427-347 B.C.).[5]

---

4. See his *Proslogian.*
5. See especially his *Phaedo.*

1. The Argument from the Immortality of the Soul

The first argument was based upon the supposed self-evidence of the immortality of the soul.

It is evident that the soul is immortal. Mortality involves corruption, the disintegration of its parts. An apple ceases to be if it is broken, cooked, or rots. The soul is simple; it has no parts. Therefore, it cannot corrupt. (Of course, it is true that God could annihilate the soul by a special act of His will. But this we trust He will not do; what He has made He sustains.) Now, it is evident that nothing immortal could have been produced by something mortal because nothing can give what it does not have. Therefore, the immortality of the soul betrays its creation by something which is immortal in itself. This is God.

2. The Argument from the Restlessness of the Soul

The second argument was based upon the supposed self-evidence of the restlessness of the soul.

It is evident that the soul is attracted by many things. This is seen in the many desires that men experience. Likewise, it is evident that the soul is never satisfied; men are never satisfied with anything they have, are, or know. Even as they satisfy one desire, another takes its place. Therefore, it is evident that nothing in the world can satisfy the soul. Continuing to desire more than the world can ever give, it is obviously being attracted by something outside the world and superior to it. This is God. As Augustine said: "My soul will never rest until it rests in Thee."[6]

D) A Knowledge of God from a Study of Nature at Large, The Five Ways

Although the arguments from a study of the soul were indeed perceived to prove their points, they rarely received first mention when the existence of God needed to be proved. This was the place given the arguments based upon a study of nature at large. Of these, none were more popular than those of Thomas Aquinas (c. 1225-1274). Remarkably soon after his death, each of his now famous "five ways of demonstrating God's existence"[7] had become a leading proof. Though the principles which supported these demonstrations had first been articulated by the man *he* called "The Philosopher," Aristotle (384-322 B.C.),[8] it was Thomas who put them to work for Christianity. They now follow, rephrased in order to avoid a problem of terminology which would unnecessarily hinder the purposes for which they are reported.

---

6. See his renowned *Confessions,* 1,1.
7. See his masterwork, the *Summa Theologica,* hereafter abbreviated *S. Th.* 1, q.2, a.3.
8. See his *Metaphysics,* part of the *Organon.* It should be stated that most of Aristotle's works were entitled after his death.

1. The Argument from Motion

The first "way" departs from the fact that nature is filled with things that are in motion.

It is evident that things are in motion. It is also evident that anything in motion moves because it has first been moved by something else. Of course, anything which has moved something else must have itself been moved by something else again. Each of these movers is properly called an "intermediate" mover because each had to be moved before it could itself move something else. Now, an infinite regression of intermediate movers is impossible because none of them would be the source of motion and nothing would ever have moved. Therefore, it is evident that there exists an unmoved, first or self-moving mover. This is God.

2. The Argument from Cause and Effect

The second way departs from the fact that nature involves cause and effect.

It is evident that this is a world of cause and effect; everything happens for a reason. It is likewise evident that the cause of any effect has itself been caused, and so on and so on. . . Naturally, each of these causes is properly referred to as an intermediate cause because each had to be caused before it could itself cause an effect of its own. Now, an infinite regression of such causes is impossible because none of them would possess the power to cause ("causality") and nothing would ever have happened. Therefore, it is evident that there exists an uncaused, or first or self-causing cause. This is God.

3. The Argument from "Contingent" and "Necessary" Being

The third way will describe itself.

It is evident that the things in the world are "contingent"; they come and they go. None needs to exist and, thus, all of them must have come into existence at one time or another. Now, if everything in the world must have come into existence, there was once a time when nothing in the world existed. Therefore, since from nothing, nothing comes, there must be something outside the world which has always existed, and needs to — a "necessary" being — which has the power to bring other things into existence. This is God.

4. The Argument from Differing Degrees

The fourth way was actually called the argument from "gradation."

It is evident that there are many things which bear differing degrees of the same characteristic. For example, some things are beautiful while others are more so; some are good while others are better. This betrays existence of something else which bears the most that there can be. After all, things do not get their characteristics out-of-the-blue; each must have its source and this source cannot possess any less than the most which is possible. Therefore, there must be something which has the most that there can be — something which is most beautiful and the best — beauty and goodness itself. This is God.

5. The Argument from the Direction of the World

Thomas called his fifth way the argument from the "governance" of the world.

It is evident that the world acts intelligently. The dependable passage of days, months, and seasons is ample evidence of this. Of course, the world is not itself intelligent. Therefore, since whatever lacks intelligence cannot act intelligently unless it is directed to, the world must have an intelligent director. And this, obviously, is God.

Section III: Divine Revelation

A) The Necessity of Divine Revelation

Although the natural knowledge of God was gratefully accepted, it was not thought to involve everything that could otherwise be known about Him. Indeed, Christianity had never considered itself other than a revealed religion. Its tenets were made known by special acts of God's will. These communicated truths that man would never have discovered on his own, "the mystery which was kept secret for long ages but is now disclosed" (Rom.16:25-26). For example, on his own, reflecting upon the evidence of the world, man would never have discovered the Trinity. As Jesus Himself said: "Thou hast hidden these things from the wise and understanding and revealed them to babes" (Mt.11:25). According to Justin Martyr (c.100-c.165), this was the principal proof that Christianity is superior to pagan philosophy.[9]

B) The Nature of Divine Revelation

Divine revelation was definitely understood to involve special, i.e. supernatural, and often dramatic acts of God's will. For example, to Abraham He appeared in the form of a desert traveler (Gen.18:2). To Moses He appeared in the form of a burning bush (Ex.3:2). To prophets He sometimes granted a vision (e.g. Is.1:1); to others He simply spoke (e.g. Jer.1:2). In any case, "no prophecy ever came by the impulse of man

---

9. See his *Second Apology*, especially 13; Justin was the most prominent of the second century "apologists" of whom mention has already been made (cf.p 34).

but men moved by the Holy Spirit spoke from God" (2 Pet.1:21). Finally, He spoke by sending His Son (cf. Heb.1:1-4).

Thereafter, the Holy Spirit inspired the apostles as they formulated the new faith. But, with the death of the last apostle, this special guidance ceased. As Irenaeus (c.130-c.200) said: revelation had "closed."[10] Hereafter, inspiration would guide only the interpretation of the existing sources of revelation. After all, if "public" revelation had not closed, Jesus was not the Father's final saving word.[11]

C) The Credibility of Divine Revelation

Although the credibility of divine revelation was a product of the grace that accompanied it, God also willed that its truth could be known by means of certain external signs of its supernatural origin. Such was the teaching of Origen (c.185-c.254) who explained that this was in keeping with God's desire that the realms of faith and reason co-exist in harmony even with respect to those things which could not be known through reason directly.[12] As Jesus Himself acknowledged: "unless you see signs and wonders, you will not believe" (Jn.4:48). Since the resurrection was the supreme sign, Paul could say: "if Christ has not been raised, then our preaching is in vain and your faith is in vain" (1 Cor.15:14).

1. Biblical Signs

Even apart from the resurrection and Jesus' other miracles, and the prophecies He fulfilled, biblical signs were both the best known and most convincing. For example, God caused Abraham's wife Sarah to conceive in her old age (Gen.21:1-2). He empowered Moses to invoke ten plagues upon Egypt (Ex.7-11). At the horn of Joshua, He brought down the walls of Jericho (Jos.6:20). Through the prophet Elijah, He predicted the fall of Israel (1 Kings 17ff). Through the prophet Jeremiah, He foretold the fate of Judah. Through Isaiah and others, He foretold the coming of His Son. In particular, He foretold His birth to a virgin (Is.7:14) of the house of David (Jer.23:5) in Bethlehem (Mic.5:2). He told that the Son was to suffer for our sins (Is.53). Indeed, nearly every detail of Jesus' passion was predicted. For example, the fact that His executioners cast lots for His garments (Jn.19:24, Ex.28:32), their inexplicable failure to break His bones (Jn.19:36, Ex.12:46) and the piercing of His side (Jn.19:37, Zech.12:10).

---

10. See his immensely influential *Adversus Haereses,* hereafter *Adv. Haer.* 4,28,2.

11. "Public" revelation was still to be distinguished from non-doctrinal, private communications to certain holy persons.

12. See especially the preface of his apologetic *Contra Celsum;* Celsus was the pagan author of a tract that ridiculed Christianity. Origen was the leader of what would later be called the Alexandrian "school" of theology.

The signs did not cease with the resurrection. As we have seen, the apostles performed many miracles. Jesus had given them the power to cast out demons, handle serpents, drink deadly poison, and cure the sick (cf. Mk.16:17-18). Peter was given a particularly potent sign of God's favor. All the apostles could cure the sick by the laying on of hands, but Peter could do it with the touch of his shadow (Acts 5:15). He was even given the power to raise Tabitha from the dead (Acts 9:36-41).

2. Post-Biblical Signs

The signs did not cease with the apostles. As we saw, the "lives of the saints" were filled with the stories of miracles. Almost all the saints could cure the sick. Many were the *object* of a miracle. (When beheaded for her refusal to renounce her faith, the body of St. Catherine was taken by angels to the top of Mt. Sinai.) As a sign of God's favor, death did not decay parts of their bodies. To the holders of these "relics," He would frequently grant supernatural favors. (When Thomas' secretary Reginald was sick with a severe fever, Thomas cured him with a relic of St. Catherine.)

3. Ever-Present Evidence

No miracle was more witnessed than the ever-present miracle of Christian life. By gifts of grace, God enabled untold numbers of hopelessly weak and sinful people to overcome their very selves. Though grace was most often to be seen in the faith and obedience of the typical Christian, it was especially obvious in the remarkable courage of the many Christian "martyrs." The word is from the Greek for "testimony," and from the stoning of Stephen, the first martyr (Acts 7:54-60), thousands of Christians have given up their lives in testimony to the truth of their faith.[13] As asked Augustine: "has anyone ever died rather than deny that Hercules or Romulus were gods?"[14]

Should someone deny that the lives of Christians were due to grace, the divine origin of Christianity was still proved in the moral superiority of their lives. As Tertullian (c.160-c.225) famously observed: "see how these Christians love one another."[15] As Origen observed, Christianity shows its superiority in the very fact it calls for love. Indeed, it calls man to love even his enemies, even to the sacrifice of one's life. What other religion or philosophy does that?[16]

---

13. Apparently grace gave not only courage but fortitude; it was said to have enabled St. Simeon Stylites to spend almost thirty years in prayer atop a pole.

14. See his classic work *The City of God*, 22,6 The work is especially remembered for its interpretation of history as the spread and conquest of evil with its pivot point in Christ.

15. See his *Apologetic*, 397.

16. *Contra Celsum*, 3.

Augustine was credited with the popular apologetic based not upon the lives of Christians, but upon the life, i.e. the history of the Church. According to the argument: were the Church not of divine origin, and therefore the beneficiary of divine protection, it would never have survived. Persecuted, weakened by internal division and plagued by corruption, it has not only survived, it has spread.[17]

Nonetheless, should anyone still have doubted that God did speak through the Church, or called to question anything it taught, the Church still had recourse to the Sacred Scriptures.

Section IV: The Sacred Scriptures

A) The Divine Authorship of the Scriptures

1. The Idea

That God is the author of the Sacred Scriptures had been the understanding of Christians from long before anyone could remember.

The Scriptures actually recorded God's instruction that certain things be written down (e.g. Jer.30:2). They even recorded the reason that they were written: "that you may know the truth concerning the things of which you have been informed" (Lk.1:4). Their *divine* authorship was especially evident in their content, for example, those things no human could have known (e.g. the events of creation). It was most evident in the beauty of their truth.

2. The Canon

Since the Scriptures were known to have been written over a long period of history, they were not expected to contain a list of the books which are properly included among their number. Nonetheless, there still seemed to be ample indication. The Scriptures mention one another. Jesus spoke of both the "Law," as the Pentateuch was also known, and the "Prophets" (e.g. Mt.5:17). He quoted Isaiah (Mk.3:3). Paul cited a number of the books of the Old Testament (e.g. Rom.9:25).

Though the New Testament did not speak of itself, tradition does. Justin spoke of the gospels and other writings of the apostles.[18] Irenaeus told that the gospels were *four*.[19] When Marcion (d.c.160) the "gnostic" (q.v.p.51) denied the divine authorship of the Old Testament, pointing out passages that seem to describe God as ignorant, cruel and

---

17. *Of True Religion*, 3.
18. See his *First Apology*, 1,67.
19. *Adv. Haer.* 3,11,8; Irenaeus was also the first to speak of a "New Testament" (*Adv. Haer.*) 4,9,1.

capricious, it was Tertullian who responded. Insisting upon the "unity of the Law and the gospel,"[20] he pointed out that the Church had always taught that both testaments were from the same good God and of equal authority.[21] Within a century, the Fathers of the Church had cited every biblical book. A listing of these books (or "canon," from the Greek word for "rule") was formally approved by the regional Council of Hippo in 373, and this same list was confirmed by the Ecumenical Council of Carthage in 397 (DS 186[22]).

B) Verbal Inspiration

The divine authorship of the Sacred Scriptures meant inspiration. As Scripture itself said: "all Scripture is inspired by God" (2 Tim.3:16). Obviously, this meant verbal inspiration — God's dictation to the mind of the human writer every word of the sacred text. It was hardly imaginable that God would have entrusted the recording of revelation to the articulation of weak and sinful men, subject to error at every step. Rather, He undoubtedly made sure that His word was faithfully reported. Some imagined that this involved an angel whispering in the author's ear. But, of course, the principal agent of "inspiration" must be the Spirit. John Chrysostom (c.347-407) saw the sacred writers as musical instruments "played" by the Holy Spirit.[23] Augustine saw them as the Spirit's "pens."[24]. It was without imagery that, in 1442, the Council of Florence declared that the Holy Spirit had indeed inspired all of the Scriptures and all of their parts (DS 1334).

C) Inerrancy

1. The Idea

Inspiration meant the inerrancy of the Scriptures in all things. After all, God could not be wrong about even the most minor of details. There was no doubt the Bible should be taken literally. Its stories were history and its descriptions of nature were science. Obviously, as Justin stated, "the

---

20. See his *Adversus Marcionem* hereafter *Adv. Mar.* 1,19.

21. See his *Adversus Praxeam*, hereafter *Adv. Prax.* 20. Praxeas was a second century "monarchist" (q.v. p. 51). Tertullian's work "against" him was actually directed against Marcion and is our best source for Marcion's thinking. Most often, as we shall see, the work of heretics was not preserved and is therefore known only through the writings, and interpretation, of those who chose to dispute them.

22. The "DS" refers to the *The Enchiridion Symbolorum Definitionum et Declarationum de Rebus Fidei et Morum*, 36th edition, a compilation of important church documents originally edited by Henry Denzinger and later re-edited by Adolf Schönmetzer.

23. See his "Homily on the Gospel of John," 1,1; John was the founder of the school of Antioch.

24. *Confessions*, 7,21.

Scriptures cannot contradict themselves."[25] Irenaeus said that they were "perfect."[26]

Many of the Fathers taught that the Scriptures tell even more than the literal truth. For example, Augustine held that Noah's ark was a pre-figurement of the Church persecuted.[27] Some found extraliteral meaning in scriptural numbers. Irenaeus went so far to say that the *four* gospels bespeak the four corners of the world to which they were meant to be carried.[28] Justin's *Apologies* attempted to prove that the Scriptures teach all of the truths of Greek philosophy — at least implicitly. Whatever the intent, Origen held that all Scripture has its "topical" sense.[29]

2. An Addendum: External Evidence of the Credibility of the Scriptures
Although the credibility of the Scriptures was said to be the product of the grace that accompanied their reading, confidence in their credibility was also to be seen in certain external sources. First of all, for the most part, the Scriptures were written by participants in the events they recorded. For example, it was Moses who received the Law and it was he who wrote it down. Furthermore, the most important biblical events were of such extraordinary nature that the witnesses to them could not have been mistaken about what they reported. For example, it was reported the sun stood still (Josh.10); who could have been mistaken about that?

The word of the New Testament authors was especially credible. Matthew and John accompanied Jesus in His public life from the beginning. They heard Him teach; they witnessed His miracles. Though the other two gospel writers did not know Jesus, they were themselves the disciples of people who did. Mark was the companion of Peter;[30] Luke was a companion of Paul.[31] Were someone to doubt the veracity of what they had written, how was he to explain that all these men, indeed all the apostles — except John — died as martyrs? And they all told the same story.

25. See his *Dialogue with Tryphon the Jew*, hereafter *Dial.* 65.
26. *Adv. Haer.* 2,28,2.
27. See his *Enchiridion*, 56. Actually, Augustin claimed that "the entire New Testament is hidden in the Old; and the Old is explained in the New" (see his *Quaestiones in Heptataeuchum*, 2,73).
28. *Adv. Haer.* 3,11,9.
29. See his "Commentary on the Gospel of Matthew," 10,14.
30. So wrote Papias (c.60-c.130), see his "Fragments," 3,39.
31. So wrote Irenaeus, *Adv. Haer.* 3,1,1.

Section V: Sacred Tradition

In 1500, no one thought that the Scriptures were the only source of revelation. For one thing, they did not claim to be. John wrote that there was much that had not been recorded (Jn.21:25). Paul also made reference to this "unwritten tradition" (2 Thess.2:14). Clement (c.96) spoke of the "rule" of tradition.[32] Irenaeus spoke of its "force."[33] Tertullian spoke explicitly of the "apostolic tradition written and oral."[34] Finally, in 787, the Second Council of Nicea officially declared that the sources of revelation were two (DS 609).

Section VI: The Church

In the end, if there was doubt about the content of Tradition, or the interpretation of the Scriptures, it could always be resolved by an appeal to Church teaching.

A) The Divine Institution of the Church

In 1500, little seemed more secure than the Church. Little was more certain than its divine institution.

As we know, God wanted the Hebrews to be His people. When they rejected this role, He desired to replace them (cf. 1 Pet.2:10). Thus, when Judas Iscariot betrayed Jesus (and later committed suicide), another apostle (Matthias), needed to be named; the fathers of the twelve tribes had to be replaced by the twelve spiritual fathers of God's new people (Acts 1:15-26). Through them, the Son would continue His mission. Therefore, Christ founded the Church, His visible "body" here on earth (cf. 1 Cor.12), His beloved "bride" and partner in the work of salvation (Eph.5:22-32).

Jesus instituted the Church when He named Peter its first earthly head. Before all the apostles He declared: "you are Peter and upon this rock I shall build My Church . . . and the powers of death will not prevail against it" (Mt.16:18). Later, He gave Peter and the other apostles the explicit commission to "make disciples of all nations" (Mt.18:19); "preach the gospel to the whole creation" (Mk.16:15).

---

32. See his "Letter to the Corinthians," hereafter Clem. 6,17. Clement was the first of the first generation of post-biblical Christian authors whose work was considered so important that they were known as the "Apostolic Fathers."
33. *Adv. Haer.* 1,10,2.
34. *Adv. Mar.* 1,21.

Though in heaven, Jesus promised the apostles: "I will be with you always until the end of the age" (Mt.18:19). "He is still head of the body, the Church" (Col.1:18). To guide the Church, He would send it His Spirit (cf.Jn.14:16). Arriving on "Pentecost," the Spirit appeared in the form of tongues of fire (Acts 2:1-4). The apostles received the power to be understood in many languages (Acts 2:6-12). With Peter as their leader, they began to preach the gospel with great courage (Acts 2:14ff). They met success immediately, converting about three thousand the very first day (Acts 2:41). This aroused the anger of Jewish leaders, including Saul. Though a persecutor of the early Church, Saul, who became Paul, was converted after Christ appeared to him on the road to Damascus (Acts 9). The first Gentiles were converted a short time later (Acts 10:45). With this precedent, Paul went to Antioch where he converted the Gentiles in great numbers, and it was there that Jesus' followers were first called "Christians" (Acts 11:26).

There was no doubt that Jesus intended His Church to remain one body (cf. 1 Cor.12), "one fold with one shepherd" (Jn.10:16), "one Lord, one faith [with] one baptism" (Eph.4:5). What else could He have intended? Indeed, He prayed to God His Father asking: "that they may be one, even as we are one" (Jn.17:22).

C) Apostolic Succession and the Papacy

1. Apostolic Succession

According to the immemorial argument, if the Church were truly to be one body, it would require a head — leadership. Without the head, the body dies. But, leadership requires authority; no one should obey a leader without authority (cf.Heb.3:10). And "there is no authority except from God, and those that exist have been instituted by God" (Rom.13:1). Plainly, this authority was given to the apostles and, for obvious reasons, it was likewise clear that Christ gave them the power to pass on their authority, as in the recorded case of Matthias and also of Timothy, who Paul appointed and became the first to be called a "bishop" (1 Tim.3:1).

Clement stated explicitly that the bishops were appointed by the apostles and given a permanent "character" so that they could appoint their own successors.[35] Ignatius of Antioch (c.35-c.107) went so far as to say that agreement with the bishop is agreement with Christ.[36] He was also the first to call the Church "Catholic," i.e. "universal."[37] The Council of Constantinople declared that the Church was "one, holy, catholic and

35. Clem. 44.
36. See his "Letter to the Smyrnaeans," hereafter Smyrn. 1,2.
37. Ibid. 8,2.

apostolic" (DS 150).

2. The Papacy

The immemorial argument was always extended to the papacy. Simply stated, if the Church were truly to remain *one*, it would require one *supreme* authority. In Peter, this was clearly provided. He was the "rock" upon which the Church would be built (Mt.16:18). He was given "the keys to the kingdom of heaven" and told that "whatever you bind on earth will be bound in heaven and whatever you loose on earth will be loosed in heaven" (Mt.16:19). Jesus, the "good shepherd" (Jn.10:11), told Peter to "feed My sheep" (Jn.21:17). Clearly, he was to be the "vicar" of Christ.

It was also clear that supreme authority had to be passed on. To whom would it go but Peter's successors as bishop of Rome? Irenaeus said that "Peter and Paul founded the Church of Rome and this Church has an authority with which all of the churches in the world must agree."[38] Cyprian (d.258) said it even more plainly asking: "he who deserts the 'cathedra' (or 'seat' or 'authority') of Peter, upon whom the Church is founded, does he really believe that he is still a member of the Church?"[39] Augustine said it most plainly: "Rome has spoken, the case is closed."[40]

When certain bishops proposed the theory that an ecumenical council is superior to the pope ("conciliarism"), Pius II (1458-64)[41] quickly condemned it (DS 1375).

D) Infallibility of Councils and Popes

Authority was all but synonymous with infallibility. (Indeed, the very word "authority," in Latin, "auctoritas," means "truth.") God would not allow His people to follow a leader in error. Neither would He allow His Church to teach error. To save it from error was one of the most important reasons He sent the Spirit, the "Spirit of Truth" (cf. Jn.16:13).

Let it be stated once again. The inspiration of Church teaching was in no way considered to compete with the Scriptures. But, as Irenaeus had argued, words on a page cannot interpret themselves. They cannot dispute the person who can claim that anything means anything. Therefore, the Scriptures require authoritative interpretation.[42] Thus did Tertullian call them the "Church's book."[43]

---

38. *Adv. Haer.* 3,3,2.
39. See his *On the Unity of the Catholic Church*, 4.
40. See his "Sermons," 131.
41. Here and hereafter, the dates for popes refer to those of their papacy.
42. *Adv. Haer.* 4,26,5.
43. See his *On the Precepts of Heretics*, 21.

Since apostolic authority had been passed on to a succession of bishops, it was also clear that the infallibility needed to uphold it had also been passed on. Irenaeus said that the bishops possessed an "unfailing charism of truth."[44] This at least meant that their councils would be inspired. The Spirit had guided the apostles in their selection of Matthias. He also inspired their decision not to require circumcision of Gentile converts; this "Council of Jerusalem" was the Church's first (Acts 15).

But, since the pope remained the supreme head of the Church, his agreement with conciliar decisions was necessary if unity were to be preserved. (This was evident from the beginning; it was Peter who convoked the Council of Jerusalem and it was he who pronounced its conclusions law.) After all, who else was to mediate disputes between bishops or groups of bishops? Moreover, as supreme head of the Church, surely the pope could speak authoritatively anytime he saw the need. Still, as Thomas made clear, his "infallibility," and that of ecumenical councils, extended only to matters of faith and morals, the scope of revelation.[45]

E) The Duties of the People

Infallibility obviously implied the duty of the people to accept Church teaching. As Jesus Himself said: "he who hears you, hears me; and he who rejects you, rejects me; and he who rejects me, rejects Him who sent me" (Lk.10:16).

The divine institution of authority also implied the duty of the people to obey. From the beginning, the faithful were told: "obey your leaders and submit to them (Heb.13:17). Paul explicitly warned that "he who resists the authorities resists what God has appointed and will incur judgment" (Rom.13:2).

F) "Outside the Church No Salvation"

Resisting the authorities undoubtedly involved a *severe* judgment.

Jesus said that a person who refused to listen to the Church should be treated as a gentile or a tax collector (cf. Mt.18:17); Paul said that the church should have nothing to do with him (cf. 2 Thess.2:14). Cut off from His body they are cut off Christ. Ignatius explained that they are cut off from the saving grace which is only shared by those in communion with the bishop.[46] Cyprian stated it explicitly: *extra ecclesiam nulla salus,* "outside the church no salvation".[47] In 1215, the Fourth Lateran Council

---

44. *Adv. Haer.* 4,26,2.
45. See his *Quodilibetum*, 9, q.7, a.16.
46. Smyrn. 8,1.
47. See his "Letters," 73,21.

formally incorporated this dictum into the body of Church teaching (DS 802). Less than a century later, in the declaration *Unum Sanctum,* Pope Boniface VIII (1234-1303) repeated the teaching, insisting that "to be saved, it is absolutely necessary to submit to the Pope"(DS 875).[48] Finally in 1442, the Council of Florence declared that "no one, not pagans, Jews, heretics , nor schismatics will be saved unless, before the end of their life, they are received into the Catholic Church"(DS 1351).

Section VII: An Apologetic For Church Teachings

Despite the duty of faith in Church teaching, the late-medieval churchmen would not have been opposed to providing an apologetic for each of the Church's individual teachings. As we have seen, the Church recognized the need to respond to those who misinterpreted revelation, or denied it (cf. p.34). Such a response would have consisted of a presentation of the evidence of Scripture, Tradition — with an emphasis on the earliest authorities - and the world. Always the project would begin with God.

A) God

1. God's Existence

We have already seen the proofs for God's existence from the standpoint of reason (cf. p. 35). Scriptural evidence supplied the rest of what needed to be defended.

It was plainly stated: "The Lord our God is one" (Deut.6:4); besides Him there is no other (cf. Is.44:6). This was clearly the teaching of Jesus (cf. Mk.12:29). It was also the universal testimony of Christian spirituality; only one God speaks to man in prayer. Besides God cannot be "God" if He shares divinity with any other being; He is *the* being upon whom all else depends. He is the one of His kind.

God's personhood would not have been defended because it had never been questioned. Every biblical word about His thoughts, feelings, acts, especially His relationship with His people, implied that He was a person. He was the living God" (Mt.16:16).

Though God "dwells in unapproachable light, whom no man has ever seen or can see" (1 Tim.6:16), it was not the Christian spirit that nothing can be said about Him. This was theology and theology had arrived at almost universal agreement as to what can be said. Indeed, Augustine[49]

---

48. *Unum Sanctum* also contained the first official statement that the Church is superior to the state.
49. See especially his *On the Trinity,* 1.

and Thomas[50] offered almost identical lists of divine attributes. It was Thomas who took pains to justify the ways in which they were known, the *via negativa* and the analogy of being.[51] In 1215, most of the attributes were included in doctrine (DS 800); the remainder did not need to be.

2. The General Attributes

The divine attributes were self-evident.

God is obviously uncreated because if He had been created He would not be God.

He is obviously self-sufficient because if He depended upon something else for His existence He would not be God. He himself told Moses:"I am who I am"(Ex.3:14).

If He was uncreated, He is eternal (cf. Gen.21:33).

If He existed from all-eternity, He is surely immortal. Indeed, "God alone has immortality" (1 Tim.6:16).

He is not made of matter. "God is spirit"(Jn.4:24).

As "spirit," He is simple. Spiritual things have no parts. Besides if He *were* composed of parts, His existence would be dependent upon them — and the stuff of which they were made. Then He would not be self-sufficient; He would not be God, the source of all being.

As the source of all being, He is perfect. He alone is good (cf. Mt.18:17). "Holy is His name" (Is.57:15). "He loves those who hate evil" (Ps.97:10).

Since limitation is an imperfection, God is also infinite.

As infinite, God is also immense. He is everywhere (cf. Ps.139:7-9).

Finally, in view of all of the above, God must be immutable. Nothing can change Him and He has no reason to change Himself. He Himself told Malachi: "I the Lord do not change" (Mal.3:6).

3. The Particular Perfections

The particular perfections were just as obvious as the general attributes.

God's perfection implies His omniscience. "God knows all things" (Job 28:24). He can see an entire lifetime at once, even before it is over (cf. Ps.139:16).

God's perfection also implies His omnipotence. He created the

---

50. *S.Th.* I, q.3-11.

51. Actually, the analogy of being was the object of some medieval debate. According to John Duns Scotus (c.1265-1308), if created things were solely analogous to God, they could not tell us anything about Him. This would only be possible if God and creation were in some way similar, sharing a "univocal" characteristic, as he called it. Otherwise, there is no way for us to move from creation to God. Thomas'followers insisted that God is superior to creation in every way. But, they still maintained that analogies give us an idea of what God is like, if not what He is.

heavens and the earth by the power of His voice (Gen.1)."[He] can do all things" (Job 24); "nothing is impossible for God" (Lk.1:37).

4. The Special Characteristics of God's Goodness

The special characteristics of God's goodness were even more evident than the particular perfections.

God's goodness was best to be seen in His infinite love. His love was best to be seen in the very fact of man's existence. God owed man nothing; it was out of love that He chose to share His life. When man sinned, He forgave him. God so loved the world that He gave His only son to be our savior (cf. Jn.3:16). "God is love" (1 Jn.4:8).

Nonetheless, God's goodness was also to be seen in His justice. He "loves justice" (Ps.37:28). He is a "God of Justice" (Is.30:18). "He shows no partiality" (Rom. 2:11).

B) The Trinity

Though the word appears nowhere in the Bible, it still seemed that the Trinity was one of its most clearly taught doctrines. After all, Jesus told His apostles to "baptize in the name of the Father and the Son and the Holy Spirit" (Mt.28:39). At creation God said: "Let us make man in 'our' image" (Gen.1:25).

The doctrine was even more clearly affirmed in the fact that the Scriptures affirm the existence and the divinity of all three persons. Everything else taught about them was the obvious implication of the simple fact of their existence as *one* God.

1. God as Father

The fact that God was "Father" was clear from His creation, rule and care for all things. Jesus constantly urged us to call God our Father (cf. Mt.6:9, Lk.11:2). God's Fatherhood was also to be seen in the divinity of His "son."

2. The Divinity of the Son

If the divinity of the Son were not evident in the miraculous events surrounding His birth (q. v. p.68), it was more than evident when He was baptized by John. It was then that God spoke from heaven saying: "This is my beloved Son with whom I am well pleased" (Mt.3:17, cf. Mk.1:9, Lk.3:22). Jesus frequently referred to God as "my" father (e.g. Jn.3:35). (If He had not claimed that He was God's Son, why was he charged with blasphemy?). Peter proclaimed Him "the Christ, the Son of the living God" (Mt.16:16).

The Scriptures also explained that Jesus is God's "only begotten son" (Jn.1:14). He is superior to the angels (Heb.1:4ff). He is God's "image"

(Col.1:15); in Him "the fullness of God dwells; (Col.1:16). He was in the form of God but He humbled Himself by being born in the likeness of men (cf. Phil.2:7-8). He existed before Abraham (Jn.8:58). He was the "Word" present at the beginning" (Jn.1:2), "through whom all things were made" (Jn.1:3, cf.1:17). He is, as the apostle Thomas came to proclaim: "my lord and my God" (Jn.20:28).

It was Justin who first explained that the Son — whom he always called the "Word," the "Logos" — was "generated," not created. He described generation in terms of fire which communicates itself but is not diminished.[52]

Despite the efforts of men like Justin, it was still to be acknowledged that the divinity of the Son had been the most troubled doctrine in Christian history. The reason: the relationship between Jesus and the Father was essentially a mystery to be accepted on faith. Naturally, there were those who would accept no mystery — except one of their own making. Valentinus (c.150) could not conceive of God made man; he held that Jesus, a man, was divinely guided, or "adopted," an idea later to be known as "adoptionism." (Valentinus was a "gnostic"; "gnosticism" was a Greek movement which combined a contempt for the material with the idea that salvation was to be found in certain mysterious "knowledge," or "gnosis," which was not available to everyone.) Sabellius (c. 200) did not see how Jesus could be both God and Son; he held that Christ was the Father made man — "monarchism." Arius (c. 250-336) did not see how the Father and Jesus could be one God. He reasoned that Christ's sonship must mean that He is subordinate to the Father. Superior to us, He is still a creature.

None of these ideas was to be accepted. If Jesus was not God, His sacrifice would not have saved us. If He was the Father, His sacrifice would not have made sense. Besides, to whom did He pray? Who had been directing creation while He had become part of it?

Not respecting these and other arguments, denials of the divinity of the Son, especially "Arianism," attracted a considerable following. It took the impassioned efforts of men like Athanasius (c.296-373) and Hilary of Poitiers (c.315-67) to arrest their spread.[53] Then, in 325, under the leadership of Athanasius, the Council of Nicea decreed that Jesus was the Son of God, "begotten not made, one-in-being with the Father" (DS

---

52. *Dial.* 61.
53. See especially Athanasius' *Against Arius* for what was to become the classic defense of the divinity of Christ.

125).[54] Finally, in 381, the Council of Constantinople formally condemned each of the heresies that we have just seen (DS 151).

3. The Divinity of the Holy Spirit

Though the divinity of the Son was more discussed, the divinity of the Holy Spirit was no less evident. The Spirit was present at creation (cf. Gen.1:2). He inspired the prophets. He descended upon Jesus at His Baptism in the form of a dove (Mt.3:16, Mk.1:10, Lk.3:22). He dwells in the faithful, making them his temples (e.g. 1 Cor.3:16-17); He brings an entirely new life (cf. Rom.8).

It was Tertullian who first said it plainly: "the Holy Spirit is the Third Person of the Blessed Trinity"; in short, "the Spirit is God."[55] When this was questioned, Athanasius explained that if the Spirit is not God, He could not make us participants in divine life. And, what was true of the Son was true of the Holy Spirit; if He was not co-eternal with the Father, and of His very substance, He would not be God.[56] But, as Basil (c.330-79) first explained, this does not mean that the Spirit had been "generated" like the Son. Since the Son must have been involved in the procession of the Spirit, He (the Spirit) must have proceeded by a different process — "spiration."[57]

Regardless of the above reasoning, a certain Macedonius (d.c.362) denied that there was sufficient reason to hold that the Holy Spirit was a distinct, co-eternal partner of the Father and the Son, one-in-being with them both. It was largely to condemn this heresy that the Council of Constantinople was called and it did declare that the Holy Spirit "proceeded" from the Father (DS 150).Then in 589, the Third Provincial Council of Toledo declared that the Holy Spirit proceeded from both the Father "and the Son" (DS 470).[58]

---

54. The phrase "one-in-being," in Greek *homoousius* represented the first time a non-biblical word was used in an official Church pronouncement; it appeared in the "Nicean Creed," a formulation of the faith that later took on an almost scriptural authority.

55. *Adv. Prax.* 12; 13. It was in this work that we find the words "Person" and "Trinity" employed for the first time with reference to the inner life of God.

56. See his "Letters to Serapion," 1,2.

57. See his *On the Holy Spirit*, 47.

58. The council inserted the phrase "and the son" in Latin *filioque*, into the text of its creed, an adaption of the creed of the Council of Constantinople, itself an adaption of the Nicean Creed. The leaders of the Eastern churches objected on the grounds that this teaching was not tradition — which they held as normative — and therefore could not be imposed as an article of faith. Western leaders pointed out that the move had the approval of the pope. This did not prove decisive because the Eastern leaders had already come to claim that the "primacy" of the pope was one of honor and not of authority. They considered the pope *primus inter pares*, "first among equals." In 1054, these, and political issues, led to the "schism," or "separation," of the Eastern churches. Though peace was made at the Council of Florence, it broke down shortly thereafeter as the bishops of Rome and Constantinople excommunicated each other. The schism still exists.

4. Three Yet One

The declarations notwithstanding, it was never thought that the full truth of the Trinity could ever be captured in formulas. The doctrine of the Trinity was "the" mystery of the Christian faith. God is absolutely three but He remains absolutely one.

We have already noted that the processions of the Son and the Spirit were in no way thought to diminish the Father; though He gave His all He retained it. Tertullian said that He had "extended" His substance.[59] This, however, did not mean that one divine stuff was shared by the three divine persons for this would mean that there were really three gods — the error of "tri-theism." Instead, as he explained, the substance, the essence of what God is is to exist as a community of three divine persons.[60]

Tertullian was also the first to explain that the unity of the divine substance is preserved by the "mutual in-dwelling."[61] This is what Jesus meant when He said: "I am in the Father and the Father is in me" (Jn.14:10). It was Athanasius who explained that the mutual in-dwelling means the three divine persons think, feel and act as one.[62]

Nonetheless, the Father, the Son and the Spirit remain absolutely distinct from one another. Not to say so would be to deny the divinities of the Son and the Spirit. This was the frequent error of "modalism," the Trinitarian version of the error of "monarchism." To combat it, Gregory of Nazianzus (329-89) pointed out that the persons remain distinct because each possesses what he called "personal properties."[63] It was Basil who explained that these consist of the uniqueness of their relations to one another within the "God-head."[64] It was Augustine who explained that the motive of God's triune existence is love.[65]

In 675, the eleventh Provincial Council of Toledo formally approved a systematic description of the Trinity which employed all of the ideas which we have seen (DS 525-532). In 1215, all were reaffirmed by the Ecumenical Lateran Council IV (DS 802-806).

---

59. *Apologetic*, 21,12.
60. *Adv. Prax.* 3.
61. Ibid. 25.
62. "Letters to Serapion," 1,28.
63. See his "Orations," 40,41.
64. See his "Letters," 38,5.

65. *On the Trinity*, 8; this same text contains the most famous of Augustine's attempts to describe the Trinity by analogy. According to his analogy from "love," love involves the natural movement from the lover to the loved and the love which unites them. Another of Augustine's analogies was founded on his reflections on the human soul, specifically the relation of its being, knowing, and willing (*Confessions* 13,11). Of course, as Augustine readily admitted, no analogy could ever do justice to the reality.

C) Angels and Demons

1. Angels

Although the Scriptures were silent as to their creation, they were replete with references to angels. Angels appeared to Abraham (Gen.18:2). They led the Hebrews to their promised land (Ex.23:20-21). The angel Raphael appeared to Tobit (Tob.3:17) while the angel Gabriel appeared to Mary and announced the incarnation (Lk.1:20). Michael was an "archangel" (Jude 9). Jesus was comforted by angels (Mt.4:11, cf. Mk.1:13, Lk.4:13). They comprise a heavenly court (e.g. 1 Tim.5:21). This was also evidence that they possessed the beatific vision. That they are spirits was evident in their supernatural ability to come and go (e.g. Mt.28:2). Their spirituality was proof of their immortality. Their rationality was evident in their ability to act intelligently. The freedom of their will was clearly implied by the fact that some of them sinned. By the 5th century, Gregory of Nyssa (c.330-c.395) had articulated all of these arguments.[66]

It was to Thomas that theology owed the rest of what it said about angels. Known as the "angelic doctor," he produced detailed descriptions of the manner of their creation, the nature of their rationality, and the extent of their free will. They occupied the place between God and man in the continuum of being. They propel the celestial bodies and serve as man's guardians, with everyone assigned at least one.[67]

2. Demons

The Scriptures spoke more about demons than they did about angels. It was a demon in the form of a serpent that tempted Adam and Eve to sin (Gen.3:1-5, cf. Wis.2:24). "Satan," their leader, even tried to tempt Jesus away from His Father (Mt.4:1-11, Lk.4:1-13). They are constantly trying to tempt Jesus' followers away from Him (cf. 1 Pet.5:8). They possess people (e.g. Mk.1:26).

Though the Scriptures did not contain an account of their sin, they did speak of "the angels that did not keep their position" (Jude 6) and were therefore cast into hell (2 Pet.2:4). (According to Justin, the demons could not be forgiven and given another chance because they had sinned without being tempted.[68]) Lest anyone claim that God had made them evil, it was expicitly taught that God had created all the angels good but that some became evil by their own doing (DS 800).

---

66. See his "Sunday Homilies," 4. Gregory was Basil's brother; together with Gregory of Nazianzus, all of Cappadocia, they were later to be known as the "Cappadocian" school of theology.
67. *S.Th.* 1, q.54-58.
68. *Dial.* 88.

D) The Creation of the World and Man

1. The Creation of the World

What was more apparent than creation? The world was all around; where did it come from? It had to have come from somewhere; this was the conclusion of all the proofs for God's existence. The Bible provided the only possible answer: "In the beginning God created the heavens and the earth" (Gen.1:1). On the first day He created light (1:3-5). On the second day He separated water and dry land (1:6-8). On the third, He planted all kinds of vegetation (1:9-13). On the fourth, He made the sun, the moon, and the stars (1:14-19). On the fifth, He filled the sea with fish and the sky with birds (1:20-23). On the sixth, He created the animals and Adam, the first man (1:22ff).

Though Genesis did not say that God created the world out of nothing, it was no less clear. If there was anything that God did not need to create, such a stuff would depend upon Him. This, of course, is impossible; God would not be God if He were not the uncaused cause of all existence. As early as the second century, Hermas said so in exactly these terms.[69]

Created by the all-good God, the world was surely created "good" (cf. Gen.1:31).

Nonetheless, it was also quite evident that something had gone wrong. Suffering and death are everywhere; people are ignorant and ruled by passions; there are wars, plagues, famines, and floods. Given belief in an all-good God, all of this was bound to cause confusion and, as it proved, erroneous conclusion. Observing that it is the body — and matter generally — that makes suffering possible, Mani (c.216-76) concluded that matter could not have been created by God. Following Marcion (cf. p.41), he held that matter was created by an evil "demiurge," co-eternal with the all-good God.[70] For a time, the followers of Mani (the "Manicheans") succeeded in winning over formerly faithful Christians.[71] Moreover, their thinking had a definite influence over Christian thinkers. Though Origen did not believe in a demiurge, he held that God had first created only souls and only later created matter as a place for their punishment.[72] Priscillian (c.370) believed that God made only matter

---

68. *Dial.* 88.
69. See the "Mandates" of his Shepherd, 1.1.
70. Actually, both Marcion and Mani followed in the very ancient tradition of Zoroaster (c.600 B.C.) who taught that there are gods of good and evil.
71. Augustine was a Manichean for a time.
72. See his *Peri Archon,* 2.9.

he believed that souls were the divine substance itself, extended to men just as the Father had extended Himself in the processions of the Son and the Spirit.

Even though Origen's ideas so plainly contradicted Genesis, they were not condemned until Pope Vigilius did so in 537 (DS 403). Even though Priscillian's ideas involved the claim that men are minor gods, his ideas were not condemned until the Council of Braga met in 551 (DS 455-63). And these condemnations did not put an end to the controversy. Instead, a contempt for the world attained a considerable popularity in the doctrine of the "Cathars,"[73] and more specifically a branch of that movement called "Abigensianism."[74] It was to condemn these movements that the oft-cited Fourth Lateran Council was called. It decreed that not only had God made all things, visible and invisible, but it insisted that He had made them "out of nothing" (*ex nihilo*) and He had made them *good*. (This was the thrust of DS 800).

Since God was God, there was no possibility that He had created out of loneliness or a desire for creativity. His existence as the Trinity surely fulfilled any need He might have felt for either community or creativity. He could not need to create for any reason. But, in the light of what He did do — the creation of beings that owe Him deference, and have available the reward of eternal life — it was evident that He had created in order to demonstrate His glory (cf. Ps.19:2) and, as Irenaeus put it, "to have someone on whom to shower His gifts."[75]

2. The Creation of Man

As we have already said, on the sixth day God created Adam. He made him in His own "image" (Gen.1:26). He fashioned his body out of the dust of the earth "and breathed into his nostrils the breath of life" (Gen.1:27). This was his soul. It was spoken of in Scripture (e.g. Ps.42, Mt.10:28, 1 Thess.5:23). Besides, its existence was self-evident.

The soul was indeed self-evident. Man sees and otherwise senses himself to have a body. The body is obviously a material thing; it can be seen and touched; it is subject to nature just like everything else that man can see. Of course, each of these sights or other sensations is experienced by a part of him that he neither sees nor touches. This part thinks and feels; it is the essence of who he is. It is nothing at all like a material thing; it is a spiritual thing. This is the soul.

Adam's soul was obviously created with rationality, free will and

---

73. The word is from the Greek for "pure."
74. The word is from the name of the region of southern France where the movement arose.
75. *Adv. Haer.* 4.14.1.

natural immortality. All three are evident in ours.

That Adam enjoyed the beatific vision was evident in the fact he and God talked together (e.g. Gen.2:16). It was the reason he was created. That this involved the gift of sanctifying grace was evident in the fact that no creature would ever be given the natural ability to comprehend God. It would make him a minor god. This Adam was not but, according to Irenaeus, he was still "a supernatural image of God."[76]

Of course, the beatific vision was not all that Adam received. Though Genesis did not say so, it was still certain that Adam received freedoms from ignorance, other fallibilities, uncontrollable emotions, other frailties, suffering and bodily death. If not, God would have been responsible for evil. Thus did Tertullian explain that evil was man's fault; this was the basis of his rebuttal of Marcion's claim that evil means that there are two gods (cf. p. 55).[77] As Augustine explained, if Adam had not been preserved from every weakness, God would have been responsible for his sin.[78]. Not surprisingly, Thomas provided the most exhaustive description of what was now called the state of "original justice," carefully delineating the distinctions between the supernatural gift of sanctifying grace, the preter-natural gifts and natural perfections that Adam surely received.[79]

Genesis also told that God gave Adam a paradisiacal garden, Eden, in which to live. Since it was not good for him to be alone, He gave him a "helper," Eve, whom He fashioned out of one of Adam's ribs (Gen.2:18-24).

3. An Excursus: The Soul

Although the first 1500 years of Christian history had seen almost universal agreement that man has a soul, the late-medieval thinker also knew that there had been no such agreement as to the nature of the soul or its relation to the body.

a. Plato and Augustine

The first attempts to deal with the question of the soul were known to have dated from the days of ancient Greece. For most of the time between then and 1500, the dominant opinion was that of Plato.[80] Plato shared the immemorial Greek philosophic attention to the fact

76. *Adv. Haer.* 2,33,4.

77. *Adv. Mar.* 2,6.

78. See his *Retractions,* 1,8. Augustine's definitive statement of man's original condition is found in *The City of God.*

79. *S. Th.* I. q.95.a.1.

80. See especially his *Phaedo, Timaeus and Republic.* Plato credits Socrates, his teacher, with much of what history credits him. Since Socrates did not write, we do not know the extent to which Plato's thought was his.

that everything is always changing. According to an adage already ancient when Plato heard it: "you can never step twice into the same river."[81] To Plato, this meant that secure, true knowledge of the world was impossible; after all, knowledge of the world became obsolete the moment it was acquired. But, Plato could not help but feel that he did possess true knowledge. Therefore, since knowledge must involve something that does not change, it betrays the existence of perfect things of which things in the world are imperfect replicas. Attributing the imperfection of worldly things to an imperfection inherent in matter, he concluded that there is a world of perfect things, the world of "forms," which is strictly spiritual. Since material things imitate the forms, only the forms are fully real. (Such a metaphysic would later be called "idealism" — the idea that ideas are most real.) We have true knowledge when we see past the material and, seeing what it is that makes the thing what it is, we see the spiritual thing which has served as model.

Actually, according to Plato, to see the form is to remember it. Accepting the already ancient distinction between body and soul, Plato believed that the soul once lived in the world of the forms. But, for some tragic reason, the soul was imprisoned in a body and required to live in the world of matter. This is the only reason that a knowledge of the forms is possible. This is also the reason that the soul wants more than the world can give.

Here was the basis of Augustine's argument from the restlessness of the soul (cf. p. 36). Replacing the world of the forms with God, Augustine held that even though the soul had not enjoyed a previous existence with God (as Origen thought) God had still "infused" it with a knowledge of Himself; this was awakened through reflection and, of course, grace. Understandably, Augustine shared Plato's contempt for the body to the extent that the Christian doctrine of creation would permit him; he held that the body was a material thing for the soul to inhabit and rule.[82] This contempt was encouraged by his reading of Paul's letters and, in particular, Paul's frequent identification of sin and the "flesh" (cf. Rom.8). His *Confessions* make clear that Augustine identified the flesh with the sexual desires which were the source of what he considered the most contemptible of all his sins.

Platonic thinking soon led to a much more than intellectual contempt for the body and the material world generally. Zealous groups devised regimens designed to enable their members to live a "totally" spiritual existence while still on earth. For example, the followers of Priscillian

81. History credits Heraclitus (6th century B.C.) with this saying.
82. See his *De Quantitate Animae*, 13,22.

disavowed marriage. There were even short-lived attempts to live without food.

In time, problems of a more philosophical nature began to emerge. Plato and Augustine held that the body and the soul are two totally different kinds of things, one material the other spiritual, with absolutely nothing in common except existence. But, they also claimed that the spiritual rules the material while the material affects the spiritual, for example, when fire causes pain. An obvious question posed itself: how do these two totally different kinds of things affect one another? The body does not respond to argument; the soul does not respond to touch. How do they communicate? Furthermore, what about the idea that the soul is constrained in a body — what does this say about the Christian belief that God created the body and is planning to resurrect it?

b. Aristotle and Thomas Aquinas

Centuries were to pass before a solution to the problems with Platonism would win general acceptance. Ironically, this solution had originally been offered by Plato's own pupil, Aristotle.[83]

Aristotle shared Plato's concern about the effect of change upon the human ability to know the truth. Moreover, he was also concerned about what the Greeks had long called "the problem of the one and the many." The world was a wonderland of many things; it contained an enormous variety of inanimate objects, plants and animals. Yet, as Aristotle could not but help think, reality was still "one." After all, boiling water became air; leaves eventually returned to the earth from which they had evidently come. Though things are different, they can change from one to another; how can this be?

Agreeing with Plato: knowledge needs to involve something that does not change — which must mean that there are forms — he did not agree that the forms exist in a world of their own. He saw no reason to postulate the existence of such a world — to deny that what we see is fully real. He held that the forms exist *in matter*. The forms are immaterial, but it is their nature to form matter, a stuff common to all things whose nature it is to receive form and never exists without some form and *vice-versa*.[84] For example, the form of the perfect tree — or, perhaps better, "treeness" — forms a certain quantity of matter into an individual tree. The degree to which the matter has accepted the form is the degree to which it is a

---

83. See especially his "Metaphysics."
84. It was for this reason that matter was also called "potency" with form referred to as "act," the ability to utilize potency. It is also to be mentioned that, for Aristotle, "motion" included the movement from potency to act.

perfect specimen of what it is, in the case of our example, a perfect tree. In other words, the form gives a thing its substance, the essence of what it is, while matter is responsible for what Aristotle called "accidents," the changeable characteristics which give a thing its individuality. (Aristotle's metaphysic was therefore to be called "hylemorphism" — "matter and form-ism.") Knowledge takes place when many individual things are seen or otherwise perceived and the form which is common to them is "abstracted." Thus, for Aristotle, knowledge originates in one's experience of the world, not the discovery of ideas latently present in the soul.

Aristotle's insistence that the world is fully real was evident in his interest in science and, in particular, his attempt to explain change. He attributed all change to the coalition of the following four causes: 1) the material cause, the matter involved; 2) the efficient cause, the worker who works upon the matter; 3) the formal cause, the form which is imparted by this work; and finally 4) the final cause, the end for which the work is done. (The latter two were attributed to the uncaused cause.) [85]

The rigor of Aristotle's thought extended to his reflections on human action, especially its "ethical" dimension.[86] He held that the motive of every human act is happiness. But, in the pursuit of happiness, man can be "virtuous" or not. The man of virtue is he who, faced with the question of how to act, chooses the "mean," the middle course between two of the "extremes," or "vices," that are always possible. In other words, faced with the question of how to behave in battle, he is neither cowardly nor foolhardy, but brave. Determinable by reflecting upon the extremes, the mean is best seen by observing the already virtuous man.

For reasons that surely include the fact that Aristotle's thought was simply ahead of his time — a fact surely more clear to the modern thinker than the medieval — the ancient mind favored Plato. Thus, as the conquests of Alexander the Great (356-323 B.C.) carried Greek thought throughout the eastern Mediterranean and beyond, it was Plato's philosophy that they carried.[87] Although the history of thought was still to hear from the "hellenistic" rejection of Platonism — in favor of the simple philosophies of the "Cynics" (who rejected society in the attempt to be true to self), the "Skeptics" (who rejected everything), the "Stoics" (who attempted to conform their lives to "nature"), and the "Epicureans"

---

85. See his "Posterior Analytics."

86. Aristotle's definitive reflections on the quality of human action are found in his *Nicomachian Ethics*. The word "ethics" still refers to principles of human action which can be distinguished from more "moral" ones which are based explicitly upon religion.

87. Ironically, Alexander was a student of Aristotle.

(who held that the pursuit of pleasure is the supreme good) — the main lines of Plato's thought had regained prominence by the time that Julius Caesar (d. 44 B.C.) and his successors brought philosophy to the rest of the Mediterranean.[88] During the first Christian centuries, it gained an even greater hold on the Mediterranean mind. Justin knew that he had no choice but to accept much of what Platonic thinking involved, claiming that Christianity not only included but surpassed it. Origen was judged to have accepted too much of it. Augustine seemed to have struck the perfect balance; his was the legacy of the early middle ages.[89] Aristotle's thought was all but forgotten. Had it not been rediscovered by the Moslems who had gained control over a number of the lands which had once been under the influence of the Greeks, it might have been forgotten forever. Instead, in the work of the Islamic philosophers Avicenna (980-1037) and Averoes (1126-98), the medieval West was finally presented with a possible solution to the problems which Platonism had always involved.

Nonetheless, at first, the "new" philosophy met suspicion and hostility. It was new; it contradicted a way of thinking which had been accepted for centuries. It contradicted the work of *Saint* Augustine. Still, the new philosophy appealed. In its insistence that the forms — which the medievals called "universals" — exist in matter, it narrowed the gap between what is seen and what is believed. It took this world seriously. Furthermore, it appeared to explain the hitherto inexplicable rapport between body and soul.

The latter of these advantages was not at first apparent. When Aristotelianism was first applied to man, many of its proponents, notably Alexander of Hales (c.1186-1245) and Bonaventure (c.1217-74), taught that both body and soul were composed of matter and form. They therefore postulated a "spiritual matter" and a form of the soul.[90] Obviously this did nothing to explain the mysterious relationship between body and soul. But, when Albert (the Great, c.1200-80) declared that the immaterial form of the body *is* the soul, an explanation finally appeared to have been provided. The form of the body was already an

88. For the sake of completeness, it should be mentioned that much of the credit for the survival of Platonism goes to Plotinus (c.205-70) whose *Enneads* were to have an indirect but profound effect upon subsequent Christian thought.
89. It should also be mentioned that the work of Dionysius the Pseudo-Areopagite (c.500) and the better known Jewish philosopher Boethius (c.480-c.524) also contributed to the fact the medieval West inherited Platonism.
90. See Bonaventure's "Commentary on the Book of Sentences," II. d. 17 a. 1. The book of "Sentences" by Peter Lombard (c. 1100-60) was the first comprehensive systemization of theology. It therefore acquired a special authority; most of the leading medieval thinkers felt compelled to write commentaries on the work. *All* are hereafter abbreviated In Sent.

immaterial thing. It also contained the "powers" for which the soul *per se* was known.[91]

This was the idea that Albert imparted to his most famous pupil, Thomas Aquinas. Agreeing with Aristotle that matter gave individuality, or what he called "existence," to the "essence" of a species which was contained in its form, Thomas also agreed that matter never exists apart from some form. He insisted, however, that forms can exist apart from matter. After all, what were the angels except pure form?[92] Certainly the soul of man could exist by itself, at least temporarily. There had to be "separate (from matter) susbstances"; doctrine demanded it. Therefore, Thomas taught that the soul could exist apart from matter even though it is a form "ordered" to a body. He then offered the most complete description of the soul and its powers that had ever been attempted.[93]

Thomas accepted that all knowledge originates in experience. Following Aristotle, he also observed the four causes, attributing the formal and final cause to the Uncaused Cause. (God was actually said to "contain" each of the forms. This was what made the analogy of being possible.) Obviously, Thomas also believed that God made matter.

Thomas also accepted Aristotle's description of the virtuous man, at least as far as what he called the "natural," not exclusively Christian, virtues were concerned (q.v. p. 75).

***

The teaching authority of the Church ultimately sided with Thomas. Even though the Archbishop of Paris (the bishop of the place were he had taught) condemned some of his ideas shortly after his death in 1274, in 1311 the Council of Vienna declared that "the soul is the form of the body." The council also reaffirmed the immemorial belief in its rationality, free will and natural immortality (DS 902). Thomas was declared a saint in 1323. By 1500, his thought *was* thought.

E) The Original Sin and Its Consequences

To the late-medieval mind, the truth of the Church's teaching on original sin was only slightly less obvious than its teaching on creation. God had undoubtedly created the world good and something had undoubtedly gone wrong. Genesis offered the only answer: in order to test his obedience, God told Adam that he could eat the fruit of any tree in the

---

91. See his *On Man*, 1.7.
92. Each angel was likened to an individual species of creature here on earth.
93. *S. Th.* 1.q.75-83.

Garden of Eden except one, the tree of the knowledge of good and evil.[94] He warned him that if he did, he would die (Gen.2:17). Soon thereafter, a serpent approached Eve and told her that, rather than die, she would become like God if she ate of the forbidden fruit (3:15). This serpent was the devil in disguise (cf.Wis.2:24). Eve gave in to this temptation and ate of the fruit, and gave some to her husband who ate of it too (Gen.3:6).

Swiftly did God respond. Expelling Adam and Eve from the Garden of Eden, He cursed the rest of the earth telling them: "thorns and thistles I will bring forth to you, and you shall eat of the plants of the field. In the sweat of your face you shall eat bread till you return to the ground, for out of it you were taken; you are dust and to dust you shall return" (Gen.3:18-19). There was no doubt; "God did not make death" (Wis.1:13). It was "ungodly men by their words and deeds that summoned death" (1:16). This was not God's plan; "God created man for incorruption and made him in the image of His own eternity" (2:23). But Eve succumbed to temptation and "because of her we all die" (Sir.25:24). Nonetheless, since Adam was to be the father of the entire human race, he bore the principal responsibility for what had happened. Thus could Paul say that "sin came into the world through one man, the death through sin . . ." (Rom.5:12).

Since we are Adam's descendants, we share his punishment. Irenaeus could even say: "we all share Adam's guilt."[95]

Of course, this was already obvious in the fact that we all must suffer and we all must die. It was also apparent in the fact that we are ignorant, otherwise fallible, uncontrollably emotional and otherwise frail. As Tertullian had explained, if the freedoms from such things had not been part of our original endowment, God would be responsible for evil (cf. p. 55).

As Tertullian also explained, if a disordered will was not a punishment, God would be guilty of *our* sins.[96]

If someone should deny that he is a helpless sinner, the Scriptures correct him: "everyone sins" (1 Sam.8:46); "if we say we have no sin we deceive ourselves" (1 Jn.1:8); "we all make many mistakes" (Jas.3:2). "No man is righteous before Him" (Ps.143:2). In sin are we conceived (cf. Ps.51:7).

---

94. It might be helpful to note that not all of the Fathers thought the original sin involved the eating of fruit. Some thought that it was a sexual sin. Nonetheless, all the Fathers did agree it was especially one of "pride."

95. *Adv. Haer.* 5.16.3.

96. See his *De Spectaculis*, 2.

F) The Early History of Salvation

Though there was no record of God's decision to restore man to the destiny for which he was created, the Scriptures still appeared to supply ample information from which to infer His plan for salvation.

1. The Creation of Individual Souls

Adam and Eve gave birth to Cain, Abel and Seth (Gen.4). Genesis did not need to state that God had created their souls directly. A spiritual soul could not have been passed along with the material body which human parentage contributes to the creation of a new person. This would imply that the spiritual was somehow dependent upon the material. This is impossible because the spiritual is superior to the material. A lower cannot produce a higher; nothing can give what it does not have.

The above argument notwithstanding, certain thinkers, notably Tertullian, were known to have maintained that the soul is passed on through the father's seed.[97] In 498, the persistent popularity of this opinion occasioned its condemnation by Pope Anastasius II (DS 360).

2. The Early History of Man

Adam lived to be 930 years old. By the time he died, the world was populated (cf. Gen.5). But, sin had also spread and God came to regret what He had created. Thus did He cause the great flood that killed every living thing except Noah, his family, and the male and female of every species who were saved in Noah's ark (Gen.6-9).

When the world had repopulated, men returned to their sinful ways. In their pride, they attempted to build the tower of Babel, an attempt to reach heaven. God thwarted their plans by confusing the one language that everyone once spoke (Gen.11).[98]

3. The History of the Chosen People

Generations passed before God revealed Himself to Abraham, telling him that He had chosen the Hebrews to be His people (Gen.12). (They were to be consecrated to Him by circumcision, Gen. 17.) God warned Abraham of His impending destruction of the evil cities of Sodom and Gommorah, instructing him to flee into the desert (Gen.19). It was there that God caused Sarah to conceive in her old age; the child's name was Isaac. After a time, God decided to test Abraham's faith by commanding him to sacrifice Isaac. Abraham accepted God's command, but, just before he was about to carry it out, God sent an angel to stop him (Gen.22). Isaac had two sons, Esau and Jacob. Though Jacob was the

---

97. See his *De Anima*, 25,27; even Augustine was suspected of this opinion.
98. The one language was supposed to be Hebrew.

younger, he tricked Esau out of his birthright (Gen.27). God now changed Jacob's name to Israel and he became the father of the twelve sons who became the fathers of the twelve tribes (Gen.30). Joseph, the youngest, was his favorite. Envious, his brothers sold him into slavery in Egypt. But, God had given Joseph the power to interpret dreams and he used it in order to gain the favor of Pharoah. Joseph was eventually made ruler of Egypt (Gen.34-41). When famine struck the promised land, he brought his family to live with him (Gen.42).

After a time, there rose a pharaoh who was not favorable to the Hebrews. Not only did he force them into slavery, but, fearing their numbers, he ordered that all their male babies should be killed (Ex.1). At this, the mother of Moses hid him in a basket and put him afloat in the Nile. He was found by Pharaoh's daughter who made him her own. When he killed an Egyptian for beating a Hebrew, he fled into the desert (Ex.2). It was there that God appeared to Moses in the form of the burning bush, giving him the task of liberating His people (Ex.3). Moses went to Pharaoh and asked him to let the Hebrews go. It was Pharaoh's refusal that occasioned the ten plagues (Ex.4-11). To protect His people from the tenth — the killing of the first-born of every family — God told Moses to tell the people to partake of a meal consisting of an unblemished lamb whose blood they should sprinkle above their doors. In this way, the angel of death would know which homes to pass over. (Thereafter, each year, this event would be commemorated by the partaking of another "Passover" meal, Ex.12.) Finally persuaded, Pharoah let the people go. He soon changed his mind, however, and set out to get them back. To make possible their escape, God parted the Red Sea only to close it, killing Pharaoh's pursuing troops (Ex.14).

Now, in order to test them, God took forty years to lead His people through the desert to their promised land. He fed them with "manna" and gave them water from a rock (Ex.18). He then led Moses up Mount Sinai and it was there that He explained the covenant and taught the Law. Though it featured "ten commandments,"[99] it actually regulated all aspects of the people's life. It even specified "clean" and "unclean" foods (Ex.21-24). It prescribed the manner of divine worship, calling for animal sacrifices offered by priests who were either sons of Moses' brother Aaron or members of the tribe of Levi (Ex.25-31; Lev. and Deut.).

99. "You shall have no other gods before me; you shall not take the name of the Lord your God in vain; you shall keep holy the sabbath day; honor your father and mother; you shall not kill, commit adultery, steal, bear false witness against your neighbor, covet your neighbor's wife, or goods (cf. Ex.20:1-17).

Meanwhile, the people, who had grumbled all along, turned to other gods, actually asking Aaron to make them a golden calf which they might worship (Ex.32). When Moses returned from Mount Sinai, he destroyed the calf and successfully begged God to forgive His people (Ex.34).

Arriving at Canaan, the promised land, God chose Joshua to lead the people in its conquest (Josh.). After the land was divided among the twelve tribes, He chose certain "judges," such as Samson and Gideon, to rule them (Judg.). Later, at the request of the people, He established a monarchy calling upon Samuel to name Saul Israel's first king (1 Sam.9). To succeed Saul, He chose David whom He had enabled to slay Goliath, a giant (1 Sam.17). Since David's rule saw to the great prosperity that the kingdom attained, God promised that his descendants would rule forever (2 Sam.6). David's first descendant, Solomon was renowned for his wisdom and he built a great temple in Jerusalem (1 Kings.5). Unfortunately, Solomon's sons were not so wise and, under their leadership, the people became unfaithful. Not only did they cease to obey the Law, they turned again to other gods, especially the Canaanite god "Baal." Therefore, God punished them, dividing the once great kingdom in two, Israel and Judah. To Israel, God sent the prophet Elijah and others. When Israel failed to repent, God saw it fall to Assyria (Kings, Amos and Hos.).

To Judah, God sent many prophets. Through men like Isaiah, He taught His people to hope for salvation. Through men like Jeremiah, He called them to keep their part of the covenant. When Judah still failed to repent, God saw it fall to Babylon. The temple was destroyed and the people were carried off to exile. But, as we know, God did not forget His people and the prophets continued to encourage them. Isaiah promised that a "remnant" would one day return to the promised land (Is.10). Jeremiah promised that God would make a "new covenant" with His people (Jer.31); Ezekiel promised them a "new spirit" (Ez.36-37). In time, God enabled Daniel to gain the favor of the Babylonian king and the lot of his people improved. Finally, when Babylon fell to Persia, Daniel persuaded the Persian King Darius to allow the exiles to return home (Dan.). Soon thereafter, the Persians were themselves conquered by Alexander the Great. After Alexander died, Judas Maccabeus led God's people (who now were called the Jews) in a revolt. Thus did they regain their independence though not their former greatness (1 and 2 Mac.). They retained their independence until the entire Mediterranean was conquered by the Romans.

The Romans still ruled the Jews when the time came for the Son to become man. In final preparation for this event, God enabled Elizabeth to bear a son despite her advanced years (Lk.1:5-25). He became John the Baptist whose mission as Christ's herald had been foretold (Is.40:3-5; Mt.3:3, Mk.1:2-3, Lk.3:4-6).

4. The Immaculate Conception

The Scriptures did not say that Mary was "immaculately" conceived. But neither did they say that she had ever sinned. What is more, the angel Gabriel told Mary that she was "full of grace" (Lk.1:28). She must have been. The Son of God should not have been conceived by a sinner; she could not have been allowed to pass on to Him the stain of original sin. Thus did Augustine exempt her from his insistence that everyone is stained by original sin[100] (q.v. p. 77). This troubled Thomas; he held that the glory of redemption would be compromised if God had otherwise remitted original sin. It was Duns Scotus who responded with the argument that it was not apart from Christ that Mary had been spared, but on account of the anticipated merit of a sacrifice that she in part made possible.[101] The Church eventually sided with Duns Scotus. In 1477, Pope Sixtus officially declared Mary the "immaculate conception" (DS 1400).

5. An Addendum: The Assumption

Mary's "assumption" was an obvious implication of the immaculate conception. Since Mary was immaculately conceived, she was not bound to sin. Moreover, the grace of her immaculate conception surely included all the grace needed to keep her free from sin throughout her life. Therefore, at the end of earthly life, there was no reason that she should not assume her place as queen of heaven. Thus was she assumed both body and soul into heaven. This was Church Tradition. Gregory of Tours (538-539) was the first to write it down.[102].

6. The Virginal Conception

The Scriptures spoke explicitly of the virginal conception. Mary was a "virgin" (Lk.1:27). She conceived by the power of the Holy Spirit (Lk.1:35). This had been prophesied (Is.7:14). Moreover, were the Son not conceived by the Holy Spirit, God would not have been His Father. Thus, as early as the Council of Constantinople, the virginal conception was part of the creed (DS 150.)

---

100. See his *On Nature and Grace*, 36,42.
101. In Sent. III, q.1, n.4. For her part in the plan of salvation, Mary would later be called the "co-redemptrix" and the "mediatrix of all graces."
102. See his *Book of Miracles*, 1.4.

7. Another Addendum: The Perpetual Virginity of Mary
The perpetual virginity of Mary was not only the teaching of Tradition, it was the product of the simplest theological reasoning. Since Mary was chosen to bear God's Son, in a special way, she was His own. It would not have been fitting for anyone to violate her virginity. Moreover, if she had had other children, the product of relations with her husband Joseph, the circumstances of Jesus' conception might have been confused. Therefore, with Joseph's consent, she must have remained a virgin throughout her life. Indeed, God must have maintained her virginity even in childbirth; surely, her virginity must have been at least as perfect as the virginity of those who follow her example. This was the reasoning of Epiphanius (c.315-403) who was the first to say that she remained a virgin both in the act of giving birth ("in partu") and afterwards ("postpartum").[103] Official declarations followed shortly thereafter. In 449, Pope Leo affirmed that Jesus' conception in no way affected Mary's virginity (DS 291). Exactly two hundred years later, the First Lateran Council declared that she was still a virgin after Jesus' birth (DS 503).

8. The Birth of Jesus
The accounts of Jesus' birth were probably the Bible's best known.

When Mary was discovered to be with child, Joseph planned to put her away, but, in a dream, God told him not to (Mt.1:18-25).

"In those days a decree went out from Caesar Augustus that all the world should be enrolled" (Lk.2:1). Because He was a descendant of David, Joseph had to take Mary to Bethlehem, David's city, in order to register (Lk.2:4-5). Because there was no room for them at the inn, they stayed in a manger; it was there that Jesus was born (2:6-7). Shepherds tending flocks in nearby fields were summoned by angels to worship Him (2:8-14). Some time later, the infant was visited by three wise men from the East; they had seen the star that God had sent to proclaim Him and they had followed it in order to give Him gifts of gold, frankincense and myrrh (Mt.2:1). Unfortunately, on route they had met the puppet king Herod and told him of the birth. Jealous of his own limited power, Herod ordered soldiers to kill all the male children in Bethlehem, two years and under. But, God visited Joseph in another dream, warning him to take Mary and the child to Egypt. There they stayed until Herod died; then they were told to return to Nazareth (Mt.2:3-23).

---

103. See his *Against Heresies*, 88,18.

G) The Incarnation

1. One Person, Two Natures

The Scriptures had no need to stress that Jesus was also man. He was "born of a woman" (Gal.4:4), a descendant of Adam (cf. Lk.3:23-38) and Abraham (cf. Mt.1:1-16). He was the "Son of David" (e.g. Mt.9:27). He was the "Son of Man" (Mt.24:27) whose coming in glory had been predicted (Dan.7:13). He suffered both spiritually — at Gethsemane (e.g. Mt.26:38) and physically — on the cross (e.g. Mt.26:63). He was "a man like us in all things but sin" (Heb.4:15). If He was not, He could not have been "the one mediator between God and man" (1 Tim.2:5, cf. Heb.7:17).

Despite the testimony of Scripture, the "docetists" still denied that Jesus was really human; they held that humanity was unworthy of God and taught that Jesus' humanity was appearance only. (They explained that the Son came — that the Son was the Father's revealer — because the Father was "too" great to reveal Himself.)

It was Ignatius who responded: "There is one physician, God in man, life in death, from God and Mary . . ."[104]; in other words, if Christ was not God incarnate, He could not have redeemed us. For this reason, Justin said that He was composed of the Logos, body and soul.[105] Tertullian said that Christ was the union of two "substances" — one human, one divine[106] — in one "person."[107] It was Origen who explained that Christ was the *complete* union of two "natures" in one "hypostasis" — one thing.[108] As he also explained, a truly hypostatic union is forever.[109]

Despite the teachings of the Fathers, Apollinarius (c310-c.390) could not see how Jesus' soul and divinity — two spiritual things — could occupy one body. Thus, he denied that Jesus had a human soul. Soon thereafter, the Council of Constantinople condemned his view, and that of the docetists (DS 151).

Unconvinced and undaunted, Nestorius (d.c.451) was sure nature implied personhood; thus he taught that Jesus was actually two persons. Nestorius' teaching also involved the denial that Mary should be called "Mother of God" ("Theotokos"). Since she was simply the mother of his human personhood, she would better be called "Mother of Christ" ("Christotokos").

---

104. See his "Letter to the Ephesians," 7,2.
105. See his *Second Apology*, 10.
106. See his *De Carne Christo*, 18.
107. *Adv. Prax.* 27.
108. *Contra Celsum*, 3.
109. See his "Commentary on the Gospel of John," 2,6,4.

Led by Cyril of Alexandria (d.c.444), The Council of Ephesus (431) condemned Nestorius and affirmed that Mary should indeed by called "Mother of God"(DS 252). The council also declared that Jesus was one "hypostasis," (DS 253).

Despite the teachings of the Council of Ephesus, Eutyches (c.378-454) denied that Christ possessed a humanity like our own; he held that His divinity had "absorbed" His humanity and "divinized" it. For this reason, Eutyches' followers were called "monophysites," Greek for "one nature."

This was not acceptable. As Tertullian had taught two centuries earlier, Christ's two substances, or natures, must have been distinct and unmixed. Were they not, He would have been some strange being, neither God nor man. He would not have been the God-man who died as God for man.[110] Therefore, in 451, at Chalcedon, a council met to condemn monophysitism (DS 300); Christ was officially declared "true God and true man" (DS 301) and His divinity and humanity were declared unmixed (DS 302).

Despite the teaching of the Council of Chalcedon, Sergius (d. 638) taught that Jesus' human will was constantly subordinated to its divine counterpart; this came to be known as "monothelitism." Since this was an obvious if watered-down reaffirmation of monophysitism, it was condemned at the First Lateran Council in 649 (DS 516).

2. Jesus' Intellect and Will

Since Jesus' divine and human natures were distinct and unmixed, He must have had two intellects and wills.

Jesus' divine intellect gave Him the beatific vision. Thus, though on earth, He could converse with His Father (e.g. Jn.17). He constantly demonstrated supernatural knowledge. He knew the unspoken thoughts of others (e.g. Mk.2:8). He knew the future; for example, He knew that Peter would deny Him three times (Mt.26:30-35, Mk. 14:26-31, Lk.22:31-34, Jn.13:36-38). Athanasius said that He actually knew everything but feigned ignorance because His humanity would not have seemed real otherwise.[111]

Though He must have known everything He wanted to, Jesus' human intellect still provided Him the knowledge of experience; He therefore "increased in wisdom" (Lk.2:52). "He learned obedience through what He suffered" (Heb.5:8). He allowed Himself to learn in this way in order to maintain His solidarity with the rest of humanity.

Needless to say, His divine will could never sin.

---

110. *De Carne Christo*, 5.
111. *Against Arius*, 3, 42-46.

Though His human will was liable to sin, it never succumbed (cf. Heb.4:15). Clement of Alexandria (c.150-c.215) said that even though Jesus had been tempted (cf. Mt.4:1-11, Mk. 1:9-11, Lk.4:1-13), He never felt the slightest impulse to sin.[112]

It was Athanasius who taught that Christ had a "perfect" humanity; what else would the Father have given Him?[113] Later, some would insist that Jesus was the best of anything a man can be — the best carpenter, the best sailor, etc. . .

H) The Life and Mission of Jesus Christ

1. The Life of Jesus

Except for the account of His parents finding Him in the temple when He was twelve (Lk.2:41-52), the gospels had little to say about the first thirty years of Jesus' life (cf. Lk.3:23). But they did appear to provide an all but complete history of His public life.

Although He had done nothing for which to repent, Jesus began His public life by allowing John to baptize Him in the Jordan river. At this, the Spirit descended upon Him in the form of a dove (Mt.3:13-17, Mk.1:9-11, Lk.3:21-22). Then, the Spirit led Him into the wilderness for forty days and nights of fast and prayer. There the devil tried unsuccessfully to tempt Him (Mt.4:1-11, Mk.1:12-13, Lk.4:1-13). Returning from the wilderness, He performed His first public miracle, changing water into wine at a wedding in Cana (Jn.2:1-11). He then called His first disciples, the men who were later to become His apostles (Mt.4:18-22, Mk.1:16-20, Lk.5:1-11, Jn.1:35-51).[114] They followed Him on His first trip to Jerusalem (Jn.2). There He encountered Nicodemus, the Pharisee. (Pharisees were experts in the law. They and the Sadducees — another school of experts — and the scribes, made up the intellectual establishment of Jesus' day, Jn.3:1-21). This was only the first of His many dealings with the Pharisees. Jealous of their own religious authority, they constantly criticized His efforts to reform the faith of His day. They criticized Him for associating with sinners (Mk.9:9-13, Mk.2:13-17, Lk.5:27-32), not requiring His disciples to fast (Mt.9:14-17, Mk.2:18-22, Lk.5:33-39), and healing on the Sabbath (Mt.12:1-8, Mk.2:23-28, Lk.6:1-5).

Eventually Jesus returned to Galilee (Mt.4:12, Mk.1:14, Lk.4:14).

---

112. See his *Stromata*, 6,71: Clement was Origen's predecessor in the School of Alexandria.

113. See his *On the Incarnation*, 1,16.

114. They were Simon, Andrew, James and John sons of Zebedee, Philip, Bartholomew, Thomas, Matthew, James son of Alphaeus, Thaddaeus (or Jude), Simon the Zealot, and Judas Iscariot (cf. Mt.10:1-16, Mk.3:13-19, Lk.6:12-16, Acts 1:13).

There He delivered sermons on the mount (Mt.6-7), the plain (Lk.6:17-49), and the shore (Mk.4:1-9). "He taught ... as one who had authority and not like the scribes" (Mt.7:29). He taught in parables; He told the parables of the sower (Mt.13:1-9, Mk.4:1-9, Lk.8:4-8), the mustard seed (Mt.13:31-32, Mk.4:30-32, Jn.13:18-19), the lost sheep (Mt.18:10-14, Lk.15:3-7), the treasure in the field (Mt.13:44), the good Samaritan (Lk.10:29-37), the prodigal son (Lk.15:11-32), and the grain of wheat (Jn.12:24). He did many miracles; He cast out demons (e.g. Mk.1:23-28), cured lepers (e.g. Mt.8:1-4, Mk.1:40-45, Lk.5:12-16), and paralytics (e.g. Mt.9:1-8, Mk.2:1-12, Lk.5:17-26). Miraculously He fed five thousand people (Mt.14:13-21, Mk.6:32-44, Lk.9:10-17, Jn.6:16-21), walked on water (Mt.14:22-33, Mk.6:47-52, Jn.6:16-21), and raised Lazarus from the dead (Jn.11:1-44). He foretold His passion and resurrection on the third day (e.g. Mt.17:22-23, Mk.9:30-32, Lk.9:43-45, Jn.2:19). He predicted the persecutions that His disciples would one day endure (Mt.10:17-25, Mk.13:1-13, Lk.21:12-19). He also predicted the division of families that would take place on account of His name (Mt.10:34-36, Lk.12:51-53). Then, in a prefigurement of His future glory, He was "transfigured" before Peter, James and John (Mt.17:1-9, Mk.9:2-10, Lk.9:28-36).

For Passover, Jesus returned to Jerusalem. His fame having preceded Him, He entered the city in triumph (Mt.21:1-9, Mk.14:1-20, Lk.19:29-38, Jn.12:12-18). This aroused the envy of the chief priests and they plotted to kill him (Mt.26:2-5, Mk.14:1-2, Lk.22:1-2, Jn.11:47-53). Knowing they would succeed, He ate His last supper His disciples. (Mt.26:17-29, Mk.14:12-25, Lk.22:7-20, Jn.13:1ff). That evening, betrayed by Judas Iscariot, Jesus was arrested, brought before Caiaphas the high priest, and tried for the "blasphemy" of His claim to divinity (Mt.26:47-75, Mk.14:43-72, Lk.22:47-71, Jn.18-27). The next day, He was brought before Pontius Pilate, the Roman, governor of Palestine, who sent Him to Herod, the son of the king who tried to kill Him when He was an infant (Lk.23:6-12). Herod had Jesus mocked, spat upon, beaten and scourged. He then sent Him back to Pilate who, finding Him guilty of no crime, appeared before the people and offered them a choice: he would release either Jesus or an insurrectionist named Barabbas. By now, however, the people had been turned against Jesus by the chief priests and elders who told them to demand His death. Washing his hands of the whole matter, Pilate acceded to their wishes (Mt.27:11-26, Mk.15:2-15, Lk.23:2-25, Jn.18:29-38). That day He was crucified alongside two criminals beneath the sign: "Jesus of Nazareth, King of the Jews" (Mt.27:27-50, Mk.15:16-36, Lk.23:26-46, Jn.19:17-30).

2. The Message of Jesus

Naturally, there was complete confidence in everything that Jesus taught.

Actually, by the very fact that He was sent, the Son already told of God's love. "God so loved the world that He gave his only Son that whoever believes in Him should not perish but have life eternal" (Jn.3:16).

The essence of Jesus' message was quite simple: "The Kingdom of God is at hand; repent and believe the gospel" (e.g. Mk.1:15). Time was of the essence; after all, "you do not know what day the Lord is coming" (Mt.24:42, Mk.13:35, Lk.12:40).

As was clear from His "beatitudes,"[115] Jesus had come to offer the kingdom to those who had not found fortune in this world, the poor and powerless (cf. Lk.4:18). He came to warn the rich and powerful that in the kingdom, things would be different (cf. Lk.6:24-26).

As all His parables made clear, the kingdom is all-important. He also taught that the kingdom was not of this world (cf. Jn.18:36). Therefore "what does it profit a man if he gains the whole world and loses or forfeits himself?" (Lk.9:25).

The importance of faith was paramount; "without faith it is impossible to please God" (Heb.11:6). And Jesus made clear that it was faith in His person that God expected. As He said: "I am the resurrection and the life" (Jn.11:25). "I am the way, the truth, and the life" (Jn.14:6). "He who believes in the Son has eternal life" (Jn.3:36). Indeed, "He who is not for me is against me" (Lk.11:23).

Though it was impossible to please God without faith, it was also necessary to obey God's commandments. As Jesus explained, He had not come to abolish one "iota" of the Law but to "fulfill" it (Mt.5:17, Mk.4:21, Lk.11:33). He had also come to explain it. "You shall love the Lord your God with all your heart and all your soul and all your mind. This is the first and greatest commandment. The second is this: you shall love your neighbor as yourself" (Mt.22:37-39, Mk.12:28-34, Lk.10:25-28, Jn.13:34-35). "Whoever would be great among you must be your servant, and whoever would be first must be the slave of all" (Mk.10:43-44, Lk.22:25-26). (Thus did Jesus wash the feet of His disciples, Jn.13:1-11.) "Love one another as I have loved you" (Jn.15:12). And "greater love has no man than this, that he should lay down his life for his

---

115. Blessed are the poor in spirit, those who mourn, the meek, those who hunger and thirst for righteousness, the merciful, the pure in heart, the peacemakers, and those who are persecuted for righteousness' sake (cf. Mt.5:3-10).

friends" (Jn.15:13). You must even "love your enemies" (cf. Mt.5:43-48, Lk.6:27-28). "You have heard that it was said 'an eye for an eye and a tooth for a tooth' (cf. Ex.21:24), but I say to you, do not resist one who is evil. If anyone strikes you on the right cheek, turn to him the other also" (Mt.5:38-39, Lk.6:29). Love without the expectation of return; "if you love those who love you, what credit to you is that?" (Mt.5:56, Lk.6:32).

Do nothing for show. "When you give alms, do not let your left hand know what your right hand is doing" (Mt.6:3). You must give not from your surplus but from your substance. A penny from a poor widow is worth much more than a greater sum from the surplus of a rich man (cf. Mk.12:41-44). You must be internally pure. "You have heard that it was said, 'you shall not commit adultery; (cf. Ex.20:14). But I say to you that everyone who looks at a woman lustfully has already committed adultery with her in his heart" (Mt.5:27-28). It is not what goes into a man that defies him but what comes out of him (Mt.15:10-20, Mk.7:14-23).

But "judge not, that you shall not be judged" (Mt.7:1, Lk.6:37). "Let him among you who is without sin be the first to throw a stone (Jn.8:7). You must forgive "not just seven times, but seventy times seven times" (Mt.18:22).

"He who has ears to hear, let him hear" (Mt.13:9).

3. An Excursus: The Classical Conception of Christian Life

According to its classical conception:

Christian life begins with repentance — sorrow for sins. This is founded on the fear of God, whose justice makes Him "terrible" (e.g. Ex.15:11). Fear of God is "the beginning of knowledge" (Prov.1:7); it comes together with the awareness that man is worthless dust (cf. Gen.2:7).

Faith follows. Faith is "the conviction of things not seen" (Heb.11:1). It is a gift (q.v. p. 76).

Gift though it is, faith is also willed. As Jesus said: "repent and believe" (Mk.1:15). Moreover, it was not just belief "that" but belief "in" — belief in a person who makes himself known and asks for trust.

Therefore, faith is certain; doubt is a lack of trust. As Jesus said to His disciples: "if you have faith and never doubt . . . if you say to this mountain 'Be taken up and cast into the sea,' and it would be done" (Mt.21:21).

Finally, faith is orthodox. Unorthodox faith is not salvific. Heresy makes a "shipwreck" of one's faith and allies oneself with Satan (cf. 1 Tim.1:19-20).

Obedience was no less demanding.

One must keep the commandments, all of them: the "ten," Christ's,[116] and those of the Church.[117] Every violation is a sin venial or mortal.[118] One must be "perfect" (Mt.5:48).

In their perfection, Christians were also to obey the dictates of "natural law." Natural law was the will of God as expressed in the structure of creation. It was also known through the operation of conscience. Available to the Greeks, its violation was the source of their condemnation (cf. Rom.1:18-32).

Thomas explained that natural law made possible the natural virtues whose study he had inherited from Aristotle.[119] But, as he took pains to point out, only the theological virtues of faith, hope and charity (cf. 1 Cor.13:13) are salvific.[120] Hope was faith in heaven, while charity was love without the expectation of return. Called "agape" in Greek ("caritas" in Latin), charity was distinguished from "eros" (or "amor"), the love of those desirable, and "philia," the love of friends, or family.

Since the natural virtues did not bring salvation, they were not of ultimate importance. Neither was anything else the world could offer. Actually, the world was against the Christian (Jn.15:18); at best it was a distraction from Christian life (cf. 1 Jn.2:15). Thus, Christians should be content with what they have (cf. Heb.13:5). They should even be willing to give up what they have. Self-denial was one of the most effective ways that a person could do penance for his countless sins of thought, word, deed, and omission.

Although the love of God and neighbor were both commanded, the love of God was better. God deserves all the attention we can give Him. Thus, Jesus recommended celibacy over marriage (Mt.19:12), as did Paul (1 Cor.7). Indeed, following the example of Jesus' own time in the desert, holy hermits and monks were living proof that a life of solitude was better

116. The law of love was concretized in terms of the "corporal and spiritual works of mercy." The corporal works were to feed the hungry, to give drink to the thirsty, to clothe the naked, to give shelter to the stranger, to visit the sick, to minister to prisoners, and to bury the dead. The spiritual works were to convert the sinner, teach the ignorant, counsel the doubtful, comfort the sorrowful, bear wrongs patiently, forgive injuries, and pray for the living and the dead.
117. Church law required members to attend Mass every Sunday and on holy days, to contribute to the Church, to make a confession and receive communion at least once a year, to keep certain days of fast and abstinence (from meat), and to marry only with the sanction of the Church.
118. Besides mortal sins, seven were considered "deadly": pride, jealousy, envy, lust, gluttony, anger and sloth.
119. Four of the natural virtues were called "cardinal": prudence, justice, temperance and fortitude.
120. S. Th. 1-11, q.62-63.

than a life with people.

4. The Atonement

It was clear that Jesus was sacrificed in order to atone for man's sins.

From the days of the Law, God required priests to offer sacrifices to atone for the sins of the people (Lev.16). But, He also revealed that He would send an innocent victim to take upon himself the punishment due them (Is.53). Surely Jesus was this victim; who else was innocent; why else would God's Son have suffered and died on the cross? Jesus Himself said that He had come to give His life as a "ransom" for many (Mt.20:28, Mk.10:45). He was put forward as an "expiation" for the sins of the world (Rom.3:25, 1 Jn. 2:22). He was the "Lamb of God" (Jn.1:29) whose blood established a "new covenant" (Mt.25:28, Mk.14:24, Lk.22:20). "As one man's trespass led to condemnation for all, so one man's act of righteousness led to acquittal and life for all men" (Rom.5:18). Thus, He is our "savior" (e.g. Jn.4:42). It was He who paid the price of our "redemption" (e.g. Eph.1:7).

Though there was no doubt that Jesus was our "redeemer" — the one who "bought us back" — there was still some confusion as to whom the price had been paid. Noting that Satan had been given "the power of death" (Heb.2:14), Origen concluded that it must have been paid to him.[121] Augustine objected, pointing out that God would never have paid anything to a demon. Our debt was a demand of justice.[122] It was Anselm who explained that justice demanded a sacrifice of infinite value.[123] Subsequent theology was mostly concerned with the question of whether the Son would have become man if Adam had not sinned. Thomas said no; Duns Scotus said yes.

* * *

Though the Scriptures did not say *why* Jesus descended into hell (cf. 1 Pet.3:19), why else would He except to release the just who had died before Him? How else was God to deal with men like Moses?

5. The Cause and Necessity of Grace

The completion of redemption, Christ's sacrifice was clearly the cause of grace (e.g. Rom.1:7, Jn.1:17). Besides, man was in no way entitled to grace; how else had it been won?

Grace was clearly a necessity. When Peter proclaimed Jesus "the Son of the living God," Jesus told him that "flesh and blood has not revealed

121. "Commentary on the Gospel of Matthew," 16,18.
122. *On the Trinity*, 13.
123. See his most remembered work *Cur Deus Homo*.

this to you, but my Father in heaven" (Mt.16:17). He explained that "no one can come to me unless it is granted him by the Father" (Jn.6:65). "No one can say Jesus is Lord except by the Holy Spirit" (1 Cor.12:3). No Christian should be "proud" (Rom.11:20): none have reason to "boast" (Eph.2:9). Indeed, it is only when we are weak that we are strong (cf. 2 Cor.12:10).

This was the testimony of Christian experience. Faith and obedience were never one's doing. Faith came suddenly; it was not the result of any effort. Obedience was not a matter of one's own will. When a person tried to do it on his own, he failed. It was only when he acknowledged his helplessness and prayed for strength that he succeeded. Thereupon, he received more strength than he ever expected. It was obvious that he had received supernatural help; this was grace, a supernatural power that illumined and gave strength.

Despite the testimony of Christian experience, Pelagius (d.c.420) denied that grace is a necessity. He insisted that the will could not have been *completely* disordered by original sin. It must have some power to choose good on its own; otherwise, how is man to be praised or blamed for what he chooses? Since he is, grace may be helpful but it cannot be absolutely necessary. Moreover, failing to see what purpose God served in corrupting man's will, Pelagius argued that sinfulness is transmitted by bad example — imitation. Failing to see what purpose was served by the other temporal punishments that Adam supposedly received, he even denied that Adam had been given the gifts that he was said to have lost. In particular, he held that Adam would have died a natural death whether or not he had sinned.

Augustine responded. First, he offered the traditional argument: if Adam had not been given the gifts he was said to have lost, God would be responsible for evil (cf. p. 55). Then, he pointed out that were grace not absolutely necessary — if someone could conceivably avoid sin on his own — we could not say that Christ's death redeemed mankind. Moreover, if some could have saved themselves, why did Christ need to die? Besides, it remains the truly Christian experience that man is a sinner — that salvation is utterly unmerited. This must mean that man's will is capable of no good on its own. This is "concupiscence"; it must have been a punishment for original sin.[124] Because of it, grace must be

---

124. See especially his *On the Grace of Christ and Original Sin*, especially 1. Actually, Augustine's thought on original sin, grace, and freedom is constantly restated throughout his many writings and no citations concerning these questions should be considered his first or last work.

at work before, during and after every Christian act. Nonetheless, the will must still co-operate with grace and, despite concupiscence, it does so freely[125]

The Church agreed with Augustine. In 418, the Council of Carthage declared that Adam had been punished with the complete disordering of his will and death (DS 222) which, with all his other punishments, were inevitably transmitted by propagation and not imitation (DS 223). This makes grace absolutely necessary (DS 225), providing as it does illumination and strength (DS 226).

This did not end the controversy. Still confused about the function of free will, John Cassian (c.360-435) attempted to modify the thinking of Pelagius. According to his "semi-Pelagianism," man must choose to co-operate with grace before it can work.

Cassian did not persuade. Mindful that semi-Pelagianism still involved the idea that man was capable of a certain goodness apart from God, the Council of Orange condemned it. Willing to admit that the function of free will was quite a mystery, the council declared that grace must be operative prior to prayer (DS 373), every act of obedience (DS 374), and even faith (DS 375). Unaffected was the Church's insistence that acts of obedience were meritorious and led to an increase in grace.

Thinkers now turned to the study of grace in itself. Observing the obvious difference between the desire for holiness and holiness itself, Alexander of Hales became the first to distinguish between actual and sanctifying grace. He was also the first to distinguish between sanctifying grace and the indwelling of the Holy Spirit. As he explained, were the Spirit to become part of a soul, each would be another incarnation.[126] Thomas told how sanctifying, or as he called it, "created" grace does become part of a soul. He also described the working of actual grace as he distinguished several kinds.[127]

6. The Resurrection

Even apart from grace, there could be no doubt about the resurrection. The Scriptures spoke in no uncertain terms. Jesus' tomb was found empty (Mt.28:1-8, Mk.16:1-8, Lk.24:1-12, Jn.20-1-3). The Roman soldiers ordered to guard it had scattered (Mt.27:62ff). (This proved that the disciples had not stolen the body.) He appeared to Mary Magdalene (whom He had previously freed from seven demons, Lk.8:2) and the

125. See his *On Grace and Free Will*, 29-33.
126. See his *Summa*, III, q.61. Actually, the distinction between sanctifying grace and the indwelling of the Holy Spirit was already to be recognized in the writings of Augustine.
127. *S. Th.* I-II, q.109-114.

other Mary (Mt.28:8-10). Then He appeared to two of His disciples on the road to Emmaus (Lk.24:13-35). Shortly thereafter, while they were still in Jerusalem, Jesus entered a locked room in order to appear to His apostles (Lk.24:36ff, Jn.20:19-23). Thomas, however, was absent. Doubting that Jesus had really risen, he would not believe it until he had put his hands in the wounds of the cross (Jn.20:24-29). Jesus later appeared to the apostles in Galilee (Mt.28:16-18, Jn.21:1ff). He was seen by as many as five hundred people at one time (1 Cor.15:6).

The apostles were alone when they witnessed the ascension (Acts 1:9).

l) The Sacraments

In 1500, the sacraments could not have been more sacred — or sought. Their effects were felt and there was no other way to obtain them. Jesus' personal institution of each of the seven was sure.

1. Baptism

Jesus instituted Baptism by commanding His apostles to "make disciples of all nations, baptizing them in the name of the Father and the Son and the Holy Spirit" (Mt.28:19). He warned that "unless one is born of water and the Spirit, he cannot enter the kingdom of God" (Jn.3:25). "He who is a believer and is baptized will be saved; but he who does not believe will be condemned" (Mk.16:16). Peter made clear that "there is salvation in no one else, for there is no other name under heaven given among men by which we must be saved" (Acts 4:12).

Peter also described the effects of Baptism. As he promised: "Repent, and be baptized every one of you in the name of Jesus Christ for the forgiveness of your sins and you shall receive the Holy Spirit" (Acts 2:38). Obviously, forgiveness also included original sin because, if it did not, a person would not be worthy to receive the Holy Spirit. But, the Spirit dwells within him (e.g. Rom.8:9). This makes him "holy" (e.g. 1 Cor.3:17), a "new creation" (2 Cor.5:17). He is given love, peace, and joy.[128] He is also freed from sin (cf. Rom.6:7). After all, "no one born of God commits sin for God's nature abides in him" (1 Jn.3:9). Of course, as was evident, one could still fall back to sin. As Augustine explained: "Baptism removes the shaft but the wound remains."[129]

Thomas described the "character" which Baptism imparts. Of course, the existence of this character had always been evident. After all, once a Christian, always a Christian. And Christians were a "royal priesthood"

---

128. Besides love, peace, and joy, the "fruits" of the Spirit also included patience, kindness, goodness, faithfulness, gentleness, and self-control (Gal.5:22-23). These were to be distinguished from the "gifts" of the Spirit: wisdom, knowledge, counsel, fortitude, understanding, piety and fear of the Lord (Is.11:1-3).

129. See his *De Nuptiis et Concupiscentia*, 1,28,29.

(1 Pet.2:9). Thus, in an emergency, all God's people's could baptize.[130]

Obviously, Baptism incorporates a person into the Church. As Paul said: "We are all baptized into one body" (1 Cor.12:13). According to Irenaeus, this legitimized the baptism of infants.[131] According to Tertullian, it was justified by the danger of premature death and damnation.[132]

His belief in the necessity of Baptism notwithstanding, Tertullian still held that the rule knew of some exceptions. Since Christian indoctrination often lasted several months, during which a person might well be martyred for the faith, he concluded that such a person received an unseen "Baptism of blood."[133] Augustine believed that anyone who died during this period received a "Baptism of desire."[134]

The only controversy concerned the practice of re-baptizing persons who had already been baptized by some heretical sect. Cyprian argued that since the initial Baptism did not take place within the communion of the Church, it had not been valid.[135] In several letters to Pope Stephen (d.257), he urged that anyone baptized by heretics be re-baptized. Stephen refused. After all, a Christian is still a Christian, and once a Christian always a Christian.

2. Confirmation

Though the Scriptures never used the word, nor told of the circumstances of its institution, it was still clear that Christ had instituted Confirmation. He sent the Holy Spirit to His apostles (Jn.20:22, Acts 2:1-4). Thereafter, they gave the Spirit to His apostles (Jn.20:22, Acts 2:1-4). Thereafter, they gave the Spirit to believers *already baptized* through the imposition of hands (Acts 8:14-17). Tertullian documented that Confirmation had remained the prerogative of a bishop.[136] Thomas explained that it strengthened the gifts given in baptism as the Holy Spirit was now received in a "personal" way which made the recipient a "warrior" for Christ.[137]

3. Penance and Indulgences

Since sin was still possible, and each sin cost the sinner some if not all of his sanctifying grace, it was to be expected that God would have provided

---

130. *S.Th.* III, q.66-69.
131. *Adv. Haer.* 2.22.4.
132. See his *On Baptism*, 18.
133. See his "Letters," 73.22.
134. See his *De Catechizandis Rudibus*, 3.4.
135. See his *De Lapsis.*
136. *On Baptism*, 8.
137. *S.Th.* III, q.72.

some means by which sins could be forgiven and grace restored. Jesus forgave sins (e.g. Mt.9:2, Mk.2:5, Lk.18:20). He gave this power to Peter saying: "Whatever you bind on earth will be bound in heaven, whatever you loose on earth will be loosed in heaven" (Mt.18:18). To the rest of the apostles, He was even more explicit: "If you forgive the sins of any, they are forgiven, if you retain their sins, they are retained" (Jn.20:23).

But forgiveness, or "absolution," did *not* involve a release from the punishments required by justice. Even though grace was restored, penance was still to be done. For this reason, Clement urged the faithful to submit to their "presbyters" — their priests.[138] (The word "presbyter" was literally to be translated "elder.")

In keeping with the teachings of Jesus, there was surely no sin — except the sin against the Holy Spirit (Mt.12:31, Mk.3:29, Lk.12:10) — that could not be forgiven.[139] As Irenaeus explained, certain sins could cost a person his communion with the Church but, the completion of his penance would restore it.[140] This did not prejudice the immemorial conviction that earthly penance rarely satisfied all the demands of divine justice.

The release from earthly penance, or even the punishment that earthly penance would not have satisfied, was simply to invoke the power to bind and loose. But, since justice was still to be done, the Church must be able to draw upon some source of merit with which to pay for the punishment properly due. It must be an infinite source since the power to bind and loose had not been restricted. These were the conclusions of Alexander of Hales, the first to describe an "infinite treasury of merit."[141] In 1343, Clement VI employed this idea in his insistence that the Church did have the power to grant Indulgences, even to the dead (DS 1025-26). He also explained that the treasury could never run dry, not only because it had been supplied by the infinite merits of Christ, but also because it was added to by the merits of Mary, the saints, and other pious Christians (DS 1027).

---

138. Clem. 57,1.
139. It is to be mentioned that not everyone agreed that all sins could be forgiven. Following the scriptural suggestion that there was no acceptable repentance for "apostasy," the abandonment of faith (Heb.6:4-6), the "Montanists," the followers of Montanus (c.172) insisted that apostasy excommunicated a person for life. Hermas said that apostasy and the other two "capital" sins, murder and adultery, should only be forgiven once (see his "Mandates," 4,3).
140. *Adv. Haer.* 1,6,3.
141. *Summa,* III, q.83.

4. The Eucharist

Of all the sacraments, the Eucharist was "pre-eminent." (Its "pre-eminence" officially consisted of the fact that in the Eucharist, Christ was present before the sacrament was used.)

There was no doubt that Jesus instituted the Eucharist at His last supper with His disciples when "He took bread and when He had given thanks He broke it and gave it to them, saying, 'This is my body which is given for you. Do this in remembrance of me! And likewise the cup after supper, saying, 'This cup which is poured out is the new covenant in my blood" (Lk.22:19-20, cf. Mt.26:26-28, Mk.14:22-24, 1 Cor.11:23-25). Surely, partaking of this bread and this cup was "the" source of communion with Christ and, thus, the richest source of sanctifying grace. Jesus Himself made clear that partaking of His body and blood was essential to Christian life: "Truly, truly, I say to you, unless you eat of the flesh of the Son of Man and drink of His blood, you have no life in you" (Jn.6:53).

The body and blood of Christ were also essential to the life of the Church. As Paul explained: "because there is one bread, we who are many are one body because we all partake of the one bread" (1 Cor.10:17). He insisted that Christians must be at peace with one another before they eat the "Lord's Supper" (1 Cor.11:17-22). Moreover, they must eat the bread and drink of the cup in worthy manner lest they profane the Lord's body and blood (cf. 1 Cor.11:27-29).

With time, respect for the Lord's body and blood only increased. Ignatius said that the bread is "the medicine of immortality and the antidote against death."[142] He condemned the docetists who denied that the "Eucharist" is the flesh of the savior.[143] He declared that the wine is Jesus' blood.[144] Justin said: "we do not receive common bread and wine but food that has been consecrated by words that come from Christ and make them His flesh and blood."[145] Thus, as Justin also insisted: "the Eucharist is only for those who have been baptized and continue to hold the faith of the Church."[146]

Though "transubstantiation"was not a biblical word, it was clearly

142. "Letter to the Ephesians," 20,2.
143. Smyrn. 7,1.
144. "Letter to the Romans," 7,3.
145. *First Apology*, 66,2; in chapter 65, Justin provides the first detailed description of a eucharistic ritual. Hippolytus'(c.170-c.236) *Apostolic Tradition* contains the earliest record of eucharistic prayer.
146. Ibid. 66,1; actually, during his time, Christians traveling from community to community often carried "letters of communion" stating that they were eligible to receive.

what the Bible described. Jesus said: "This is my body." As Thomas explained, if it is His body, it cannot be bread too. It is certainly not a mix of substances; then it would be neither. One substance has been changed into another without a change in the "accidents" which account for its appearance.[147]

It was clear the Eucharist re-offers the sacrifice of the cross. Jesus said: "this is my body *which is given for you.*" As Paul delcared: "as often as you eat this bread and drink the cup, you proclaim the Lord's death until He comes" (1 Cor.11:26).

Clement said that bishops had been appointed "to offer the sacrifice."[148] Justin said the Eucharist is the "pure offering" foretold by the prophet Malachi (1:10).[149] Irenaeus stated it plainly: "the Eucharist is a sacrifice offered throughout the world."[150] Tertullian insisted that the merits of this sacrifice can be applied to souls departed.[151] Duns Scotus said that the priest has the power to apply its "fruits."[152]

5. Matrimony

It was obvious that God had ordered marriage. "Male and female He created them" (Gen.1:27). He created Eve to be Adam's "helper" (cf. 2:18ff). But it was Jesus who made marriage a sacrament when He said: "What therefore God has joined together, let no man put asunder" (Mt.19:6). Plainly, He meant matrimony to be "indissoluble." "Whoever divorces his wife, except for unchastity, and marries another commits adultery" (Mt.19:9). According to Paul, Christ meant matrimony to be a sign of His love for the Church (Eph.5:20-32). Thus it must involve the grace of fidelity.

Since marriage was meant to be a sign of Christ's love for the Church, the Church had the right and duty to regulate it. As Ignatius said: "it is proper for the bridegroom and bride to contract their marriage in conformity with the rulings of the bishop."[153] Nonetheless, as Thomas explained, the ministers of the sacrament are the bride and groom themselves.[154]

6. Extreme Unction

Jesus' institution of Extreme Unction surely took place one of the many

---

147. *S.Th.* III, q.75.
148. Clem. 44.
149. *Dial.* 41.
150. *Adv. Haer.* 4,17,5.
151. See his *De Corona,* 3.
152. See his *Quodlibetum,* 20.
153. See his "Letter to Polycarp," 5,2.
154. *S.Th.* III, q.42.

times He commissioned the apostles to continue His work of healing the sick (e.g. Mt.10:1). The Scriptures explicitly recorded His instruction on the use of oil (Mk.6:13, see especially Jas.5:14).

By 416, in a letter to Decentius, the Bishop of Gubbio, Pope Innocent I explicitly called the "anointing of the sick" a sacrament (DS 216). Thomas taught that it was preparation for death.[155]

7. Holy Orders

Since we have already provided an apologetic for the ordination of bishops (cf. p. 45), we can move immediately to the proof that the apostles had also been empowered to extend some of their powers to such representatives as they saw fit.

The Scriptures contained a detailed record of the apostle's first ordination of deacons, stating specifically that this involved the imposition of hands (Acts 6:1-6). Though there was no record of the first ordination of priests, the Scriptures did say that they too were "appointed" by the apostles (Acts 14:23), receiving a "gift" by the imposition of hands (1 Tim.4:14).

Clement recalled the "appointment" of bishops and deacons.[156] (He is already on record as to the authority of the presbyters, c.f. p. 81.) Ignatius said that the Eucharist should be offered by "the one bishop with the presbyterium (the body of 'elders') and the deacons".[157]

Cyprian insisted that "priests" had also been given the power to offer the Eucharist.[158] (He employed the word "sacerdos," a word which the Old Testament used for "priest.") Since the priest does offer the Eucharist, his soul must possess the character that carries this power. (This gives him a share in the bishop's mission "to teach, to sanctify and to rule — a share of Jesus' role as priest, prophet and king.) It makes him "a priest forever after the order of Melchizedek" (Heb.7:17). Thus, as Innocent III declared: "anyone who believes and contends that he can perform the sacrifice of the Eucharist without first having been ordained is a heretic" (DS 794).

Undoubtedly, the demands of orders were accompanied by the grace needed to carry them out. Indeed, as Thomas explained, this grace made the priest an *alter Christus*, "another Christ."[159]

---

155. *S.Th.* III, q.32.
156. Clem. 42.
157. See his "Letter to the Philadelphians," 4.
158. "Letters," 63,4.
159. *S.Th.* III, supplement, q.34-40; this "supplement" was actually put together from Thomas' notes after his death by Reginald his secretary.

8. Sacraments in General

At this point, our look at the Church's teaching on the sacraments would unquestionably profit from a brief look at sacraments in general.

Though the Scriptures never speak of "sacraments," they did provide ample evidence that God should be expected to affect salvation through visible things. He had spoken through the prophets. Even when He had spoken in person, He took on the visible form of flesh in order to do so. Therefore, it was no surprise that sanctifying grace was communicated visibly. This way, its recipients could know that its most important effects had taken place. As Ambrose (c.339-97) explained, this is the reason that sacramental actions symbolize the grace that they communicate. As he observed, the use of water in Baptism is quite symbolic of the cleansing of the soul that actually takes place.[160] This idea was clearly present in Thomas' definition of a sacrament — "an external sign instituted by Christ to give grace."[161] Peter Lombard had already said that they are seven.[162]

Augustine had contributed the distinction between the visible "element," such as water, and the "word" of which sacraments consist.[163] Thomas spoke of these as sacramental "matter" and "form."[164]

Obviously, the grace conferred by the sacraments was the work of God, and not the person who performs them. In and of themselves, ritual actions accomplish nothing. It was only the fact that God had chosen to work through these rituals that made them effective. Thus, as John Chrysostom could insist, the holiness of the person who performs them was not important.[165] When the Donatists said otherwise and insisted upon the re-baptism of anyone baptized by someone that they considered unworthy, Optatus (c.370) responded with what was already the classical argument.[166]

Augustine was the first to distinguish a "valid" sacrament, which produced grace, and the effectiveness of this grace, which depended upon the disposition of the recipient.[167] Thomas was the first to distinguish between sacraments, which work "ex opere operato" (by virtue of the

---

160. See his *On the Sacraments*, especially 1.
161. *S. Th.* III, q.4.
162. *Sentences*, d.2, c.1.
163. See his "Commentary on the Gospel of John," 80,3.
164. *S. Th.* III, q.60.
165. See his "Homily on the Second Letter to Timothy," 2,4.
166. See his *Against Parmenianus the Donatist*, 5; Optatus' use of this argument preceded Augustine's more famous dispute with the Donatists.
167. "Commentary on the Gospel of John," 26,11.

action performed) and "sacramentals" which work "ex opere operantis" (by virtue of what the actions might inspire).[168] Thomas also provided the definitive statement of the immemorial idea that even though the sacraments are the work of God, i.e. the whole Trinity, they are in a special way the work of the Son because Christ instituted them in order to enable the visible continuance of *His* mission. Thus, the person who administers them does so *in persona Christi,* "in the person of Christ."[169] Nonetheless, sacraments are also acts of the Church. Therefore, their minister is still bound to do what the Church requires of the valid sacrament. He is also required to "intend" what the Church intends.

J. God's Working in the World

There was no doubt that God was at work in the world apart from grace. He was clearly perceived to intervene in human history — frequently.

1. The Efficacy of Prayers of Petition

The efficacy of prayers of petition was most evident from their frequent success. Almost everyone could tell that they had gotten something they had prayed for. After all, if God was really a loving Father, how could He not respond to the pleas of His people? "What father among you, if his son asks for a fish will instead of a fish give him a serpent. . ."(Lk.11:11). Indeed, from the time of their captivity in Egypt, God has responded to the pleas of His People (cf. Ex.2:23-25). Moreover, "the prayer of a righteous man is powerful in its effects"(Jas.5:16). Jesus said: "ask and it will be given to you" (e.g. Mt.7:7, Mk.11:24, Lk.11:9); "If you ask anything in my name, I shall do it" (Jn.14:14). Of course, faith was required; as we have seen, "if you have faith and never doubt . . . whatever you ask for you shall receive" (Mt.21:21-22).

The Trinitarian scheme of God's response to prayer was all but stated. "The Spirit intercedes for us" (Rom.8:26); the Son is our "great high priest" (Heb.4:14).

2. The Intercession of Mary and the Saints

Surely, our great high priest would himself respond to the intercession of His beloved mother and the saints who were now with Him in heaven. "The prayers of the saints are precious"(Rev.5:8). This was the testimony of the many who had prayed to Mary or the saints and had gotten what they prayed for.

Origen was the first to call the saints a "communion."[170] We can pray to them because they are also in communion with us on earth.

---

168. In Sent. IV, d.1; the status of simple "blessings" was never made clear.
169. Ibid. d.7.
170. See his *In Jesu Nave Homiliae,* 16.5.

3. Divine Retribution

God obviously chose to intervene much more often than He was asked. This was the evidence of history. When the chosen people kept the Law, they were rewarded with a good harvest (e.g. Ex.34:22). When they did not, they were punished (cf. p. 66). When Ananias and his wife Sapphira failed to give the Church all the money they had gotten from the sale of their property, they were struck dead (Acts 5:1-11).

God did not always do His own punishing. Sometimes He permitted demons to do it for Him. Augustine said that they were responsible for disease;[171] Thomas said that they were responsible for storms.[172]

4. Providence

Of course, everything that happens is still God's will. Since He is the creator of all things and their sustainer, nothing can happen apart from His will. Since He is all-good, everything happens for the best. Therefore, "do not be anxious about tomorrow . . ." (Mt.6:34). "In thy book were written, every one of them, the days that were formed for me, when as yet there was none of them" (Ps.139:16). "The Lord is my shepherd, I shall not want . . ." (Ps.23:1).

K) Human and World Destiny

Providence still meant death, and death meant judgment.

1. Individual Judgment

Individual judgment was necessary. After death, a soul had to go somewhere. Besides, how else could Jesus have promised one of the two criminals with whom He was crucified: "today you will be with me in paradise" (Lk.23:43)?

a. Heaven

Jesus promised paradise, "heaven," to all who would accept Him (e.g. Mt.5:12, Mk.4:17). Therefore, if a person was baptized (cf. Mk.16:16), his sins were forgiven, and no punishment was due, he will go directly to heaven. There he will see God and become like Him for he will see Him as He is (cf. 1 Jn.3:2). He will enjoy happiness presently unimaginable (e.g. 1 Cor.2:9). And he will never die again (e.g. 1 Cor.15:42ff).

Augustine held that the happiness of heaven is the ability to praise God without tiring (cf. Eph.1:12). He also held that heaven will be experienced in different degrees. The degree will depend upon the life a person had lived on earth. This was only just (cf. Mt.19:29-30). This was what Jesus meant when He said: "in my Father's house there are many

---

171. See his *De Divinatione Daemonum*, 3.
172. *S. Th.* 1, q.80, a.2.

rooms" (Jn. 14:2). How else could He have said that "many of those who were first will be last and many of those who were last will be first" (Mt.19:30, Lk.13:30)? But, since everyone will have their personal fill, there will be no envy.[173] Thomas agreed that heaven will be experienced in differing degrees. As he explained it, the degree will depend upon the sanctifying grace a person has obtained during his lifetime. It is grace that gives a person the "beatific vision," and through it, a "participation" in divine life. Thereupon, the happiness of heaven is the "knowledge" of God.[174] Duns Scotus insisted that it is an active ability to "love" Him.

b. Purgatory

The existence of purgatory was all but stated. It was an obvious demand of justice. And, God's goodness could not tolerate the sin-stained soul. Thus did Paul say some will be saved only through fire (cf. 1 Cor.3:13-17).

Tertullian spoke explicitly of the place where souls were detained in order to be cleansed.[176] Gregory of Nyssa was the first to call it "purgatory."[177]

c. Hell

The existence of hell was even more certain than the existence of heaven. The Hebrews called it "sheol," in Greek "hades" (e.g. Ps.9:17). Jesus called it "Gehenna." It was the place for the damned — the unbaptized (cf. Mk.16:16) or those who had committed a mortal sin and never repented (cf. 1 Jn.5:16-17). It was a place of unquenchable fire (e.g. Mt.5:21-22, Mk.9:44). "There men will weep and gnash their teeth" (Mt.8:12, cf. Lk.13.29). Nonetheless, their punishment will be eternal (e.g. Mt.25:46). Unfortunately, "the gate is narrow and the way is hard that leads to life and those that make it are few" (Mt.7:14, cf. Lk.13:24).

Even though Jesus taught that hell was eternal, certain thinkers could not believe it. They could not believe that God's mercy would permit anyone's eternal suffering. The otherwise orthodox Gregory of Nyssa even believed that the fallen angels would be reconciled to God; He did not believe that beings could exist apart from God forever.[178]

Basil responded. He explained that beings in hell are totally cut off from God and thus have no chance of repentance. They had their chance; now it was too late. The demands of justice must be respected;

173. *The City of God*, 22.
174. *S.Th.* 1, q.12.
175. In Sent. d.49, q.5.
176. *On the Soul*, 58.
177. See his *Orationes de Mortuis*.
178. See his *Oratio Catechetica*, 26.

God's goodness can permit nothing else.[179] According to Augustine, justice also demands that the pain of hell differs in degree, depending upon the sinfulness of a person's life (cf. Mt.18:6, Lk.17:2).[180]

In 543, Pope Vigilius formally declared that hell is eternal (DS 411). In 1439, his teaching was confirmed by the Council of Florence. The council also endorsed the idea that the pains of hell (and the happiness of heaven) differ in degree. It also affirmed the patristic teaching on purgatory (DS 1304-05).

d. Limbo

The existence of limbo was the one major issue which many considered an open question.

According to Augustine, humanity is a "damned mass."[181] The stain of original sin makes everyone a sinner from the moment of his conception. Why else do infants suffer even before they have committed a sin?[182] For this reason, all who die before Baptism go to hell.[183]

Thomas disagreed. He held that the inherited stain of original sin is nothing for which a person is guilty until he has committed a sin of his own. But, he did acknowledge that the stain of original sin makes everyone unsuitable to receive sanctifying grace. Therefore, he concluded that the unbaptized infant, personally guilty of nothing but still unworthy to see God, is consigned to the incomplete happiness of a "limbo."[184]

2. The End Time

The Scriptures had much to say about the end time. When all of God's enemies have been put under His feet, the Son will deliver the kingdom to His Father (cf. 1 Cor.15:24-25). "The sun will be darkened and the moon will not give its light and the stars will fall from heaven . . . they will see the Son of Man coming on the clouds of heaven and He will send out His angels with a loud trumpet call and they will gather His elect from the four winds, from one end of heaven to the other" (Mt.24:29-31). Then Christ will render final judgment on the living and the dead (cf. 2 Tim.4:1), repaying everyone for what he has done (cf. Mt.16:27). This will take place in the body so that everyone can receive judgment for what he has done in the body (cf. 2 Cor.5:10).

There was no doubt that the end would indeed involve the resurrection

---

179. *On the Holy Spirit*, 40.
180. *The City of God*, 21.16.
181. *De Nuptiis et Concupiscentia*, 2.57.
182. See his *Against Julius*, 6.67.
183. See his *Opus Imperfectum Contra Iulianum*, 3.199; "Iulianum," i.e. Julius, to whom this work was addressed, was a follower of Pelagius.
184. *S. Th.* III, supplement, q.69.

of the body. Jesus rose in the body. According to Thomas, the soul is ordered to the body (cf. p. 62). But, the body we receive will surely be far superior to the body we now possess; it will be a "spiritual body" (cf. 1 Cor.15:44). "Christ . . . will change our lowly body to be like His own glorious body" (Phil.3:21). Nonetheless, as Cyril of Jerusalem (c.318-386) made clear, our spiritual bodies will be our old bodies made new; what else does "resurrection" mean?[185] How else will we know each other?

After the dead have risen, they, and those still living, will rise into the clouds, to meet Christ in mid-air (cf. 1 Thess.4:16). There will be a "new creation" (2 Cor.5:17), "a new heaven and a new earth" (2 Pet.3:13), "a new Jerusalem" (Rev.21:2), and "God will be everything to everyone" (1 Cor.15:28), "the alpha and the omega, the beginning and the end" (Rev.21:6).

* * *

More or less, this would have been the defense of the faith of 1500.

---

185. See his *Cathecheses*, 17.

Chapter III: The Decline of the Faith of 1500

Section I: The Remote Causes of the Decline

In 1500, the faith certainly seemed secure. Yet, in 1517, Luther made public his objections to the doctrine of Indulgences and the Church began to see the steady, accelerating decline of the acceptance of its teachings which is still in progress.

Ironically, the remote causes of this decline profoundly include actions of the Church, particularly the papacy, at the height of its power.

Let there be no mistake; the late-medieval churchman was not misled about the Church's power. Even before the Empire officially fell, the Church had already assumed the role of civil government. By 450, Leo I (the "Great") was ruler of Rome.[1] By 600, Gregory I (also the "Great") ruled much of what is now Italy. What is more, thanks to what had indeed been the remarkable success of many missionaries, half of all medieval lords were bishops; the rest were no less responsive to papal authority.[2] It was this that made possible the Crusades.

During the seventh century, the rapid rise of Islam had involved not only the spiritual but also the military conquest of many then Christian lands. These included the Palestine of Jesus' life and mission, an affront and embarrassment to Christian Europe. Therefore, in 1096, Pope Urban II called for a crusade to free the "holy land" from Moslem rule. He called for armies to be raised throughout Europe and offered an Indulgence to anyone who would join them. Many did and, in 1099, they gained control of the holy land. Soon thereafter, the Moslems captured it back. This began a series of seven more crusades which ended in 1291, a failure.

Nonetheless, the Crusades did have a permanent effect on Europe. Prior to the Crusades, Europe had changed little in the five hundred years since the fall of the Roman Empire. Subsequently to be called the "Dark Ages," the fall of the empire had meant the almost complete decline of

---

1. Leo is remembered for persuading Attila the Hun not to sack Rome.
2. The official assertion of Church over civil authority was said to date from Christmas Day of the year 800 when Leo III crowned Charlemagne "Holy Roman Emperor." In this act, Leo supposedly "invested" Charlemagne with the Church's power of civil government. (He supposedly did this in order to free the Church for more spiritual concerns.) When, in 1076, the reigning Holy Roman Emperor, Henry IV, attempted to assert civil control over the Church — demanding the power to appoint local bishops — Gregory VII (1021-1085) deposed Henry, restoring him to power only after he had acknowledged that the pope's power *was* supreme.

civilization. Except for the little learning which took place in monasteries,[3] few people could read and write. The vast majority were "serfs" scraping out a meager existence within a self-contained, isolated "manor" in the service of a local lord and the knights he employed for their protection. The lords were subject to other lords within the "feudal" system of alliances which more or less kept order.

The Crusades initiated a chain of events that changed all this. The call for a crusade and the organization which it required led to a greatly increased level of communication among feudal powers. This, coupled with a new-found demand for the goods, such as spices, which were discovered when the crusaders went eastward, led to a rapid increase in trade. This spelled the end of the "barter" system as the demands of trade spurred the redevelopment of money. This made possible the accumulation of wealth. It also freed people from agriculture and saw to the emergence of crafts. As more and more people stayed home from the fields, cities began to take shape. The rise of cities, together with the increase in communication, led to the rise of national states. This both caused and was fostered by the development of national languages as eventually manifest in the work of men such as Dante Alighieri (1265-1321) whose *Divina Comedia* had much to do with the standardization of medieval Italian.

This was only the beginning. From the crafts emerged a newly intensive practice of the arts and, eventually, the sciences. With the accumulation of wealth, patronage became possible; promising talent was afforded the possibility of full-time employment at something other than growing or making. The growth of cities resulted in a pooling of talents, a sharing of ideas and, not surprisingly, rivalries which propelled progress in every field of human endeavor. The general result of all these developments was the "Renaissance" of Western Europe, a period of artistic and scientific activity which soon surpassed anything the world had ever known.

This was also an age of geographical exploration. Encouraged by the possibility of increased trade with the East — and sustained by the wealth which eastern trade had already produced — the Venetian merchants

---

3. Christian monasticism originated in Egypt. Conceived by Anthony (c.251-356), it involved the pursuit of spiritual perfection away from the distraction of life in society. Shortly thereafter, at the instruction of Basil, monasticism took on the institutional character of life under a "rule" designed to foster spiritual perfection. Monasticism was introduced to the West by Benedict (480-543) whose rule extended to almost every aspect of life in the monastery. It specifically required some form of manual labor, be it work in the fields or the transcription of the Scriptures or other ancient texts. This preserved many that would otherwise have been lost.

began to commission expeditions farther and farther eastward. When Marco Polo (c.1254-c.1324) returned from his overland journey to India and China[4] to tell of the great wealth which he had found there, most of the emerging European powers became interested in an economical, i.e. water route East. To this end, Prince Henry "the Navigator" of Portugal (1394-1480) sponsored a number of attempts to sail around Africa to get to India. Henry's patronage was directly responsible for Vasco Da Gama's arrival in India in 1498. By way of competition, it was also responsible for Christopher Columbus' Spain-sponsored "discovery" of America in 1492.[5] Twenty years later, these voyages made possible Magellan's successful circumnavigation of the globe. This proved that Columbus was right; the earth is round.

Geographical discoveries confirmed the growing conviction that there was no limit to what man might discover or do. So did the achievements of men like Leonardo Da Vinci (1450-1519) and Michelangelo Buonarotti (1475-1564), both of Florence, the unofficial capital of the Renaissance.[6] It was here that the Renaissance passed the point of no return.

Needless to say, the developments that gave birth to the Renaissance had their effect on the Church. The increase of wealth supplied the Church with money for projects of all kinds. The breakdown of life in isolated communities saw the founding and rapid growth of unsequestered, "mendicant" (or "begging") religious orders such as the Dominicans, founded by Dominic in 1220, and the Franciscans, founded by Francis in 1223. Almost immediately, in an attempt to bring learning to the newly forming cities, these orders founded universities in Paris, Bologna, Salamanca, and Oxford, to name but the first. It was here that Christian Scholasticism would be born.

But, the developments that gave birth to the Renaissance also made life more difficult for the Church. The increase of wealth gave power to people other than churchmen. With the rise of cities and, thereupon, national states, the Church was soon to be overtaken in temporal power. With the death of Innocent III (1198-1216), a churchman would never again be the dominant Western leader. The relationship between the

---

4. In China Marco Polo met Kublai Khan, grandson of Genghis Khan, who, to the chagrin of the Europeans, had conquered an empire far larger than that of Rome.

5. Actually, the evidence indicates that about the year 1000, Leif Erikson of Scandinavia had already been the first European to reach the Western Hemisphere. Of course, the Asian-born American Indians had already been there approximtely fifteen thousand years.

6. But, the Renaissance spread throughout the continent and beyond. It was found as far away as England, in men like William Shakespeare (1564-1616) who gave a new dramatic form to the English language.

Church and society was changing.

The most significant change took place at the level of ideas. The pursuit of the arts and sciences led to an increasingly critical attitude toward the truth. This, together with specific artistic and scientific achievements, led to a critique of the idea that the world is an accursed place to be endured while salvation, man's only hope for happiness, is to be pursued. The world was becoming a place of great potential to be explored for all it was worth. And, the conscious focus of man's attention was beginning to shift; once it was God, it was now becoming *himself*.

Let it be clear. Not only did these changes involve only the smallest percentage of the population, but even where they did occur, they were almost imperceptible. Though Niccolo Machiavelli (1469-1527) did startle the intellectual world of his day with *The Prince*, a treatise on the acquisition and maintenance of power which advocated the axiom: "the end justifies the means," Leonardo poured his soul into the Last Supper while Michelangelo struggled to put the dome atop St. Peter's Basilica in Rome.

Nonetheless, a change had taken place. And, with remarkable swiftness, there was to emerge a modern mind that would repudiate almost everything that its predecessor held "sacred." Of course, despite its swiftness, the abandonment of the medieval mind still required several "steps." What each of these involved, we shall now see.

Section II: The Decline of Confidence in Scholasticism

The first step in the decline of Christian Scholasticism was the decline of confidence in scholasticism, its philosophical base. Though this has been the least noticed of all the steps we shall see, it remains the one that underlies all of them.

A. Scholasticism After Thomas

Thomas made philosophy a science — an almost exact science. And, not only had he explained reality, he provided the means of its continuing exploration. His successors took up the task; they endeavored to explain things with ever more completeness. Naturally, they sometimes disagreed. There was debate as to whether two or more kinds of a given thing, such as apples, betrayed the existence of two or more forms, or simply one form existing in different ways. There was also a difference of opinion as to when change involved one form present in different degrees, or the change from one form to another. What of the change of an acorn to an oak tree?

Not surprisingly, the passion for completeness was not restricted to philosophy. Quite apart from the famous debate as to how many angels can dance on the head of a pin, the science of theology had many questions to be answered. There were numerous attempts to explain how God could be one yet three, and how Jesus could be true God yet true man. There were similar efforts to reconcile grace and free will. Theologians further distinguished the kinds of grace while churchmen decided which acts led to its greatest increase or loss. Studies of the sacraments concluded that the body of Christ was present in any visible particle of the Eucharistic host and, when received, would perdure in a person for approximately fifteen minutes.

B. Nominalism

In its attempt to be complete, Christian Scholasticism drew the increasingly critical eye of those bothered by the fact that it involved so much that was so far from common experience. Eventually, the critique fell upon the central idea upon which the scholastic world-view was built, the idea that all things are composed of matter and the immaterial form which accounts for the commonality of similar things and the unchanging nature which makes them knowable.

As was discussed, Aristotle agreed with Plato that the demands of knowledge required, and therefore betrayed, the existence of unchanging, immaterial forms (cf. p. 59). Unlike Plato, however, he saw no need to postulate a world of forms far from the world which we experience. Wanting to narrow the gap between what was seen and what was believed, he held that the forms were in the matter that made up the things with which we deal. Inarticulately, he invoked what would later be called "the principle of economy," i.e. never explain with more principles that which can as completely be explained with fewer. In other words, postulate as little as possible.

The principle of economy was first articulated by Durandus of Saint-Pourçain (c.1275-1334), a relatively little known medieval thinker who was also the first to employ it in a denial of the existence of forms.[7] To this end, it was more famously employed by William of Occam (c.1285-1347), who called it the "razor."[8] He and Durandus had concluded that the postulation of immaterial forms was superfluous. They argued that the commonality of similar things is simply similarity. Their common "essence" is man's idea which should still be considered valid knowledge.

7. In Sent. II, d.3, q.5.
8. See especially his *Summa Logicae.*

Supporting this point of view was the fact that the postulation of immaterial forms involved so many problems. What *are* they? (What would a "perfect" hammer be?) What of the problems of "kinds" and "change"? What of the fact that some things appear to involve several forms at once? (Isn't a hammer a stone and a stick, and isn't a stick still part of a tree?) What if a thing is broken in two; does one form become two? Besides, how *do* the forms form matter? Where do they come from; where do they go? In short, the idea of forms presented too many problems — and it was not necessary.

Occam also argued against the idea of matter — pure matter. He insisted that it was not necessary to postulate pure matter as the principle of individuation. Individuality does not need to be explained because only in individuals is there existence. There is no "man" nor "manness" but simply our abstraction of what is similar about many individual men. Thus, the universals exist in name only. This was "nominalism," from the Greek word for "name."[9]

The abandonment of the distinction between matter and form was also the abandonment of the distinction between substance and accident. The substance of a thing was its form, its essence which perdured despite change. Nominalism means that a thing changed is a different thing.

C. Problems with the Proofs for the Existence of God

The decline of scholasticism was not restricted to a critique of its distinction between matter and form. The increasingly critical attitude toward everything soon involved a growing doubt about the many proofs for the existence of God. After all, if the great thinkers had been wrong about reality, they could also be wrong about its maker.

1. The Ontological Argument

It has already been stated that the ontological argument never enjoyed widespread acceptance (cf. p. 35). Thomas did not accept it. In its inference that the very idea of God (a perfect being) implied His existence (because it is better to exist), it appeared to assume the assertion that it supposedly proved. Moreover, as was pointed out to Anselm, if the argument was true, it could be used to prove that there is a perfect everything, for example, a perfect island. Though Anselm insisted that this is not true because perfection is not part and parcel of the idea of island, his rebuttal failed to sway the majority opinion because it

9. Nominalism is not only to be distinguished from "realism" (the idea that universals exist in matter) but it is also to be distinguished from the "conceptualism" of men like Abelard who held that somewhere there had to be something that substantiates the commonalities revealed by conceptual thinking.

remained to be proved that what can be thought must *be*.

2. *The Augustinian Arguments*

As was stated, the Augustinian arguments rarely received first mention when late-medieval theologians attempted to prove the existence of God (cf. p. 35). Now the reasons were becoming clear.

The argument that the immortality of the soul implied the immortality of its maker was jeopardized by the simple fact that the immortality of the soul no longer appeared proved. Though the soul did not appear to be composed of parts, it was by no means clear that its apparently impossible corruption was the only way for it to die. In its spirituality and workings, the soul was really quite mysterious. Perhaps it could die by some uniquely spiritual means; it certainly seemed to.

The argument that the restlessness of the soul betrayed an extra-worldly object of desire was critiqued for two reasons. The restlessness of the soul might just be its natural condition; it might just be the nature of the thing to want, and always to want more. Besides, not everyone testified to this experience; some claimed to be content. It hardly seemed possible to build a proof out of an insistence that everyone was unsatisfied by life whether or not they would admit it.

3. *The Five Ways*

Even the irrefutable five ways (cf. p. 36) found their critics. Occam had problems with three.

He was not convinced by the "Argument from Differing Degrees." To his perception, it is simply that natural causes can produce a given characteristic in differing degrees. The fire which makes things hot can also make them hotter.

William was no more convinced by the "Argument from Motion." He challenged the assertion that an infinite regression of finite movers is impossible. He claimed that if this regression *were* infinite, a source of motion would not be necessary.

The denial of the Argument from Motion led to a critique of the "Argument from the Direction of the World." If motion *were* eternal, some motions would surely have assumed the cyclic character which has previously been mistaken for the direction of some intelligence. How else are we to explain the fact that the world also exhibits a certain undirectedness — a random character which accounts for natural disasters and freak accidents?

William did not deny the validity of the "Argument from Cause and Effect." He agreed that causality implied an uncaused cause. He also agreed that creation betrays its dependence upon a "necessary" being.

These arguments combined in what remained a popular proof for the existence of God: Everything requires its cause; nothing comes from nothing. The world is here; it must have come from somewhere. It cannot have caused itself; therefore, it must have had an extra-worldly cause or maker. This is God.

Later nominalism was not so sure. Under continuing scrutiny, the arguments that William accepted did not appear to yield the certainty of a "proof." They seemed true but it was still possible to dispute them. It was possible to imagine a contrary position. Perhaps something *can* come from nothing; was it really possible to prove otherwise? Soon, all of the arguments for the existence of God came to be regarded as "probable" but not conclusive.

D. Trouble with the "Science" of Theology

It was not long before "probabilism" gave way to a contempt for apologetics. The impossibility of proof had come to be considered an effect of original sin, an anticipated punishment for man's prideful attempts to know it on his own and avoid the submission of true faith.

It was not long before a contempt for apologetics gave way to a denial that theology was a "science." Reacting against the proliferation of the highly detailed theological treatises that presented God in the most impersonal of terms — not to mention its reliance on "false" philosophy (cf. Col.2:8) — thinkers like Nicholas of Cusa (1401-64) began to insist that scientific theology is a hopeless attempt to express the inexpressible and to explain a truth which is a mystery grasped only vaguely, and only by means of religious experience.[10]

Section III: The Decline of Confidence in the Church: The Reformation

A. The Medieval State of Religious Life

Acknowledging the essential falsity of any generalization, it remains safe to say that, by 20th century standards, the medieval state of religious life left a good bit to be desired. Although the vast majority of people were baptized Catholics, the faith of the people was simple, shallow, given to superstition and its ultimate manifestation, magic. This was the reason that most people sought the sacraments. Where there was prayer, it was usually prayer for miracles addressed to Mary and the saints. Conceived

10. See especially his *The Clever Fool.*

as minor deities, Mary and the saints were much more approachable than the Almighty Three who demanded perfection and were ready to condemn anyone, even for sins committed unknowingly, accidentally or involuntarily. The fear of hell was very real. To escape hell, or an especially agonizing amount of time in purgatory, and to get the best possible place in heaven, the faithful sought to accumulate as much grace as they could get. They were especially eager to do anything that the Church prescribed for this purpose.

Actually, in their simplicity, the people depended upon the Church to direct almost every aspect of their lives. Naturally, this led to abuses. This was especially to be expected in light of the corruption that had begun to engulf the Church once the Empire fell and churchmen assumed the role of civil government with all of the power and wealth that this involved. This magnified the problems that normally attack institutions when they become big, influential and old.

One of the biggest problems was a clericalism which exalted the ordained and led to the idea that "lay" people[11] were second-class Christians whose role was strictly obedience. The priestly role of the ordained — especially the idea that the ordained is an *alter Christus* (cf. p. 84) — led to the idea that he should be treated as Christ, a human focus for the people's respect for God. This justified the very comfortable life that clerics could now expect. Obviously, this made ecclesiastical office attractive to many men of poor motives. Once in office, many of them plotted to keep the power in the family by the appointment of relatives to the growing ranks of ecclesiastical positions (nepotism). Others desired to increase their wealth by the sale of such positions (simony). Obviously, these practices spurred a further decline in the quality of the clergy, a group whose morals were beginning to scandalize even the most trusting of the simple people who were theoretically entrusted to their care.

It was inevitable that scandal would soon involve theology. Mostly inspired by greed, certain churchmen began to engage in the creation and sale of spiritual "goods." Up for sale were a variety of powerful relics, statues, and even blessings. Those not truly sorry for their sins could make up for their "attrition" with almsgiving. Indulgences were also for sale; you could buy one for yourself or for your loved ones.

Of course, despite its problems, the Church still saw to the survival and spread of Christianity. It had some Christian influence on everyone and it provided a spiritual home for a number of exceptional Christians

11. Actually, the word "lay" is from the Greek for "people."

whose faith was far ahead of its time — and ours. Of these, some even had the vision and courage to call for institutional reform and spiritual renewal. Gregory VII led a reform, while the spirituality of Francis of Assisi is still at work today. Unfortunately for the Church, though these and other efforts did help, they were not enough to bring about the global reforms that were needed. The collective weight of the Church's institutional sins was too much to be undone by the zeal of far too few. The situation continued to deteriorate. Its spiritual authority diminished, the Church became prey to the newly emergent national states. Indeed, by 1309, the Church — and particularly the papacy — was so weakened that the King of France was able to remove the pope from Rome and keep him in Avignon, France, for his own "protection." There the papacy remained until 1377 when Catherine of Siena was able to persuade Gregory XI to return to Rome. But, the "cardinals"[12] who remained in Avignon elected a rival "antipope." For forty years there were as many as three popes at the same time. When, in 1417, the Council of Constance finally settled the question, electing Martin V the rightful pope, it was a badly discredited office that he assumed.

Nonetheless, discredited or not, the papacy remained a powerful position which was desired by certain men for all the wrong reasons. By a variety of wrongful means, some of these men managed to obtain it. Thus did the papacy reach its perigee in the succeeding notorious reigns of Innocent VIII (1484-92) and Alexander VI (1492-1503).

B. Religious Humanism

It should not be thought that the general failure of reform efforts succeeded in crushing the spirit of reform. The Church has never been without those who call it to greater holiness. Neither has there been a time when the zeal for reform had not caused some to abandon the Church and to set out on their own. This had been the case with the Montanists (cf. footnote p. 81) and the Donatists (cf. p.85). In time, both were suppressed. Medieval times had already seen the Wycliffites and the Hussites meet the same fate; John Hus, the founder of the Hussites, was burned at the stake in 1415.

The burning of dissenters undoubtedly encouraged reform-minded people to bide their time and be careful about what they said. Thus, as the Renaissance gave birth to an increasing number of such people, a concern for personal safety gave rise to a quiet movement of thinkers which was

12. Cardinals are at least titular members of the clergy of Rome who, from about 1050, have had the right to elect the pope. As a "college," they are the caretakers of the universal Church when there is no pope.

later to be known as "Religious Humanism." Mindful of Church authority but imbued with the Renaissance spirit of inquiry, the religious humanists led a cautious re-examination of Christian truth.

To a great extent, this involved a return to the scriptural texts which was part and parcel of the return to the library which characterized the Renaissance generally. Beginning with the rediscovery of Greco-Roman literature,[13] it required a newly intensive study of ancient languages which soon came to include the Greek, and later Hebrew, of the Bible. This made it possible to bypass the Latin of the Vulgate as the Scriptures were studied in the original.

The Scriptures did not shed a happy light upon the medieval state of religious life. Popular beliefs and many Church practices began to pale as their scriptural and even traditional bases were found wanting. Men like Desiderius Erasmus (1466-1536) began to decry the situation both in word and in print. His *The Praise of Folly* provided a testament for religious humanists throughout Europe. This was possible now that Guttenberg, his contemporary, had invented a printing press with movable type. Nonetheless, he and the other humanists remained Catholic, believing or, at least, claiming that the Church was worth reforming.

C. Luther

1. The Circumstances of Luther's Initial Break with the Church

Martin Luther was born in 1483. In 1505, he entered the Augustinian Order of monks in Erfust, in what is now Germany. That same year Julius II commissioned the building of a new St. Peter's.[14] It was to be the greatest edifice the world would ever know. In order to raise funds, Indulgences were offered to anyone who would contribute. Agents were sent to all parts to exhort the faithful to avail themselves of these spiritual goods. Meanwhile, Luther was doing his studies at the newly founded University of Wittenberg. It was there that he became acquainted with the Scriptures, Tradition and the writings of Augustine, the spiritual founder of his order. It was there that he embarked upon the period of suffering and searching upon which so much of his theology would eventually draw.

In 1517, John Tetzel, a particularly aggressive preacher of Indulgences, came to Wittenberg.[15] Luther objected to what he was offering and

13. Among those rediscoveries: the epic poetry of Homer (c.8th cent. B.C.) and the orations of Cicero (106-43).

14. The old St. Peter's was built by Constantine during the 300's.

15. Tetzel is remembered for his reputed saying:"When a penny in the coffer rings, a soul from purgatory springs."

challenged him to debate the idea of Indulgences *per se.* His objections took the form of "ninety-five theses" which, according to legend, he affixed to the door of the Schlosskirche in Wittenberg in order to publicize his position. In short, Luther objected to Indulgences because he did not believe that the Church could release man from God's punishments. He supported his objection by pointing out that the Scriptures say nothing about Indulgences. It was also for scriptural reasons that he went on to list a number of areas, both theological and practical, which required reform. He encouraged the people to read Scripture, something that was officially discouraged for the fear that it would lead to the spread of uninformed and dangerous ideas.

It took three years for Leo X to respond. Finally, he issued the letter *Exsurge Domine* which condemned most of what Luther had proposed. Also he ordered Luther to recant the condemned propositions. When Luther refused, Leo ordered him arrested. Luther's life might have ended then and there were it not for Frederick III, the Duke of Saxony, who offered him protection. It is not to be denied that Frederick was one of a number of German nobles who saw the case of Martin Luther as an opportunity to weaken papel influence in his land. Under Frederick's protection, Luther denied the authority of the pope, and went so far as to call him the "antichrist" (e.g. 1 Jn.2:18). Taking advantage of the newly invented printing press, he published a trilogy of works which became the testament of his now radical reform movement.[16]

2. Luther's Theology

Though he had ostensibly broken with the Church over the question of Indulgences, Luther's problems with Catholic theology proved to be far more extensive. Clearly, as Luther would later claim, they had their origin long before the Indulgence controversy brought them to the fore.

Luther began to part company with the Church during a period of great frustration over his own failure to avoid sin. Initially terrified, he eventually became convinced that sin could not be avoided — the effects of original sin were too severe. Still sure that God is no liar, that out of His love and mercy He offers man salvation, Luther concluded that all that man can and must do is accept it. He must admit that he is a helpless sinner and have faith, faith that Jesus died to save him.

---

16. See his *To the Christians of the German Nation, The Babylonian Captivity of the Church,* and *On the Freedom of Christians.* Notably, these were the first works of such a kind to appear in the vernacular. Luther is also responsible for the first complete translation of the Scriptures into German, a feat which had much to do with the emergence of modern German.

This was Luther's doctrine of "justification by faith alone" (*sola fide*). In what he would later call his "tower experience," it hit him while he was reading Paul's Letter to the Romans where it says: "no human being will be justified in [God's] sight by works of the law" (Rom.3:19). "The righteousness of God [is] through faith in Jesus Christ . . . there is no distinction, since all men have sinned and fall short of the glory of God, they are justified by God as his gift . . . through the redemption which is in Christ Jesus whom God put forward as an expiation by his blood to be received in faith" (3:22-25). "We hold that man is justified by faith apart from works of the law" (3:28). "Abraham believed and it was reckoned to him as righteousness" (Rom.4:3, cf. Gen.15:6). Therefore, "if you confess with your lips that Jesus is Lord . . . You will be saved" (Rom.10:9).

Luther supported his position from his interpretation of other scriptural texts (especially the Gospel of John, e.g. 3:15) and the writings of Augustine (especially his writings on the effects of original sin, cf. p 77). Indeed, after reading Augustine on original sin, he articulated his doctrine of the "depravity of man" — the idea that not only is man in utter need of God's grace but, even should he receive it, he is still incapable of a life pleasing to Him. For this reason, Luther made much of the Pauline word "justified"; he denied that faith brought the sanctifying grace that made one holy. Instead, he insisted that justification was a legal sort of status which was granted to a person who had done the little he could do in order to reconcile himself with God. Little was indeed the word; according to the doctrine of the depravity of man, man on his own did absolutely nothing to deserve his salvation, even his co-operation with grace was itself its product. Did not Jesus say: "apart from me you can do nothing" (Jn. 15:5)? "For by grace you have been saved through faith; this is not your own doing, it is the gift of God" (Eph.2:8). This was the doctrine of "justification by grace alone" (*sola gratia*). It also meant that there is nothing a person can do to merit an increase in grace.

Since Luther's teachings departed so drastically from contemporary Church teachings, it was necessary that he find a new supreme source of Christian truth. Not surprisingly, he found his source in Scripture alone; this was the doctrine *sola scriptura.*[17] Agreeing with those who denied that theology was a science (cf. p. 98) — an obvious implication of the

---

17. In declaring the supremacy of the Bible, Luther also favored a change in its contents — the canon (cf. p. 41). Certain Old Testament books, most notably the two books of Esdras, were not part of the most ancient Hebrew manuscripts. They were known from the *Septuagint*, the Greek version of the Old Testament. Luther did not believe that these books were of the same status as the rest of the Scriptures. Called the "Apocrypha" (the books "outside" the canon), some would later insist that they be dropped from the Bible entirely.

doctrine of the depravity of man — but acknowledging that the Scriptures were liable to anyone's interpretation, he insisted that the Holy Spirit endowed Scripture with a "living voice" (*viva vox*) which guaranteed that the true believer would interpret it correctly.

In this implicit exaltation of the individual over the institution, Luther both endorsed and advanced the Renaissance emphasis on man. This, however, did not mean that Luther denied that Christians should belong to a church, "the" church; the Scriptures plainly stated that they should. But, he favored a new church structure, one that did not confuse the church's pronouncements for the Word of God.

He also favored a church with much less ritual. Lack of scriptural evidence led him to deny Jesus' institution of all the sacraments except Baptism and the Eurcharist. He was especially contemptuous of the sacrament of holy orders for which he blamed the rampant clericalism of his day.[18] Declaring that a person was "ordained" only to serve,[19] he insisted the efficacy of sacraments depended upon the faith of the people. Though he did affirm the real presence of Christ in the Eucharist, he denied transubstantiation for which he saw no biblical basis. Moreover, to him, it was obvious that bread and wine remained what they always were; he therefore held that the presence of Christ is *in* the elements, an idea he eventually called "consubstantiation." But, he denied that the presence of Christ perdures in the elements after the eucharistic service; therefore, the reservation of the eucharistic bread is not necessary. Not surprisingly, for all of the reasons that one might presume, Luther denied that the mass is a sacrifice; he pointed out that the Scriptures specifically state that the sacrifice of Christ was an offering once and for all (cf. Heb.7:27).

Despite the rapidly deteriorating situation, there were still a number of serious efforts to reconcile Luther and his followers with the Church. Unfortunately, neither side was willing to see the truth of anything the other side had to offer. Indeed, they had come to define themselves in terms of their differences. It must also be mentioned that a certain sector of German nobility favored a complete break with Rome as a way to increase their political independence. On the other side, Rome was often more interested in maintaining its political influence in these territories

---

18. Luther renounced his own ordination and also the celibacy which had become the rule for priests about five hundred years earlier.

19. Luther was especially interested in the supression of the priestly title "father," pointing out that Jesus Himself had said: "...call no man your father on earth..."(Mt.23:9); he advocated the scriptural title "minister," i.e. "servant" (Rom.13:6).

than in the religious matters at hand. In any case, hope for reconciliation was all but lost when, in 1530, the reformers formally established their doctrinal positions in the "Confession of Augsburg." Though efforts at reconciliation would continue, it soon became obvious that they were not to succeed. The "Protestant" Reformation was history.

D. Later Protestantism

1. Zwingli

Not all of the 16th century reformers were Luther's followers. Though they all admired his ground-breaking efforts, some did not feel that he had gone far enough.

The first to reform the Reformation was Ulrich Zwingli (1484-1531), a former priest who, in 1522, brought Protestantism to Switzerland. Invoking the doctrine of *sola scriptura,* he denied the existence of purgatory. Invoking the doctrine of *sola gratia,* he also pointed out that no one is any more guilty, any more in need of purification than anyone else. This means that no one is any more saintly than anyone else; therefore, neither Mary nor the saints occupy any sort of special place in heaven. (Obviously, this meant that esteem for their relics was mistaken.) Not surprisingly, Zwingli found no scriptural basis for belief in either the immaculate conception or the assumption; He did not deny the virginal conception.

Despite their agreement about the "living voice" of Scripture, Zwingli and Luther became embroiled in a bitter dispute about the proper interpretation of the accounts of the last supper. Finding no basis for belief in the Real Presence of Christ in the Eucharist — not even consubstantiation — Zwingli held that Christ's presence is merely symbolic.[20] Luther found this abhorrent and the issue permanently divided the two reformers. It would not be the last of the issues to divide Protestantism.

2. Calvin

Among subsequent reformers, none was to have the influence of John Calvin (1509-64). Renouncing his Catholicism in 1535, soon thereafter, he published *The Institutes of Christian Religion,* perhaps the most widely read of all the reform tracts. The work is best remembered for what it says about "predestination" — the idea an individual's eternal destiny is predetermined for him by God even before he is born regardless of anything that he could ever do. Calvin read Paul to state explicitly that God "predestined" some for glory (cf. Rom.8:29). They were "chosen" (Col.3:13)

---

20. Zwingli's attack of Luther's position is found in his *Commentary on True and False Religion.*

"from the beginning"(cf. 2 Thess.2:13) "before the foundation of the world" (Eph.1:4) in God's "eternal councils" (Eph.1:11) "in virtue of His own purpose"(2 Tim.1:9). Thus, Christians are God's "elect"(Rom.8:33). What could this mean?

Because of the disordering of our will, Augustine insisted that our every good impulse is the product of grace. But, he also insisted that our co-operation with grace took place freely (cf. p. 77). Of course, Augustine also acknowledged that God could have given anyone enough grace to ensure a saving result; he explicitly acknowledged that even Judas could have been given enough grace to withstand the temptation that eventually caused him to betray Jesus.[21] Therefore, as Augustine had to admit, since God knows exactly how everyone will respond to a particular grace, the result is an act of His will; in other words, He chooses to save some and not others.[22] The saved were probably chosen to replace the fallen angels.[23]

Thomas also felt compelled to admit predestination; but, he believed that those saved and those condemned — and the different degrees of grace or pain which they received — were determined to satisfy God's passion for order, in particular, His desire that everything exist in different degrees.[24]

Augustine and Thomas agreed that, regardless of the reason, it was still God's right to save only those He chose; after all, everyone was rightly damned.

Having no patience with the mystery of free will, Calvin held that man's will is so corrupt, it is not free. Therefore, he taught that grace is irresistible whenever it is offered. Thus, when it is offered, when there is faith, a person can know that he was chosen. Therefore, since he was chosen apart from anything he could ever do, nothing he could do could cost him his salvation; he can be certain he is saved. He does not need to live a Christian life. He does not even need to try, but the good Christian does, but only out of gratitude. How else could Paul write: "All things are lawful for me"(1 Cor.6:12)? How else could Augustine say: "Love and do what you will?"[25]

Despite the liberality that his theology seemed to license, Calvin and his followers demanded from themselves a very disciplined lifestyle. This was partly gratitude and partly to prove they had been chosen.

Calvin's theology spread quickly. In fact, it carried the Reformation

21. *On Grace and Nature*, 7,8.
22. See his *On the Predestination of the Saints* for his most complete treatment of the idea.
23. *The City of God*, 22,1.
24. *S. Th.* 1, q.23.
25. See his "Commentary on the Letters of John," 7,8.

to more places than did Luther's. After a time, Calvin was invited to rule the city of Geneva according to his teachings. There he set up a government by a council of elders which would later serve as the model for "presbyterian" communities whenever Calvin's thinking attracted a following.

3. England

From England came a different sort of blow to the catholicity of the Church. When the Reformation first hit Germany and Switzerland, England remained solidly Catholic. Its king, Henry VIII (1491-1547) was actually a staunch opponent of the reform movement and wrote an anti-reformation *Defense of the Seven Sacraments.*[26] During the tumultuousness of the first decades of the Reformation, however, Henry became unhappy in his marriage to Catherine of Aragon. Dutifully, he sought an annulment,[27] something he could obtain only from the pope, Clement VII. Unfortunately for Henry, Clement was in the "protective custody" of Charles V, the Holy Roman Emperor and Catherine's nephew. Not surprisingly, the Pope refused to annul the marriage. Finally, in 1534, after several more petitions had been refused, Henry had parliament pass the "Act of Supremacy" which declared him the supreme head of the Church in England, thereafter the "Anglican" Church. (The annulment was granted.)

During the remainder of Henry's lifetime, the Church in England remained Catholic in all things but allegiance to the pope. Under the reign of his daughter Elizabeth I (1533-1603), however, the combined influences of independence and Reformation saw the gradual change of practice and even doctrine; the Church in England became distinctly Anglican in character. When, in 1570, Pope Pius V excommunicated Elizabeth, the English Church became Anglican in fact.

Nonetheless, Anglican theologians remained troubled by the scriptural and traditional arguments in support of the papacy. This evidence was particularly problematic because Anglican theology had retained a number of traditionally Catholic doctrines and practices on much less evidence. For some, the solution to this problem came to involve the idea that the pope held the position of highest "honor." (This was already the Orthodox idea, cf. footnote p. 52.) For others, it involved the idea that the pope did have the authority to speak for the whole Church, but not

26. In gratitude, Rome awarded Henry the title "Defender of the Faith," a title the British monarchs still claim.
27. An annulment is an ecclesiastical declaration that a lawful marriage contract was not made. Thus, a marriage annulled never existed.

the supreme authority and infallibility to which he currently laid claim. Instead, they argued the supreme authority in the Church was meant to be shared by the bishops who, in the territories of their own responsibility, were subject to no one; this was the "episcopal" model of Church government.

4. Evangelicals

As the major figures debated the issues, the reforming of the Reformation also continued quietly. Beginning with the "Anabaptists" (or "re-baptizers") — who broke away from Luther because they did not accept infant baptism — small but fervent groups of "evangelicals" abandoned belief in everything which was not essential to the gospel of personal salvation.[28] Sure that grace comes only through faith, they decried all the sacraments and ritual in general. They saw ritual as a distraction from true worship. Thus, they attempted to purge their worship of ritual elements. Insisting that no one speaks for God, they would have no ecclesiastical offices. Finally, following the biblical prohibition of "graven images" (Ex.20:4), they declared sacred images to be idolatry — and a distraction — and they forbade any attempt to depict God or the major moments in the history of salvation.

* * *

Despite their attempts at ultimate reform, even the evangelical groups were to experience division. Disputes arose not only over doctrine but questions of morality, public and private. Division also occurred over questions of the structure, governance and demands of community life.[29] A major division occurred over the "pentecostal" idea that true Christians must be open to the prompting of the Holy Spirit as heard in those who spoke in tongues (e.g. 1 Cor.14:4). This horrified the "fundamentalists" who heard such murmuring as madness. It led to the split between these groups which still exists.

E) The Church's Initial Response to the Reformation: The Counter-Reformation

1. The Council of Trent

The many movements which followed Luther eventually made clear to most churchmen that the Church was indeed in need of reform, at least as far as practice was concerned. Moreover, there were even some who were

28. Occurring everywhere the Reformation went, perhaps the best-known, at least to English-speaking people, were the "Puritans" who played an important role in founding what was to become the United States of America.

29. The best known of the reform movements which departed from a dissatisfaction with practice, not doctrine, was "Methodism," founded by John and Charles Wesley in 1729.

in doubt as to the degree that the Protestants were doctrinally wrong. In any case, a council was needed. Nonetheless, years passed before a pope could be persuaded to call for one. The delay was caused by the combined effect of three things: 1) In the beginning, Church leaders believed that the Reformation was just another heretical movement that the Church would outlast; they truly believed that it would go away as long as they held their ground. 2) For any institution big and old, change is difficult. Finally, 3) the Popes feared a revival of the idea that an ecumenical council was superior to the pope. Though "conciliarism" had been condemned (cf. p. 46), its revival was always a possibility if a number of bishops gathered together. This was perhaps the main reason that, despite a rapidly deteriorating situation, a council was promised but constantly postponed.

Finally, fearing a complete loss of authority in Europe, Paul III called for and opened a council in Trent, in Northern Italy. The council met for three long sessions (from 1545-47, 1551-53, and 1562-63) under the authority of Julius III, Paul IV, and Pius IV. No other council in Church history had ever met to consider so many serious problems. No other would render so many decrees which are still viewed as the definitive statements of Church teaching.

First, the council called attention to the fact that the doctrine *sola scriptura* was not scriptural. Moreover, what else but the Church's Tradition had determined the canon? Thus, the fathers declared that there were *two* sources of divine revelation — Scripture *and* Tradition. They then endorsed the existing canon and declared it forever closed (DS 1502-03).

Next, the council reaffirmed the Church's classical — and uncontested — teachings of God, the Trinity, angels and demons, and creation. The fathers then reaffirmed the classical doctrine of original sin. Still insisting that Adam's punishments were passed on by propagation, not imitation, the fathers also maintained that these included concupiscence — Mary excluded (DS 1511-16).

The council now faced the central issue of the Reformation, the question of justification (DS 1521-50). Acknowledging that faith is the beginning of salvation, the fathers also declared that faith demands the completion of obedience. (Indeed, they held that faith without obedience is worse than no faith; after all, the person with no faith knows no better.) They insisted that obedience was both possible and necessary; the will was wounded, not destroyed (DS 1536). Otherwise, what would be the value of faith?

The fathers were sure that the Scriptures supported their position.

They were especially supported by the letter of James. "What does it profit, my brethren, if a man says he has faith but has not works? Can his faith save him? If a brother or sister is ill-clad and in lack of daily food, and one of you says to them, 'Go in peace, be warmed and fed,' without giving them the things needed for the body, what does it profit? So faith by itself, if it has no works, is dead" (Jas.2:14-17). "Even demons believe — and shudder" (2:19). "Was not Abraham our father justified by works when he offered his son Isaac upon the altar?" (2:22). "A man is justified by works and not by faith alone" (2:23). Besides, Jesus had explicitly taught that keeping the commandments was necessary in order to enter the Kingdom of God (cf. p. 73). Indeed, as He also said: "not everyone who says to me, 'Lord, Lord,' shall enter the Kingdom of heaven, but he who does the will of my Father who is in heaven" (Mt.7:21). As John said: "He who says 'I know Him' but disobeys His commands is a liar" (1 Jn.2:4). "Whoever does not do right is not of God nor he who does not love his brother" (1 Jn.3:10). Paul himself said that God "will render to each man according to his works" (Rom.2:6). He mentions several kinds of sinners who will never enter the kingdom of God (cf. Eph.5:5).

Clement stated it explicitly: "Those who keep the commandments are saved."[30] Why else did Jesus teach commandments? How could God fail to punish sinners or to reward those who do their best? What is more important than what we do? What would the world be like if people really believed that acts would not be rewarded or punished? Moreover, how could the Church — guided by the Spirit — have been wrong for 1500 years?

The necessity of obedience implied the necessity of perseverance. Thus, "the rash presumption of one's own predestination must be avoided" (DS 1540). After all, holiness can be lost. There are "mortal" sins (cf. 1 Jn.5:16). Indeed, even faith was sometimes lost. There is apostasy (cf. footnote p. 81). (The Protestants held that true faith would never be lost — why would it?) Jesus Himself warned: "he who endures to the end will be saved" (Mt.24:13). Paul promised: "If we have died with Him, we shall also live with Him; if we endure, we shall also reign with him" (2 Tim.2:11-12).

Since no good was possible without actual grace, and man was totally undeserving and incapable of earning grace, it was rightfully reaffirmed that salvation is utterly unmerited. But, since grace requires the co-operation of free will, good acts still obtain a certain merit just as sins deserve a certain penalty. This was the reason that Jesus could call

30. Clem. 58,2.

salvation a "reward" (e.g. Mt.6:4). (He had even acknowledged that almsgiving could remit sin, (Lk.11:41, cf. Tob.12:9.) Furthermore, since each good act deserves a reward, each one surely brings about an increase in the sanctifying grace that makes one holy. Naturally, justice also demands that each sin brings about a decrease in grace. This is how "the rich get richer and the poor lose the little they have" (Mt.13:12, Lk.8:18).

Having dealt with the central issues, the council turned to the remainder of the issues that the Reformation had raised. For all of the classical reasons, it formalized the traditional teachings on each of the sacraments, including their efficacy (DS 1600), the fact that there are seven (1601), and the fact that they work *ex opere operato* (1608). The Eucharist received special attention; reaffirmed were the teachings on the Real Presence (1636), transubstantiation (1642), the sacrificial nature of the mass (1738-42), and the idea that its merits can be applied to specific causes or persons living or dead (1743). This was the perogative of the priest whose ordination conferred an ontological character which carried the power to offer the Eucharist (1764-77). Also reaffirmed were the existing teachings on purgatory (1820), the intercessory power of Mary and the saints (1821), Indulgences (1835), and the value of the veneration of religious relics and art (1822-23).

This is not to say that the council changed *nothing*. On the contrary, it involved a number of reforms designed to correct the abuses which had fanned the Reformation. It called the people to spiritual renewal and it called the clergy to a new emphasis on the preaching of God's Word.

2. The Later Counter-Reformation

As much as it did, the Council of Trent neither exhausted nor concluded the Church's own attempts at reform and the containment of the Protestant Reformation. Paul III personally decreed a number of reform measures; it was he who revived the ancient "Inquisition." It was he who assigned the task of Counter-Reformation to the "Jesuits" founded by Ignatius Loyola in 1534.[31] Thereafter, this zealous group led the most successful — if sometimes brutal — efforts to recapture the faith of formerly Catholic lands or to prevent still Catholic lands from "falling" to the Protestants.[32]

Paul's immediate successors, Paul IV (1555-59) Pius IV, (1559-66),

---

31. The Jesuits were actually co-founded by Ignatius and Francis Xavier (1506-52). Francis is best remembered for the missionary work which established the Church in Asia.

32. Of the non-Jesuits involved in the Counter-Reformation, Francis de Sales (1567-1622) is the best remembered; Francis is remembered for his attempt to improve the piety of the Christians in the lands that remained Catholic.

Pius V (1566-72) and Gregory XIII (1572-85) each led a reform of his own. (It was Paul IV who established the "Index of Forbidden Books."[33]) All restrained the Reformation through effective politics. Politics were important because the religious profession of the common people was actually determined for them by local lords. **Protestant** lords required their subjects to embrace their form of Protestantism while Catholic lords forbade any change.

Tragically, papal politics were not so successful as to prevent — if they did not encourage — the "Thirty Years War" in which Catholics fought Protestants from 1618 to 1648. When the "Peace of Westphalia" finally ended the conflict, the denominational lines were clearly drawn and since have dried.

Section IV: The Decline of Confidence in Christianity: Scientism

A) The Rise of Modern Science

The Reformation did not leave Europe any less *Christian*. Indeed, on account of the attention given the faith because of the Reformation, it was more committedly Christian than ever before. Yet, the progress that gave rise to the Reformation did not cease with it and, in the form of the rise of modern science, this progress was soon to cause a decline in Christianity itself.

1. Old Science

No accounting of the rise of modern science can take place without an understanding of the science from which it emerged. No accounting of the old idea of science can take place without an understanding of the old conception of "nature" which followed from it.

According to its pre-modern conception, nature was essentially mysterious. Its true workings were known to God alone. It was generally dependable, but it was also available to frequent divine intervention, including that which was initiated by ritual and prayer.

Old science followed from this conception of nature. Science was nature's description and categorization. Where it *did* involve explanations (e.g. the bigger the rock, the faster it falls[34]), it mostly involved the repeating of principles reported by the venerable and virtually unquestioned sources of truth which had seemingly existed from time immemorial — the Bible

---

33. Gregory is best remembered for his reform of the calendar that still bears his name.
34. The bigger rock had the greater desire to rest upon the earth.

and the few ancients whose writings had survived the collapse of the Empire. From the Bible came the description of creation and whatever else might be read between its lines. From Pythagoras (6th century B.C.) and Euclid (3rd cent. B.C.) came all that one could want to know about mathematics. From Ptolemy (2nd cent. A.D.) came the elaborate system of "epicycles" that accounted for the motion of the lights that revolved around the earth. From Galen, his contemporary, came an inventory of the organs and their secretions which accounted for man's moods. Of course, upon their discovery, the writings of Aristotle provided the four causes which were now observed to operate in all change.

2. The Rise of New Science: the Renaissance Reconsidered
We have already considered the general causes of the explosion of arts and sciences known to history as the Renaissance (cf. p. 92). Let there be no misunderstanding. Though the Renaissance is best known to history as a time of artistic activity, it was no less a period of scientific progress.

Spurred by the demands of trade and city life, it began with inventions that changed the face of Europe. The 1100's brought the Gothic arch and the European-style invention of wind and water wheels which ground grain, turned saws and ran metal works. The 1200's brought the invention of the mechanical clock — and the beginning of a Machine Age. Within a century, the invention of the compass would make possible the age of exploration. This led to the discovery (in China) of gunpowder and, by 1350, the invention of the cannon which sealed the fate of the walled city. One hundred years later, Gutenberg invented the movable type which made the Reformation possible.

Well before the Reformation, however, a revolution of another kind was already in progress. Encouraged by the availability of resources, the inquisitiveness born of the time to think, and the optimism owed to practical success, medieval scientists began to explore ever wider fields of study.

What was now needed was a method that could guide study. The first to suggest one was Roger Bacon (1214-97), a Franciscan priest. Guided by his own success in study of lenses he had obtained from the Orient, he said that science first involves the gathering of data — something best done by doing experiments.[35] This allows the scientist to pursue the objects of his interest and to formulate theories with the maximum data at his disposal. Bacon also insisted that perennially accepted principles

---

35. See his *Opus Maius*. Bacon was undoubtedly inspired by Robert Grosseteste (c.1175-1253) who preceded him in the study of light.

should be subject to the verification of tests.

Bacon's ideas were troublesome to the men of his time. They betrayed an interest in the world that was thought unbecoming a churchman, if not any Christian. Even more troublesome was his denial that old ideas, however venerable, should be presumed true. It was for both of these reasons that he was involved in a renowned intellectual battle with Bonaventure, his religious superior, who warned him to stay away from science.

Although the suspicion of science was quite common, the appeal of progress could not be resisted. Therefore, the ancients *were* put to the test and often they failed. Then, at the turn of the 17th century, the scientific suspicion of venerable principles reached the point of no return when Simon Stevin dropped two different sized cannonballs from the tower of Pisa and proved none other than Aristotle wrong; in everyone's sight they hit at exactly the same time.

What now was needed was a method by which to justify scientists in their abandonment of ancient ideas that could *not* be tested. Coincidentally, it was Francis Bacon (1561-1626), no relation to Roger, who provided such a method. Arguing that all principles must proceed from evidence, he insisted that principles be the product of "induction," the movement from the evidence to a principle that accounts for it, not "deduction," the interpretation of the facts according to principles arrived at from "higher" reflections.[36] Here was a method that followed from nominalism — and the principle of economy. Bacon invoked his method in denying that Aristotle's four causes are the explanation of all change.

It is to be acknowledged that, even before its articulation, Bacon's method had already been practiced by pioneer scientists like William Gilbert (c.1540-1603) and Leonardo Da Vinci. Gilbert is remembered for his study of magnetism, while Leonardo is remembered for his study of everything — including certain of his projects that were soon to lead to a new view of scientific explanation.

Fascinated by the human body, Leonardo undertook the dissections which led to his explanation of how the body works. Notably, this explanation involved a description of the body's inner working — the working of its parts. In this, nature was itself explained. And this was only the beginning.

Fascinated by motion, Leonardo did experiments with the trajectory of cannonballs which inspired Galileo Galilei (1564-1642) to do his own

---

36. See his *New Organon.*

experiments resulting in what he called the "laws" of falling bodies. (Notably, in describing the results of this study, Galileo was to become the first to advance a scientific formulation of the idea that motion is "natural." He predicted that if a falling body was not stopped by the earth, its motion would continue indefinitely, a theoretical fact he referred to as "inertia.") More importantly, in speaking of scientific "law," he became the first to articulate the idea that nature had its ways that one could count on.

3. The Emergence of an Age of Reason: The Enlightenment
Thanks to Galileo, a new idea of nature had emerged. Mysterious no longer, nature was now available to explanation. Furthermore, as nature was studied — as experiments were done and repeated — the scientist's sense of the dependability of nature grew, and grew more articulate. Reflected in the writings of Francis Bacon, this increasingly articulate sense that nature is dependable not only meant that nature was available to explanation, but it also meant that nature was available to the manipulation of man for his own benefit.[37]

Clearly, these developments marked man's increasing confidence in his ability to know and, in particular, the power of his own "reason," the power that lets him know.

Rarely defined even by those who spoke of it, reason has always been thinking in accord with good "reasons," or "evidence," according to self-evident principles of its evaluation. The importance of reason was also self-evident. How else were divergent opinions to be evaluated? What else was to save man from having to believe anything he hears — or anything he wants?

What was new was the success which was obtained and expected from observation, especially experimentation and testing. Thus, it was fast becoming "scientific" to accept only the evidence of some form of observation — the data of one of the five senses. Here was a new standard of proof positive. Its adoption was proclaimed to be the abandonment of the primitive ways of the past. It was proclaimed to be the dawn of what was soon to be called the "Age of Reason" or the "Enlightenment," a period whose dominant thinkers enjoyed a great optimism for all that humanity would accomplish now that man had seen the light of reason — of reason alone. It is this that we are calling "Scientism."

---

37. See especially his *The Great Instauration.*

B. Science Confronts Christianity

Scientism was bound to cause trouble for Christianity. But, this was bound to take time. Indeed, even with the increasing sense of the dependability of nature, it was still easy to imagine that God could intervene in His creation — and did. With the passage of time, however, and the increasing articulation of the scientific way of thinking, some began to think twice about the many miracles reported around them. Even so, the Bible was still respected for what it reported. Then, something happened that was to change forever the way it was viewed.

1. The Galileo Incident

When first he thought about it, man thought the world was flat and the center of the universe. The Earth certainly looked flat; it certainly seemed to be the center of the universe. How remarkable it was that there were ancients who had problems with both these ideas. The apparent orbit of the lights in the sky raised the problem of imagining what was beneath the earth or beyond its edges, while the "retrograde" (or the occasional "backwards") motion of some of the lights that would later be identified as planets was simply confusing. As early as the 3rd. century B.C., Eratosthenes proposed to solve the first problem by suggesting that the earth was round. Some five hundred years later, Ptolemy devised the system of "epicycles" — his idea that the lights that orbit the earth also orbit an invisible point in space — which appeared to solve the problem of retrogarde motion.

Though Eratosthenes' theory was largely to be forgotten — until it was proved true by Columbus' accidental discovery of America — Ptolemy's theory was not only remembered but it became the almost universally accepted explanation for the lights that might otherwise confuse the idea that the earth is the center of the created universe.

It took Copernicus (1473-1543) to suggest an entirely new idea. Reflecting on what was to him the unsloved problem of retrograde motion, Copernicus realized that if the earth and the other "planets" revolved around the sun, the problem of retrograde motion would be solved in the simple understanding that they had orbits of different diameters. The otherwise inexplicable orbits about invisible points in space would become an optical illusion produced by their different paths and speeds.[38]

Copernicus' theory had the advantage of simplicity. Seeing the earth within the larger scope of celestial space, he explained the evidence with a theory that required few postulations, and did not require an inexplicable

---

38. See his *On the Revolution of the Heavenly Bodies.* Actually, it must be acknowledged that Eratosthenes' contemporary Aristarchus had proposed a "heliocentric," or "sun-centered" theory that was simply forgotten.

type of motion that never occurs in common experience. (Ptolemy's theory postulated 79 epicycles.) Once Johann Kepler (1571-1630) predicted retrograde motion precisely — proving that the planetary orbits were really ellipses and not circles as Copernicus had thought — the principle of economy was clearly on the side of the new view.

It was Galileo who provided conclusive proof. In 1610, in his own experiments with lenses, he developed the telescope. Shortly thereafter, out of curiosity, he turned it upon the heavens not knowing what he would find. The results were historic. Jupiter did not appear to be a star; it appeared not to give light but to reflect it. Furthermore it was orbited by four satellites, apparently moons like our own. Through Galileo's telescope, the system was a microcosm of the sun-centered unverse of Copernicus.

Under the title *Sidereal Messenger,* Galileo announced to the world that Copernicus was right. To his surprise, the Inquisition condemned his views. To the view of the churchmen of his day, the Bible made clear that the earth was the center of the universe. Genesis taught that the earth was made four days before the sun, the latter merely a light in the sky (1:16). During the war with the Amorites, God empowered Joshua to stop the sun in *its* path by holding out his arms (Josh.10:12). Besides, man was the pinnacle of God's creation; his home undoubtedly occupied the central place in the universe.

Galileo begged his inquisitors to change their mind. He asked them to look through his telescope in order to see the evidence for themselves. They flatly refused and ordered him not to publish again. He heeded their warning until 1632, when he became the first man to observe the phases of Venus. The geometry of light and darkness made clear that Venus was not revolving around the earth. He published again.[39] One year later, under the threat of torture, he recanted.

In 1664, in the document *Speculatores Domus Israel,* Alexander VII formally condemned the Copernican universe. It was the last gasp of a futile effort. The combined work of Copernicus, Kepler, and Galileo would not go away. The condemnations notwithstanding, other scientists built telescopes and they saw what Galileo had seen. They discovered that Mars was not a star and that Saturn had rings as well as moons of its own. Besides, heliocentricism explained everything from the four seasons to newly discovered shadows on the earth's moon. Just as the idea that the earth is flat had given way to the more complete picture required by the evidence, so too the limited perspective of belief in an earth-centered

39. See his *Dialogue on the Two Great Systems of the World.*

universe had given way to a more comprehensive view once men were broadminded enough to see it. In the process, the credibility of the Church had suffered another setback. But, more importantly, for the first time, the credibility of the Scriptures had been called into serious question.

2. The Emergence of Major Problems with the Scriptures

The Galileo incident was only the beginning. The issue had been broached, the formerly unquestionable truth of the Scriptures had been questioned, and the result had not been favorable to the eyes of an "enlightened" society. Moreover, if they were wrong about one thing, could they not be wrong about another? This opened the larger question of whether the Bible should be presumed true. In other words, did it really merit the presumption of truth now denied to every other ancient source?

Under the scrutiny of these new questions, the Bible was now examined as if for the first time. In honesty, one had to admit that it was filled with stories that would never have been taken as true if they had been found anywhere else. It spoke of a talking serpent that talked man into sin. It told of a world-wide flood, and an ark. It said the sun stood still. What a miracle! But miracles were violations of the laws of nature, and — to the scientist — they were no longer in evidence. What was in evidence were legends created in ignorance and repeated uncritically by the simple folk who were a present reminder of times past. The Scriptures had come from times long past. Who could know that they had not originated this same way?

Possibly such questioning would have remained just that, at least for a longer time, were it not for two of the other products of Renaissance progress — the rediscovery of Greco-Roman literature and the age of exploration.

For most of the medieval period, as for centuries prior, the Scriptures were unquestionably sacred. They had always been around; they had always been inspired and they had always been believed. They were the only religious writings that people knew.

In the rediscovery of Greco-Roman literature, the West rediscovered Zeus (whom the Romans called Jupiter), Poseidon (Neptune), Hermes (Mercury), and many others. But, the mere fact that certain gods were once believed in and written about was not sufficient reason to believe they actually existed. It did not warrant belief in something so extraordinary, especially when the stories about them were so easily accounted for. They were myths, "silly myths" (1 Tim.4:7), the obvious products of man's primitive, i.e. pre-scientific imagination.

With the age of exploration, it became clear that myths were man's way to explain his world, and give structure and hope to his life. The explorers found myth everywhere and, unlike the myths of the ancient Greeks and Romans, these stories were believed by people now. Furthermore, as Europeans became more familiar with the Near East and India, they discovered venerable religions — especially Islam and Hinduism — which were held with a fervor that seemed to match if not surpass that of Christianity. Each had its sacred books.[40] Nonetheless, venerable if not beautiful though they were, these books still bespoke man's pre-scientific imagination. They were too easily explained by human nature. They were not supported by sufficient evidence to warrant their belief.

Were the Scriptures supported by such evidence? It surely seemed fair to ask. After all, both the Hebrews and early Christians were as human as anyone. And they were as ancient as most.

Under this scrutiny, the Scriptures began to look more and more like myth. They said that Daniel slew a dragon, that David slew a giant, that Jonah spent three days in the belly of a fish. And there were other signs of human authorship — and surely not divine. Genesis did not say that Eve gave birth to a girl but, if she did not, how was the world populated? Why was Cain, her first-born, afraid of a world that was already populated (Gen.4)? Plainly, in places the Bible was not well written and it was inconsistent. There are two different — and differing — accounts of creation (Gen. 1 and 2).[41]

Following Marcion (cf. p. 41), if unknowingly, the critics began to observe that the God of the Old Testament was nothing like Jesus' supposedly all-loving Father. He became angry, regretted His creation, and sent the flood that wiped out almost every living creature. He led His people in the slaughter of thousands even though He could have as easily have given them land by bloodless means. He was the jealous and exacting God of the Law.

Moreover, even the New Testament was inconsistent. Though Matthew, Mark and Luke told one story, John told another. Only in John does Jesus go to Jerusalem twice; John's account of the resurrection

---

40. The sacred book of Islam is called the Koran; it is said to have been dictated to Mohammed by the angel Gabriel. Sacred to the Hindus are the "Vedic" hymns, *Upanishads* and, to some, the *Bhagavadgita*. The earliest elements of the "Vedic" hymns date to approximately 2000 B.C.
41. The break with England had involved an overt scriptural contradiction. Henry claimed that to "marry his brother's wife" was prohibited by Lev.18:16. Rome responded that to do so was required by Deut.25:5.

is notably different from that of the others and he does not report the last supper.[42] John's Jesus is referred to with different words (such as "Word") which insinuated a distinctly different idea of who Jesus was. Furthermore, to an uncommitted observer of the Catholic-Protestant debate, Paul and James *did* appear to have very different, even opposing theologies of justification.

In any case, the New Testament was almost as poorly written as the Old. Its Jesus was an artificial figure — and not even friendly (cf. Mt.21:18-20).

All in all, the Bible had begun to look like a very human book, the product of human nature not unlike all of the other sacred books that Christians found so easy to disbelieve.

Thinkers began to ask themselves whether there is sufficient evidence to believe the Bible is a special case — or to believe it solely as history. Of those who asked, most did not think so. If someone should disagree, surely the burden of proof was on them.

3. The Emergence of Major Problems with Christian Beliefs

The emergence of major problems with the Scriptures was obviously a problem for Christianity. The problem was only aggravated by the post-Reformation emphasis upon the biblical basis of Christian beliefs. But, the problem would not have been as serious as it was were it not for the fact that increasing numbers of critical thinkers were beginning to have major problems with Christian beliefs *per se*.

Certain beliefs had always presented problems. The simultaneous affirmation that God is absolutely one and distinctly three was not only an acknowledged mystery, but it was a mystery which had proved too mysterious for many of otherwise good faith. The incarnation was just as mysterious; how could someone be both God and man at the same time? What about the mystery of grace; how does grace *not* compromise free will; how does the doctrine of predestination *not* compromise belief in God's infinite goodness?

Furthermore, if God is so good, why did he require the sacrifice of His only Son in order to forgive man for his sins; how could justice require anything of a God who is the author of everything? Besides, how did *Christ's* sacrifice make-up for *man's* sins?

Even if one could solve the problem of redemption, one was still left with the problem of the reason it was needed — original sin. The

---

42. Actually, discrepancies in the gospels had always been observed; as early as the year 150, Tatian had attempted their synthetic reconciliation in a combined gospel called the *Diatessaron*.

Renaissance man did not feel fallen. He thought well of himself, his powers and his future. This left him quite confident to question the justice of a universal condemnation of humanity which also left man helpless to avoid sin even before he is born — especially when he does not ask to be born — leaving him liable to eternal damnation.

Hell was a problem in itself. Despite the demands of justice, how could the all-loving God condemn even one of His creatures to an eternity of terrible suffering? The problem was compounded by the fact that most of the people who have ever lived — or who are alive at present — have never heard Jesus' name. What of the people who died before Jesus was born? Catholics had to deal with the fact that their faith appeared to insist upon the condemnation of people who might have had faith, but not the sacraments.

God's goodness was especially questioned in light of evil. Since the doctrine of original sin was already under seige, it was not credibly invoked as the Christian excuse for the fact that the all-good God made a world in which everyone born must suffer and die.

In God's providence there are earthquakes, floods, famines and diseases. It allowed the "Black Death"(bubonic plague) which wiped out over a third of 14th century Europe. Too often bad things happened to good people — and *vice-versa*. So often sinners prospered to the end of long and apparently happy lives while the saintly suffered and died young. To the faithful, and even those who were victims of divine retribution, this meant that they must have done something to deserve their punishment. To an increasing number of critical thinking people, however, there was no real pattern to be observed. Instead, as more and more was learned about nature, much of what was once considered divine retribution was now considered the rather predictable product of natural causes.

The same was beginning to appear true of God's response to prayers of petition. Despite the biblical assurances to the contrary, prayers were *not* answered at least as often as they were.[43] So often the most intense, lifelong or churchwide prayers — for the best of things — seemingly fell on deaf ears. To the faithful, even those who had been badly disappointed, this meant that God knew better. To the scientifically minded, however, the randomness (and heartlessness) of events was better explained by the simple fact that nature has its ways which are indifferent to man's desires. It was science, not prayer, that would cause

---

43. But the Bible (and scholastic philosophy) also insisted that God is immutable (cf. p. 49). How were prayers expected to change Him?

nature to co-operate with man's desires and his hopes.

As progress was made, faith suffered as hope increasingly concerned the here and now. And, hope in heaven was becoming less sure. After all, no one has ever come back. Besides, where is heaven; what is it? Perhaps a "perfect" life is too good to be true.

4. The Emergence of Major Problems with the Belief of Christians

Even considering the emergence of problems with the Scriptures, and Christian beliefs *per se,* the decline of confidence in Christianity might not have happened as fast as it did were it not for the fact that these crises were accompanied by the emergence of major problems with the belief of Christians — the decline of confidence that Christians were people to be taken seriously in anything they thought.

Though the problems were in evidence for centuries, it was the Reformation that brought most of them to the fore.

The apologetic from the survival and success of the Church had obviously been dealt a serious blow. Moreover, thinkers now took a new look at the entire history of the faith. Now, the almost constant corruption, history of heresies and many schisms made them wonder. What about the rise of Islam in which God had evidently allowed the almost complete defection of what was once Christian North Africa? Though it might be answered that this largely took place at the point of a sword, one would still be given to wonder why God had allowed it. Furthermore, as the new breed of "modern" historian was apt to point out, the conversion of the barbarians — the ancestors of the Christian masses of medieval Europe — took place under no less duress.

The apologetic from the sanctity of Christian lives also suffered on account of the Reformation. Catholic-Protestant disputes were waged in mutual hatred. In the name of God, Christians spilled blood, the blood of their fellow Christians. Not only did this spectacle cause some to wonder where grace was — those not already wondering "what" grace was — it also caused them to question whether grace was really necessary for goodness. The age of exploration had brought Christians into contact with many non-Christians; and many were fine people who had great faith and character which rivaled that of the saints. Furthermore, with the decline of confidence in Christianity, the same could be said of many who professed no faith at all. This was especially telling because, unlike Christians, they could not be accused of the selfish motive of their own salvation.

Furthermore, in the light of this wider experience, many began to question just how holy a Christian life really was. Apart from the selfishness, shallowness, and superstitiousness of the common Christian, the lives of Christian leaders were rarely models of virtue. High-sounding in their preaching, they were often hypocritical in their conduct. The best were hardly free of sin and few appeared at peace. Most often they were ignorant even as to the basis of their own beliefs; almost always they knew little of what man was lately doing and provincially claimed they did not need to. Yet, though men of faith who should have felt more secure, they refused to look into Galileo's telescope.

For all of these reasons, the credibility of Christianity suffered. But, it was because of faith, because faith was the basis of Christian belief, that Christianity lost the respect of the scientifically minded. The experience of faith was no longer considered sufficient evidence to warrant its acceptance.

Faith was untestable. It was easily explicable without resorting to an unseen act of God. If the theologian insisted that faith was self-validating — the religious experience in which God had told him "Jesus is Lord" — how could he respond to the Moslem who claimed to be equally certain of the religious experience in which God told him "There is no God but Allah and Mohammed is His prophet?"[44] After all, more Christians have become Moslems than Moslems have become Christians. How could he respond to the Hindu who insisted that his religious experience reveals that God is not a Person? How could he respond to the scientist who remembers his own religiosity as something he has rightfully outgrown? By what right could he insist that *his* experience was uniquely God-given, or more informative, or better interpreted? If he would not accept the burden of proof, he would effectively have declared that reason cannot be brought to bear in human affairs. This would ultimately be self-defeating because, without reason, he has no means to make a case for — or against — anything.

5. The "Enlightened" Understanding of Christianity

Clearly, by the end of the 1600's, confidence in Christianity had begun to suffer a slow but steady decline among the educated, "enlightened" elite of Europe. This meant that a natural explanation for its existence and hold upon the religious life of the West had to be advanced. This did not appear to be a problem.

Thousands of years ago, most peoples were simple of mind and prone to imagination. In their imaginings, they invented remarkable stories which became true by the time they were told twice. In time, these stories

---

44. The essential Islamic confession of faith.

became the basis of religion — a primitive people's need to have *some* explanation of life at large. In the case of the Hebrews, the religion was Judaism.

After a time, there appeared a certain Jesus of Nazareth, a great man. Desiring to reform Judaism of a burdensome passion for a law which it had developed, Jesus attempted to simplify the law in the commandment: "do unto others as you would have them do unto you." Moreover, He proclaimed a "universal brotherhood of man" which appealed to people in a society of class distinctions that put most at the bottom of the ladder. Naturally, the established religious leaders of His day branded Him a heretic and had Him put to death. Unwilling to abandon His attempt to reform, a group of His followers declared that He had risen from the dead — some may even have believed it. (This would explain the possibility that there *were* some martyrs — though not nearly as many as Christianity's self-written history predictably claims.) In any case, Christianity was their idea. For a coincidence of other historical reasons, not the least of which was the decline of the Roman Empire, the new religion spread. For other historical reasons, it became the religion of Europe just as Islam became the religion of the Middle East and Hinduism became the faith of India. But, it was now time for a true brotherhood of men based on truths immediately available to all — the dictates of reason.

* * *

Despite the increasing prevalence of the enlightened opinion, it would hardly be accurate to suggest that it quickly became the opinion of all the educated. It was definitely the minority view. Furthermore, even where it was held, it did not always involve the complete disregard for the historical character of the Bible, especially when it came to the New Testament.

The Old Testament was easy to ignore. It concerned a *very* ancient people. And, despite the traditions which conveniently accounted for almost every book, the authorship of all of them was questionable. Finally, its claims were much more outrageous than those of the New Testament; it told of a catastrophic fall that disordered all creation, a universal flood and the day the sun stood still.

To be sure, the New Testament had troubles of its own. It spoke of many miracles, not to mention Jesus' resurrection from the dead. But, even in the telling of its most extraordinary tales, it seemed much more true to life. It should have; after all, it was written by people much less ancient. It was based upon the recollections of people who did know

Jesus. And the gospels were in general agreement, even John. And who could be sure that their authors did not die as martyrs for the new faith? What else could explain the fact that Christianity did survive serious persecution and still it did spread?

Given the facts, certain critics felt compelled to admit that there must have been some historical basis for most of the New Testament events, even the most extraordinary. Remaining sure that the laws of nature had not been broken, they devised alternate explanations. All Jesus' miracles became faith-healings, a phenomenon only now being seen for its effectiveness among the simple-minded sort who could as easily be "cursed" into almost any ailment. The resurrection was an hallucination or, perhaps, Jesus did not die upon the cross; were not the guards surprised to find that He had expired after only three hours (Jn.19:31-33)? Perhaps, as the guards had claimed, Jesus' disciples had stolen His body (Mt.28:11-15). The first modern thinker to suggest just this was Hermann Reimarus (1694-1768).[45]

Such theories were the work of people who had lost faith in Christ and Christianity. They were devised by people who had abandoned faith in the name of a scientific criterion of truth that still required them to supply a natural explanation for everything Christian regardless of how remarkable, or ridiculous, it might appear. Ironically, it would be the work of committed Christians that opened the door to much less remarkable, much more plausible, natural explanations for everything biblical.

C. The Rise of Modern Biblical Criticism

Inevitably, scientism began to affect the thinking of Christians who did not see its demands as sufficient reason to abandon their faith.

As it became obvious that there were major similarities between the Scriptures and other ancient writings of undoubted human origin, it had begun to become clear that the biblical writers had made a definite contribution to the content of their writings. In other words, they were authors, not merely transcribers. Perhaps inspiration had taken place without their knowing it. In the light of this idea, it was clear that the Scriptures could be studied as any other text. This was the beginning of the scientific study of the Scriptures, or "modern biblical criticism," as it was later to be called.

1. Studies in the Old Testament

Modern biblical criticism was first applied to the Old Testament. Of the

---

45. Reimarus' views come to us from Gotthold Lessing, his student at the University of Wittenberg.

two testaments, the Old appeared to involve much more that needed to be explained.

The first truly scientific Scripture scholar was Richard Simon (1638-1712), a convert to Catholicism, a priest, and an expert in biblical languages. Simon began his work in an attempt to sort through the many, sometimes differing scriptural manuscripts in order to determine the original, true text. Then, by studying key words as they are used throughout the Scriptures, other ancient texts and patristic writings, he endeavored to discover the precise meaning of these words. This led to a new awareness that the Hebrews were not the Greeks; they were more concerned with prose and poetry than with philosophic precision. Linguistic study also led to a new awareness of the differences in style which distinguished the different Old Testament books and even parts of books.[46]

Acknowledging that there were indeed two accounts of creation, Simon also observed that Genesis had two distinctly different ways of referring to God. In certain chapters, He was called "Yahweh" (which was related to the verb "to be"), His personal name. (Too holy to be spoken, when it appeared, the Hebrews read "Adonai," i.e. "Lord.") In other chapters, He was called "Elohim" (a word in plural form which was evidently related to "El," the common semite word for "god"). With this evidence, Simon concluded that Moses was not the only author of the Pentateuch. It was instead a composite, the product of what was probably a long period of oral tradition, writing and rewriting. Simon's superiors had his book placed on the Index.

With this, the scholarly initiative passed to the Protestants. There was also a shift in the method of study. Simon had concentrated on the text itself. Now, scholars were increasingly convinced that there was more to be learned by reflecting upon the historical specifics which must have shaped the way the Hebrews thought and wrote. That the Hebrews *were* people of their time and place was now evident in what they did write. How else was one to explain that their God had commanded them to kill witches (Ex.22:18) and to slaughter entire peoples (Deut.20:16-17)? How else was one to explain that He encouraged them in what was plainly a pre-scientific fear of menstration (Lev.15:19-30)?

In view of what was easily imagined about the life of Near Eastern cultures, it was now to be presumed that Hebrew writings were indeed the product of a long period of oral tradition. It was also to be presumed that

46. See his *Histoire Critique du Vieux Testament*

they *were* written from the hindsight of many centuries, surely the product of all the exaggeration to be expected of a primitive people remembering their past. Moreover, as a primitive people, surely they engaged in some of the myth-making which is characteristic of every other.

2. Studies in the New Testament

Though scientific methods were first applied to the Old Testament, it did not take long before they were also applied to the New. Once again, it was Richard Simon who paved the way. Again he did comparisons devised to determine the true texts and their proper translation. Again he employed the study of language and literary forms in order to understand their authors.[47]

Simon observed that though the early Christians were not Hebrews, they were Jews. They may have written in Greek, but they were still semites. (Actually, Matthew's gospel was thought to have been written in "Aramaic," the linguistic successor of ancient Hebrew and the language spoken by Jesus. Mark's gospel was thought to be an abridgement of Matthew.) In any case, the early Christian writings involved marked differences in style and theme, if not theology. This was now read to reveal the human involvement in their composition.

Some of the differences finally began to look like disagreements (cf. p. 110). Of course, some early Christian disagreement had always been in evidence. The Bible itself told of the disagreement between the groups that would later be called the "judaizers" and the "hellenists" (Acts 15). Now, Ferdinand Baur (1781-1860) would claim that the entire New Testament is a product of early Christian struggle over the doctrine of the new faith.

Baur contended that this apostolic struggle was won by Paul, to whom he attributed the lion's share of Christian doctrine, even more than Jesus. He also argued that Paul's influence was itself the product of the Greek thought prevalent during his day, especially gnosticism. This he saw in Paul's descriptions of life in the somewhat mysterious "spirit." Moreover, Baur insisted that by "spirit," Paul intended no reference to the Third Person of the Blessed Trinity; belief in the Trinity came much later as did all of the complex doctrines which became orthodox Christianity. Actually, it was the lack of complex doctrine and, more importantly, the ample evidence that Paul believed that Jesus was soon to return (e.g. 2 Thess.4) which led Baur to conclude that Paul's letters were the first New Testament writings. (Scholars would later support this conclusion by pointing out that if Paul had known of the gospels, he

47. See his *Histoire Critique du Texte du Nouveau Testament.*

would surely have made some reference to them.) Where the "Pauline" letters did not bespeak the expectation that Jesus was soon to return, Baur pointed out differences in style and theology which proved that they were not written by Paul. Attributed to Paul well after they were written in order to gain authority, most of the Pauline letters — and most obviously the letter to the Hebrews — were written by unknown others.[48] (Actually, research now uncovered significant patristic doubt about the Pauline authorship of Hebrews, for precisely Baur's reasons.)

Questions of gnosticism and authorship were not only raised with regard to Paul. John was already suspect. Not only did John speak of Jesus as the "Word" who was with God and who was God (Jn.1:1-4), but his gospel spoke of the mysterious "rebirth" of one who was begotten from above (cf. Jn.3). His writings also bespeak a contempt for the world (e.g. Jn.15:18, 1 Jn.2:15). Actually, to some scholars, differences in style and theology proved that not all the "Johannine" writings were written by the same person. In any case, even if they were, he was surely not the young, semite which the gospels describe. This supported the idea that his gospel was no account of history. (When research uncovered the fact that the Gospel of John was missing from early canons and, in some cases, explicitly rejected, this conclusion was apparently confirmed.)

With the passage of time, the other gospels would not fair much better. The human involvement in their composition was identified in what were now seen to be marked differences in style and theology. Yet, what would ultimately prove to bring about the degradation of their value as history was their agreement.

It was true; despite the differences, the gospels of Matthew, Mark and Luke were notably similar. Called the "synoptic" gospels, often they parallel each other word for word. Prior to the rise of modern biblical criticism, this was explained by divine inspiration; if God was the author of the gospels, surely they should agree. Now, in the age of enlightenment, a natural explanation was necessary. Therefore, the gospels began to be studied with this in mind. In time, the comparison of the texts began to yield the idea that, contrary to tradition, the Gospel of Mark was the source of both the gospels of Matthew and Luke. (There was no real evidence that there had been an Aramaic Matthew and the tradition was too easily explained by the uncritical presumption that the author of Matthew's gospel was the apostle.) Furthermore, since Matthew and Luke shared a significant amount of material which was not found in

---

48. See especially his *Paulus, der Apostel Jesu Christi.*

Mark, it was also concluded that they had drawn upon a second common source — called "Q" from "quelle," the German word for "source" — which has been lost. With the realization that the original ending of Mark's gospel has also been lost — with vv.9-20 an obvious addition — it was evident that the gospels were written well after the events.

The synoptic theory apparently proved that the gospel writers were not contemporaries of Jesus. It also appeared to prove that the gospels were the products of time, of oral tradition, writing and rewriting. Given human nature, this surely meant that they were the products of exaggeration unto outright story-telling if only for the sake of religion. Here was a plausible natural explanation of Jesus' miracles and fulfilled prophecies — even His divinity. After all, didn't the Egyptians divinize the pharaohs; didn't the Romans divinize the emperors?

Actually, human nature was already in evidence. In Mark, Peter is accredited with the confession: "You are the Christ" (Mk.8:27-30). In Matthew, Peter not only calls Him the Son of the living God, but he (Peter) is made head of the Church and given the keys to the kingdom of heaven (Mt.16:13-20). In Mark, when Jesus dies, the curtain of the temple is torn in two (Mk.15:38). This otherwise undocumented event was an obvious attempt to make a point. In Matthew, not only is the curtain torn but the earth shook, tombs were opened and the bodies who had fallen asleep were raised and appeared to many (Mt.27:51-53).

The relationship of human nature, time and the truth — and, as well, the practice of attributing works to authoritative names — was especially in evidence in the newly rediscovered Christian "apocrypha."[49] There were gospels of Peter, Philip, Thomas, Bartholomew, Jude, Matthias, and the "Twelve," as well as a variety of "Acts." Written during Christianity's second century, these works told incredible tales.[50] The later the work, the more incredible the tale, and the more gnostic the theology.

Reflection on the relationship of human nature, time and the truth led to a growing sense that one must distinguish the Christ of the gospels from the Jesus of history, a figure about whom we actually know very little. First employed by Reimarus (cf. p. 125), this distinction was used to explain his idea that the Jesus of history was a political revolutionary (the only kind of "messiah" that was ever expected) whose failure could not be accepted by

---

49. Religion surely explains the fact that the *Protoevangelium of James* took pains to tell about Mary's parents Joachim and Ann.

50. Some were also bizarre. The *Infancy Gospel of Thomas* told of the boy Jesus' habit of making real birds out of clay; when the other boys made fun of Him, a single glance struck them dead.

his followers. Having met failure on earth, they turned to hope in heavenly kingdom. This was not Jesus' idea. Neither was the great commandment. It was not even original; contained in Leviticus (19:18), it was called the "great commandment" by the rabbi Hillel just before Jesus was born.

Taking the distinction between Jesus and Christ to the extreme, Bruno Bauer (1809-82) declared that it was doubtful that Jesus, or even Paul, ever lived.

Most scholars felt that men like Reimarus and Bauer had gone too far. They were also more sympathetic to the first Christians. According to David Strauss (1808-74), the New Testament showed that the first Christians were people of true faith, if zealous imagination. He believed that they believed that Jesus had risen from the dead. The resurrection accounts concretized this conviction. The gospels expressed their faith. But as documents of faith, the gospels cannot be read to reveal the real life and teaching of Jesus.[51]

3. An Addendum: Liberalism

Many found the results of modern biblical criticism far too persuasive to be ignored. Unconvinced that Christianity should be abandoned, however, certain thinkers, mostly Protestant, attempted what they came to consider a new phase of the Reformation, a new way to approach the true essence of Christianity, and to believe only that. Needless to say, they favored a rather free, or "liberal," reading of texts and, hence, their movement was called "Liberalism."

Much was now expendable. All of the most philosophically explained doctrines were rejected as man-made additions to the true message of Jesus. The sacraments were the result of the human desire to manipulate the divine and to be sure of what only faith should be sure. They were also the product of a gradual process. For example, gradually, as Jesus' disciples continued to take their meals together — as they did when He was with them — they transferred their heightened sense of His presence among them to the food they ate in common, especially inasmuch as partaking from the one loaf and cup had become a sign of *their* communion. This did not mean that they had always been a "church"; Jesus did not plan to establish a church; He was simply trying to reform Judaism. (But this was *not* a reason to presume that God had written the Old Testament. The Old Testament was truly primitive and, despite the best efforts of Jesus' disciples, it did not prefigure him; there were very few references to a messiah of any kind, much less the God-man of later theology.) Jesus'

---

51. See his very influential *Life of Jesus.*

followers became a church because Jesus' attempt to reform Judaism had failed. The scriptural accounts of His appointment were written in order to sanction something that had actually happened by natural causes.

Needless to say, the liberal view represented a great deal of agreement with the modern scientific reluctance to believe that the laws of nature would ever be broken. This caused a questioning of all of Jesus' miracles, including the resurrection.

Moreover, in something of a submission to the growing contempt for any sort of supernatural, even faith was now to be described in natural terms. Affirming the modern opinion that reason does not confirm faith, at least not in a *positive* sense, thinkers began to search for another natural source. Friedrich Schliermacher (1768-1834) was the first to find one. He held that more could be known than what was known through reason, claiming that feelings are informative. He said that faith is a "sense for the infinite" and a "feeling of absolute dependence."[52]

Not surprisingly, the liberal movement also involved a new approach to Christian morality. When last we considered Christian morality, it was built upon the notion of law (cf. p. 75). God had revealed many laws; these determined right and wrong. Now, with the new view of the sources of revelation, it began to be insisted that there is only one imperative — love. In any case, it was also to be argued that right and wrong are "relative" to the individual — relative to his judgement of what is true for him. This opinion came to be known as "moral relativism."[53]

Section V: The Decline of Belief in God

Despite liberal efforts, the first generation of a-Christian thinkers saw no reason to accept faith. But, this did not mean that they saw no reason to believe in God.

A. Deism

The first generation of a-Christian thinkers believed in God. In fact, it appeared positively un-scientific not to. The argument from the need to explain the world (cf. p. 97) still seemed valid.

But, now that nature appeared so dependable — that its laws would never be broken — it also seemed that God had left the world to follow

---

52. See especially his *Religion, Speeches to Its Cultured Despisers.*
53. A less individualistic form of relativism came from the enlightened understanding of the cultural character of religion (cf. p.123). Known as "cultural relativism," this was the idea that right and wrong are relative to the ethical framework provided by culture.

the laws he had given it. This was "deism."

To the minds of men like Voltaire (1694-1778), deism accounted for everything — the world, its dependability, and the fact that the random character of its many events is indifferent to the good of man. It clearly established reason as the supreme principle of human guidance.

According to men like Jean-Jacques Rousseau (1712-78), deism was hardly un-Christian. It called Christians to the true sincerity possible in the absence of the promise of heavenly rewards. It freed Christianity from the myth and superstition that had previously obscured its call for liberty, equality and fraternity.[54]

Although most of the first deists professed respect for Christian virtues, even these were not without their critics. Edward Gibbon (1737-94) blamed Christian passivity for the collapse of the Roman Empire, a tragic event which put the Church in charge of society and cost Europe centuries of progress.[55] Contending that Christianity was a rationalized failure to cope with life's realities — especially death — its survival and spread were explained away. And now, Christians were *derisively* called "sheep." It was time for people to shake off their fears and live their lives accepting responsibility for what happens in the world.

The contempt for Christianity professed by men like Gibbon did not become the norm for enlightened thinkers. Christianity's perceived call for universal brotherhood was still admired. This, however, was often coupled with the conviction that "all religions are really the same," calling man to essentially the same virtues regardless of the variety of now unnecessary ways in which they justified their point.

* * *

Under the influence of writers like Rousseau, the burgeoning middle-class of his native France was stirred to a passion for political freedom. In 1789, the passion burst forth in the French revolution. Led by men imbued with the ideals of the enlightenment, the revolutionaries were not only impatient with Christianity but they were also avowed enemies of the Church whose affiliation with the monarchy was historic. Churchmen were executed; churches were closed and Church property was confiscated. Though the rise of Napoleon (1769-1821) improved the relations between Church and state, this was due to Napoleon's desire to use the Church to further his political ends. In fact, Napoleon all but embodied the

---

54. Rousseau is best remembered for his belief that man in the "state of nature" is good only to be corrupted by living in society.
55. See his *The Decline and Fall of the Roman Empire.*

Enlightenment and his military successes served to spread its ideals throughout Europe. These ideals later spawned the revolutions which brought an end to the age of all-powerful, or "absolute," kings in Europe. Not only did this mean trouble for the Church, it appeared to prove that it was man and not God who would make the world a better place.

B. Atheism

For some, deism moved quickly to atheism.

Deism was a product of the principle of economy. It followed the judgment that Christianity involved much more than was warranted by the facts. But, deism accepted the idea that the world required a Creator. In the name of reason however, it was inevitable that some would question this contention, and, for the first time ever, respected thinkers would answer "no."

The arguments which Occam accepted (cf. p. 97) were accepted no longer.

To argue from cause and effect was to ignore the fact that change was now explained in terms of natural law.

To argue from the fact that nothing in the world is "necessary" was to fail to see that even though individual things come and go, this did not need to be true of the underlying stuff of which the world is made.

To argue that the world had to have its maker — to insist that everything must come from somewhere — is to create the question: "who made God?" If God always was, why not the world? Would it not be more economical to believe in the world? After all, the world is here, where is God? If there is a God, why was evil built in to His creation?

Thus did men like Denis Diderot (1713-84)[56] conclude that belief in God is problematic and unnecessary. For the first time in human history, there was "atheism" — positive disbelief in God. Reason and self-reliance seemed to have triumphed.

* * *

With the rise of atheism, certain thinkers set out to create a concrete replacement for religion, one which acknowledged that man was his own God. Auguste Comte (1798-1857) devised a "Religion of Humanity" complete with doctrines glorifying man and reason, feast days and rituals. Comte's ideas, however, did not generate much interest. The enlightened elite professed nothing but the pursuit of pleasure. Thus, in recommending the "greatest good" — the venerable ethical principle which states that we should always do whatever will bring about the

---

56. Diderot is also remembered as an author of the famous *Encyclopedie*, an ambitious attempt to compile all of human knowledge.

greatest good — John Stuart Mill (1806-73) argued that we should do whatever will bring the most pleasure to the most people. Moreover, according to Mill, what we do can only be judged according to the "utilitarian" principal which says that the rightness of an act is determined by its consequences.[57]

Mill is also remembered for the "libertarian" principle which says that "just" government must give maximum liberty to the individual.

Section VI: The Decline of Confidence that Man is Something Special

A) The Changing Attitude Towards Man

Man was always sure that he was something special. Though the Greeks knew that he was an animal, he was the *rational* animal. Rationality proved that he had a soul. Of course, as spirit, the soul was still a mystery.

Modern science had no patience for mystery. The soul was not about to stand in its way. Why should it? After all, the body was part of nature subject to natural laws. Why not the soul?

Actually, man was no longer said to have a soul. Now the spiritual aspect of his existence was simply his "mind," nothing of immortal nature, not even something significantly different from the "spiritual" life of other animals.

With study, man and other animals were inevitably to be compared. Naturally, similarities were observed. After all, other animals have intelligence, they seem to feel pain and to pursue pleasure as man does. It began to appear that man is different only in degree. He is just another object of study.

B) The Special Problem of Free Will

The presumption that natural laws explain spiritual life immediately involved the abandonment of the belief that man has free will.

Actually, the scholastics had their own problems with free will. Even apart from the problems of grace (cf. p. 106), it was by no means clear how the Cause of all causes does not bear the ultimate responsibility for everything that happens. Did providence somehow exclude human actions and, if it did, how was God still to be considered the ultimate

---

57. The "utilitarian" principle was first articulated by Jeremy Bentham (1748-1832). But it was Mill who explored it, attempting to deal with the difference between short and long-term consequences. He is also remembered his attempt to distinguish different qualities of pleasure.

cause of everything? Here was another mystery.

Here was another unacceptable mystery — and it was unnecessary. Man had finally come to realize that his will was not free. It had taken a long, long time.

Except for acts of physical compulsion or intimidation, the Greeks saw freedom in anything a person did of his own choosing. Of course, they also saw a certain relationship between act and circumstances; if a person were struck, he would likely strike back. If he were hungry, he would be more likely to steal. This was what made possible talk of "human nature." But hunger was not the cause of stealing because many who were hungry did not steal.

With time, however, observers also began to see a certain relationship between a person's acts and the circumstances of his past. It was hard *not* to notice that thieves usually came from "bad" homes, while the products of "good" homes were normally good people. Of course, this did not mean that a person's past *produced* his actions; after all, some bad people came from good homes and some good people came from bad homes. Circumstances might be responsible for the strength of certain "tendencies"[58] but they did not *cause* action; there was an exception to every rule.

But, with the deepening conviction that everything has its natural explanation, exceptions came to be seen as the fault of the rules — the fact that human nature is much too complex to be described by simple rules gained from casual observation. Attempts to refine the rules became the science of "psychology." It was soon conceived to discover the psychological "laws" which explain, and therefore predict, human "behavior." In other words, science had concluded that circumstances *do* cause, or "determine," action. Man's will is not free. A person is not responsible for what he does or who he is.

Section VII: An Introduction to Materialism

The conviction that natural laws explain everything, even the human mind, was not long in leading to materialism. After all, what is nature but matter in motion?

---

58. The scholastics spoke of "inclinations." They also talked in terms of "habits," acquired inclinations. Habits were naturally the product of repetition, and supernaturally the product of grace; sanctifying grace was also called "habitual" grace.

A) A Sketch of the History of Materialism

Like every other idea, or so it may seem, materialism was first suggested by an ancient Greek. In this case, it was Leucippus of the 5th century B.C., as reported by his student Democritus. According to Leucippus, all things are composed of matter — the underlying substance that explains how things can change from one to another. Matter cannot be divided indefinitely. No rock can be broken into an infinite number of smaller ones. Eventually, one would come to indivisible units, or "atoms," which are eternally in motion. (Hence, Leucippus and Democritus were known as the "Atomists.") Though made of the same substance, atoms differ in size, shape and texture. They comprise everything, including man. Since man is part of nature, he too consists of atoms; his mind, the atoms of his head, are simply the smoothest. He can see (or hear, etc.) because objects give off some of their atoms which move through space through the eye (or ear, etc.) and strike the atoms in his head.

Despite what would later be considered the attractiveness of materialism, Platonism still became the philosophy of Greece. Indeed, the materialism of the ancients was completely forgotten; it was only rediscovered as something was needed to fill the metaphysical void left by the demise of scholasticism.

The first modern thinker to propose a materialism was Thomas Hobbes (1588-1679).[59] Most impressed with the precision of Galileo's laws, Hobbes set out to show that motion could explain everything. Like the Atomists, he held that mental processes are the motion of matter in the head. To explain the constancy of motion, he held that everything is a "body" — that the universe is completely filled with matter whose motion is sustained by constant collision.[60]

Rene' Descartes (1586-1650) articulated the materialism already implicit in the practice of scientific explanation (cf. p. 114). If the explanation of things in nature involves a description of the working of their parts, it should ultimately involve a description of the motion of matter, the parts of the parts. In other words, things in nature are machines. Given the laws of motion, this would explain everything.

Descartes shared Hobbes' belief that the world is, as he called it, a "plenum" filled with matter whose constant collisions keep things moving. Unlike Hobbes, he did not believe that matter could explain the

59. Hobbes is best remembered for his reaction to Rousseau's thinking on personal liberty. He argued that unregulated liberty brings chaos, a fact which has already required the masses to cede there liberty to monarchs who thus rule by "divine right."
60. See his *De corpore.*

mind. Unimpressed with the scholastic idea that reality consists of two mutually dependent substances (cf. p.59), he insisted that reality consists of two totally different substances; it is a "dualism" of matter and spirit. Matter is a substance "extended" in space; spirit is not.[61]

Descartes paved the way for scientists to agree with Hobbes. Speaking not of the motions of thought *per se,* they began to speak about the machine-like function of the brain. Speaking specifically of the incredibly complex "physiological" processes of which it is capable, they began to insist that these processes explain mental life.   Among the first to articulate such a theory was Julian de La Mettrie (1709-1751), a doctor who was to offer specific physiological explanations for various mental phenomena.[62]

B) The Support of Modern Science

Materialism clearly appeared to be supported by modern science. Not only did it appear to have provided a mechanistic explanation of man, it appeared to have provided a mechanistic explanation of matter.

Empedocles (5th cent. B.C.) believed that there were four "elements" — earth, air, fire and water, mixtures of which made up everything. For twenty centuries, this idea satisfied scientific interest. It was not to satisfy modern science. Beginning in the work of Robert Boyle (1627-91), modern chemists[63] began to describe a number of substances in terms of chemical "properties." Boyle's specialty was gases and his correlations of pressure and volume became the first chemical laws.

Building upon the work of men like Boyle, Antoine Lavoisier (1743-94) began to analyze the newly identified substances. Many proved to be "compounds" made of smaller elements, some of which made up more than one. In the end, he distinguished 23 elements which he believed to be the building blocks of all substances. Moreover, during his experiments, Lavoisier discovered that the weight of all the involved elements was the same before and after the chemical interactions by which compounds were broken down. This led him to conclude that matter is neither created nor destroyed but instead takes different forms — the law of the

---

61. See his *Principles.* Descartes' "dualism" inspired Gottfried Lebniz (1646-1716) in his attempt to re-unify reality. His was a "monism" involving the idea that everything is made of indivisible "monads" which contain the essence of reality within them. This makes it difficult to judge whether he is to be considered a materialist or not.

62. See his *L'Homme machine.*

63. The designation "modern" can best distinguish chemistry from its predecessor alchemy, the rather un-scientific mixing of substances in hope of discovering a formula for gold. Un-scientific though it was, alchemy was unintentionally responsible for much of the data which the first modern chemists had at their disposal.

conservation of matter. This law gave significant support to the materialists' contention that matter explains everything.

John Dalton (1766-1844) appeared to complete the picture. Following the Atomists, he realized that the elements cannot be divided indefinitely into smaller and smaller quantities. Thus, there must be a fundamental unit of each one, an "atom" (to borrow a word) which he pictured as a round, hard little mass that obeyed the laws of motion.[64]

Once Dalton had identified the fundamental units that obey the laws of motion, a truly complete explanation of everything had apparently become possible. How? Galileo's laws had already been explained.

We have already taken note of Galileo's theory of inertia, the idea that motion naturally continues indefinitely if unimpeded (cf. p. 115). This was the first scientific statement of the idea that nature could have a life of its own. It was Isaac Newton (1642-1727), however, who provided the thinking which was ultimately taken to prove that nature could account for itself — completely.

Newton was pondering the idea of inertia when he was struck by the idea that it was best described in terms of "force" (or "F"), the energy a body has because it has weight and is in motion.[65] Immediately, this led to the observation that force has a direction that, in a collision, involves the transfer of force from one object to another to an extent proportional to the directness of the collision. Thus the equation $F = -F$. Then, he observed that the force of an object is best described as its weight (or "mass" or "m") multiplied by its acceleration (or "a"), not its velocity, but the energy required to produce this velocity, the amount of energy evident in its change in velocity. Thus $F = ma$. Finally, in order to explain the laws of falling bodies, Newton postulated "gravity" — a force of attraction affecting all bodies, including the earth itself. Obviously, the force of gravity was proportional to the mass of the object. (We can now see that "mass" can be distinguished from "weight," the force of gravity upon a given mass.) The force of gravity upon a given mass can be determined by the law $F = G \frac{m^1 m^2}{r}$, where G is the mathematical value of the effect of gravity, and r is the distance between any two objects.

Remarkably, in the above *three* laws, Newton had provided a natural explanation of all motion. Already convinced that the complex creatures were simply complex machines, he had apparently explained the motions that made them go. The universe is a grand machine run by gravity.

---

64. See his *New System of Chemical Philosophy*.
65. See his *Principia Mathematica*.

Newton's three laws of motion left only the less studied phenomena of heat, light and magnetism to be explained.

Heat did not appear to be a problem. Heat had long been considered the collective, or "aggregate" effect of matter in motion. Atomic theory provided a picture that made this easy to imagine. When Prescott Joule (1818-89) offered evidence that the total heat imparted to an experiment could be accounted for as the experiment ran its course, a fact he formulated in a general law of the conservation of energy, the identification of heat and motion was apparently proved.

Light was a problem. Newton thought that light was a stream of material particles which escaped from a larger mass.[66] But, light did not always travel as should be expected of a particle governed by the laws of motion; it curved around corners and filled a room. Christian Hrygens (1629-95) thought that light is a disturbance in the invisible "ether" which he believed to fill space. Taking the form of a "wave," it left the object in a pattern similar to the one which is created by a stone thrown into a lake, or better, the sound wave which disturbs the air or other matter. This eventually gave rise to the measurement of light in terms of frequency and wavelength.[67]

Magnetism remained a problem. As we saw, William Gilbert observed that certain substances, which he called "electrics,"[68] bore the mysterious energy of magnetism. According to Benjamin Franklin (1775-1836), electrics bore either positive or negative "charges."[69] Alessandro Volta (1745-1827) used one of each to make the first battery. This enabled the creation of an electric "current," a sustained form of the mysterious sparks which had always puzzled man. This led Andre Ampère (1775-1836) to the theory of electromagnetism, the idea that magnetism is itself a form of a larger category of energy — "electricity." When electric current was discovered to behave like a wave, James Clerk Maxwell (1831-79) was led to the electromagnetic theory of light, the idea that light is another form of electricity.

Although the materialist had to admit that the existence of electricity, a

---

66. Newton's study of light resulted in his invention of the prism which apparently broke light into the "spectrum" of its constituent colors. This was important because it made possible the eventual invention of the "spectroscope" which would prove instrumental in the chemical analysis of anything that gives off light.

67. It is to Thomas Young (1773-1829) that we owe the mathematical description of light we still employ.

68. The word was Greek for the "amber" which was one of its best sources.

69. Franklin is also remembered for flying the kite which proved that lightning is not a bolt from heaven.

pure form of energy, somewhat spoiled the simplicity of a materialism involving only matter and the laws of motion, still he was undaunted. After all, energy was still a "physical" thing. It was not spiritual. Together, matter and energy would surely be shown to explain everything.

Apparently, matter and energy had already explained life.

Building upon the work of Leonardo, William Harvey (1578-1657) had discovered that blood circulates in a closed system pumped by the heart.[70] Not only did his discovery disprove Galen (cf. p. 113), it provided an unmistakable example of the mechanistic function of the body.

It was already obvious that the body, that all living things, were made of matter. When living things died, they decomposed, the result was quite chemical. Plants were known to need material from the ground in order to grow. They had lately been discovered to give off the oxygen animals cannot live without. Animals eat plants. They need to drink water.

Study continued. Living things were analyzed down to the slightest tissue. When Matthias Schleiden (1804-81) turned the telescope — in the form of the "microscope" — down upon these tissues, he discovered cells, complex structures with constant internal activity. In these, he had discovered the building-blocks of plants. It was Theodore Schwann (1810-82) who discovered that cells are the building blocks of animals, including man.

The analysis of cells soon revealed that all are composed of chemicals, mostly compounds based on carbon. Moreover, their internal activity consists of chemical reactions which break down and produce compounds and heat like any other. Thus, when Hermann Helmholtz (1821-94) showed that the laws of the conservation of matter and energy extended to these reactions, the mechanistic character of life appeared proved, at least to the materialist.

* * *

Progress in biology also had practical results. It led Louis Pasteur (1822-95) to discover the bacteria which turned milk into poison. In this discovery, modern medicine was born and, soon, it was to offer cures for a number of diseases which had always been killers. Progress in physics had already led Michael Faraday (1791-1867) to discover the "induction" which enabled the invention of the electric motor. Other inventions, such as the steam engine, had already led to the "Industrial Revolution" which made a variety of goods available to people who would never have had them otherwise. And, surely, progress had just begun.

C) Certain Aspects of 19th Century Materialism.

As is likely obvious, when materialism was first conceived, it was

70. See his *On the Motion of the Heart.*

considered the most un-Christian way of thinking about the world.

Not even a machine, materialism left man no more than matter in motion. This was called "reductionism." In other words, the laws of psychology can best be explained in terms of the laws of physiology. In turn, the laws of physiology can be "reduced" to those of biology. Surely, the laws of biology can be reduced to the laws of chemistry; this project had already begun. The laws of chemistry were already reduced to the laws of physics. Such were the conclusions of Paul Heinrich Dietrich d'Hollbach (1723-1789) whose *System du nature* became the bible of 19th. century materialism.

Materialism also meant determinism that everything is determined by the motion of matter according to the laws of physics. Therefore, according to Pierre Simon de Laplace (1749-1827), if one could know the exact position, trajectory and acceleration of every particle of matter in the universe, one could also predict the future and report upon the past perfectly.[71]

The appeal of materialism was its simplicity; it explained reality without the postulation of unseen anythings. It did away with the mystery of the soul. In particular, materialism offered a solution to what had come to be called the problem of mind and body — the problem of their interaction.

Plainly mind and body did interact; fire caused pain while fear caused nausea. Alcohol caused drunkenness. If mind and body were two totally different kinds of things, how did this happen? This was a problem. It was one of the major problems with hellenism (cf. p. 59). Scholasticism did not solve it. Scholasticism simply insisted that the immaterial gave form to the material. But, it did not explain how an immaterial form could ever move the material; neither did it explain how the material could move the spiritual. Materialism avoided the problem; it insisted that the spiritual *is* the material. It accounted for everything with the one thing whose existence was evident.

Materialism was the triumph of scientism.

Section VIII: Skepticism

Materialism was definitely the triumph of scientism, the insistence that truth depends on evidence — the tangible testable evidence of the five senses. But soon thereafter, the critical attitude out of which it was born began to look with an increasingly critical eye at the credibility of the only

---

71. See his *Essai philosophique sur les probabilites.*

evidence which science accepted. With increasing skepticism, thinkers began to question the validity of sense evidence and the basic principles of its interpretation.

Less a movement of society, "skepticism" was more a movement of individuals, the dominant figures of modern philosophy. With the collapse of scholasticism, they were not only concerned to replace its metaphysic, but they were most concerned to know how *not* to replace it with another system that would ultimately fail the test of truth. Thus, after a hiatus of almost two thousand years, philosophy returned to an overriding interest in the questions of the origin of knowledge and a way to be certain.

A) Descartes

Though a pioneer of modern materialistic thought, Descartes was unconvinced that science is a sure path to truth. After all, scientists were wrong at least as often as they were right. They frequently disagreed and there was rarely indisputable evidence that anyone was right. Moreover, upon reflection, it had to be admitted that even the five senses are apt to be mistaken. If a person passes from the cold into a warm room, he will feel that it is warmer than it really is. People sometimes see things that are not really there. Indeed, a person can legitimately wonder whether his entire experience of the outside "objective" world is the product of his dreams, or an hallucination imparted to him by some evil power. (This idea — that my experience of the outside world is an illusion — is called "solipsism.") Upset with this uncertainty, Descartes set out to discover what he could know for sure. Questioning the truth of anything that he could call to mind, he eventually concluded that there was only one thing he could not question — the fact of his own existence as a thinking, questioning being. In the very act of questioning, he indisputably experienced himself as existing and able to think. This is the meaning of his famous axiom: "cogito ergo sum" ("I think therefore I am ")[72].

Descartes considered the "cogito" an expression of "pure-reason" — a self-evident truth which is inherent in the mind. (In identifying such a truth, he followed Plato.) He also held that the truths of mathematics are self-evident. In other words, it is self-evident that one plus one equals two. (Describing reason in terms of the self-evidence of certain truths would later be called rationalism.) This was not to say that self-evident truth exhausted the scope of knowledge. After something of a restatement

---

72. The "cogito" was the result of what Descartes called "methodic doubt"; see his *Discours de la methode.*

of the ontological argument for the existence of God (cf. p. 35), Descartes argued that our "clear and distinct" ideas of the world must correspond to reality because, if they did not, God would be an evil deceiver which, by definition, He is not.

Though he may well have believed that he had found a reason to believe in God, and with God, a reason for confidence in experience, Descartes had seriously compromised the credibility of both. His methodic doubt established a new criterion for certainty and the simple fact of personal existence was the only truth that passed the test. Against this criterion, everything else was reduced to the status of a "belief."

B) Spinoza

Descartes' ideas were bound to cause controversy within the intellectual circles of his day. The first to offer a rebuttal was Baruch Spinoza (1632-1677), a Jew who was eventually to be excommunicated (from Judaism) for his ideas. Willing to admit that the senses can never be certain, he was still convinced that we can have knowledge — that we can have an idea of reality which we can trust. Thus did he declare that reality consists of ideas. The physical characteristics of the world are some of the ideas which it involves. Here was a pure "idealism" (cf. p. 58).[73]

Spinoza's pure idealism gave considerable support to his own restatement of the ontological argument. He further argued to a number of the traditional divine attributes, especially God's infinity. Reflecting on God's infinity, Spinoza concluded that it surely excluded the existence of anything apart from God. He therefore concluded that everything, including man, is part of God. We are not only made *by* Him, we are made *of* Him. This idea would later be known as "pantheism."

C) Locke

Neither rationalism nor idealism was attractive to the scientifically minded of their day. But, Descartes' thought elicited a response.

The first to respond was John Locke (1632-1704).[74] Utterly convinced of the importance of the testable evidence — evidence available to the mutual inspection of several testers — Locke decried the contention that the mind is born with certain ideas built-in. He specifically disputed the idea that mathematics provides knowledge. Mathematics is simply a

---

73. See his *Ethics.* Another pure idealism was later, more popularly proposed by George Berkeley (1685-1753).

74. Locke is best remembered for his thoughts on government which were eventually employed in the justification of the American Revolution. It was Locke who first stated that governments rightfully exist to protect the life, liberty and property of the individuals in society. Therefore, laws must be expressions of their collective will, i.e. democracy.

system of related definitions. Its statements are "true" for convention's sake, like language. Following Aristotle and Thomas, he insisted that all knowledge begins with sense experience. He went so far as to insist that man's mind is a *tabula rasa,* a "blank slate" until it is written on by experience.[75]

Locke established "empiricism," the idea that knowledge is the result of nothing other than sense experience. Sense experience produces what he called "simple ideas," those ideas of the world which cannot be broken down, i.e. defined in terms of any others, such as "round" or "red." These were the basic data of memory and reflection, the building-blocks to be recalled or combined in the mind's possession of "complex ideas," such as "apple," or even something so complex as "causality."

Locke is also remembered for his distinction of the "primary" and "secondary" qualities which objects possess. The primary qualities are essential to an object's perception. For example, a geometrical shape is a primary quality; if an object did not possess a certain shape it could not be perceived for what it is. Moreover, two or more observers can point to this shape to show that they perceive the same thing. They cannot point to a secondary quality, for example, a color or an odor; no one can know whether another person perceives the same thing. Secondary qualities may well be caused by the mind.

D) Hume

Just as the epistemology of Descartes led to the critical reaction of Locke, the epistemology of Locke elicited the critical reaction and epistemology of David Hume (1711-76).

Inasmuch as Locke assumed that the mind knows how to synthesize data in a way which is truly informative about the world, Hume held that he was not a true empiricist. He asked: how do we know that the way we combine simple ideas in the creation of complex ones reflects the way things really are? Agreeing that all knowledge is the result of sense perception which, as he said, produces the "impressions" out of which complex ideas are put together, he argued that the *way* impressions are put together had to come from somewhere. Since the mind knows nothing of its own, its ways had to be learned, the result of repetition, habit. But, there is no reason to assume that these habits correspond to what is really true of the world itself.[76]

Hume's epistemology was a denial of causality. According to Hume,

---

75. See his *Essay Concerning Human Understanding.*
76. See his *Treatise on Human Nature.*

belief in causality is produced by the constant conjunction of certain events. This gives rise to the habit of expecting their conjunction and, eventually, the idea that one must follow the other — because of causality. But, we have not seen causal forces. We have seen one event follow the other. This does not prove that it had to. Indeed, someday it may not; we do not know. We only know what we immediately experience.

Hume's insistence that we know only what we immediately experience even compromised belief in the one thing of which Descartes was sure, the existence of one person doing the questioning, the "self." According to Hume, mental life is a "bundle" of perceptions, a succession of states. There is no real evidence that there is really a person behind them. The idea "I am a person" is but a momentary thought, one of the mind's many learned mistakes.

E) Kant

1. *"The" Distinction*

Immanuel Kant (1724-1804) was one of the few thinkers who read Hume's work; he was the only one who realized that Hume's empiricism invalidated the findings of science. In his denial of causality, Hume had denied the very thing that gave nature its dependability — and predictabiity — without which scientific knowledge is simply knowledge of what was, not of what is. In other words, if there is no real, binding reason to believe that natural laws must hold true, we really know nothing. It was for this reason that Kant set out to prove that Hume was wrong. Specifically, he set out to prove that the mind is not the passive recipient of the ideas which arise from its perceptions.[77]

Pointing out that the rise of a habit presumes that the mind must have some inherent power to associate similar events, Kant did show that the mind could never be completely passive. Indeed, as he also pointed out, every perception presumes the complex mental processes without which nothing could cause sight, sound, smell, taste or touch.

As Kant soon realized, however, this meant that there is a distinction between the thing perceived and the content of its experience. Thus, we do not know the thing in itself (which Kant called the "nomenon") but only the thing as it has affected the mind (the "phenomenon"). We cannot know what the mind has done to the data it has received. We cannot know if the thing is not something totally different from our perception. In effect, Kant pointed out that the entire perception of reality consists of

---

77. See his *Critique of Pure Reason.*

Locke's secondary qualities.

Ironically, in his attempt to prove Hume wrong and to establish a basis for true knowledge, Kant succeeded in proving — at least to himself — that we know nothing about what is really out there. Naturally, he found himself agreeing that there is no basis for belief in causality. Furthermore, with reference to the function of causality as the backbone of traditional proofs for the existence of God, he declared that even if causality were somehow proved, it would not provide a basis for belief in God. Information gained from this world is useless in forming a picture of any other world. We cannot know that what works here would work there. Obviously, this principle also invalidated attempts to know God by analogy.

2. An Addendum: The Moral Argument for the Existence of God.

Although Kant's epistemology led to his declaration of the invalidity of most of the traditional philosophical approaches to God, Kant was still a believer. Moreover, he maintained that his belief was in accord with reason. Though one cannot prove God's existence from a study of the world, one did have recourse to God in the study of oneself. (In this, he followed Augustine, cf. p. 35.) He believed that one could prove the existence of God from the experience of conscience. This was his "moral argument for the existence of God."

In the stirrings of conscience, it is evident that man experiences the reality of "right" and "wrong," "good" and "bad." In this, he experiences the reality of law because it is only inasmuch as he obeys or breaks a law that his act is right or wrong. Now, the person of conscience knows that the laws which he experiences in conscience are not of his own making. If they were, he would not experience them as binding. Therefore, they must have been made by something, or someone, higher than himself. This is God.

Kant's conception of moral goodness — to act in accord with law, or principle — was the basis of what was soon to become his popular idea of the proper way for a person to determine the good of himself.[78] Since a principle is binding, it must be binding on everyone. Therefore, to determine the good, one must ask: what if this were binding on everyone — or not?

Though Kant's ideas on morality were quite popular, his moral argument for the existence of God did not persuade the disbelievers of his day.

---

78. See his *Foundations of the Metaphysics of Morals.*

Scientists had already explained religious sentiment as the psychological product of fears and desires. Moral sentiments were to be explained in the same way. (Besides, feelings are not facts.)

Philosophers could remind Kant that the inference from moral feelings to an extra-personal lawgiver was at least as invalid as the move from the world to its cause which he himself had criticized.

F) Philosophy after Kant

Kant was surely one of the pivotal figures in the history of thought. His ideas were the subject of all his immediate successors' careful inspection and, to a certain extent, all of their philosophies were reactions to his claim that the world out there was unknowable in itself. This means that philosophers after Kant can be grouped into two general categories: those who rejected his major ideas (the majority) and those who accepted them.

1. *Thinkers Who Rejected Kant*
a. Hegel and Schopenhauer

The first thinker to reject Kant's critique of the possibility of metaphysics was Georg W. F. Hegel (1770-1831). Agreeing with Spinoza — that we do have contact with what is really true — he also followed Spinoza in pantheism. But, Hegel's pantheism insisted that God, or "Spirit," or "Reason," is constantly becoming. This process follows a "dialectic" pattern. We begin with a "thesis." This gives rise to its opposite, the "antithesis". (After all, as something comes into existence, the possibility of its *not* existing has also been created.) Their conflict produces a "synthesis." This becomes a new thesis and the process begins again.[79]

Like Hegel, Arthur Schopenhauer (1788-1860) was both an idealist and a pantheist. In his view, however, the ultimate reality is not "Reason" but "Will."[80] Reality is striving, not learning. Moreover, since reality is constantly striving for ever more, it (and we) can never be satisfied. While we exist, we are bound to suffer from dissatisfaction and should therefore do all we can to extinguish our desires. In this thought, Schopenhauer betrays hs indebtedness to Buddhism (q.v. p.269).

b. Feuerbach and Marx

The idealists were not the only ones to insist that they had contact with the world as it really is. Materialists were quite convinced that they had contact with what is real. Ludwig Feuerbach (1804-72) declared that, in

---

79. Hegel's actually quite complicated system was expounded throughout his voluminous writings beginning with his *Phänomenologie des Geists.*
80. See his *Die Welt als Wille und Vorstellung.*

man, matter became conscious and earned the right to consider itself the ultimate reality. Feuerbach is best remembered for his insistence that religion is the result of man's inarticulate belief in his own divinity.[81]

Though a materialist, Karl Marx (1818-83) was profoundly influenced by Hegel's idea that reality was involved in a dialectic process of becoming. Impressed with what becoming, i.e. progress, had lately accomplished, especially in terms of material, i.e. consumer goods, Marx was appalled by what he considered the injustice of a class society in which the many work for the good of a few. Attributing this to the fact that a few own the means of production ("capitalism"), he insisted that justice would be obtained when these were owned collectively ("socialism"). This would be a classless society in which all share equally the fruits of their collective labor. Marx' study of history assured him that this was inevitable. At the same time, he also insisted that it would not happen apart from human effort, specifically in the form of the revolutions that would bring down the present order and establish a new one, "communism." This was his "Dialectical Materialism."[82]

Marx' thought is especially noteworthy because his was the first philosophy to involve 1) a call for social action, and 2) the idea that the state is the supreme social institution — indeed the supreme good. He considered religion the "opium" which allowed, if not encouraged the "masses" to endure a life of drudgery.

2. Thinkers Who Accepted Kant
a. Kierkegaard

To certain thinkers, the many new philosophies only served to prove that Kant was right: reality is out of reach. Some of these thinkers would follow Kant in a "Christian" response to the problems that this involved. Uncertain about everything and wracked with anxiety over the prospect of his death, Søren Kierkegaard (1813-55) claimed that man's only hope is faith. For Kierkegaard, however, unlike Kant, faith is a "leap" into the unknown; it is a non-rational decision to believe recommended by the simple fact that belief offers a hope that non-belief does not.[83]

---

81. See especially his *The Essence of Christianity*.
82. See his *Communist Manifesto*. Marx wrote in collaboration with Friedrich Engels (1820-95).
83. See especially his *The Concept of Dread*. Actually, Kierkegaard was not the first to claim that faith is taking a chance that one will never die to regret. This was already the "wager theory" of Blaise Pascal (1623-62). Kierkegaard has received first mention with regard to this idea because it was his formulation of it which occurred in specific response to the proposition that the traditional sources of truth were no longer reliable.

b. Nietzsche

Of course not everyone who agreed with Kant followed Kierkegaard in a Christian response to the questions which this raised. For some, a leap of faith was out of the question; faith was far too far to leap. (Indeed, for some, the very fact that faith had to be an act of the will was reason not to believe in a God who would put man in this position.) Seeing no other alternative, Friedrich Nietzsche (1844-1900) declared that nothing is intrinsically true or false, good or evil ("nihilism"). He challenged the people of his day to accept the fact that they must make their own values, even their own truth. He, like Marx, criticized Christianity for its encouragement of submission and resignation. He exalted the "superman," the person who had the courage to make his own values and the will to force others to accept *his* way.[84]

* * *

By the middle of the 19th century, the intellectual sector of society had before it a very bewildering diversity of views from which to choose. Scholastic agreement was gone. The modern mind could agree only that the old philosophy and the older faith had seen their day.

Section IX:
The Church's Initial Response to the Modern Mind

The Church identified the modern mind with all of the apparently un-Christian ideas we have examined. The first to elicit a response was the idea that all religions are essentially the same, and just as able to afford salvation to their adherents. Called "indifferentism," it was condemned by Leo XII in 1824 (DS 2720). Gregory XVI (1831-46) confirmed this condemnation and added his own censure of "rationalism" — any idea that reason is the supreme arbiter of truth (DS 2730-32).[85] Gregory also condemned a number of the propositions of Georg Hermes (1775-1831), a Catholic who tried to reconcile Christianity and Kant (DS 2738-40).

This was only the beginning. In 1854, the same year he proclaimed the doctrine of the Immaculate Conception, (*Ineffabilis Deus,* DS 2800-04), Pius IX (1846-78) issued his own condemnation of indifferentism (*Singulari Quadam* DS 2866). (His, however, did specify that the Church's teaching on salvation outside the Church did not apply to people living before or far from Christian truth, in "invincible ignorance," as Pius called it.) Then, in 1864, Pius issued a sweeping "Syllabus" of all

---

84. See especially his *Thus Spoke Zarathrustra.*
85. Gregory is also remembered for his condemnation of the ideas of Fèlicité Robert de Lamennais (1782-1854). Lamennais was a churchman who nonetheless argued for the separation of Church and state. Lamennais argued against any law that gave preference to an official state religion.

the errors which his predecessors and he had previously condemned (DS 2901-80).[86] He denounced deism, pantheism, and denials of the historical character of the Scriptures. Also condemned was materialism (DS 2958). The syllabus even condemned socialism in all its forms, especially communism (DS 2891).[87]

The syllabus did not stem the tide of intellectual disaffection with the faith. Indeed, if anything, the sweeping condemnations only served to fan the fires of discontent among the educated of the era. And this was not the Church's only problem. The forces in favor of a separation of Church and state had succeeded in gaining the repeal of statutes requiring affiliation with the official faith — even in Italy. There, these same forces were working for unification of the country. They were busy mustering the military force which would wrest political control of the "Papal States" from the pope.[88] Despite this threat — or because of it — Pius IX called for an ecumenical council to meet in the Vatican. This First Vatican Council met from 1869-70.

The council began at the beginning. First, it reaffirmed the traditional teaching on God, His attributes and, to contradict the popularity of various forms of pantheism, the absolute distinction between Himself and His creatures (DS 3001). It reaffirmed that God had created all things material and spiritual. In the face of materialism, the council specifically insisted that God had created things that were purely spiritual, the angels and human souls (3002). (Materialism was eventually to be condemned by name, 3022.) To contradict the popularity of deism, the council insisted that events were directed by divine providence (3003).

With this, the council fathers turned to epistemological questions. They affirmed not only the possibility but the certainty of a natural knowledge of God (3004). This was a response not only to the atheists, but also the "fideists" who, disturbed by the theological struggles, denied that faith had its rational basis. In response to the rationalists, the fathers insisted that divine revelation was necessary for the knowledge of certain truths (3005). Then, they redeclared that revelation was safely preserved in the inspired, inerrant Scriptures and also Tradition (3006) as explained by the magisterium. (3007).

86. Pius' first catalog of errors was contained in the letter *Qui Pluribus* (DS 2775-86) which he issued during the first year of his pontificate.
87. Communism had already been condemned in Pius' earlier document *Quanta Cura* (DS 2890-96).
88. The "Papal States" were the last vestiges of the territory whose political administration had fallen to the Church after the fall of Rome. Consisting of the land around Rome all the way across the Italian peninsula, they were both a political and geographical obstacle to the Italian unification movement led by the patriots Mazzini, Cavor and Garibaldi.

The council also reasserted the supernatural origin of faith (3008). Though it maintained that faith has its rational basis in miracles and prophecies (3009), it still insisted that faith requires grace (3010) which is meant to give faith in Church teaching (3011) which is necessary for salvation (3012). The council insisted that faith and reason cannot contradict each other (3017) but, since they originate in God, the one author of all truth, they support one another (3019).

Of all the teachings the council issued, none has received more attention than its teaching on the papacy.[89] Declaring that the church was founded upon Peter as its earthly head (3053-55), it insisted that his authority was passed on to his successors as bishop of Rome (3056-58). Thus, the bishop of Rome has supreme authority over the universal Church (3059-64). Therefore, God guarantees that whenever he speaks for the Church as pope (*ex cathedra*) on a matter of faith or morals, he is infallible (3065-75).

Shortly thereafter, the imminent invasion of Italian unification forces caused the council to adjourn. As it happened, the papal forces were defeated and the Papal States were incorporated into a united Italy. In response, the pope took up a self-proclaimed exile behind the walls of the Vatican. There he and his successors remained until 1929 when Pius XI and the Italian government (under Mussolini) reached the agreement in which the papacy recognized the legitimacy of the government in exchange for Italy's recognition that the Vatican would remain outside its jurisdiction, an independent nation.

* * *

As is known to history, the teachings of the First Vatican Council did not end the intellectual disaffection with Catholicism. Indeed, it was only to continue at an accelerating pace. Part of a much larger problem, an ever increasing percentage of the educated sector was finding no use for any form of Christianity — or religion. The rest of society, however, was largely unaffected. There were still faithful and there were *more* faithful than ever before. The age of exploration had been followed by a veritable explosion of missionary activity, especially Catholic, particularly in South America. To the minds of most churchmen, all was well enough; the Church was still at the center of people's lives and soon the modern heresies would go the way of so many before them and the Church would resume its rightful place at the uncontested forefront of world leadership.

89. Not only from without but from within, the papacy was under attack. Still remembering the independence that their Church had enjoyed during the revolution, certain French theologians had proposed the idea that national churches should govern themselves. Called "Gallicanism," it was another form of Anglicanism (cf. p. 107).

Chapter IV: The Impact of Evolution

Section I: The Theory of Evolution

Even as Vatican I was taking place, the scientific debate was settling the future of a theory that was soon to change everything.

A) A Sketch of the History of Evolution

As the "Introduction" made mention, Anaximander had spoken of evolution by the 7th century B.C. Sharing the common Greek conviction that reality is "one"(cf. p. 59), he concluded that the various species must be the diversifications of one primordial prototype. Since no one had seen this happen he further concluded that the process of diversification must have been a gradual one, a process of evolution.

Like materialism, evolution was not popular with Greek thinkers. They did not see the need for such a theory. The rise of Christianity put the issue firmly to rest. There it remained until the modern period.[1] Then, with the conviction that there is always a natural explanation, thinkers again began to wonder about the diversity of species, especially in light of their similarity. Once again, gradual change, evolution appeared to be the only natural explanation.

Gradual change clearly appeared to be nature's way. Georges Buffon (1707-88) the "father" of geology, offered evidence of the "evolution" of the earth.[2] (He was also the first to offer scientific evidence that the earth was much older than the biblically based figure of several *thousand* years.) Perhaps it is surprising that Immanuel Kant offered a theory of evolution of the heavens. Now that Galileo had proved that stars are other "suns," Kant said that they were the result of the mutual gravitation of matter in space.[3] The idea of mutual gravitation was Newton's; so too was the invention of the prism that would eventually make possible the spectroscopic discovery that stars are collections of hydrogen (cf. footnote p. 139).

Progress in the study of living things also argued for evolution. The comparative analyses of animals and plants, especially the life's work of

---

1. Actually, it should be acknowledged that even so orthodox a churchman as Duns Scotus had wondered whether some diversification of primitive species might explain the emerging awareness that there were many more species than could have fit, two by two, into an ark of imaginable size.
2. See his *Geology.*
3. See his *Natural History of the Heavens.*

Carl Linnaeus (1707-78),[4] appeared to prove that all were related. Evolution was even observed in the fact that the species fit into a pattern of ascending structural complexity. All that was needed was a theory to explain it.

Such theories were soon suggested. Among the most discussed was that of Jean-Baptist Lamarck (1744-1829). Observing that complex creatures are distinguished by their possession of parts or powers which are *useful* to them, he declared that the use of any internal structure strengthens it, causing it to develop, while its disuse will weaken it, causing it to disappear. Then, when a given improvement is possessed by both sexes of a pair that mate, they pass it on to their offspring.[5] Where the demands of different environments led to the use of different parts or powers, the diversification of species took place. For example, because the only available food was in the trees, to eat, the forerunners of modern giraffes had to crane. Thus did they develop long necks.

B) Darwinism

Lamarck's theory did not strike scientists as sufficient to explain evolution. For one thing, Lamarck did not explain how the use of a certain structure could result in a development that could be passed on to an offspring who had never used this structure. It appeared that another explanation for evolution was needed. Here Charles Darwin stepped into history.

Darwin was born in 1809. In 1825, he took up the study of biology with an eye on a career in medicine. In time, however, biology became a self-sustaining interest and Darwin became a biologist. In 1831, he made his now famous voyage to South America on the *Beagle*. It was during this expedition and, in particular, his visit to the Galápagos Islands, that he discovered certain species of birds found nowhere else. Unable to understand how this could be, he was moved to consider evolution as an explanation for the origin of species.

He was immediately sympathetic to Lamarck's idea that the environment was the principal cause of evolution. After all, what else could explain the existence of species particular to a place? But, he also agreed with his scientific colleagues who were unconvinced that Lamarck had supplied a plausible explanation of the way the environment spurs this process.

Amid his reflections, in 1838, Darwin remembered the *Essay on Population* by Thomas Malthus (1766-1834). In this work, the author

4. See his *Systema Naturae*.
5. See his *Philosophie zoologique*.

observed that all creatures, including man, are constantly engaged in a struggle for survival because their population grows "geometrically," as the many offspring of a single couple each bear many offspring while the available food to feed them increases only "arithmetically," as limited resourses are only somewhat better exploited. In other words, despite the geometric growth of population, there are only so many trees in which to find food, only so much land to farm.

Malthus provided Darwin with the idea he needed. If creatures must compete for a limited supply of food, only the strongest, the fastest, the smartest will survive. A disparity of gifts is given to any litter. Nature selects the survival of only the "fittest."

It was now obvious how evolution took place. Having won the struggle for survival, only the fittest mated to pass on their natal strengths. Over the course of many generations, this saw to the steady structural improvement of the species. It eventually led to the development of entirely new structures as old ones so improved as to be able to do new things. Naturally, different environments favored the development of different strengths and, therefore, the eventual development of whole new species. The evidence was accounted for.

For some twenty years, Darwin gathered evidence to support his theory, and to elaborate it, extending its ability to explain particular phenomena in greater and greater detail. Then, on July 1, 1858, sparked by Alfred Wallace, a biologist whose studies had brought him to confirm Darwin's conclusions, he reluctantly[6] presented his theory to the Linnaean Society in London. A year later he published *On the Origin of Species by Means of Natural Selection*.

In light of the changing attitude towards man, it should not be surprising that Darwin did not doubt that evolution explains man. Man is subject to natural laws like everything else. He bears a definite resemblance to other animals both structurally and behaviorally. He bears a striking resemblance to the family of primates. Undoubtedly, he is a member of this family sharing the same ancestors. In 1871, the same year that the pope was declared infallible, Darwin published *The Descent of Man* which stated this explicitly.

---

6. Darwin had correctly anticipated the controversy that his theory would create and he was admittedly afraid to be the center of it. Prior to the discoveries of Alfred Wallace, he had decided to publish his theory posthumously.

Section II: The Conflict of Christianity and Evolution

A) The Conflict

We have already seen the reasons that evolution was bound to be perceived as a threat to Christianity. It appeared to contradict the Bible. It did not appear to require God. And, finally, in speaking of the emergence of a higher from a lower, it certainly seemed to support the materialist's contention that there is nothing in man that cannot be reduced to matter in motion. Christians were horrified, Catholics included.

Let there be no mistake. The Church had always taken Genesis literally. The first Christians would not have known how else to take it. The Fathers frequently referred to the six days of the creation.(Augustine explained that God chose *six* days because six is the *perfect* number; both the addition and multiplication of its factors, 1, 2 and 3 equal itself.[7])The scholastics were just as sure; according to the *Roman Martyrology,* genealogies and other scriptural information indicated that the universe was created in 5199 B.C.[8]

Protestants were even more commited to biblical liberalism. The Bible was their sole source of truth. If it was wrong, where did that leave them?

B) The Church's Initial Response to Evolution

1. *Uncritical Objections*

Mention has already been made of the deluge of denunciation that met the publication of *The Origin of Species.*

Samuel Wilberforce, Anglican bishop of Oxford, wrote that "the principle of evolution is absolutely incompatible with the Word of God."[9] Various others declared that "Darwinism is an attempt to dethrone God... which does open violence to everything the Creator has told us in the scriptures of the methods and results of His work... If the Darwinian theory is true, Genesis is a lie and the whole framework of the book of life falls to pieces, and the revelation of God to man as we know it is a delusion and a snare."

7. See his *De Genesi ad Letteram,* 4, 2.

8. Anglican biblical scholar John Lightfoot (1602-75) determined that the universe was created in 4004 B.C. on October 1, at exactly 9:00 A.M. G.M.T.

9. All of the following condemnations of evolution were compiled by Andrew Dickson White in his remarkably comprehensive study *A History of the Warfare of Science and Theology in Christendom.* Published in 1898, the work was itself an important contributor to the struggle.

Henry Cardinal Manning (1808-92), Archbishop of Westminster, declared that Darwin's theory is a "brutal philosophy [in which] there is no God and the ape is our Adam." When, in 1877, a certain Dr. Consantin James wrote a refutation of *The Origin of Species*, Pius IX wrote to commend him stating that Darwinism is a "system which is at once repugnant to history, to the tradition of all peoples, to exact science, to observed facts and even to reason itself."

As was stated, most of the denunciations involved a caricature of the theory, the most common involving the idea that one fine day two monkeys gave birth to a human baby. Always, it was argued that the theory was inadmissible because it contradicted the Bible and the Faith.

2. *Scholastic Objections*

Not all of the objections were so uncritical. From the rational heads of certain churchmen came criticism much more challenging. Invoked were a number of scholastic principles:

1) Evolution is impossible because it violates the principle that a higher cannot come from a lower. Nothing can give what it does not have.

2) Evolution is impossible because it would involve a virtually infinite number of immaterial forms. Finally,

3) Evolution is impossible because it describes an imperfect creation filled with species destined for extinction. This is incompatible with belief in a perfect and all-good God.

3. *Scientific Objections*

Churchmen also made use of objections to Darwin's theory raised by respected members of the scientific community.

1) Having the scientific passion for proof, they questioned whether Darwin had really supported his theory with sufficient evidence. Though Darwin did offer impressive evidence of the evolution of certain minor traits, it was by no means clear that this evidence could support the global claims which he made. In particular,

2) Many scientists did not see how the gradual strengthening of a given structure could ever lead to the development of a totally — functionally — new structure. Natural selection could easily explain the development of taller trees or faster rabbits, but how could it explain the development of the eye? After all, the eye is nothing like anything else in the body; it is *very* sophisticated; and it would not have been of any use until it was in good working order. (Darwin himself admitted that the eye caused him considerable consternation.) Furthermore,

3) Lamarck was criticized because he did not explain the way in which improvements were passed on. But, Darwin did not explain the way in

which improvements were created. In the absence of such explanation, how could any evolutionary theory impose its picture on reality? Finally,

4) It seemed that there are too many missing links. But, it also seemed that there are too many species, especially simpler ones.

Section III: Increasing Pressure from Old Problems

A) The Continuing Decline of Confidence in the Scriptures

Despite the objections, Darwin's theory of evolution still appealed to the scientifically minded of his day. The scientific objections did not seem to present unresolvable problems for what was otherwise a sensible solution to a question never before answered. The other objections were not perceived to have any validity at all. This was particularly true of the principal obstacle to its acceptance — the Scriptures. Confidence in the Scriptures was still on the decline.

1. The Old Testament

For the most part, the question of the credibility of the Old Testament was already closed; the theory of evolution was simply icing on the proverbial cake. For all of the reasons that have already been stated, most of the educated elite were already convinced that the Old Testament was the product of a primitive people's need for stories with which to explain the world and themselves. Its continuing study only made them more certain.

Students of the text like Julius Wellenhausen (1844-1918) all but proved that the Pentateuch was indeed the result of the weaving together of several more primitive documents.[10]

Historical studies all but proved that each of these documents was written from the hindsight of many centuries. For example, Edouard Reuss (1804-91) observed that the law spoke to a long-settled society and would not have made sense to the desert-wanderers to whom it had supposedly been given. Inspired by such discoveries, men like Hermann Gunkel (1862-1932) gave rigorous scientific form to the idea that all the Old Testament writings were the product of a long period of oral and written tradition.

Moreover, as scholars continued to study the other peoples of the ancient Near East, they began to conclude that not only were the Hebrew

---

10. Wellenhausen's "documentary" theory was so supported by literary evidence that the general idea was no longer disputed by reputable scholars.

writings myths, they were mostly borrowed. Textural evidence was immediately available. For example, the "nephilim" (also translated "titans") of Genesis (6:4) were discovered to be the very un-Hebrew half-god, half-men described in the writings of much more ancient cultures. Then, in 1876, in the successful translation of recently discovered Babylonian inscriptions, George Smith (1856-1906) apparently proved that all of Genesis had been borrowed. In *The Gilgamesh Epic,* the older Babylonians also described the earth as a void. "Marduk" separated the water from dry land. He created the first man, Gilgamesh, from clay. Gilgamesh also fell from grace and was punished with death. His descendants were almost wiped out by a great flood; the descendants of the survivors were thwarted in their attempt to build a tower to heaven.[11] Not unlike Moses, Sargon was saved by being sent down a river in a basket. (But the "Law" was given to King Hammurabi.)

The Hittites claimed that God offered *them* a covenant. The Sumerians claimed that God ordained *their* monarchy. All these peoples had their prophets.

And all these peoples had their gods, i.e. a god of their own — at least one. Nonetheless, they also accepted the existence of other people's gods — occasionally they even worshipped them. By their own confession, the Hebrews were no different. Actually, the Egyptian cult of Aton (c. 1400 B.C.) was "monotheistic" long before the Judaism of later history.

Of course, the most incriminating evidence against the historicity of the Old Testament remained the modern sensitivity to the fact that there was almost no evidence to support any of its most remarkable claims. For example, archeology offered no evidence of the ten terrible plagues that supposedly devastated Egypt.

Archeology even offered positive evidence that the Bible was wrong; for example, during Abraham's time, there were no Chaldeans (Gen. 11:28).

2. The New Testament
Study also continued to undermine confidence in the New Testament.

The study of the text led William Wrede (1859-1906) to his famous conclusion that Mark's gospel was a literary work meant to be a gradual revelation of the fact that Jesus was the messiah.[12] This was the birth of "redaction criticism," the scientific study of the ways in which the

11. Modern linguistics had already ridiculed the idea that all the world's languages derive from Hebrew (cf. footnote p. 64).
12. See his *The Messenic Secret of the Gospel.*

theologies of each of the evangelists had affected their use of available material. This study all but proved the synoptic theory of gospel formation, confirming the fact that the gospels were the product of tradition.

The probable effects of this process were scientifically formulated in what Johannes Weiss (1863-1914) called "form criticism." This study all but proved that the gospels were the product of theology and exaggeration. (Actually, according to men like Adolf Harnack (1851-1940), theology *is* exaggeration; it is a forced, philosophical addition to the gospel message.[13])

Historical studies also appeared to verify the thesis that the first Christians had help in the formulation of their faith. Most disturbing was the accumulating evidence indicating that much of what was supposed to be unique about Christianity had its predecessor, or parallel, in what Richard Reitzenstein (1861-1931) called the Hellenistic "mystery" religions.[14] It had become clear that in the Near East of Jesus' time, there was no shortage of salvific cults founded by divine humans. Alexander of Abonoteichos was also called the "Son of God." Apollonius of Tyana was raised from the dead; his disciples swore to it. So did the disciples of Attis; he was raised three days after he was put to death. Under scrutiny, many aspects of the community life of the early church resembled that of the "Essenes," a community with rigorous moral standards who separated themselves from the Judaism of Jesus' day.[15] The cult of Mithras practiced a form of worship which closely resembled the Eucharist.

The wider study of "Comparative Religion" was also disconcerting. Confucius had rendered a negative formulation of the "golden rule" (do not do to others what you would not have them do to you) over five hundred years before Christ. Zoroaster had predicted a virgin-born savior. Krishna is the re-occuring incarnation of Vishna, one of the three principal personalities of the essentially impersonal Hindu God. The Mahayana Buddhists believe that there have been many Buddhas, each an incarnation of "karma," the law that orders the universe. Moreover, the continued study of the religious experience of the pious people of all faiths revealed a deep spirituality that was both rich in content and reflected itself in conduct quite holy by Christian standards. There were many Muslim martyrs — many died at the hands of Christians.

---

13. See his *The History of Dogma.*
14. See his *The Hellenistic Mystery Religions.*
15. The Essenes were the people who preserved the Dead Sea Scrolls. Discovered in 1947, the scrolls proved that history had inherited a very ancient text of the Old Testament.

Even the study of geography provided problems. Despite the testimony of Mk.7:31, Tyre is *South* of Sidon.

* * *

With a summary of all that modern scholarship had uncovered, Albert Schweitzer (1875-1965) was moved to declare that — Strauss was right (cf. p.130) — we cannot know the historical Jesus.[16]

Rudolph Bultmann (1884-1976) agreed; he insisted that the historical Jesus was lost beneath the faith of the first Christians. But, we can affirm *their* faith; in other words, we can have faith in their faith. This is Christianity's only hope.

3. An Addendum: Modernism

Bultmann's work was perhaps the ultimate manifestation of Liberalism (cf. p.130), a movement which was entirely Protestant in its proponents. With the continuing pressure of scientific progress, however, increasing numbers of Catholic thinkers were coming to the conclusion that they had to accept some of what it involved.

Concluding that the Scriptures did contain myths, these thinkers still insisted that these myths told religious truths. They were the first to claim that Genesis was meant to tell the truth of the fact of creation, not the means by which it was accomplished. In the defense of this idea, George Mivart (1827-1900) explained that once evolution had reached a certain point, God intervened in the direct creation of the first human soul.

Facing the challenge brought by men like Harnack, Alfred Loisy (1857-1940) explained that even though the Fathers, if not the Scriptures, reflect "additions" to the faith of the first Christians, if not the verbal teachings of Jesus Himself, they still took place under the guidance of the Spirit and were thereby revealed. In other words, even if Jesus did not explain His pre-existent Sonship — or was not even aware of it — or did not institute the sacraments, the Church's innovation of these ideas had revealed them. Now, Loisy argued, the Church must again "modernize" its doctrine under the guidance of scholarship.[17]

The "modernists" also held that moral theology must move away from absolutes. They held that right or wrong is actually to be determined by the unique set of circumstances that bear upon anyone's decisions.[18]

Modernism also called for changes in practice. Its proponents specifically insisted that the Church must move away from centraliziation

---

16. See his famous *The Quest for the Historical Jesus.*
17. See especially his *L'Evangile et L'Eglise.*
18. This idea was later to re-emerge under the mid-twentieth century title "situation ethics."

of authority and uniformity in worship.[19]

Not surprisingly, modernism met with condemnation. In 1900 — the first year of the twentieth century — the Inquisition(now called the"Holy Office") required Mivart to recant his attempt to reconcile evolution and creation. In 1907, in the encyclicals *Lamentabili* and *Pascendi,* Pius X (later St. Pius X, 1903-14) condemned modernism by name. The next year Loisy, already suspended from his teaching post, published a "reflection" on these encyclicals and was promptly excommunicated. One year later, the Pontifical Biblical Commission[20] declared that questioning the historical character of the Genesis account of creation — the creation of Adam out of dust, and from his rib, Eve, their life in the garden of Eden, and their fall at the temptation of a demon in the form of a serpent — was not "safe"(DS 3512-19). Finally, in 1910, Pius X decreed that all clerics must take an oath against modernism (DS 3537-50).

* * *

The oath against modernism did nothing to dissuade the scientist. And, it was still the scientific conclusion that Christianity was the product of human nature[21] just like every other religion.[22] To some, the natural origin of religious belief was reason for a "Religious Argument for the Existence of God." Most scientists, however, were more inclined to see the natural origin of religious belief — no matter how universal — in terms of ignorance and wishful thinking.

B) The Continuing Decline of Belief in God

1. The Fact

Evolution only accelerated the decline of belief in God.

In its apparent explanation of the origin of species — which would surely lead to an explanation of life — it gave credence to the idea that nature could account for itself.

Natural selection, working as it did through the struggle for existence and death, dramatized the fact that the world is not a place that would

19. According to the proponents of "Americanism," Church discipline should reflect the needs of local culture.

20. Founded by Leo in 1902, the Commission was charged with reviewing the results of scholarship with respect to orthodoxy.

21. See especially *The Varieties of Religious Experience* by William James (1842-1910). James is especially remembered for his idea that the "validity" of religious beliefs consists of whether they "work" for the person who professes them.

22. Ironically, even Christian studies of comparative religion appeared to support the idea that all religions are essentially similar. In *The Idea of the Holy,* Rudolf Otto (1869-1973) described the universal experience of God as an encounter with a "mystery" which is at once awesome and fascinating.

ever have been created by an all-good God. In other words, evolution made the problem of evil worse.

Furthermore, never before had the natural course of world events seemed more indifferent to man's well-being. Science was the only way to bring it under control. It was science that had transformed the world with the automobile, airplane, electric light, telephone and radio. It was the work of scientists, soldiers, politicians and businessmen — not the prayer of pietists — that would continue to make things happen.

Or, so it seemed to an increasing number of enlightened atheists.

Seeing life as an opportunity, and a challenge, and accepting it for its own sake, and not for some heavenly reward, the enlightened atheist was himself accepting reality. The religious showed their true colors in their irrational reaction to evolution; they were cowards who could not accept death, or even life.

2. Developments in Philosophy

a. Positivism

The source of enlightened atheism, scientism was finally formulated by philosophers.

The "positivists," also known as the "Vienna Circle," brought together by Ernst Mach (1838-1916), taught that reason is strict adherence to the dictates of "logic." Always considered the self-evident principles by which inferences are evaluated,[23] the positivists insisted that logic means that every statement is either true or false with nothing in between.[24]

In the wisdom of science, the positivists insisted that no statement is true unless it can pass the empirical criterion — a test with sensible results which is open to the inspection of several observers. The positivists also insisted that no statement can even be called true unless it can be tested, at least in principle. In other words, the statement: "There is life on Mars" can be true because we can imagine how the statement might be tested, and, one day, it probably will be. But, the statement: "There is a God" cannot be true because there is no way in which this statement could ever be tested, even in principle.

Charles Peirce (1839-1914), a thinker largely unknown during his lifetime, took the principle a significant step further. Troubled by the constant confusion and disagreement about what statements really mean, Peirce was concerned to provide a criterion not only for truth but

23. According to Aristotle, the basis of logic is the "law of non-contradiction": nothing can be what it is not in the same way at the same time.
24. See especially his *Science of Mechanics*.

for meaningfulness. He insisted that the meaning of a statement can only be discussed in terms of the "practical consequences" of its truth or falsity. Thus, the meaning of the statement "This is hard" consists of whether or not the object will hold up under a pre-agreed pressure. But, what about the statement "There is a God"? How do we determine the meaning of such a statement? In the absence of a way to be clear about what the statement means, it is actually *meaningless*.[25]

Peirce came to be considered the founder of "pragmatism," a philosophy better known for its quasi-ethical recommendation to "do what works."

b. Linguistic Philosophy

Soon after the positivists opened up the question of "meaning," a specialized discipline calling itself "linguistic philosophy" took the question to its supposedly logical conclusion. Originating in the work of Ludwig Wittgenstein (1889-1951), linguistic philosophy concluded that most of the great philosophical problems were the result of the mis-use of language.[26] According to Wittgenstein, words derive meaning from two sources: 1) things: the objects, characteristics, or actions to which they refer, and 2) the language system which relates words that refer to things. We get into trouble when we take things out of context or try to find a meaning for a word apart from the way in which it is meant to be used in the system. For example, we ask an improper question if we ask "what" is time. According to the system, "time" relates to "when"; it does not relate to "what." Thus, the question "what is time" has been a philosophical problem for nothing. So have most of the major philosophical problems.

Linguistic philosophy following Wittgenstein went one step further. Insisting that name-words refer to something one can point to, they pointed out that words like "God" have no reference. Barely definable even by those who use them, these words are really meaningless.

3. An Addendum: Agnosticism

At this point in the discussion, it should be stated that the actual rise of modern atheism hardly involved the smooth and orderly passage from one idea to the next which the systematic presentation of these ideas might have suggested. Actually, the reasons for disbelief differed from person to person. And they emerged only slowly. Only painfully did increasing numbers come to realize that there was more to the issue than they may have wanted to believe. But, for most of these people,

---

25. See especially his *How to Make our Ideas Clear.*
26. See his *Tractatus Logico-Philosophicus.*

this was experienced *not* as the embrace of atheism in a positive sense, but as doubt.

Naturally, as doubt increased, so did the reluctance to identify oneself as a believer. Thus, increasing numbers became increasingly willing to say that they did not know if there is a God. They described themselves as "agnostic." Moreover, affected by the rise of skepticism, increasing numbers were becoming increasingly convinced that they could not know if there is a God — that the existence of God is in principle unknowable. This was the original meaning of the word "agnosticism" when it was coined by Aldous Huxley (1894-1963).

C) The Continuing Decline of Confidence that Man is Something Special

Although the decline of belief in God spread steadily,[27] the decline of confidence that man is something special did not follow at quite the same rate. Some resisted the idea that man is simply an object of scientific study, a machine, no more than matter in motion. Indeed, this idea generated a counter-reaction, a multi-faceted movement later known as the "Romantic Revolt." First manifest in music — in the transition from Bach to Beethoven to Brahms, in literature — in the works of Byron, Keats and Shelley, and in the painting of the Impressionists, this movement asserted the emotional, supposedly neglected side of human existence, and proclaimed the richness of the human spirit. It implicitly begged for a stop to the continuing dissection of man under the knives of many sciences. But the scientists had just begun. Psychology led the way.

1. Progress in Psychology
a. The Latest Developments

Through the work of Wilhelm Wundt (1832-1920), the nascent science of psychology began to acquire a vocabulary all its own. Wundt was the founder of the "structuralist" school which dealt with the mind as a whole, describing it in terms of the nature and inter-relatedness of various processes. Particular attention was devoted to the processes

---

27. Actually, the steady decline of belief in God was occasionally punctuated by periods of religious "revival." Mostly conservative Protestant, revival movements followed wars or other social upheavals and declined with the restoration of social stability. A major revival followed World War I and this one came complete with apologetics. The work of Karl Barth (1886-1968), it was a repudiation of the liberal Protestant embrace of science and called for a return to the reformers' idea that original sin had corrupted man's reason and left him helpless but to have faith.

involved in sense perception, reflexes (q.v. p.251), and learning (especially memory).

Soon thereafter, Sigmund Freud (1856-1939) opened up a whole new field of psychological study. Using hypnosis in order to treat people suffering from inexplicable psychological illnesses, Freud discovered the "subconscious."[28] Concluding that all behavior is rooted in the subconscious, he specifically explained that behavior results from the interplay of the "id" (the source of all desires, the fundamental of which is sexual, the "ego" (the person conscious of what he knows) and the "super-ego" (the principally subconscious influence of societal expectations). Not surprisingly, Freud was completely convinced that the interplay of these forces was completely determined.

Freud's psychology became the first of many, rather bold attempts to explain everything with just a few principles. Following Freud, both Alfred Adler (1870-1937) and Carl Jung (1875-1961) saw the subconscious as the principal source of behavior though they differed with Freud, and with each other, as to the fundamental desire. Adler said it was the desire to avoid the feeling of "inferiority" experienced as guilt; Jung said it was the desire for survival, the function of what he called the "libido."[29] William McDonald (1871-1938) was the first to suggest what would eventually become the popular thesis that man is motivated by a "hierarchy of desires." As he satisfies his most fundamental desire (which is probably survival), he moves on to "higher" needs which bespeak the extent of his psychological development.

In the retrospect of history, it should not be surprising that disagreement was to cause a critique of psychological method. This, together with the fact that human experience was impossible to describe in "positivistic" terms, led James Watson (1878-1958) to insist that the only data of psychological study is observable behavior and the circumstances which bring it about. Watson was the founder of the "behaviorist" school of psychology; it was devoted to the correlation of "stimulus" and "response." Needless to say, this approach had no room for free will.

Even before behaviorism was explicitly formulated, evidence was being gathered to support its most deterministic claims. Experimenting with the sequences of stimuli that could bring about certain behaviors, Ivan Pavlov (1849-1936) "conditioned" his dogs to expect that they

---

28. See especially his *The Interpretation of Dreams.*
29. Jung is also remembered for his platonic-sounding theory that all men are born with certain primitive ideas which he called "archetypes."

would be fed at the sound of a bell. As the experiments proved, the dogs began to salivate — before seeing the food — whenever he rang the bell.

The behaviorists insisted that a person is conditioned by the events of his past — the cause of his every response to a new one. Disinterested in the unknown world of the mind, they came to insist that the mind contributed nothing but the simple instinct to avoid pain and to perpetuate pleasure as informed by some power to associate similar events.

To the minds of other psychologists, the behaviorist's simplification of psychology appeared to neglect the experienced complexity of mental life. In what amounted to a rebirth of structuralism, "gestalt" (in German, literally "shape") psychology returned to a study of the whole. This led to the development of "personality" theories which described the characteristics and causes of specified "types."

Although the personality theorists saw man as quite complicated, they still contributed to the growing confidence that human behavior is indeed the product of natural causes which determine every human act.

b. Sociology

The attempts to explain human behavior were not long in leading to the realization that "society" was a major contributor. This led to the realization that not only does society influence the individual, but society predictably infuences itself in ways that can be studied. Specifically called "sociology" for the first time by Auguste Comte, it was Herbert Spencer (1820-1903) who created the categories that gave this discipline a character of its own.

Continuing study showed that society is subject to a form of evolution.

This was reason enough for sociology to draw a negative reaction from religious leaders. Soon there was even more. Religion was among the societal realities to attract the interest of sociologists. According to Emile Durkheim (1858-1917) religion is the product of a society's desire for identity.[30] Known as "totemism," Durkheim's theory was only the first of many which attempted to explain religious phenomena — particularly ritual and priesthood — in terms of social dynamisms having nothing to do with the ordination of any god.

2. Progress in the Biological Sciences

If the progress in psychology appeared to confirm what was already believed about determinism, progress in the biological sciences surely seemed to give evidence of the materialism by which this determinism was

---

30. See his *Elementary Forms of Religious Life.*

now explained.

Studies in anatomy continued to uncover evidence that the body is a machine, albeit a machine of fantastic complexity. Harvey's discovery of the circulatory system (cf. p. 140) was followed by the description of the respiratory, digestive, and nervous systems. That the body appears to have very few moving parts was now explained by the way it works through chemistry, bio-chemistry.

The brain was the object of particularly important studies. Discovered to involve the chemistry of electricity, electro-sensitive instruments were now used in order to identify the structures involved in each of its different abilities. Soon, it was actually being "mapped" with the areas involved in the various forms of sense perception and motor control especially well-identified. Though much remained a mystery, it still appeared that it would be no more than a matter of time before physiology could explain every aspect of mental life.

Meanwhile, progress was also providing a material explanation of the function of the cells which make up the brain and every other living thing. Studies in both plant and animal physiology began to yield the identification of a variety of internal cell structures. Of special importance was the discovery of the cell "nucleus" whose role in the integration of the cell's internal activity was also observed to initiate the "division" by which cells reproduce themselves. Not only did this complement the mechanistic explanation of cell life, it described a mechanism which could explain the way that parents pass their particularities on to their offspring. This was more than helpful to the idea of evolution.

Actually, the study of "heredity" was already in progress. Gregor Mendel (1822-84), a priest, observed that there was a predictable pattern to the way in which the peculiarities of the bean plants in his garden were passed on to those of their progeny. This led Francis Galton (1822-1911) to develop the concept of "genes" — cellular structures which contain the seeds of certain traits and must be involved in the processes of reproduction. It was August Weismann (1834-1914) who penetrated the cell nucleus to discover the "chromosomes" which contained the genes that Galton had predicted. Evolutionists were delighted with the discovery that the genetic "code" is the same in all creatures.

The discovery of chromosomes did not end the analysis of cells. It was soon to be discovered that individual cell parts were made of "amino" acids. By the 1950's, when Crick and Watson explained reproduction in terms of the structure of DNA,[31] the structure and function of most of the

31. Deoxyribonucleic acid, the particular amino acid out of which chromosomes are made.

other cell parts were already known.

Together with contemporary developments relating chemistry and physics, it appeared that the sciences *had* been reduced to physics, and that human life had been reduced to the motion of matter.

Section IV: The Inevitability of Evolution

A) The Accumulation of Evidence

Despite the increasing pressure of all the old problems, it is by no means clear that Christianity would ever have accepted evolution were it not for the accumulation of evidence which supported it directly.

1. Biological Evidence

The following biological evidence had come to be all but universally accepted by those who were qualified to evaluate it:

1) All living things can be grouped into the broader and broader categories that surely betray their common ancestry. In other words, each category, such as "mammal," represents the ancient creature that first developed something different, in this case, warm blood.

2) The classification of creatures clearly forms an ascending chain of beings which reveals the improvement of something inherited which is quite similar to something still possessed by a "lower" creature. The human hand is the most obvious example of this phenomenon.

3) There are "vestigial" organs — inherited remains of an organ once important but now unused. For example, certain cave creatures bear the remains of eyes even though they have never seen light; the human coccyx is undoubtedly the remainder of a tail bone.

4) Embryology has observed that from conception to physical maturity, many creatures pass through what is now recognized as the prior stages of their evolutionary development. For example, the human embryo grows and then loses a tail. As a "tadpole," the frog-to-be passes through its ancestral existence as a fish.

5) Certain species are unique to isolated areas. Obviously, they have evolved under the influence of local conditions. Darwin's birds are still the classic example of this phenomenon which has since been observed all over the globe.

6) Finally, there are fossils, not simply the remains of ancient creatures now extinct, like the dinosaurs, but the physical remains of creatures who were plainly the primitive forms of present-day species. What but evolution could possibly explain the skeletons of Peking, Java, Neanderthal, and Cro-Magnon man?

Of course, some did attempt alternative explanations, however ridiculous, for all the biological evidence. For example, some insisted that fossils are the remains of species not saved from the great flood. But the alternatives always involved too much that was not in evidence.

2. The Evidence of Nature

Even apart from the biological evidence, there was ample evidence that evolution is nature's way. Some form of evolution — of natural, gradual change — was seen to explain the present state of almost everything.

Modern astronomy (q.v. p.308) was confirming the evolutionary ideas of Kant and others. It described the mutual gravitation of hydrogen and its ignition in star birth. It described the exhausting of a star's hydrogen and the attendant explosions which create the so-called "heavy" atoms that are spewed out in star death. It described the coming-together of these atoms in the formation of planets. Modern geology provided proof[32] that the earth is about five billion years old and has evolved through many "ages."

Notably, just as astronomical and geological evolution were linked in a description of the birth of planets, geological and biological evolution were linked in a description of the origin of life. Geological evolution described the origin of the chemical "soup" which characterized the earth's earliest ages. It was this soup that bred the amino acids which were now known to be the building-blocks of life. Biology provided several theories to explain their origin, together with sensible, if general, theories of the way in which the complexification of their structure might have led to the first cell. The discovery of the "virus" — which bears some but not all of the distinctive characteristics of life — appeared to prove that some such theory was true. The discovery of single-cell organisms (like the Amoeba) had already supplied a link in the explanation of the origin of multi-cell creatures.

Still debated was (and is) the question of whether animals came from plants (the "autotroph" hypothesis) or developed independently (the "heterotroph" hypothesis).

The generally accepted time-table was (and is) as follows:

About two billion years ago, amino acids began to form. The first cells appeared about a billion years later. By 500 million B.C., there were multi-cell sea-creatures; by 250 million, the first land-creatures had emerged. By 75 million, mammals had developed; primates appeared at

---

32. The "proof" was actually provided by chemistry. The discovery that carbon decays ever so slowly, but dependably, makes possible the "dating" of anything that contains carbon.

about 40 million. The first "hominids" (creatures who walked upright and had an "opposable" thumb) date from about 4 million. By 2 million, "Homo Habilis" had appeared. At 1 million, he was succeeded by "Homo Erectus." Modern man, "Homo Sapiens" dates from about 250,000 B.C.[33]

Evolution was even seen in the development of man's personality while the progress of society is clearly analogous to that of the individual.

Societal progress has also involved a direction describable in its own terms:

Slowly man moved from food-gathering to food-production. (This allowed for leisure, and learning.) Meanwhile, he had learned to make and use simple stone tools. This was the Early Stone Age; it is reckoned to have ended about 15,000 B.C. By then, man had also developed language. From then to about 10,000 B.C., the Middle Stone Age, he developed writing. He also learned to make and use complex tools and he used them to build the first free-standing structures. By about 5000 B.C., the New Stone Age, he began to live in cities. About a thousand years later, he learned to extract metal and an Age of Copper had begun. Within a thousand years, it was succeeded by an Age of Bronze. The Iron Age began about 1000 B.C. By then, human history had become history.

Even apart from the evidence that evolution is nature's way, the following are also to be observed:

1) Nature should be expected to work through gradual change. Gradual change involves dynamisms that are still seen to be at work. And, in the graduality of the way they work, they can most easily be imagined to have done all that is reputed of them. Finally,

2) As a *natural* theory, evolution accounts for the data postulating as little out of our experience as possible. It provides a natural explanation where once there was none. It answers the ancient, pre-scientific demand for some explanation of life in its diversity which was once satisfied with a story that is not supported by nearly sufficient evidence to warrant its extraordinary claims.

B) New Ways to Explain Evolution

In addition to the accumulation of evidence, the credibility of evolution was also supported by the suggestion of new ways to explain it.

We have already examined the question of whether natural selection is sufficient to explain all that has supposedly happened (cf. p. 156). As we saw, though most of Darwin's colleagues did agree that natural selection played a significant role in the development of individual species, there

---

33. Cro-magnon man disappeared about 25,000 B.C.

was no such agreement that this one dynamism could explain all the complex structures of which creatures consist. The problem of the development of what was functionally new, such as the eye, etc., was especially perplexing. Something more than natural selection was needed.

1. DeVries

The first important theory to complement natural selection was advanced by Hugo DeVries (1848-1935). A student of the new science of genetics, he discovered that the transmission of traits from parents to offspring did not always result in the transmission of traits which either of the parents possessed. Sometimes something went wrong. Speaking of the accidents as "chance mutations," he held that they accelerate natural selection inasmuch as they produce wholly new characteristics which would only be passed on if they proved helpful to the creature who possessed them.

Subsequent studies in cell physiology identified the various ways in which chance mutations can take place. Thus, DeVries' theory was not only supported as an explanation of the generation of evolutionary improvements, it was supplied with an explanation of the way in which these improvements — at least those generated by the process of cell division — are passed on to succeeding generations.

2. Other Dynamisms

Not everyone was at all confident that chance mutation could complete the accounting for evolution. Continuing studies of mutation showed that it happened rather infrequently; even more rarely did it involve dramatic change. When it did, the resulting creature was usually sterile. Moreover, how plausible was it that mutations would just happen to produce the fantastically complex structures upon which even the simplest living things depend? How imaginable was it that they could account for such things as the brain and miles of well-placed wiring that make up the nervous system — what were the odds?

These were just some of the reasons that the credibility of evolution required the suggestion of other dynamisms that might have propelled it. Fortunately for evolution, others were available:

1) Apart from the struggle for a limited supply of food, natural selection was certainly spurred by other environmental circumstances such as climate,[34] or the presence of competitors or predators, etc.

---

34. Indeed, "neo-Darwinism" conceives of spurts of evolution spurred by major environmental changes such as the "ice ages" that have descended upon the earth every so often. Also called "punctuated equilibrium," neo-Darwinism contradicts the presumption that evolution is always taking place.

Moreover, natural selection was surely encouraged by certain developments unrelated to food-gathering, such as longevity or the ability to reproduce, which would obviously have had their effect on the survival of a species.

Besides, who knows whether special circumstances — that can no longer exist — favored the survival of certain species or their development of a certain trait?

Furthermore, reflection on the struggle for survival has led to the realization that nature is a system of very inter-related happenings. Not only do creatures co-exist, but they depend upon each other for their existence. For example, studies of the so-called "food-chain" have proved that the death of one species is the loss of the food for another and can lead to a disruption of the whole "ecology" (natural balance) of a given place. With this in mind, the fact that there are so many different species is easily explained; not only do they not compete, they complement one another. Of course, the fact that the similar species *do* compete — for the same food, territory, etc. — would seem an adequate explanation for the fact that there are missing links.

2) Studies of the theoretical history of life indicate that the present bespeaks a stability which was a long time in the making. Thus, though the earliest ages of life history are largely unknown, it is likely that there was a time when creatures were much more prone to change than they are now. Finally,

3) In the tradition of Lamarck, it is to be considered likely that science will one day discover a mechanism to explain the way (or ways) in which improvements gained during the lifetime of a creature — and were somehow invented by the path of progress — were somehow fed back into the structure of its chromosomes. Although no such mechanisms have yet been discovered, evidence that at least one does exist is often obtained experimentally, for example, in the experiments with rats who must learn their way around a maze but whose offspring know just where to go from birth. (What else would explain any animal instinct?) If one or several such mechanisms had developed, each would surely have become constitutive of living things. Who knows what they might be? Perhaps the answer will involve the fact that there is a constant "turn-over" in most of the cells which make up most creatures. Perhaps the life of the creature can affect this process. Though few scientists presently feel that they are even close to such a discovery, science has just begun its attempt to explain evolution.

C) Response to the Remaining Objections

1. Scientific Objections

The preceding sub-section spoke to many of the scientific objections that Darwin's theory initially elicited. Speaking primarily to the all-embracing objection from the apparent insufficiency of natural selection as Darwin explained it, the sub-section suggested a number of complementary dynamisms. Some also involved a response to the particular difficulty of imagining the evolution of an organ functionally new.

It is also to be stated that the difficulty in imagining the evolution of something functionally new often proceeds from a failure to appreciate the extent to which graduality is the very name of the process. Evolution involves a truly *inconceivable* time-scale, involving *billions* of years. There is little that would not seem possible of slow change over such a long period, especially when we consider that change is one of the few constants by which nature can be characterized.

Moreover, the evolution of something functionally new never meant that it suddenly appeared with its present structure. It surely had its prehistory as a primitive form of what it is now. The eye surely had its prehistory as a most primitive light-sensitive structure — itself the descendant of the earliest sensory organs which detected only touch — itself the descendant of the simple fact that creatures are inevitably affected by their environment.

Upon reflection, it is also clear that the evolution of organs and systems did not take place as *isolated* events. Surely, one change often led to a number of inter-related improvements.

Any discussion of the "odds" of evolution must take into account the fact that calculations normally — but wrongly — admit of only one way a given event could have taken place. It is with this in mind that one must judge the sometime claim of anti-evolutionary scientists to the effect that the formation of even one amino acid took place against odds of millions to one — a claim used by others to prove that God was the necessary "Director" of the process.[35] In considering any claim of this sort, it is especially important to remember that the actual odds of a given event are largely unknown. Given the fantastic number of variables which are involved in any event, not to mention the fact that the most remarkable evolutionary events took place long before conditions were what they are

---

35. The so-called revolutionary argument for the existence of God is normally conjoined to the observation that man occupies what appears to be the central position in creation midway between the micro and macro-scopic.

now, any declaration of the length of evolutionary odds which is held to disprove the process — or to prove God's existence — must be viewed as scientifically irresponsible.

Finally, it is important to remember that the contemporary inability to provide an exact description of evolution hardly disproves the existence of the process. Indeed, an exact description of the process will always be wanting. This is true of the scientific explanation of anything; it is no reason to disbelieve what *is* evident from the facts we *do* have. For all the preceding reasons, it soon came to be seen that a blanket denial of the idea of evolution was a pitiful example of closed-mindedness rooted in intellectual cowardice.

2. Scholastic Objections

Though the scientific debate held most of the attention, the scholastic objections to evolution were still to be answered.

To the objection that a lower cannot beget a higher because nothing can give what it does not have, it was simply to be responded that, *au contraire,* it can, as is evident every time parents give birth to a baby who grows up to be bigger or brighter than they are.

To the objection that evolution implies a denial of the existence of immaterial forms, it was simply to be responded that nominalism had already proved that they are not necessary (cf. p. 95). Modern science had simply confirmed that they were not needed in order to explain things.

To the objection that evolution implies an imperfect creation, not only was it to be responded that the presumption of creation is an invalid source of argument, but even if the universe has been created, the "imperfection" evident in evolution need not be considered a mistake.

3. Uncritical Objections

Most of the uncritical objections to evolution, involving as they do traditional Christian truths, do not stand up under scientific scrutiny. The question as to whether they still have validity — and what facts they really bring to bear upon this discussion — is largely the topic of all that follows.

Section V: A Crisis and Its Resolution;
A New Theology of Scripture

A) The Crisis

With the accumulating evidence for evolution, the conflict between Christianity and modernity reached the crisis stage. It had apparently been proved that there is no soul, no God and certainly no credible book about Him, much less by Him. Catholics were especially put upon because it appeared that Church teaching had been proved wrong. To deny the evidence would be to fly in the face of reason itself.

Churchmen did not have this option at their disposal. This would contradict the longstanding Catholic tradition of respect for reason (cf. p. 34). As we saw, the author of faith is also the author of reason. It was unthinkable that He would contradict Himself. This was the reason that faith and reason were mutually confirming, even if faith gave the greater, more immediate, more certain knowledge. Moreover, since reason was indeed man's greatest natural gift, it was impossible that God would ask man to deny it. Indeed, as history tells, even the most rabid of anti-scholastics did not claim that faith contradicted reason. (Neither did they attempt to construct a system closed to otherwise irrefutable facts.)

B) The Emergence of a New Theology of Inerrancy; The Distinction between the Essence of the Truth and Its Expression

1. A Solution to the Problem of Genesis

Faced with the impossible situation created by the accumulating evidence for evolution, increasing numbers of churchmen finally saw their way clear to accept the liberal, modernist idea that the Genesis account of creation did not need to be taken literally in order to reveal that God was indeed responsible for all that there is.

Evolution was a natural explanation of the diversity of life. At best, it might be extended to explain the origin of life. It did not account for the existence of nature. The opinion of the atheist notwithstanding, this was still to explained. Thus, there had to be a God, a Creator. He had simply chosen to create by means of evolution. Genesis was simply meant to convey the fact that He did create.

Let there be no mistake. The new idea was not accepted without struggle. At first, many hoped that the historical character of Genesis could be preserved by insisting that the story corresponded to the facts once one realized what God *really* meant by the word "day." Claiming that man had misunderstood that a day to God is much longer than a day to man, and pointing out that the details of what happened during each day were omitted from the account, some claimed that Genesis was an account of evolution.

Attractive though it was, this idea was not to withstand the scrutiny of honest examination. One could not help but notice that Genesis said that God created light before He created the sun (1:3); it spoke of the moon as having light of its own (1:16). Moreover, its order of creation did not follow the facts; birds did not come before land animals. Woman did not emerge out of man's rib. Plainly, if it was anything, Genesis was a story, a myth, albeit a myth which told the truth of creation. But it was not the literal truth.

2. Precedent for Non-literal Interpretation

In view of what was required by evolution, proponents of the new theology of the inerrancy now pointed out that there is much precedent for non-literal interpretation. Even apart from the "topical" sense of Scripture (cf. p. 43),[36] certain statements had never been taken literally.

It was never taken literally that the Lord is a "rock"(Ps.18:2). This was poetry. It was never taken literally that God "walked" in the Garden of Eden (Gen.3:8). This was simply an "anthropomorphism," one of many places that God was described in terms *too* human. It was not to be taken literally that there were really "strange gods" not to be put before the Lord (Ex.20:2); this was but one of an even larger number of the uses of "allegory." This was what made it possible to accept the discovery that the sun did *not* move about the earth.

Many of Jesus' moral teachings were not taken literally; surely they were meant to exhort. Did Jesus really mean that to be a follower one had to sell everything one had (Mt.19:21)? How could He have meant that "anyone who does not hate his own father and mother and wife and children and even his own life, he cannot be my disciple" (Lk.14:26)? Even though He said: "turn the other cheek" (Mt.5:39), was there not a right of self-defense which even permitted one to kill, permitting nations to engage in a so-called "just" war?

Theological reasoning had even "qualified" Jesus' doctrine. Though *He* did not admit of exceptions to the rule that "unless one is born of water and the spirit he cannot enter the kingdom of God" (Jn.3:5), His Church did.

How had the Church come to understand His promise "ask and you shall receive" (e.g. Mt.18:19, Lk.11:9)?

What of His apparent mistakes? Was He to be taken literally about the fact His hearers would live to see the coming of the kingdom (Mt.16:24, Mk.9:1)?

What of His statement that He, God, did not know the time of its coming (Mt.24:36)?

---

36. The medievals knew four senses of Scripture. Every statement had its literal sense while certain statements also referred to Christ (their "Christological" sense), man (their "tropological" sense), or the kingdom (their "eschatological" sense).

3. The Formulation of the New Theology

In view of all the above, Christian leaders began to insist that the Bible was never meant to be taken literally — at least not always. The reason: in order to make Himself clear, God had employed man's own ways of using words. Thus, when the "expression" of truth recommended it, God had used non-literal forms. Of course, what He intended to express, the "essence" of the truth, was still to be taken literally. And this was still inerrant.

4. The Church Approves the New Theology

Needless to say, the Church's approval of the new theology took time. This was surely to be expected. It took time to study the new ideas and to anticipate the possible implications of their adoption. Besides, given its self-conception, the magisterium was bound to be conservative. After all, the Church was commissioned to pass on God's truth, not to rewrite it. Indeed, the new theology was especially feared because it meant that man would be taking the risk of deciding what God did and did not mean. And it would open the door to a denial of the literal truth of anything.

But, after an honest evaluation of the precedents already set, it was clear that the door had already been opened. Thus, as the weight of the evidence for evolution continued to mount, it became clear that the time for change had come; the continued credibility of Christianity would permit nothing else. Therefore, as the new theology was better and better formulated, as churchmen became more and more accustomed to thinking in the new way, approval was cautiously given. In 1943, Pius XII (1939-58) issued the encyclical *Divino Afflante Spiritu* (DS 3825-31) which acknowledged the Scriptures did employ non-literal forms and encouraged the linguistic, literary and historical studies aimed at their proper interpretation. Then, in 1950, the same year that Pius infallibly proclaimed the doctrine of the Assumption (*Munificentissimus Deus* DS 3900-04),[37] he officially permitted the teaching of creation by means of evolution so long as it was maintained that God created Adam's soul directly (*Humani Generis*, DS 3875-99).

C) The Emergence of a New Theology of Inspiration; The Distinction between the Essence of the Truth and Its Understanding

1. Theology Moves Forward

As we already know, even before the Church's approval of the new

---

37. Notably, in proclaiming the Assumption, Pius cited the evidence of "Sensus Fidelium," the "sense of the faithful." Inspired by the Holy Spirit, it was seen in popular devotion to the Assumption everywhere and throughout history.

theology of inerrancy, theologians were already articulating the new theology of inspiration which followed the realization that God's use of human literary forms must have involved His use of the human writer to a greater extent than had hitherto been imagined.

Let it be clear. When the distinction between the truth and its expression was first articulated, it involved no more than the idea that different means of expression were simply "different." But, continued reflection soon showed that they could also involve a difference of sophistication. Genesis was a simple story. And it was similar to the stories, the myths, used by all ancient peoples to explain the world. Plainly, it was a story *for* a primitive people. Moreover, it was so similar to myths of other primitive peoples that theologians had to admit: it was a story *by* a primitive people; the author was a person of his time. In other words, the author of Genesis probably believed that creation took six days. It was *his* idea that light was created before the sun. It is not *our* idea.

2. Implicit Precedent of Interpretation Contrary to the Author's Intent
In the retrospect of wisdom, it became clear that scriptural statements once interpreted at the pain of extensive theological argumentation actually involved interpretation contrary to the author's intent — at least partly.

The nature of anthropomorphism notwithstanding, how else was honesty to explain the fact that God was often described in what were now seen as less than the best of human characteristics? It had been centuries since the better theologians had believed that "vengance" was the Lord's (e.g. Deut.32:35). How could He "regret" (Gen.6:7)? "Anger" (Ex.4:14) was now a sign of immaturity.

Our understanding of Jesus' moral teachings notwithstanding, how else were we to make sense of His rejection of so much of the Old Testament's supposedly "perfect" law (Ps.19:7)? It was against Jesus' law to demand an eye for an eye and a tooth for a tooth (Mt.5:38). He explicitly overruled *Moses* in His forbading of divorce (Mt.19:3-9). (Indeed, what of the fact that He gave Moses credit for the Law?)

How else were we to make sense of what was now the truly ample evidence that the first Christians believed that Baptism was essential to salvation, or that the kingdom was indeed coming soon? Paul made clear that *he* expected the kingdom to come soon (e.g. 2 Thess.4, 1 Cor. 15:51). If he had known better, why didn't he say so? The absence of an answer was a profound addition to the evidence that all of the Scriptures were the product of some very human limitations.

3. The Formulation of the New Theology

Interpretation contrary to the author's intent did not need to be a denial of the idea of inspiration. But it did mean change. Actually, the classical idea was already troublesome. It involved a rather dramatic sort of miracle that robbed the human author of what was now the evident humanity of his role as the person through whom God had put His truth into human terms. Therefore, the author was now imagined to have been given an idea — probably unbeknownst to him — which he did his best to understand and express for the sake of his fellows. The "idea" was the "essence" of God's truth; it was to be distinguished from its "understanding" in the mind of its human mediator even if the progress of understanding proves that he was in some way wrong. Now, this did not mean that God's care did not extend to the human author's expression of the idea. Undoubtedly, God made sure his limitations did not result in an errant statement of the essential truth as it needed to be understood then and now.

But, let there be no mistake. The new theology involved a potentially great distance between the truth and the text, even to the point of the assertion of interpretations dramatically contrary to the literal intent of the scriptural author, even to the point of admitting that he was wrong about certain things that *he* may have thought were important. And in view of scriptural problems old and new, little would be taken for granted, the stories in the gospels not exempted. After all, there is no insisting that what is true with regard to one part of the Bible could not be true of others. Nonetheless, scholars were still confident that they could gain a better idea of what God had really meant to reveal, and what had really happened.

4. The Superiority of the New Theology

Plainly, the new theology of inspiration involved even greater risk than the new theology of inerrancy.

Nonetheless, the new theology was supported by too much evidence. It responded to the old and new problems with the Scriptures. It explained the difference between the Old and New Testaments. It explained the discrepancies within the New. It explained the fact that the Scriptures looked like myth. It excused literary and historical errors and it even gave response to what now appeared to be bad theology. Indeed, where once it was necessary to insist that "Jesus didn't mean it," even if the literary evidence clearly suggested that He did, one could now suggest that "Jesus didn't say it."

Of course, one could still deny that there were problems, explaining them away with fantastic excuses that some still chose to invoke. But this was a blatant violation of the principle of economy, the use of a fantastic explanation where a simple one was now available. This explanation, the new theology of inspiration was in accord with reason and left good reason to believe that the Scriptures are God's word.

As an added benefit, the new theology would now make it possible to move beyond any number of the scripturally based positions to which Christians had historically been committed regardless of what was now their better judgement. Now, Pauline statements that "it is well for man not to touch a woman" (1 Cor.7:1), "women should keep silence in churches" (1 Cor.14:34), "wives should be submissive to their husbands" (Eph.5:22) while "slaves should remain obedient to their masters" (Eph.6:5) were to be understood in terms of the culture of the ancient Near East. And these and other scriptural injunctions could be interpreted to Christianity's *credit* because they could be read to represent progress even if they did not anticipate all the progress that would one day be made. The completely modern ideas would have been too much for the people for whom they were originally written.

C) Major Results of the New Theologies

1. Critical Method

The new theologies of inerrancy and inspiration legitimized the use of the critical method of scriptural interpretation which, as we have seen, had actually been taking shape for several centuries. Also called modern "exegesis," it involves the scientific effort to determine the true "context" of scriptural statements, a procedure also known as "hermeneutics." First formulated for use by Catholic scholars by Marie-Joseph Lagrange (1855-1938),[38] critical method is conceived to answer what have become two distinct questions: 1) What did the author really mean, and 2) What did God really reveal?

The first step, "textural criticism," involves the attempt to determine the true reading of the original text. Pioneered by Richard Simon, all the most ancient copies of the scriptural texts are compared in order to determine the true original. (The oldest New Testament fragment dates from the mid-second century, the oldest complete copies are about two centuries younger.[39]) This study has happily revealed that we possess the vast majority of scriptural words just as they were written. Where there is some disagreement, the result of a mistake in copying, either accidental

---

38. Lagrange was the founder of the *Ecole Biblique*, the first school of modern Catholic biblical scholarship.

39. They are the Codices "Vaticanus" (which is kept at the Vatican Library) and "Sinaiticus" (which is kept at the British Museum).

or on purpose — for some theological reason (as was apparent in the fact that some versions of Lk.2:33 read "Joseph and His mother" while the more ancient texts read "His father and mother"), genuine detective work has resulted in general agreement about the reading of the original text. Very few of the most important passages are disputed.[40]

Upon a determination of the original text, the next step becomes translation and with it "linguistic criticism." Once again, comparative analysis, based not only on the Bible but other ancient and patristic texts, is used in order to determine not only the exact translation of individual words, their "denotation," but also their "connotation" in special circumstances of their use. This obviously provides important insights into the minds of the persons who employ these words.

Thereupon, "literary criticism" begins. Already the subject of much discussion, it provides the most immediate information about the context of a given scriptural statement.

Literary criticism gives way to "redaction criticism." Based upon the study of the whole text — with special attention to structure — it also involves the comparison of the text to other works of a similar kind in order to determine the author's characteristic theology and style. This provides a way to determine whether a certain word, passage, or even chapter has been added by later redactions. (An especially important element of New Testament studies, it was bound to be fruitful because all these works concern the same things and several were written by the same person, Paul.)

Redaction criticism feeds a study of the effect that transmission has upon ideas, "form criticism." Looking for the effects of faith and other less illustrious influences on the formation of theology and the telling of stories, it also involves the comparative studies that identify literary dependency and it complements redaction criticism in determining the time and place of a work's composition. (The study of the New Testament is simplified by the fact that all of its works are more recent and all were written during a relatively short period.)

Form criticism has its place within the larger embrace of "historical criticism," the study of events, such as wars, or conditions, such as culture, which have had their effect upon the content of anything written during a given period. It also attempts to identify the influence of a people's contact with others.

---

40. Notably, repeated attempts to prove that the word "water" was added to Jn.3:5 have failed to prove anything but the fact that it appears in the oldest texts we possess.

This brings us to "religious criticism." Based on a study of the aspects of religion which are universal in man, or nearly so, it attempts to identify what is typical, and naturally explicable, and what may not be.

2. *Concessions to the Critics*

The adoption of critical method was already a concession to much of what the critics had been saying for centuries. Even so, its results have come to be respected by the leaders of virtually all denominations.[41]

a. The Old Testament

It is now all but universally acknowledged that the Hebrews were indeed a primitive people and largely typical semites. They were not concerned with philosophy.[42] Instead, they used stories in order to understand their world and themselves, and to feel that they were chosen by at least one of the gods whose existence they acknowledged.

In view of all of this, it is clear that there was no one by the name of Adam or Eve who lived in a paradisiacal garden at the dawn of creation. Neither was there a talking serpent, a great flood, or a tower of Babel.

There may not have been an Abraham, Isaac, or Jacob. In any case, the stories about them are largely legendary, responding to the Hebrews' need to explain their origins. There may have been a Moses, who lived in Egypt about the year 1300 B.C., but the story of his leadership of the Hebrews in Egypt is surely a highly embellished account of events which are actually lost to us. Though he likely did lead at least one tribe of Hebrews back to their homeland, most of the tribes were already there. Joshua did not lead them in its conquest. (Of course, the newcomers must have fought for living space; and they and the other Hebrews were constantly squabbling with other peoples.) About the year 1000 B.C., however, a king David did unify the tribes and led them to local dominance.

---

41. No accounting of the results of specific studies could be contained in a work of this kind. Collectively, these results are best displayed in various reference works. Of Catholic authorship, the first of these was the *Dictionary of Biblical Theology* edited by Xavier Leon-Dufour, originally written in French. Originally in English are the *Dictionary of the Bible* written entirely by John L. McKenzie and the *Jerome Biblical Commentary* edited by Raymond E. Brown, Joseph A. Fitzmeyer and Roland E. Murphy. Among the best respected Protestant works is the *Interpreter's Dictionary of the Bible.*

Modern theology is documented in excellent encyclopedic works such as the *Sacramentum Mundi* edited by Karl Rahner, originally written in German, and *The New Catholic Encyclopedia,* available only in English.

Also to be endorsed is the *Oxford Dictionary of the Christian Church* edited by F. L. Cross.

42. It can well be agued that the Hebrews were not capable of philosophy. They had no word "is"; they had ways to say "was" and "will be," but not the "is" with which the Greeks spoke of a thing in itself.

David did not write the Psalms. Songs of prayer composed by many people, the Psalms were the products of a long period of oral tradition and bear the remnants of the most primitive thinking of which the Old Testament consists.

Shortly after the establishment of David's kingdom, someone of the religious establishment wrote the so-called "Jahwist"[43] document which proposed to explain the people's history to date. Drawing on centuries of oral tradition — and affected by all the influences that one would expect — it was followed by the composition of three other collections of the stories that the people had previously passed on by word of mouth. Called the "Elohist," the "Deuteronomic," and the "Priestly" documents, each was partly and somewhat haphazardly, incorporated into the present Pentateuch which actually included the book of Joshua. This was done by priests attached to the second temple in the fifth century B.C. — after the exile. Also written at this time were the books of Judges, Samuel and Kings.

The first prophetic books were also written at this time. Prophecy, however, was much older and it was common to semitic peoples. The prophets came from outside the establishment mainly to critique it. There were many prophets and many bad ones (e.g. Jer.23:9ff). Some, however, attracted a following making it possible that they would be remembered. But, in most cases, many years would pass before recollections of what a prophet said were written down. The majority of prophetic writings were composed between the 4th and 2nd centuries B.C. This was long after all the prophets were dead. Thus, there can be no doubt that most of their more detailed predictions were written from the hindsight of what actually happened. In some cases, a tradition of uncertain origin was given an author; thus, some of the more remarkable prophetic characters (like Job and Jonah) probably never lived.

The first prophetic book was that of Amos which, like Hosea, originated in Israel. The first prophetic book which originated in Judea was Isaiah. But, the present book which bears his name is actually the product of three different authors, with three different theologies, contributing chapters 1-35, 36-39, and 40-66 respectively.

The prophetic writings were followed by Sirach, the Proverbs, the Canticle of Canticles and the books of Job, Ecclesiastes and Wisdom. Collectively known as "wisdom" literature, they were not written by

---

43. It was "so-called" because of its characteristic use of the word "Jahweh" (from the German spelling of what in English is rendered "Yahweh") in reference to God.

Solomon. Written and rewritten by a variety of authors, they reflect a concern for "wise" living which was common to the semites of this time. In the sophistication of their content, however, they also betray the influence of Greek thought. They contain the first biblical attempts to deal with the problem of evil. It is in the book of Wisdom, written only two hundred years before Christ, that we find the first real evidence of a belief in life after death. Prior, we have evidence of only a vague belief in a place where the dead go to be dead. "Sheol" by name, it was not the fiery "Gehenna" of Jesus' time. For most of their history, the Hebrews (who became the "Jews" after generations of inter-marriage) did not believe in a heavenly life after death. Instead, they believed that God's favor was to be seen in a long and prosperous earthly life.

The remainder of the Old Testament writings were composed during the final two centuries before Christ. Of these, the book of Daniel should receive special mention. The author-subject is probably legendary, not only because the stories about him are so remarkable, but also because the book contains several different types of material.[44] Of these, the most unusual is Daniel's vision of the future, a so-called "apocalyptic," which betrays the hellenistic influence of its heavy use of symbolism.

It was no longer insisted that the Old Testament is to be read as the explicit, progressive revelation of Christ. Most if not all of the supposed references to Jesus now saw their *immediate* explanation in terms of persons, events or theologies contemporary with their writing. (Here was a sensible explanation for the fact that Jesus was *not* named "Immanuel," cf. Is.7:14.) Indeed, it was even acknowledged that the promise of a messiah — even political — was not a major Old Testament theme. It was a teaching of the great rabbis who lived just before Jesus.[45]

b. The New Testament

Naturally, the adoption of critical method also involved concessions to the critics of the New Testament.

Immediately confirmed was the conclusion long held by some: the New Testament was not written until a significant time after the events of which it told. Its oldest writings were definitely written by Paul.

The first of Paul's writings were his two letters to the Thessalonians. Written during the early 50's, they were intended to encourage the Christian community of Thessolonia to persevere under persecution.

---

44. It also contains the only scriptural material written in Aramaic.
45. Initially, preserved only in the oral form of the "mishna," the teachings of the great rabbis were later preserved in the written form of the "Talmud."

They also display Paul's concern for what he perceived as the excessive legalism of this community. Paul's letters to the Galatians, Corinthians[46] and Romans were written during the late 50's. The letter to the Galatians was the first of Paul's theological discourses on salvation through faith. Paul's first letter to the Corinthians was written in response to licentiousness which had evidently followed his insistence that the people let the Spirit guide them. The second letter to the Corinthians is especially concerned with the afterlife and some scholars do not believe that it was written by Paul. The letter to the Romans is most concerned with the issue of Gentile Christianity. It stresses justification by faith, not the Mosaic law. It also contains the most extensive Pauline discussion of "life in the Spirit." In the light of the latest scholarship, it is clear that when Paul wrote of the "spirit" ("pneuma" in Greek, "ru'ah" in Hebrew for "wind") he had in mind a typically ancient idea of God's "power" at work. Paul was an ancient, and a Jew, but he *was* at the vanguard of the attempt to make Christianity intelligible to the people of the larger Greco-Roman world. The letters to the Philippians and Philemon were the last of Paul's writings. The co-called "Christological hymn" in the letter to the Philippians (2:6-11) was not written by Paul but was added much later. Its developed Christology contrasts with Paul's rather simple insistence that Jesus was the "Christ," the "messiah," the "anointed one."

The letters to the Ephesians, Colossians and Hebrews were all but certainly *not* written by Paul. This is apparent in their distinctive styles and theologies, all of which feature rather sophisticated statements of the divinity of Christ. The letters to the Ephesians and Colossians were written during the later 60's but they do betray Paul's influence. The letter to the Hebrews is quite original; it did not even bear Paul's name until quite late and is missing from early canons. It features a sophisticated theology of Christ the mediator between God and man.

The so-called "pastoral" epistles — the letters to Timothy and Titus — concern Church life. All were written during the late 60's, but not by Paul.

This same period saw the composition of the first letter of Peter, but almost certainly not by Peter. The letter was written to teach and encourage certain communities in Asia Minor (Turkey). The second letter of Peter was definitely not written by Peter. The latest of all the New Testament writings, it was not composed before the year 100 and may well have been written as late as 125.

---

46. We have two; there were probably four.

The letters of James and Jude may date anywhere from the late 60's to the 80's. There is no positive evidence linking either to an apostle. The letter of James is the most notable for its obvious reaction to the Pauline emphasis on faith. Both letters represent independent sources of Christian thinking.

The first gospel was that of Mark. It was probably written in Italy during the late 60's. It features a relatively simple presentation of the Christian message with a notable insistence on miracles as proof that Jesus was the messiah.

The early dating of Mark contributed to and confirmed the synoptic theory of gospel formation (cf. p. 128). And the accumulation of evidence in support of this theory confirmed the general conclusion that the gospels took shape somewhat slowly through oral tradition and several written stages. It was specifically concluded that the passion narratives came first, as independent accounts, while the infancy narratives were the last additions to the present gospels. It was only later that they were given the name of some authority.

Matthew the apostle was not the author of the gospel of Matthew. Written during the mid 70's, originally in Greek, its author was probably a Syrian Jew. Its principal purpose was to prove that Jesus was the promised messiah — the fulfillment of the Law — to make faith in Christ acceptable to pious Jews.

Luke was written about the same time; there is no agreement as to where. Luke — almost certainly the author of the *Acts of the Apostles* — wrote for Gentile Christians. His gospel describes the progress of truth to Jerusalem, the revelation to the Jews, while the book of Acts describes the progress of the truth to Rome, the revelation to all peoples. He was particularly concerned to show that Jesus held out salvation not just to every people, but to every class of people, especially the poor.

All the synoptics call Jesus the "Son." But, it must also be mentioned that such a "title" was not unknown to the pre-Christian Jew. The good man was a "son of God" (e.g. Sir.4:10). Every man was a "son of man" (e.g. Ez.2:1). The great king promised Israel had to be a "son of David" (cf. p. 66).

Though the gospel of John also calls Jesus the "Son," it features the insistence that He was the pre-existent "Word." This concept does bear the influence of Greek thought.[47] And this is not the only evidence of

---

47. This influence may have been mediated by the personification of Wisdom — as a woman — as described in the book of Wisdom (6:12ff), particularly as interpreted by the Hellenistic rabbi Philo (c.20 B.C.-c.50 A.D.).

Greek thought in John's gospel. It is evident in John's identifications of Jesus with any concept ("truth," "life," "light," etc.) and in his claim that Jesus said that the Father and He exist "in" each other. (It also betrays the early Christian contempt for unconverted Jews. And it was for apologetic reasons that they are blamed for Jesus' death.) Written no earlier than the 90's, and possibly as late as the year 100, and probably in Asia Minor, the apostle John was not the author. Chapter 21 was added to the original, but not by the original author. Indeed, not all the Johannine writings have the same author; the second two of the three letters that bear his name were definitely written by someone other than the author of the gospel. Nonetheless, in the similarity of their thought, there is some evidence that they belonged to an informal Johannine "school." In any case, in their insistence that faith reflect itself in action, it is clear that none of them was a gnostic. The Johannine contempt for the world was principally a response to worldliness, and persecution.

There is no identifying the author of the book of Revelation, an apocalyptic from start to finish.[48]

It was now clear that all of the New Testament writings, including the gospels, were the result of the very human influence on the transmission of truth. All were written long after the facts, by people who did not know Jesus. They betrayed the use of remarkable stories to make their points or to answer questions that were important to the first generations of Christians. There can be no doubt that what *we* would call exaggeration is in evidence. Indeed, with particular reference to the infancy narratives, one could now identify genuine Christian myth. Actually, even beyond their differences (cf. p. 68), and obvious apologetic motive (Bethleham was David's city), they had always been problematic because they told of fantastic events which somehow had no effect on Jesus' later life.

There was now good reason to doubt that most of Jesus' miracles really happened and to question whether He really said much for which He was quoted.[49] And, once it was discovered that parables were a teaching tool used by all the great rabbis, some scholars insisted that even these were written for Him. (Even the so-called "Lord's Prayer" was probably not Jesus' own. Essentially a prayer for the coming of God's kingdom, it betrays the faith of first century Christians awaiting Jesus'

---

48. Its "visions" are now recognized to have drawn heavily upon human imagination. This has justified the Catholic contempt for the inumerable "millenarians" who have dwelt upon its reference to a thousand years (Rev.20:4-5) in an attempt to predict the end of the world.
49. It was especially clear that words had been put into Mary's mouth (Lk.1:46-55) and Zechariah's (Lk.1:68-79). This gave a special sacredness to what were liturgical prayers.

return.) Admittedly questionable was His explicit intention to found a church, and only more so His naming of Peter as its head. Also questionable was the existence of a twelve-member apostolic group; since the early Christians considered themselves God's new chosen people, they may have felt the need for twelve founding fathers. (And the listings of the twelve did not even agree, cf. footnote p. 71.) Scarcely secure was the classical claim of Jesus' deliberate institution of seven sacraments; indeed, it was by no means clear that the Church conceived of any "sacraments."

3. Scriptural Support for the Essentials of Christian Belief

Despite the number and importance of concessions to the critics, critical method also gave churchmen a scientific basis to assert that the Scriptures did support at least the essentials of Christian, even Catholic, belief.

a. The Old Testament

Although the Hebrews were a primitive people who acknowledged the existence of many gods, their religion called them to worship only one. Moreover, their's was never the very primitive "polytheism" that sees a different god behind every important natural phenomenon. Neither did their religion involve the worship of images.

More importantly, their religious history is a story of remarkable progress. At first, the Hebrews believed that Yahweh was their own god, the warrior who protected them from the gods of other people. With time, defeat and exile, they came to see Him at work in everything that happens, guiding their history. Eventually, they came to see Him behind everything, the God of all peoples. This was the "radical"[50] monotheism that did prevail in Jesus' time. It was not common.

The Hebrew's moral thought was also uncommon. From the beginning, Hebrew law bore a remarkable concern for "justice." (The principle "an eye for an eye..." *limited* retribution; "vengeance" was *left* to the Lord.) With time, however, there developed an even more remarkable realization; God desires not burnt offerings but a "contrite heart" (e.g. Ps.51). He asks His people to "do justice, love kindness and walk humbly with [their] God" (Mic.6:8).

Of course, it was still to be acknowledged that the Old Testament cannot be read to involve an explicit, progressive revelation of Christ. But, in a modern adoption of extra-literal interpretation (cf. p. 43), what was now called the *sensus plenior* (or "fuller sense") of certain passages

---

50. A "radical" is like an absolute; it knows no qualification.

was said to be revealed by the fact of subsequent Christian interpretation. In other words, the author of the second addition to the book of Isaiah may not have intended his statements about the suffering servant to be a prediction of the globally consequential sacrifice of Christ, but the fact that the first Christians read him to say so is enough to justify the claim that this is what *God* meant.

b. The New Testament

Critical method provided churchmen with a scientifically sound means by which to obtain evidence that the reported events of Jesus' life and contents of His teaching are historical. Admitting that the gospels were not only written decades after the reputed events, but were indeed documents of faith and not history strictly speaking, they articulated principles by which to bridge the distance of time and faith and identify the historical basis of the stories that were later to be told.

The principles were indisputably scientific. They followed the scientific presumption that everything can be — and needs to be — explained. Thus, the very fact that there is a New Testament is evidence of something. Surely, the human authors of these texts wrote for some reason. Surely, they believed some of what they wrote. Therefore, the first principle involves "Inexplicability by Alternative": the simple fact that whatever is written is probably true if there is no good reason not to believe it.

Immediately, the first principle offers us all but certain knowledge that Jesus, a Jew, did live as an itinerant preacher in Palestine during the first decades of the age that was ultimately to be named after Him. After all, the Christian movement did not appear out of mid-air. It required a founder and no one else was ever mentioned. Instead, Jesus is not only mentioned, but He became the object of its worship within two decades of His death.

If the existence of the New Testament, and the Christian movement generally, is not accepted as sufficient evidence that Jesus lived, it would have to be admitted that no knowledge of history before the camera could ever be accepted.[51] The real questions concern the specifics of what is said about Him. This quest is informed by other principles:

2) "Centrality": The more central a story or teaching is within a writing, or the more common one is within the New Testament, the story or teaching is more likely more true. This principle especially encourages belief in the historicity of anything that was never in any way contradicted.

Together the writings of the New Testament make clear that the essence of Jesus' message was indeed His proclamation of the coming of God's kingdom. This immediately implies the importance of repentance, faith (at least in "God") and, most of all, love. Not only are these the central themes of all the early Christian writings, it is safe to say that if Jesus had *not* taught them, the subject of the New Testament would have been the first person who did.

It is also clear that Jesus must have insisted that God is our Father — our loving Father. The coming of the kingdom cannot be conceived otherwise.

3) "Antiquity": The sooner after the events an account was written, it is less likely affected by transmission. For this reason, the authentic letters of Paul and, among the gospels, Mark's, are to be considered the primary sources of what actually happened.

4) "Detail": The more detailed an account is, it is more likely true. This lends particular credibility to the passion narratives.

5) "Consistency": Specific accounts of what a scriptural person said or did are more likely true if they are consistent with the pattern of what would be expected from him. For example, this principle would support the story of Jesus' forgiving His executioners while still on the cross (Lk.23:34).

6) "Conformity": Accounts of the way things were are more likely true if they conform to what would be expected from the situation as indicated by common sense or the history of the period. This principle provides evidence in favor of much of what is generally said of Jesus' life as an itinerant preacher in Galilee. His conflict with the Pharisees, and the

---

51. The argument has also been made that we actually have *less* reason — or perhaps only slightly *more* — to accept accounts of the lives of Roman Emperors. In any case, evidence has been provided by some of the same people. Luke speaks of Augustus (2:1) while several Roman authors mention Christ: Suetonius placed the followers of "Chrestus" in Rome by about the year 50 (see his *Life of Claudius,* 25,4). Tacitus blamed them for the fire that devastated the city in 64; he also mentioned Christ's crucifixion under the rule of Pontius Pilate (see his *Annals,* 25,44,2-8). About the same time, Josephus, a Jewish historian, mentioned the stoning of "James, brother of Jesus called the Christ" (see his *Antiquities,* 2,9,1).

people's expectations of a kingdom of earthly glory. Finally,

7) "Non-Conformity": Accounts of the unusual, even the extra-ordinary, are more likely to be true if they cannot easily be explained by appeal to what would normally be expected from the culture or the "creative" effects of man and time. Here we find evidence that not only did Jesus teach the law of love, but He did so in a truly radical way. In His insistence on love extending even to enemies — even when justice would demand otherwise — it is clear that the Judaism of His day had *not* been put in His mouth. Indeed, in the light of the Judaism of Jesus' day, there is also evidence of His proclamation of the coming of the kingdom. The expectation of an afterlife was not the common presumption of most Jews. (The Sadducees did not believe in the resurrection of the dead, cf. Acts 23:8.) It was no reason to give up one's life.

This same principle can also be used in order to support belief in Jesus' divinity. Even though most of Jesus' titles — especially those that refer to Him as "Son" — had their less than divine connotation (cf. p. 186), each was used with respect to Jesus in a divine-sounding way. Moreover, His recorded references to His Father sounded exclusively personal; He is even recorded to have referred to His Father as "abba," i.e. "daddy" (e.g. Mk.14:36, cf. Rom.8:15), an expression which the Judaism of His day could not have conceived. More importantly, Jesus is not called a "prophet." His death suposedly saved the world. Shortly after His death, He was spoken of as "Lord" (e.g. 1 Thess.1:1), the proper substitute for God's unspeakable name (cf. p. 126). Considering the radical monotheism of the Judaism of Jesus' time, this was more than remarkable.

Belief in Jesus' divinity was both betrayed and supported by the equally important belief in His resurrection. Shown to be an essential element of Christian faith from the very beginning, especially in the evidence of the writings of Paul (cf. 1 Cor.15), it was "the" event that explained the survival of the Christian movement after the death of its founder reportedly sent His disciples fleeing. The account of their cowardly flight did not appear to be a story that they would have invented. (Actually, neither would the story of His crucifixion; to Judaic thinking a man executed is "accursed" by God, cf. Deut.21:23.) The story of the empty tomb provided a separate line of argument: if told strictly for apologetic purposes, it should not have featured women; Jewish law did not accept their testimony. Furthermore, no tomb ever became a shrine. Christians were obviously convinced that Jesus was not there. He had risen from the dead and appeared to the "apostles"; this was the reason they bore this title and the authority that went with it (1 Cor.15:9; see also Acts 1, 21-22).

Catholic scholars found new evidence to support Church teaching about the Church. That Christians were meant to be a "Church," i.e. "ecclesia," or "assembly," was evident in the very fact that they *were* a church from the very beginning. And, it was clear that they considered themselves a "body" — "the body of Christ" (cf. p. 44). It was also clear that Peter was its leader. A fact acknowledged by Paul, his sometime *rival* (cf. Gal.2:7), it was even more apparent in the scriptural accounts which were plainly meant to justify his position (cf. p. 46). (The very fact that the first Christians reported that his name had been changed from "Simon" to "Peter," i.e. "rock," was evidence that he possessed a position of unique importance.) Remarkably, much of what was claimed about Jesus' deliberate institution of the Church was now explained with the aid of Loisy's ideas on the relevatory role of the Spirit in the Church (cf. p. 160). Now not surprisingly, they were also used to support belief in institution of the seven sacraments. Though the sacraments had some basis in the events of Jesus' life, they actually emerged as sacred actions as the Church took up His mission under the guidance of the Spirit. A notable exception concerned His institution of the Eucharist; studies of the story of the last supper, especially as reported in 1 Cor.11, led scholars to insist that they had discovered any of the actual words of Jesus ("ippissima verba" as they were called), they were the words: "This is my body; this is my blood."

***

How remarkable it was. A little over a century after the publication of *The Origin of Species,* a new approach to the Scriptures had gained the acceptance which enabled the experts to respond to problems that had troubled credible Christian belief for centuries prior. Although literalism had to be abandoned, the sanctity of the Scriptures did not. Though they could no longer be read to provide so many details, they now revealed the essence of faith more clearly than ever before. Christianity had taken a giant step forward.

Section VI: A New Theology of Church Teaching

A) The Idea of Doctrinal Development

Though the new theology of Scripture may have been a great step forward for Christianity, it was not immediately obvious that it was a great step forward for Catholicism. Indeed, it caused a grave problem for the classical theology of Church teaching. We have already seen documentation of the fact that the classical theologies of inerrancy and inspiration involved a very literalistic understanding of what the Scriptures were and how they were to be read (cf. p. 155). As late as 1920, in the encyclical *Spiritus Paraclitus,* Benedict XV would insist that inspiration extends to both religious and "profane" matters making sure that everything the Scriptures say is the historical truth (DS 3652-53). Of course, as we have also seen, when evolution was first put forward, not only was the theory condemned by Catholic churchmen, but the attempts to reconcile the theory with creation were officially rejected.[52]

1. The New Distinctions Applied to Church Teaching
In the light of the new theology of Scripture, a new theology of Church teaching was now needed.

As we are already aware, the Church simply applied the distinctions between the essence, expression and understanding of the truth to the expression and understanding of its teachings. Surely Church teachings were not to be taken any *more* literally than the Scriptures. Rather, it was now to be acknowledged that Church teachings were also the result of God's speaking through persons who remain who and what they are, their limitations notwithstanding. Thus, just as inspiration preserved the truth essential to salvation, divine guidance guaranteed that the essence of the truth would not be lost in its interpretation. And, surely, the Church should be expected to grow in its understanding of the essence. But, this did not "change" doctrine; if it did, there would be no reason to believe the Church right now. It was the "development" of doctrine; the essence which had always been affirmed, if implicitly, that had become better understood and better expressed.[53]

2. Implicit Precedent for the Development of Doctrine
From the very moment that the idea of doctrinal development was articulated, the evidence of Christian history was seen to confirm it.

It was obvious the classical system of doctrine had developed. After all, if the early Fathers did consider the Holy Spirit to be the Third Person of the Blessed Trinity, why didn't they say so? Now this was no scandal.

Studies of Christian history also made clear that controversy was

---

52. As early as 1860, the Provincial Council of Cologne had condemned any notion that the human body was the product of evolution.

53. The term "development of doctrine" originated in the writings of John Henry Newman (1801-90), a convert from Anglicanism whose eloquent writings about his conversion paved the way for many others. According to his conception, however, the development of doctrine involved the articulation of truths that were always known explicitly.

instrumental in the formation of doctrine. It was Marcion whose thought required the Church to decide upon a canon. Arius and Pelagius required the Church to come to terms with issues which were only settled when *their* positions were unacceptable.

Study was likewise responsible for a deepening of the awareness that theological progress had involved differences among orthodox thinkers. The "schools" were newly distinguished for their characteristic approach. The Alexandrians were inclined to see things "spiritually" and "symbolically." In reaction, the Antiochenes were more "realistic" and concerned about orthodoxy. Western theology was most "legalistic" and it was most rigorous.[54]

The ambiguity of orthodoxy became especially evident in the time it took for certain ideas to be condemned, or replaced, as Augustine's entire world-view was now seen to have been replaced by Thomas. This was the occasion for the realization that Christianity must be distinguished from the world-views which it has been required to interpret.

Of greatest importance was the evidence that even *declared* doctrine had developed. Supported by centuries of Christian thinking, the Council of Florence had declared that outside the Church no one can be saved (cf. p. 47). The Baptisms of blood and desire notwithstanding, the unchurched were surely damned. But, with the age of exploration and the attendant discovery of peoples all over the world who had never so much as heard the name of Jesus, the condemnation of the non-baptized came to be seen differently. It did not seem just; not having had the opportunity to make the choice for Christ and the Church, how could God condemn them? Even man would be more just than this. (To the argument that man's justice is not necessarily God's justice, it was simply responded that there is no idea of justice that does not begin with man's — and from there goes "up.") Faced with this dilemma the Church eventually decided that the necessity of Baptism did not apply to those who had no fair chance to be baptized. Since they too receive grace — after all "God wills all men to be saved..." (1 Tim.2:4) — they could be saved by their primitive faith and response to conscience. As we saw, this position entered formal teaching under Pius IX, who said that non-Christians of far away places live in "invincible ignorance"(cf. p. 149). This statement was contained in the same letter that contained his first condemnation of indifferentism, an affirmation of the idea that there is "normally" no salvation outside the Church.

54. In what was now seen to have been a remarkable concession to the pluralism of valid approaches, the Council of Florence had acknowledged that neither the *filioque* nor the Greek idea that the Spirit proceeds "through" the Son completely captures the truth which both ideas attempt to express (DS 1300-02).

Nonetheless, this new explanation of the old teaching was a major development.

3. The Formulation of the New Theology; A New Theology of Revelation

The first *acknowledged* development of doctrine was the new theology of Church teaching.

In its formulation, the new theology first attempted to account for the idea that truth was now spoken of as an "essence." To do so, it invoked what was proclaimed to be the biblical idea that revelation is "personal." Not consisting of lifeless truths (the so-called "propositional" model of revelation), it consists of a person, God revealing Himself. This He did gradually as persons do. When finally man was ready, God revealed Himself fully, "in" person, in the person of Christ (cf. Heb.1:1-4). Here was good reason for the differences between the Old and New Testaments. Moreover, since the truth is a person (cf. Jn.14:6) — whom different persons are bound to see somewhat differently — there were bound to be differing views of Jesus within the New Testament. Together, they provide a view from all sides — a more complete view of the fullness of revelation.

Though Jesus was indeed the fullness of revelation, the recipient of the revelation was still man. Therefore, its full understanding was not to be expected. What was to be expected was that man would grow in its understanding. Entrusted to the Church, revelation was meant to be reflected upon and passed on, and this was meant to lead to the development of doctrine and a reform of practice which would be signs of the Church's spiritual growth. This was the true meaning of the ancient dictum *Ecclesia semper reformandum* ("The Church is always reforming").

Originally passed on in the form of oral tradition, the truth was already the product of reflection by the time it was first written down. It continued to develop *after* the Scriptures were written and it is still alive today. In other words, the Church has a "living tradition." The magisterium serves to guide this tradition by determining its parameters. The infallibility of the magisterium is evident in the simple presumption that the Spirit guides the Church.

The new theology of Church teaching had apologetic appeal. Not only did it explain the facts leaving infallibility intact, but it employed these facts in a documentable assertion that Scripture was the product of tradition. And, it excused the lack of scriptural support for doctrines which the reformers had abandoned. Though they *were* the product of theological reasoning, so were doctrines which the Scriptures taught explicitly. This was no demeaning of the Scriptures. They were still seen to have been inspired. They were inspired in order to provide a basis for the ongoing development of doctrine which must continue if the faith is to grow with humanity.

The time was right and Vatican II adopted much of what the new theology of Church teaching had to offer. Stating specifically that revelation was God communicating Himself (*Dei Verbum,* Ch. I), the Council actually went so far as to abandon the idea that the sources of revelation were two, Scripture and a distinct unwritten Tradition, and spoke instead of the one Tradition, a living one, that includes them both and the acts of the magisterium (Ch. II). The Council then gave formal support to the recognition that the Scriptures have their human element which must be taken into account if they are to be interpreted correctly (Ch. III).[55]

4. An Addendum: The Distinction between the Ordinary and Extraordinary Magisterium

Before we consider the important doctrinal developments that now followed, we would do well to examine the uniquely modern distinction between the "ordinary" and "extraordinary" magisterium.

First, let us be clear that doctrinal development was not understood to allow the Church to unteach doctrine. It was not imagined to involve a change in what the Church was knowingly trying to communicate at any time in the past. This is called the "irreformability" of doctrine and it was insisted on when infallibility was formally declared (see especially DS 3020). It was not imagined that infallibility could mean anything else.

It was largely for this reason that infallibility was insisted on only insofar as a pope or ecumenical council deliberately intended to declare a doctrine, or "dogma," binding on the conscience of the faithful. These were considered "extraordinary" acts of the magisterium. Few in number, they were *not* recognized to include any moral teachings. They were distinguished from "ordinary" acts of popes, non-ecumenical councils, papal and regional commissions, and local bishops. These *were* reformable.

It served the Church to make this distinction. The initial conflict between evolution and Christianity involved certain rather uncompromising declarations about such things as the creation of Eve from Adam's rib and the existence of the talking serpent. The conflict was resolved using

55. Contemporaneously, Paul VI (1962-78) issued an instruction to the Pontifical Biblical Commission which explicitly acknowledged that gospels are the products of three definite periods of formation: the preaching of Jesus, the recollection of the apostles, and the writing of the first Christians (see his *Sancta Mater Ecclesia*).

concepts once condemned. Moreover, as the newly painstaking studies of everything had uncovered, the history of the papacy had involved a number of acts which would have compromised the concept of infallibility if it were extended too broadly. After all, Galileo had been condemned. Furthermore: Pope Liberius had signed an Arian creed. Pope Gelasius had condemned transubstantiation. Based on a literal reading of Psalm 15, several popes had condemned loans at interest while, based on Exodus 22:18, Innocent VIII had encouraged the burning of witches. Gregory XVI had condemned railroads. Now each of these teachings could be seen in the context of its time and, without elaborate argument, replaced.

B) Important Developments

Even as the new theology of Church teaching was being formulated, several important developments were already taking shape. Notably, the most important involved a reform of the one teaching whose historical development was one of its most important precedents — the doctrine "Outside the Church No Salvation."

1. The Continuing Development of the Doctrine
"Outside the Church No Salvation"

When last we encountered the doctrine "Outside the Church No Salvation," it already had been qualified by the "invincible ignorance" of people who never had the opportunity to become Christians (cf. p. 194). Said to receive grace — communicated by the Holy Spirit as all grace is — they could respond in a primitive faith in God, however they saw Him, and in the obedience of their conscience. In this way, some could be saved. But, let there be no mistake; when this idea was first conceived, it was considered the exception, not the rule. If *many* non-Christians were saved, what was the value of being Christian? What was the necessity of the Church?

With time, however, and an increasing familiarity with non-Christian cultures, the better Christian thinkers began to realize that to see a vast difference between us and them was the most narrow-minded sort of provincialism. Moreover, reflection on the correlation of culture, faith and conscience made clear that non-Christian religions were hardly incidental to the religious lives of their adherents. They learned about God and right and wrong *through* these religions just as Christians learned about them through Christianity. Faced with what seemed to be a Christian version of indifferentism, Christians needed some way to maintain the truth of their conviction that Christ and the Christian way were essential to salvation. Churchmen needed some way to retain this essentiality for the Church.

Soon a way was found. It came to be insisted that, in all cases, the Spirit actually communicates Christ. This involved a little-known element of Justin's theology that provided just the insight that theologians needed.

Justin was convinced that Christ was indeed "the" truth, the "Logos," the "Word" of truth itself (cf. p. 51). But, he was still bothered by what he could not help but see as the truth of much of Greek philosophy. Unwilling to compromise his belief that Christ was "the" truth, God's perfect expression of Himself, Justin insisted that it was He to whom God had entrusted the whole task of revelation. (Thus, it was really the Word who spoke to the patriarchs and the prophets.) This was the reason He had participated in creation (cf. Jn.1:1-4). But, not only did He do the work, He was its model. Therefore, it is really Christ who anyone sees to the extent that he perceives any truth. For this reason, Justin suggested that the Greeks could rightly be called "Christian."[56]

Justin's thinking encouraged Karl Rahner (1904-84) to insist that all the world's religions have as their object an imperfect perception of Christ even though their adherents do not know it, and would probably disagree. They should therefore be called "anonymous Christians."[57] Rahner was actually to conclude that implicit Christian faith is possessed by a person who accepts any truth, especially the truth of the fact of his own humanity. This he saw as an inarticulate form of repentance — essentially a submission to something greater.

The idea that Christ was bigger than Jesus offered Christianity a way to escape the problem of insisting that its truths were only for the historically, geographically privileged. The historical Jesus became the boundless love of God made visible. (The sacraments became visible signs of the grace He gives everyone.) The idea that the Spirit was, and is, at work in bringing Christ to consciousness through all the world's religions transformed them into evidence of His action rather than a reason to deny that Christianity is special.

In view of all the above, the Second Vatican Council formally accepted much of what the new theology had to offer. The Council spoke several times of the divine origin of other world religions (see the documents *Lumen Gentium,* paragraph 15; *Nostra Aetate,* 2[58]; and *Ad*

---

56. See his *First Apology,* 46, 2-3.

57. See his "Anonymous Christians."

58. In paragraph 4, the council speaks of the Church's special bonds with Judaism. Declaring that Jewish people did not inherit the guilt of Christ's death (despite the testimony of Mt.27:25), the council laments the anti-semitism that has been justified on this ground.

Gentes Divinitus, 3). It all but stated that these religions are vehicles of salvation.

During the council, Paul VI was even to speak of the sincere faith of the atheist whose honest pursuit of the truth had been misguided by misinformation (see his *Ecclesiam Suam*). Indeed, in view of the obvious evidence, it was now to be acknowledged that the essential holiness of such persons might well surpass that of professed Christians.[59]

Still claiming to be the community of the faithful outside of which no one would be saved, the Church now held that all men of good will are "ordered" to the Church whether or not they know, or want to be (*Lumen Gentium,* 16). In its own mind, the Church's idea of itself had grown as did its conception of Christ.

The doctrine "Outside the Church No Salvation" had developed considerably. In the face of charges that the Church had changed its teaching, churchmen insisted that the historical formulation of the teaching was meant to affirm the essentiality of the Church *per se* and actually condemned only those who left it knowingly. (The biblical insistence on the necessity of faith in Jesus was now seen as the only way that the primitive Church knew how to affirm the fact that Christ was indeed "the" way to salvation.) Though the modern formulation of this idea was admittedly quite different, it was still insisted that there was a definite "continuity" between the formulations of the teaching old and new.

2. Religious Liberty and Ecumenism

The new formulation of the teaching "Outside the Church No Salvation" obviously meant that the Church's position on a number of issues would need to change with it. Immediately affected was the teaching on religious liberty.

When last we heard of religious liberty, Gregory XVI had condemned Félicite' Lammenais, one of its leading proponents (cf. footnote p. 149). Gregory's condemnation of religious liberty was confirmed by Pius IX whose "Syllabus" included the *error* that "it is good that is some Catholic lands the law has allowed people emigrating there to exercise publicly their own cult" (DS 2978). Considering what was then the Church's understanding of the requirements of salvation, this made sense.

But salvation now required following one's faith. Thus, it seemed the Church should promote religious liberty. This was precisely the position that men like John Courtney Murray (1904-67) took to Vatican II.

---

59. Indeed, it was now insisted that those who closed their eyes to the evidence and were unwilling to accept the modern understanding of salvation may have less faith than many atheists.

Thanks to their efforts, the council was persuaded to declare religious liberty a "human right." The document *Dignitatis Humanae* was entirely devoted to this teaching.

The Church was now convinced that it should strive for peaceful co-existence with differing belief systems. To this end, it should talk with leaders of other religions in an attempt to identify the points upon which they already agreed. Termed the "inter-religious dialogue," this would also be the best way to continue the work of evangelization. So taught the decree *Ad Gentes,* the Council's attempt to revitalize the missionary activity of the Church, an activity whose motive was now seen as the Church's duty to give everyone the opportunity to know the Christ who is already the object of whatever faith they have.

Remarkable though the preceding developments may have been, surely they did not surpass the changes in attitude towards what would soon be called the Church's separated "brothers," the Orthodox and Protestant Churches. The Council of Florence had specifically stated that neither schismatics nor heretics will be saved unless, before the end of their lives, they are reconciled to the Church. This was precisely the attitude that had prevailed ever since. The Reformation set Protestants *against* Catholics and, as far as the Church was concerned, reconcilation still meant that the Protestants had to rejoin the Church. If they did not, they were at least as damned as pagans, and maybe more so; after all, they had heard the truth but rejected it.

But now that they had come to an appreciation of the religiosity of non-Christians, churchmen were bound to grow in their appreciation of the sincerity and good Christian faith of non-Catholics. According to men like Yves Congar (b.1904),[60] it was time for the Church to acknowledge that all Christians were truly brothers in the same Christ. Moreover, in view of the fact that the Church had come to adopt some of the positions of those who had left it (such as the Protestant encouragement of the private devotional reading of Scripture), the Church should even admit that the Spirit had given the dissidents something to say. (This was possible within the context of the idea that everyone has some perception of a truth which no one possesses perfectly.[61]) Finally, since the dissidents obviously existed in real communities of faith — which was surely the work of the Spirit — they should be dealt with as "churches" even if they were not in communion with the one true Church.

60. See his *Divided Christendom.*
61. This is the reason that disputes are best settled when persons strive to see each other's point of view.

The work of men like Congar culminated in *Unitatis Redintegratio*, Vatican II's decree on the Catholic principles of Christian unity, or "ecumenism." (The term dated from the Protestants' attempts to achieve their own unity which had begun about a century earlier.) Acknowledging that the "separated" were indeed brothers, the Church actually apologized for its share of the "scandal" of disunity. Moreover, in view of the recognition that there is an element of truth present in the perceptions of all sincere believers, it declared that unity is best pursued by dialogue. Acknowledging that non-Catholics could form churches[62], it defined its relation to these churches in terms of a "hierarchy of truths" which was also meant to lead Christians to realize the degree to which they were already in agreement.

* * *

In the meantime, the Council's general efforts to renew the Church's own faith-community life resulted in the adoption of a number of what would previously have been considered Protestant ideas. In the name of what was officially called "pastoral" concern, the Church reformed its "liturgy" (with the aim of improving the people's understanding and participation), "ministry" (with the aim of forming clerics willing and able to be a true *Alter Christus* — who came to serve — while newly encouraging all God's people to share in His work), and government (with the remarkable aim of establishing structures through which, to a certain extent, even authority could be shared). All in all, a definite *rapprochement* had begun.

3. A New Conception of Christian Life

Actually, not only did the new teaching on the salvation of non-Catholics lead to the lessening of tensions — and practical agreement — between Catholics and Protestants, it also led to a *rapprochement* in terms of doctrine, the one doctrine that most divided them, the question of justification.

The new theology of the salvation of non-Christians became the common property of both Catholics and the more "liberal" of what would eventually be called the "main-line" Protestant denominations.

62. Actually, "churches" having all the earmarks of "the" Church, with the exception of the communion with the pope (the Orthodox and Anglicans), were distinguished from "ecclesial communities" which had sacrificed some of what made them a bonafide church according to what was considered the revealed model of what a church should be. The Orthodox were further distinguished from the Anglicans whose "orders" were not considered valid since Leo XIII declared that they were not conferred with the fullness of what was intended by the Church (*Apostolicae Curae, DS 3315-19); see also Vatican II's Orientalium Ecclesiarum*).

The power of the arguments was too compelling to be denied even though the new theology involved the admission that explicit faith in Christ was not required for salvation. Moreover, as it became clear that explicit faith, even in God, should not be required, it also became clear that it was only in the conduct of a person's life could there be seen the evidence that he did submit to something. This seemed very sympathetic to the Catholic idea that it was only in obedience that the Christian showed his true colors. But, how was one to identify obedience from culture to culture? There was only one thing the Christian had a right to expect from everyone — love.

But, love originates in God who loved us first.

The person must decide whether to love Him back, to accept God's love, something very sympathetic to the Protestant notion of justification.

This is what Rahner would call exercise of one's "fundamental option."[63] But, since it involves the whole person, it must involve his whole life. It must be lived out. And, as it is, it may grow, or it may diminish and die out. It is man's lifelong response to grace, a lifelong process of conversion and growth. (Pure Protestantism is perceived to neglect man's life before and after a moment of conversion.) Loving God involves obedience because love makes concrete demands. This, however, was a change; no more was it love out of obedience, it was obedience out of love. Man is "called," not commanded to love. (Scrupulosity was now bad.)

Now faith and obedience could be seen as differing degrees of man's response to God's love. God offers Himself to man. Man's response begins with repentance, his recognition that he is not God. It becomes faith, the recognition that God is, that God loves, that God loves me. It continues with the faithful, on-going acceptance of this love which consists of loving God, showing it, and loving God's other children — ever more deeply.

The new perspective on faith and obedience gave a new perspective to the evidence of Scripture and Tradition.

We have already seen the texts which speak of the essentiality of "obedience" (cf. p. 109). Read in the light of recent developments, it became clear that, in every case, to obey was to love. The synoptics said that the love of God and neighbor was the summation of the law. But, as John explained, love followed belief; he who believed in Jesus would do His works (cf. Jn.14:12). He who loves Jesus would obey His commandments (cf. Jn.14:15). Thus, as the letter to the Galatians had

63. See his "Fundamental Option."

said all along: "faith expresses itself through love" (Gal.5:6).

Actually, as modern Scripture scholarship now showed, Paul's theology of justification by faith was principally his response to the question of whether Gentile converts to Christianity should be required to observe the Mosaic law with all of its many elaborate prescriptions. Of course, he also condemned any legalism that insinuated that salvation was a matter of external observances and not the internal conversion of one's heart. Though conversion was first manifest in faith, Paul never meant to imply it should not include love, a true love manifesting a sincere faith expressing itself in concrete acts of unselfish giving. As he himself said: you could have faith great enough to move mountains but, without love, you are nothing (cf. 1 Cor.13:1-13).

This was the reason that Augustine could say "Love and do what you will (cf. p. 106). Though the importance of love was soon to be obscured by the increasing institutionalization of the Church — and its attendant concern for law — love remained at the heart of the true Christian. Then, with the renewal of Christian spirituality in modern mystics like Teresa of Avila (1515-82), the essentiality of love reappeared. John of the Cross (1542-91) would write that love is the essence of the self-surrender that makes possible the "union" with God which is man's true destiny.[64] The importance of love was clearly present in Vatican II (see especially *Lumen Gentium*, 42).

Not surprisingly, the re-emphasis of love had its effect on Catholic moral theology. Reflected in the work of men like Bernard Häring (b.1912), pains were now taken to show that specific laws were necessary implications of the law of love.[65] Where it had begun to appear that a specific law was too specific, it was actually recommended that the law be changed.

The new perspectives also led to a distinction between a violation of the law and sin. Anticipated in Thomas' insistence on the supremacy of the "informed" conscience — i.e. the voice of conscience as it speaks when a question is considered correctly[66] — the Church now could admit the possibility of a sincere but malformed conscience. This meant that even though acts are "right" or "wrong," it is *motive* that decides whether or not the person who commits them is "good" or "bad." (No longer were

---

64. See especially his *The Spiritual Canticle.*
65. See his *The Law of Christ*; actually Häring's work had its inspiration in the voluminous moral writings of Alphonsus Ligori (1696-1787), the founder of the "Redemptorist" order of which he is a member.
66. *S. Th.* I, q.79, a.13.

there automatically "mortal" sins, now there was "grave matter" and'full consent.) New attention was accorded the old conviction that God asks no more than one's best; and one's best will differ from person to person. And "to those to whom much is given much will be required" (Lk.12:48).

C) The Development of Christian Evolutionism

The theological progress that followed the reform of the Church's teaching on the salvation of non-Catholics was only the beginning.

1. The Development of a Theology of Secularity

It was several centuries in the making, but the time had come for a theology of secularity — a theology of a positive attitude toward earthly existence.

As we have seen, the scholastic — and hellenic and biblical — understanding of Christianity did not involve a very positive view of life on earth (cf. p. 75). The world was fallen, its goods were distractions from God. Therefore, attempts to make life better were not only destructive of spiritual life, they were surely futile.

Of course, as history would have it, such attempts proved *not* to be futile and, as they were increasingly successful, the goods they provided to increasing numbers proved to be *too* good to be forsaken for the sake of the increasingly obscure value of their renunciation. Indeed, if nothing else, modern progress had actually freed man from many of the mundane struggles which had hitherto served to preoccupy energies which might now be turned to spiritual pursuits.

Moreover, the widespread enjoyment of these goods, particularly those which were the products of human labor, was beginning to fuel membership in activist organizations such as the Communist Party whose members perceived that their struggle for a better world necessarily involved an abandonment of the secular negativism of Christianity and its attendant passivity.

The increasing popularity of the Communist movement undoubtedly encouraged Leo XIII's groundbreaking encyclical *Rerum Novarum* (DS 3265-71). The encyclical was groundbreaking for two reasons: 1) it spoke to an issue for which there was no direct biblical reference, and 2) it implicitly affirmed the increasingly secular concerns of modernity. Indeed, even though "the love of money is the root of all evils (1 Tim.6:10), the laborer was still entitled to a "just" share of the fruits of his labor. Though the encyclical also affirmed the "right" of private property, it marked the beginning of the Church's concern for social reform.

Rerum Novarum was a first step. But, it did not address the classical idea that worldly pursuits are distractions from God. Of course, in its insistence that the goods of the world must be distributed justly, it implicitly acknowledged that they were "good." The modern experience had made it impossible to assert otherwise. Therefore, theologians finally began to take seriously an idea that had already been articulated.

It had long been insisted that everything was "of" God and "like" Him to the extent that it is good. Therefore, it was simply to be asserted that the exploration and enjoyment of creation are proper means to know God so long as the explorer did not mistake the created for the Creator —the modern understanding of idolatry.[67] With the insight of the new theology of Christian life, any true interest in anything good could now be considered an implicit act of faith — an act which was never more clearly an act of love.

The burgeoning sensitivity to the fact that it was God who was loved in created things soon led to the realization that there is nothing more lovable than other people. Classically, it had been good to love others "because" they are God's children; now it was realized that "as" God's children, they are lovable. It is the Lord one serves "in" others (cf. Rom.12:11, Eph.6:7). The love of God and man were no longer considered to compete. Newly conceived was the importance of human relationships. (Relationships challenge the whole person and may do so for his whole life.) Obviously, this led to a largely novel appreciation for marriage as a state of life. This led to an entirely novel appreciation of human sexuality, a created reality rightly experienced as good and is obviously constructive of the intimacy which is the goal of married life.

The burgeoning sensitivity to the fact that it is God who is loved in others soon led to the realization that God is to be loved in "me." Classically, the person was unworthy of God's love. Now the person was encouraged to realize that God had created him good and special. (God gave his "self" worth.)Though he must not forget that God has given him everything he is — true humility as Thomas had already described it [68] — he is to love himself as the first stage of a sincere love of others. (Self-denial was now a source of spiritual enrichment, and a means of charity.)

All in all, the theology of secularity had a tremendous effect on Christian Spirituality. Now, life was for living. Being Christian was being human.

---

67. The modern opposite of idolatry is "detachment" — the recognition that things are not of ultimate importance.

68. See his *Summa Contra Gentiles*, 4, 55.

2. The Development of Theologies of Progress

The development of a theology of secularity inevitably led to theologies of progress; after all, secular goods were the obvious products of progress.

Of course, as we have seen — if sometimes paranthetically — theologies of progress, i.e. theologies of history were not new to Christianity. Justin said that history before Christ was the progressive incarnation of the Word (cf. p. 198). In *The City of God*, Augustine said that history after Christ is the gradual conquest of evil (cf. footnote p. 40). Moreover, modern theology turned to progress in order to ground its idea of the development of doctrine. But, never before was general progress described in terms of scientific or artistic achievement, and even standard of living, even apart from ending injustice, considered man's holy work on earth. Now, progress began to be described as man's co-operation in creation, the creation of God's kingdom, a work whose culmination will somehow be seen in eternity.

Even as the preceding ideas gained general acceptance, certain thinkers had already come to see societal progress as an extension of evolution, an idea which led to new conceptions of reality as a whole. Following Hegel, Henri Bergson (1858-1941) insisted that reality is forever "becoming," something new, as propelled by an "elan vital" (or "life-force") with which it was somehow imbued. [69]

Evolutionary thinking received an explicitly Christian expression in the work of Pierre Teilhard de Chardin (1881-1955). He held that the energy which propels evolution is "love," God's love. He also insisted that evolution betrayed a "direction," ever increasing unity, and a goal, "Christ," the fullness of God's love. Most controversially, Teilhard believed that the historical person Jesus was a prefigurement of the "cosmic Christ" which the world is slowly but surely becoming. [70]

Despite the controversial character of much of Teilhard's thought, his assertion that evolution betrays a Christian direction converted the idea into an apologetic for the same faith it had so recently threatened. Surely this encouraged the Second Vatican Council to acknowledge that

69. See his *L'Evolution creatrice*. Bergson is also remembered for his modern revival of "intuitionism," the idea that the demand for proof positive is essentially inappropriate to the fact that human knowing involves certain super-logical leaps which have their origin in evidence but cannot be reduced to it. Bergson's intuitionism was partly a response to the linguistic philosophers whom he felt demanded a correspondence of words and ideas which did not do justice to the essentially inexpressible contents of ideas.
70. See his *Le Phénomène humain*.

"mankind has passed from a static to an evolutionary concept of nature" (see *Gaudium et Spes*, 5). This document, the council's declaration on the Church in the modern world, was formal approval of the theology of secularity.

3. Theologies of the Corporate Nature of Humanity and Creation
In its implicit endorsement of theologies of progress, *Gaudium et Spes* also contained the Church's first official statement of the corporate nature of humanity and creation. This was inevitable; after all, what progresses except humanity, what evolves except creation?

To be sure, such thinking was not totally new to Christian tradition. Even earlier, the Old Testament gives more than ample evidence of the idea of the Hebrew concept of corporate morality and God's equally corporate retribution. (Surely the doctrine of original sin is the outstanding example of this idea.)

Nonetheless, never before had thinkers spoken of humanity as one family whose achievements and failures were somehow the product and heritage of all. Never before had they spoken of humanity as "one." They even explained it — in terms of the oneness of creation — and they described the latter in almost personal terms. (Teilhard would go so far as to suggest that evolution is in the process of the creation of an "ultra-man," an essentially single thing with human parts.[71])

Now, in the light of modern needs, theologies of the corporate nature of humanity and creation were employed in the host of attempts to render modern reformulations of all of the classical doctrines which progress had called into serious question.

***

Evolution had been Christianized. Evolution had become a major element of the new ideas with which theology was finally to respond to the centuries of Christian decline it once appeared to confirm. Truly a Christian Evolutionism had been created, and it was good.

71. See his *The Future of Man.*

Chapter V:
The Future of Doctrinal Development

Section I: The Process of Doctrinal Development

The introduction to *Christian Materialism* has already offered this author's opinion that the recent theological progress he has called Christian Evolutionism will not be sufficient to re-establish the credibility of Christianity in a modern world whose world-view is materialism, the only metaphysic in which evolution ever made sense. Thus, the creation of Christian Materialism was said to be needed. But, the synthesis of Christianity and materialism was anticipated to involve changes far more dramatic than those which resulted from the synthesis of Christianity and evolution, especially those formally approved by Vatican II. This was the reason that the introduction to Part I concluded with the promise of a look at the principles which would rightly govern the process of doctrinal development, particularly with respect to the degree of "drama" which change can involve and still be called legitimate.

A) The Creation of Doctrine

Any look at the process of doctrinal development must begin with an examination of the process by which doctrine is originally created. How else are we to obtain an understanding of the way in which doctrine develops?

1. The Necessity of Doctrine

Before we examine the process by which doctrine is created, it would surely be helpful to clarify the reason that the creation of doctrine is necessary. The question of the necessity of doctrine has some precedent in the opinion that theology is a useless attempt to express the inexpressible (cf. p. 98). It is also posed by the "indifferentist" opinion that all religions are really the same (cf. p. 132).

Temporarily prescinding from a detailed portrayal of the fact that all religions are really not the same (q.v. p. 269, 362), the question of the necessity of doctrine can nonetheless be answered now. In short, though it is easy to acknowledge that the experience — and thus the content — of faith cannot be captured wholly and totally in words and formulas, it is also to be acknowledged that no truth can be. If linguistic philosophy has shown us anything, it has shown us that language has its limitations. Nevertheless, it surely remains both possible and necessary to say what *can* be said, if for no other reason than to identify what is *not* the truth.

Indeed, without such statements, i.e. doctrine, faith would surely fall into the abyss of confusion, caprice and conflict which would soon make confident, consistent and united belief *and action* impossible.

This said, we can now turn to the specific means which have already been involved in the creation of doctrine.

2. The Rule of Faith

As modern biblical criticism has certainly made clear, Jesus left no detailed doctrinal system defining the truth and providing principles by which to direct the answering of any question which might arise with respect to it. This was left to His disciples.

Remembering His life and teaching as best they could, and guided by the content of their faith as they experienced its truth, Jesus' first disciples attempted to concretize and communicate their faith. This was the first operation of the "rule" of faith. It resulted in the production of an articulate Christian tradition which had the authority of its proximity to the actual life and teaching of Jesus.

When the need for a more detailed articulation of the faith presented itself, subsequent generations of Christians were bound by the data of tradition. But, they were bound by the data of the whole tradition, written and not, and this guided the interpretation of any one of its specific statements. More importantly, they were still guided by the rule of faith, the content of faith as they experienced its truth. This was the basis of the non-literal interpretation of many of the scriptural statements which were once excused on the basis of the claim that a literal reading was not what Jesus or God "really" meant.

3. The Rule of Reason, the Necessity of Theology
a. The Idea

Efforts to express the content of faith obviously involve reason at least inasmuch as reason is involved in the expression of anything. After all, the description of experience and its attendant ideas involves words with determinate meanings in the context of language and truth generally. Furthermore, reason must address the many implications that any idea will have in a world of inter-related truths. In other words, if our experience of God has moved us to say He "always was," we are also bound to observe that He had no creator and much, much more. This is the "rule of reason" — the science of theology at work.

Moreover, human as man is, faith is not only to be stated, it is also to be questioned. This questioning is both inevitable and, as it is experienced, good. It is good that man needs to know more, to know how, to know why; this is how he grows.

In order to question, man must see his faith within the general context of truth as he sees it, and he must utilize this context in order to learn more about what his beliefs really involve. In other words, in wondering about how it can be that God "always was," we reflect upon what it is for anything to "be" and in so doing try to determine how anything could always have been. Naturally, in doing so, we are bound by the requirement of "reasons" to hold what we do.

As Abelard showed, without reason we have no way to settle disputes in which both sides appeal to the experience of faith — the vast majority of all theological disputes (cf. p. 34). Without the requirement of reasons, these disputes would be unresolvable in principle.

Dealing with theological disputes, or simply answering questions may require the creation of terminology or even concepts which are not part of the immediate data of tradition. As the fathers of the Council of Nicea discovered long ago, the precise explanation of the relationship between Jesus and the Father — one which would not encourage a misinterpretation of Jesus' divinity in the direction of either of the then popular oversimplifications of this idea — required the creation of a new word, *homoousios*, "one-in-being" (cf. footnote p. 52). Similar disputes made necessary the use of such rationally derived terms as "substance" and "person." These were words with a more precise meaning than the terminology previously available. They were better able to express ideas which admittedly defy expression in any words. And if this were not done, the data of tradition would have been liable to serious misinterpretation.

To those who would object to the idea that Christianity should express itself in terms which involve a "philosophy," we would ask: What is philosophy except a description of the world as it is? What is Christianity if it is not an interpretation of the world? How is Christianity expected to survive in the context of philosophies that do not admit of those things, such as spirituality, freedom, etc., which its very sensibility requires?

b. Theological Method

At this point, the discussion would likely profit from a look at some of the specifics of the relationship between faith and reason: theological method.

Like any other science, theology properly attempts to account for all the data with statements which can pass an appropriate test. Like any other science, it is expected to justify both its data and the principles involved in its interpretation. This must involve evidence demonstrably applicable and sufficient; the application of principles must be consistent.

Unlike other sciences, theology accepts as data the experience of faith and the facts of Christian tradition, especially the Scriptures. Catholics see as authoritative the teaching of the Church. But, this does not mean that the validity of any of these sources — or the specifics, or the meaning of their content — is to be accepted without the need of a justification of some sort. On the contrary, in the face of the fact that religious traditions or experience can be used in order to justify anything, including a host of contradictory notions, reason requires a reason to accept the data of any religion — especially the datum of experience.

B) The Development of Existing Doctrine

Having described the general principles involved in the creation of doctrine, we can now turn to those involved in its development.

1. The Necessity of Development

Before we consider the specific principles of doctrinal development, a few words may be in order concerning the necessity of doctrinal development.

Unquestionably, the crux of the issue rests in the crisis of credibility which Christianity faced little over a century ago at the hands of the theory of evolution. Existing, immemorial ideas about the Scriptures were fundamentally tested and they failed. Were it not for the development of new theologies of inerrancy and inspiration, the Bible would not be believable to the educated and intellectually honest of today. Development was indeed necessary. Therefore, if Christianity is truly the authoritative voice of God's truth, the development of its doctrine is not only necessary, it must certainly be in accord with God's will.

Contrary to the idea that doctrinal "reforms" correct past failures and are only to be accepted with some shame and apology, it should now be clear that "developments" are just that — the forward movement of mankind toward the truth of God Himself. In light of the theologies of progress, it should now be clear that doctrinal reform has its proper place within the context of the great enterprise in which humanity is engaged.

2. The Rule of Deepening Faith

Perhaps the best way in which to describe the role of the rule of deepening faith in the development of existing doctrine would be to examine an example of one of the most notable ways in which it has already worked — the development of the doctrine "Outside the Church No Salvation."

It is not to be denied that for most of Christian history most Christians, including churchmen, were utterly sure that almost everyone who was not baptized was going to hell. This idea was consistent with their conception, and thus their experience, of God. This conception, which placed an emphasis on God's justice, was the Judaic heritage of the first Christians' idea of God.

It was only slowly that Christian spirituality, and, as we can now say, human progress generally, came to a deeper understanding of the fact of God's love. (Christianity actually came to understand that to condemn someone for failing to do something which they had no chance to do is not even just.) This caused a tension which was eventually to be relieved by the formulation of a new teaching on salvation. This new teaching was the work of the rule of deepening faith.

3. The Rule of Demanding Reason
a. The Idea

Like the rule of deepening faith, the rule of demanding reason is also best illustrated by example.

Surely reason was at work in the thinking which identified the problems with the old doctrine on salvation and, specifically, its inconsistency with the results of what was indeed spiritual progress. It was likewise at work in the deliberations which produced the synthesis of the old doctrine and the new spirituality.

But, it was also involved in the discovery of facts which the doctrine was required to take into account. Mention has already been made of the fact that the Age of Exploration had uncovered millions of people unknown to the ancient and medieval thinker. This fact had its definite effect upon the doctrine as it was eventually formulated. It is a clear case of the evidence of the world having a specific influence upon the formulation of Church teaching — and scriptural interpretation. An even better example is to be seen in the influence of evolution on the formulation of theologies of creation and revelation. History makes clear that these changes were *required* by reason. Faced with the evidence in favor of evolution, faith could still have denied the theory, explaining that some demon had forged evidence that would otherwise have persuaded. But reason would not permit it. This was the rule of *demanding* reason.

b. Further Reflections on Theological Method

The rule of demanding reason has some very definite things to tell us about the ways theology should operate from now on.

It tells us that theology must respect the competency of other disciplines. All contribute to man's ongoing attempt to understand God, the origin of all things. They may even contribute to man's attempt to understand revelation.

The rule of demanding reason also tells us that the content of revelation can no longer be presumed to involve a simple reading of tradition or one's own spiritual experience. Though it has always been understood that experience or tradition may be misinterpreted — hence the need for official Church teachings — it is now to be acknowledged that even the most straightforward of revelation's data may not have been meant to say what it seems to, or even what the Church has taught that it says.

The above can only be understood in terms of the following:

We have already discussed the question of whether Church teachings can be said to change (cf. p. 193). We have seen it insisted that the Church's teachings "develop," the essence of what they were meant to say "irreformable" even though their expression or even understanding may improve. This essence was identified in the "continuity" between expressions.

But, when we consider that continuity is seen between teachings as diverse as the old and new versions of the doctrine "Outside The Church No Salvation" — where the essence of the teaching states that the Church is essential to salvation in a mystical sense — surely some question must be raised as to the meaning of the word "development."

Must it not be admitted that doctrine *can* change? Actually, this is a question of semantics. The important question is: in future attempts at doctrinal development, where existing doctrine conflicts with the evidence of the world, how deep into the doctrine can one go in order to identify an essence that one could call the essential content of Church teaching or Christian revelation? How far from the original formulation can one go before he has effectively left the Church or created his own religion?

Section II: The Indeducibility of Developments

The question of the degree to which doctrines can develop and still be said to contain the essential content of Christian revelation can only be answered with a look at developments which have already taken place.

A) The Essence as Determined Only in Retrospect

It would appear obvious that the essence of any doctrine is determined only in retrospect. It emerges only after the old doctrine is compared to the new one; the similar elements become the essence. No amount of reflection upon the old doctrine would have revealed the new one without the light of new knowledge.

When the doctrine "Outside the Church No Salvation" was first proclaimed, the formulation specifically included "infidels" (Moslems generally), schismatics and heretics among the damned (cf. p. 47). Salvation most definitely involved overt, professed membership in the visible Church. There was no salvation for the non-baptized, non-Catholic, not in good standing.

It took centuries of deepening faith — with some help from the Age of Exploration — to bring about new perspectives which required the reformulation of the traditional teaching. Prior to the emergence of these perspectives, no amount of time spent thinking about this teaching would have brought about this development. The essence of the teaching could not have been identified until the old and new expressions, and understandings, were compared.

B) The Abandonment of Elements Once Believed Essential

Not only is the essence determined only in retrospect but, when it is, it involves the abandonment of elements of its expression and even understanding that were once believed essential.

Armed with the modern idea, the medieval reformer of the Church's teaching "Outside The Church No Salvation" would have been burned. Though its leaders would have accepted the sentence "The Church is the community of the saved," they would have insisted that this means visible membership. And this idea has been abandoned. There is no mistaking it.

There is also no requiring a "precedent" in order to argue for a reform. So far, *Christian Materialism* has made mention of several important precedents (cf. p. 176, 178, 193). Hopefully, these were helpful in showing that a given change was not so dramatic as might otherwise have seemed. But, each of these was itself, at least to some extent, without precedent. We can now see that the indeducibility of developments means that precedents should not be demanded.

* * *

At this point, the discussion requires some response to the fact that certain theologians deny that the change in the teaching on salvation was as dramatic as it appears. Making reference to the patristic teachings on the possibility of baptisms of blood and desire, as well as the fact that the formal statements on salvation were meant to speak to specific crises of Church unity, these theologians would have us believe that the Church never held that non-visibly-baptized, non-Catholics were not saved.

It is surely true that historical circumstances *did* occasion the formal teachings on salvation outside the Church.[1] It is also true that these teachings were *not* meant to teach the damnation of the millions of unevangelized. But, let us make no mistake, their damnation was already presumed. Taught in Scripture, it was a fact that Christian history took completely for granted. To be Christian was to be saved. Patristic thinking on alternate forms of Baptism concerned those who had already professed Christian faith and lacked only the external rite. (Medieval thinkers developed the doctrine of limbo out of a conviction that this rite was essential.) The first person to suggest anything resembling the idea of "invincible ignorance" was Francisco Suarez (1548-1617). If one should argue that the classical doctrine bespoke an ignorance of the wider, non-European, non-Christian world, how is one to explain the fact that once the new world *was* discovered, missionaries were expected to give up their lives attempting to baptize as many as possible?

It is clear. The Church has abandoned something that was once an extremely important element of its teaching, one which had formerly motivated martyrdom. In the process, the Church has acknowledged that the essence of one of its teachings involves "less" than had once been thought. Of course, it is not necessary to acknowledge that the Church now "knows" less. Not only has its understanding of the teaching improved, the improvement has opened the door to ideas about the Church much more profound and informative than any that would have been possible prior. In the same fashion, the abandonment of biblical literalism required the Church to concede that it did not know what had happened on a given day of creation, but it opened the door to a host of profound ideas about what creation has actually involved.

Progress requires the abandonment of elements once believed essential. Growth always leaves something behind.

C) Continuity as Confidence in the Church

The fact that the essence of the doctrine is determined only in retrospect, and may indeed involve the abandonment of elements once believed essential, surely calls into question the classical understanding of infallibility. After all, it explicitly contradicts the notion of irreformability,

---

1. But, let it be pointed out that the Church has never allowed the effect of historical circumstances to diminish its faith in God's providence. The history of the great councils of the ancient Church is replete with evidence of the interference of the emperors in doctrinal matters, particularly with regard to forced compromises designed to keep the peace. Constantine required the compromise of Nicea (cf. p. 52); Justinian (483-565) demanded the condemnation of the Montanists (cf. footnote p. 82). The Spirit was still perceived to be at work.

hitherto considered essential to infallibility (cf. p. 196). Temporarily prescinding from a definitive statement on this issue — a postponement which must await the exposition of much more data — presently it can be pointed out that the divine guidance of Church teaching has not been denied by what has been said so far. For one thing, the Church's old teachings have obviously been the vehicle by which modern versions have been born. In view of this fact, the case can easily be made that the old teachings accurately represented the ideas in question given the mentalities, the spiritualities, which represented the state of humanity at their time.

As to the question of "continuity," especially in light of the fact that the old and new versions of any teaching can be so dramatically different, it is to be acknowledged that even though the past formulations of a given teaching do not allow the prediction of a new one, they do betray the direction of God's guidance. Moreover, given God's guidance, continuity is faith in the Church, faith that the Church is doing as well as it can right now, faith that it will continue to make progress.

D) The Possibility of a Change of Mind

Faith in the Church does not need to mean that it cannot change its mind. Perhaps this is not clear. After all, one could argue that faith in the Church means that the Church would never have rejected a truth which was once available.

Sensible though this would seem, it is also to be acknowledged that the Church's teachings are designed not only to express the truth but to present it to the people effectively. Therefore, if some were ready for a certain truth but most were not, the Church can be understood for not accepting it. That this has happened is evident in the Church's dealing with evolution.

It is also evident that the Church can adopt positions which look like compromise with critics and reformers once condemned. To its benefit, the Church has adopted much of modern biblical criticism. Its unintentional collaboration with the Protestants has produced a new and better conception of Christian life (cf. p. 201). These things happen because the whole truth is possessed by no one, a fact particularly obvious in the liturgical, ministerial and ecclesiological reforms which the Reformation inspired (cf. p. 201). But, the initial rejection of these reforms also had its truth; given the historical circumstances, it was as well as the Church — the whole Church — could do.

E) The Essence as Contained in the Doctrinal System, Not Individual Doctrines

A concern for the whole Church leads us to realize that the essence of any individual doctrine needs to be seen in the context of the whole faith — the entire doctrinal system by which the faith is expressed. Already we have seen the modern emergence of the distinction between the pronouncements of the ordinary and extraordinary magisterium (cf. p. 196). This was an admission of the fact that the faith is bigger than any one doctrine, none of which stands alone, all of which have their meaning in the context of the whole, some of which are more central than others in terms of their role within the doctrinal system.

Therefore, now that we acknowledge that elements once considered essential to a given doctrine can be abandoned during the course of its development, the time has come to acknowledge that the future of doctrinal development may involve the virtual abandonment of all mention of an individual doctrine except in terms of its historical importance as part of a past formulation of the doctrinal system.

Section III: The Suspension of Belief

A) The Necessity of the Suspension of Beliefs

Since the essence is determined only in retrospect, and may involve the abandonment of elements once believed essential, it is now to be acknowledged that relatively little should be held irreformable. Considering the dramatic changes that the proposed synthesis of Christianity and materialism promises to involve, it should hopefully be clear that the attempt to achieve this synthesis must involve a Christianity willing to suspend beliefs that it has always considered essential. This willingness, if unspoken, made possible the reforms which have already taken place. An openness to consider the possibility that anything is reformable will make possible continued, necessary reform.

B) Unsuspendable Beliefs

Although it will indeed be necessary to consider the possibility that "anything" is reformable, it is still to be acknowledged that certain beliefs are necessarily implied by the very fact that one is engaged in a search for the essence of *Christian* beliefs.

1. The Absolutely Unsuspendable Beliefs

Of course, any search for the essence of religious truth implies that there is, in fact, a God, a being upon which all else does depend.

Of course, any search for the essence of Christian truth implies that the founder of the Christian movement, Jesus, was uniquely God's spokesman. If not, there would be no reason to search Christian tradition for any truth that could not more easily be found and upheld by any individual's reflection and personal credibility.

Moreover, since the primary source of information about Jesus and His teachings is contained in what we call the New Testament, it must also be assumed that these writings contain the essential truth of His message, at least implicitly. If this information were not available, there would be no basis upon which to employ Jesus' credibility in the assertion of anything Christian.

If one is to engage in Catholic doctrinal development, one must also presume the uniquely divine origin of the Church, the only fact which gives basis to the presumption that the history of Church teaching is a uniquely authoritative manifestation of the theological progress to which this work hopes to contribute.

2. The Almost Unsuspendable Beliefs

The preceding were "absolutely" unsuspendable because they were logically implied by any thought that there is a point to the process of doctrinal development. The following are to be considered "almost" unsuspendable because not only have they always been essential to the spiritual experience that *is* Christianity, but, were they to be abandoned, it is hardly imaginable that anyone would want to engage in this enterprise.

Despite the historical emphasis put upon God's justice, mature Christian spirituality has always centered upon the fact of God's infinite love.

Also, Christian spirituality has always involved the belief that, as a sign of God's love, Jesus died on the cross. Obviously, this presumes some special relationship between God (the Father) and Jesus. Although the history of theology has involved denials that this relationship involves Jesus' "divinity," and, even more specifically, the idea that He was "God made man," it has almost never involved the denial that Jesus was not, in some sense, God's "son."

Belief in Jesus cannot be distinguished from faith in His principal teachings: His proclamation of the coming of God's kingdom and His call to love — the possibility of salvation. Most essentially, this is Christianity.

* * *

This completes the minimum with which we can begin. It is not nearly all that the Church would expect us to affirm. What we can affirm we shall see. Thus must we consider the metaphysic which will settle the question.

Part II: Materialism

Introduction to Part II

We must now consider the necessity and nature of the materialism which is to interpret and be interpreted by the Christianity whose essence has now been established. This was the stated purpose of Part II.

In order to accomplish its purpose, Part II will proceed as follows: Chapter I will attempt to demonstrate "The Inevitablity of a True, though Creative, Materialism." It will give particular attention to the creative aspect of matter in motion, the "space" in which we shall hopefully find room for a Christian interpretation of materialism. Chapter II will be a study of man in the light of these perspectives; this "Anthropology of Creative Materialism" will attempt to describe human nature with special attention to its more spiritual aspects, especially "knowing." Chapters III and IV will deal with the crucial questions of "Determinism" and "Personal Responsibility."

Chapter I: The Inevitability of a True, Though Creative, Materialism

Section I: The Relentlessness of Materialism

A) The Failure of the Church's Initial Attempt to Deal with Materialism
When last we encountered materialism, the Church had condemned it (cf. p. 150). Its relation to evolution was rightly perceived and it was critiqued by the same sorts of arguments (cf. p. 155).

The "uncritical" arguments claimed that materialism means that man is a machine. Thus, materialism is "disproved" by the supposedly obvious immateriality of consciousness, thoughts, and feelings.

The "scholastic" arguments centered upon the impossibility of the emergence of a higher from a lower as was supposed to happen when chemicals gave rise to cells.

The "scientific" arguments involved the observation that science had failed to provide a complete explanation of a single aspect of mental life.

As time has told, this response was not to prove sufficient.

To an increasing number of the scientifically minded, the idea that man is a machine was attractively simple and it freed the scientist from the need to explain the impossibly mysterious existence of the mind. Consciousness, thoughts and feelings were either ignored or considered curious "by-products" of material processes.

The scholastic arguments had been discredited by evolution; plainly, the higher could emerge from the lower. Moreover, the now accepted fact that the species were the product of gradual change undercut the idea that things get their identity from unchanging forms.

Evolution also dealt a severe blow to the scientific argument that materialism had not provided a complete explanation of a single aspect of mental life. Just as the absence of a complete explanation of evolution was no reason to ignore the overwhelming evidence that it has occurred, the overwhelming evidence for materialism was more than enough reason to accept the idea, at least in general terms. It was reason to pursue the scientific study of the brain with confidence that more complete explanations would eventually emerge. Indeed, with each passing day, progress was being made; this added to the evidence.

B) A Compromise Attempted and Failed: Vitalism

Though impressive, the evidence of a materialistic explanation of the mind was nothing compared to the evidence of a materialistic explanation of everything else, especially inanimate objects. With their increasingly complete chemical analysis, it was becoming more and more clear that chemicals accounted for all of their characteristics. The insistence that immaterial forms were an essential part of their composition was becoming less and less tenable. A rock was a mass of chemicals; no more needed to be said.

Under the weight of this evidence, certain thinkers attempted a compromise. Acknowledging that most things *can* be accounted for in terms of matter, they distinguished between inanimate objects and the obviously different realm of living things. Since these are "living," as chemicals are not, they must contain something uniquely living — something uniquely "vital." This was not the "form" once required of everything, but at least it was something.

Known as "vitalism," the compromise was rejected for the reasons that had already made materialism so persuasive. A uniquely vital element was not in evidence and none was needed in order to explain the life of living things. This was all the more obvious thanks to the decades of scientific progress that had followed the first formulations of materialism.

Though the major part of this progress involved the chemical analysis of inanimate objects, biologists had hardly been idle. We have already seen mention of the discovery of various cell structures, particularly those of the cell nucleus (cf. p. 167). This was followed by the discovery of the cell membrane (whose structure selects the cell's food from its surrounding environment), the Golgi Complex (whose secretions catalyze digestion), and the mitochrondia (wherein food's energy is released). This process involves the "Kreb's Cycle" — the release of phosphates from ATP.[1] In plants, it is stimulated by "photosynthesis" which has oxygen as its by-product. In animals, oxygen removes the carbon which is the major by-product of metabolism. Thus was answered the mystery of breathing.

Altogether these discoveries appeared to answer the mystery of life. Although there was admittedly much more to be learned, life processes had been penetrated. No vital — immaterial — element was needed to explain them.

---

1. Adenosinetriphosphate.

C) Another Unsuccessful Attempt at Compromise: Dualism

In view of the continuing progress of the biological sciences, the notion that matter and life were fundamentally distinct was soon so badly discredited that Christian thinkers were again compelled to make a change. Predictably, where once it was held that it is necessary to postulate a certain something extra in order to explain life, it was now held that this was still necessary in order to explain spirituality.

Perhaps the body was entirely explicable in terms of matter. After all, it was now officially admitted that evolution was probably responsible for the body. But, it was explicitly taught that evolution was not responsible for the soul.[2] The soul was made in God's image; it was immortal; it was free; it could not be ruled by natural causes.

Christian thinkers had returned to dualism; they were attempting to turn back the clock some fifteen hundred years.

For the same reasons which had already rejected previous attempts at compromise, this too was doomed to fail. Even beyond the reasoning which had led to the abandonment of dualism the first time around (cf. p. 141), there was no acknowledged evidence of a spiritual substance and no sufficient reason to postulate such a thing. Were it to be insisted that the simple fact of consciousness is evidence of the immaterial — and therefore immortal — soul, would it not be necessary to take the consciousness of animals as evidence that they, too, have such a soul?

Section II: Neo-Scholasticism

A) A New View of an Old Idea: Rahner

With the failure of all attempts at compromise, Christian thinkers found themselves upon the horns of a dilemma not unlike the one they had faced at the insistence of evolution. Science appeared to prove one thing; faith — and experience — seemed to say another. A person could not deny reason; yet, how could he deny the spirituality of experience? What of the consciousness of *self* in which he now distinguished himself from other animals? This was not a material thing. It had not proved predictable by

---

2. In accord with the immemorial tradition of the Church (cf. p. 64), *Humani Generis* insisted that God had reserved to Himself the direct creation of individual souls (cf. p.177). Pius XII also stated that he did not see how Church teaching could ever be reconciled with "polygenesis" — the idea that human evolution occurred along several simultaneous lines. The doctrine of original sin did not appear to allow for a multi-lineal evolution of humanity. Why would the sin of the father of one line condemn the rest?

physical laws. Actually, nothing except the motion of the most primitive forms of matter was successfully explained by physical laws.

Here was the key to a new idea. Admitting that matter *is* the basis of all things, certain Christian thinkers began to point out that the simple laws which explain matter in motion tell us nothing about why salmon swim upstream in order to spawn. They do not explain the way in which chemicals make up a cell. The cell may be made only of chemicals but, when organized in the *form* of a cell, these chemicals constitute something more, something whose holistic life—and the laws which explain it—cannot itself be explained by a simple appeal to chemistry. Indeed, it is the form of the cell that organizes its chemicals and tells them where to go. It is the reason that individual chemicals will enter and exit but the cell remains. It is the reason that laws of biology will never be "deduced" from a study of the laws of chemistry. Biology involves a study of the whole that cannot take place until it exists. Therefore, according to members of the newly emergent school of "Transcendental Thomism,"[3] lower-level realities should be said to "transcend" themselves when they are organized into forms which are obviously higher, a process that creates something new. But, it should not be said that the lowers explain the highers for it remains true that nothing can give what it does not have. It is the form that explains the working of matter, not *vice-versa*.

Here was a true, if "neo, scholasticism."

According to Karl Rahner, the new movement's most illustrious spokesman, matter is "self-surpassing." It gives nothing that it possesses of itself. God enables it to exist in the ever more complex forms that culminate in man. Betraying the influence of Pierre Teilhard—who had spoken of evolution as the complexification of matter until and beyond its self-awareness in spirit—Rahner explained that evolution is the transformation of matter by spirit; man is the "self-transcendence" of matter as spirit. Thus, man is indeed one, an "incarnate spirit," a unity with corporality and spirituality. (Remarkably, it was now declared that man had rediscovered the "biblical" understanding that man is "one.") Form is spirit—the Spirit of God bringing about His image in matter.[4]

---

3. Transcendental Thomism is to be distinguished from the more literal revival of Thomistic philosophy which followed *Aeterni Patres,* the encyclical in which Leo XIII established Thomism as the official philosophy of the Church (DS 3135-40). Best represented in the work of Jacques Maritain (1882-1973) and Etienne Gilson (1884-1984), it involved a definite suspicion of all forms of compromise with modern thinking.

4. See especially his *Spirit in the World.* See his *Hominization* for his claim that the new idea of how God creates frees us from the need to postulate a scientifically troublesome interruption in the visible processes of nature in order to hold His direct creation of individual souls.

B) A Supposedly Supportive Development in Modern Philosophy:
Phenomenology
1. The Idea
Even before neo-scholasticism became the new metaphysic of educated
Christianity, there had already occurred a development in modern philoso-
phy that would eventually be considered supportive.

Materialism had failed to impress not just Christian thinkers. To some
others, it did not do justice to all that humans experienced. Indeed, experience was neglected as an object of study. Such was the conclusion of Ed-
mund Husserl (1859-1938). Agreeing with Kant: the mediation of the senses
puts an insurmountable barrier between man and the world around him,
Husserl argued that a informative analysis of reality should consist not
of a theoretical description of the matter upon which it may or may not be
built, but rather a descriptive analysis of that which we do know immediately—consciousness.[5] Attempting to put his ideas into practice, Husserl
began to "observe" his own consciousness in action and to describe his
findings in terms suited to the project. This led to the first "scientific"
descriptions of such things as the "mind's eye," the mental passage of one
thought to another, and the content of emotions. Husserl's thought struck a
number of thinkers as an alternative to what they also perceived as the
"soul-lessness" of materialism. The result was the rise of what was soon to
be called "phenomenology"—the study of phenomena as experienced.

In time, the "phenomenological" approach was adopted by certain
churchmen. Initially wary because it might be used to deny the existence of
the outside world—a contradiction of the doctrine of creation—the phenomenological approach did share the neo-scholastic experience that there is
more to life than matter in motion. Therefore, as long as the data of experience are insisted to have their origin in something true of the outside world,
phenomenology could be understood to complement the new Thomism. In
claiming that it does, Bernard Lonergan (1904-84) reminded the scientist
that nothing he accepts as data *are* data until they are experienced.[6] Thus, no
data concerning matter can compel man to deny the experience of his
spirituality, or to reduce it to the matter which is truly "real." Indeed, since
the immediate datum of our experience is that of ourselves as "subjects,"
self-conscious, spiritual beings who experience themselves as interested in
the systematic explanation of the world around them, we actually have more
reason to assume that matter is a contrived concept by which we have
attempted to make sense out of something which is, in essence, a far more

5. See his *Ideas.*
6. See his *Insight.*

complicated reality.

Lonergan was particularly critical of 19th century determinism (cf. p.140). Calling attention to the scientific "experience" that not only were the laws concerning highers not deducible from those that predicted the behavior of lowers, he pointed out that they were less dependable; they admit of more exceptions. This he called "emergent probability." Lonergan insisted that this emergent unpredictability is to be interpreted as a natural correlation between complexity and freedom so that as one ascends the levels of organization, laws became more and more general until all hopes of an exact science are properly abandoned in man, whose freedom from law is an experienced fact. Actually, Lonergan distinguished between the "psychological," or "reflexive" level, where a certain predictability was possible, and the "spiritual," or "reflexive" level, where it was not.

2. An Addendum: Existentialism

If phenomenology can be described as reflection upon the data of consciousness with reference to science, its principal philosophical progeny, "Existentialism," can rightfully be described as such a reflection with reference to life. Somewhat anticipated in the thought of Søren Kierkegaard with a Christian result (cf. p.148), the practice of global judgments about human existence was now more popularly to be explored in non-Christian directions.

Convinced of the wisdom of the phenomenological approach, Martin Heidegger (1889-1976) recommended that philosophy abandon all attempts to determine what reality is "made of"; he insisted that only our experience is truly real. Declaring that Greek philosophy had mistakenly asked the question: what is "being," meaning, what substance is common to all things; he asked: what is be-ing, i.e. what is it to be, especially as humans experience it?[7]

Among the answers he offered was the idea that human "be-ing" involves a certain "thrownness," i.e. existence without prior agreement to be, a sudden and surprising fact which is utterly mysterious. Being is likewise "being-in-the-world," the experience of existence as inseparable from the experience of existence within a larger reality than oneself. It is also "being-with-others," the fact that being is shared by others like oneself. It is "being-toward-the-future," life constantly lived in anticipation of times coming. It is simultaneously "being-towards-death," life lived in the at least implicit knowledge that it will come to an end—nothingness. According to Heidegger, an "authentic" life, the best of what human life can be, is a life

---

7. See his *Being and Time*.

lived in accord with the truth, especially the acceptance of death.

Death figured prominently in the popularization of existentialism, a largely French movement which had little regard for philosophical technicalities and was solely concerned with an articulation of what was fast becoming the modern despair over the pointlessness of progress and of life in general. Not only had science failed to provide "utopia"—the "perfect world" it had once promised—such a world was no longer to be expected. Indeed, some argued that progress, scientific and otherwise, had only made things worse. The inventions that had given rise to the Industrial Revolution had also been responsible for the rise of impersonal cities and the physical and psychological damage they now did to the vast majority of their inhabitants. There had been two world wars, both made more terrible by science. The second had concluded with a triumph for modern physics, the atomic bomb that now made possible humanity's self-destruction.

The failure of faith in the world left little for those who had long since lost faith in God. With no hope in eternity, nor esteem for temporal—and therefore temporary—and essentially valueless success, and bored with the shallowness of a life spent in pursuit of pleasures that so quickly lost their appeal, they despairingly concluded that life was indeed a pointless, i.e. "absurd" and often painful journey from non-existence to nothingness.

Despite their despair, the "absurdists" found that a person still needed something to give his life meaning—a reason to do or be something. In words more than reminiscent of Friedrich Nietzsche, Jean-Paul Sartre (1905-78), the informal movement's most celebrated spokesman, insisted that man's only if minimal hope for a meaningful life is to create a value system of his own and press onward toward his self-appointed purpose until death comes to end the game.[8]

Section III: An Intermezzo: Materialism and Modern Physics

At this point, something must be said about what modern physics has to say about any metaphysic which insists that matter can explain anything; after all, what is physics but the study of matter? A look at this study is also important because recent developments have given some thinkers the idea that materialism has been disproved.

---

8. See especially his *Being and Nothingness*. It is to be noted that most of the absurdists used the vehicle of fiction in order to make their point. See especially the works of Albert Camus (1913-60).

A) The Rise of Modern Physics

Our look at the rise of modern science began with its comparison to old science (cf. p.112). In like manner, our look at modern physics cannot but be clarified by its comparison to "old physics," the way the physical world was viewed until this century. This would essentially involve the comparison of the old and new conceptions of 1) space and time, and 2) the stuff of which the universe is made.

1. The Changing Conceptions of Space and Time
a. Euclid and Newton

The classical conceptions of space and time were the implicit presumptions of the ancient mind long before Euclid (c. 300 B.C.) wrote the *Elements*. Taking for granted that the universe is always to be measured in terms of up, down, North, South, East, and West, i.e. *three* dimensions where the shortest distance between two points is a straight line (such that no two parallel lines would ever meet), Euclid described geometry in the most exact of terms. Time was not a consideration; time was time; it simply passed.

These were the ideas of space and time that Newton inherited almost two thousand years later. Indeed, he explicitly presumed space was "absolute"; in other words, even if an object were alone in the universe, it could still be said to move, and to move a determinate distance. Newton also assumed that time was absolute; it passed at a uniform rate, second per second, throughout the entire universe.

b. Riemann and Einstein

Its longevity notwithstanding, the classical conception of space actually began to be questioned as soon as it became clear that the flatness of the earth is an illusion—that the surface of the earth is that of a sphere. In the hopes that a geometrical description could be provided for curved surfaces, mathematicians set out to discover whether the predictable patterns of measurable distances upon which such a geometry would be based were there to be found. This was achieved by Georg F.B. Riemann (1826-66). In his geometry of curved surfaces, parallel lines did meet.

"Non-Euclidian" geometry led to the decline of the classical conception not only of space but also of time through the mind of Albert Einstein (1879-1955). Taking up the question of the propagation of light, he was disturbed by the failure of experiments designed to detect the "ether" which was supposedly its medium (cf. p.139).

In 1887, Albert Michelson (1852-1931)—who had already achieved the first verifiable measurement of the speed of light (approximately 186,000 miles per second)—and E.W. Morley attempted to detect ether in the effect upon the speed of light that should be caused by the rotational movement of the earth toward and away from certain celestial light sources. But they found that the speed of light was always the same. This should not have been.

Reflecting on this paradox, Einstein came to a number of conclusions that were soon to startle the scientific world. In the absence of evidence of ether, he concluded that all motion is "relative," i.e. things can only be said to move in relation to other things. In other words, if an object or system were alone in space, it could not know that it was moving. This is the reason that the laws of physics are not affected by the motion of a given system.

Galileo had already observed: within every "frame of reference," i.e. a system in which everything is moving at a constant velocity, the laws of motion are relative; unaffected by motion, they are always the same. This was what made it possible to play cards in a carriage once the horses have finished accelerating.

Now, in view of the Michelson-Morley experiments, Einstein extended this relativity to the motion of electromagnetic radiation. But, if the speed of light is unaffected by the motion of its measurer or its source, it would appear that the faster he is going, relative to the source, the slower must be passing the seconds with which he measures the light. Thus, time is relative to the speed of light; or perhaps space is; after all, the effect would be the same.[9] This was the "Special Theory of Relativity." It also involved the idea that since it is impossible to know whether to blame space or time for the relativistic effects, the relation of systems was better described in terms of "space-time," an idea which also meant the abandonment of the classical concepts of space and time. (The so-called "dilation" of time was later to be measured by super-accurate clocks carried aboard spacecraft moving at extraordinary velocities.)

Einstein's ideas about space and time were initially more interesting to the popular mind than his relation of mass and energy. Certain thinkers, however, knew better. In his extension of classical relativity to electro-magnetic radiation, he had implicitly united Newtonian "force" (as in the equation $F=ma$) to energy. Convinced that nothing can move faster than light—a limitation already "scientific" given the finite velocity of the means of measurement—Einstein rendered the equation $E=mc^2$ where c is the speed of light. This mathematical prediction of the convertibility of mass into energy led to the development of the atomic bomb which does just that.

(It is to be noted that, if the speed of light is indeed the velocity of something without mass, its finite velocity is the speed of pure energy.)

9. Actually, equations describing such an effect of velocity on space had already been advanced by Hendrik Lorentz (1853-1928) who explained the effect with the rather conventional idea that velocity caused a certain "compression" of the thing moving.

The Special Theory was solely concerned with frames of reference in uniform motion. Therefore, soon after its publication, Einstein sought to extend it—to predict the effect of acceleration on the moving system. Given his relation of mass and energy, he concluded that increased acceleration, i.e. energy, increased mass. Furthermore, struck by the fact that the push of acceleration cannot be distinguished from the pull of gravity, he decided that gravity was directly related to energy. Thus, he predicted that light would bend when passing by a great mass. (With starlight and the sun, this was later proved.)

Notably, Einstein's now "General Theory of Relativity" also involved the conclusion that simplicity recommended the abandonment of the idea of "force." Given the relativity of space-time he had already postulated, he insisted that physics should better say matter simply bends the space-time in its vicinity. In other words, planetary orbits are not the result of a competition of forces but, instead, the fact that bodies follow straight paths in the curved space that surrounds a great mass.

(It can therefore be said that inertia is the result of the fact that a mass is the center of its own universe while energy can be considered the transit of no space in no time.)

Einstein's Special and General theories not only proved themselves in the experiments that he devised in order to test them, they have been incorporated into microscopic physical theories designed to explain how matter is the stuff which makes up all things. These fed Einstein's own attempt to explain all of physical reality in what he believed was a single law which he hoped to call the "unified field theory." Though he did not succeed, microscopic physical theorists are still pursuing this goal.

2. The Changing Conception of the Stuff of the Universe
a. Progress in Modern Atomic Theory

Progress in modern atomic theory had not ceased with Dalton (cf. p.138).

Working with this theory, Amadeo Avogadro (1776-1856) observed that the smallest amounts of any substance are comprised of the same elements *in the same proportions*. This suggested that atoms could somehow combine in the form of a "molecule."

Meanwhile, the description of the elements began to betray a certain pattern which indicated that atoms are themselves combinations of something even smaller.

The description of the elements culminated in the work of Dmitri Mendeleef (1834-1907) whose "periodic table" demonstrated that the elements, their weights and their properties are mathematically related. (This led to the prediction of elements which were later discovered.) Then, in 1895,

Wilhelm Roentgen accidentally discovered the X-rays which led Pierre and Marie Curie to discover the radium which emits this "radioactive" radiation as it slowly changes into lead.

Encouraged by this unmistakable evidence that atoms are indeed composed of something smaller, Ernest Rutherford (1871-1937) proposed the theory that eventually cracked the atom. Simultaneously attempting to explain electricity, he theorized that the atom is composed of a relatively massive and positively charged "proton," an equally weighty but uncharged "neutron," and an almost weightless and negatively charged "electron." He pictured an atom "nucleus" of protons and neutrons orbited by a number of electrons generally equal to the number of protons. Conceived to work by momentum and gravity, the Rutherford model also appeared to explain how atoms can combine in the form of a molecule; they can share or lose electrons in "covalent" or "ionic" bonding.

b. Quantum Theory

The Rutherford atom was an attractive explanation of many of the facts but there were problems with it that remained unresolved. Pictured as a mini-solar system that obeyed Newton's laws, one could not but wonder: why did it not run down? In the face of this problem, science was again advanced by accident.

Max Planck (1858-1947) was doing experiments designed to determine the patterns in which electro-magnetic radiation is emitted from a "black body" source—a source that did not reflect radiation. Expecting energy to be emitted continuously, he was surprised to find that energy was actually emitted in discrete units. This suggested that waves are based on something "particular." Perhaps this could resolve the problem of their propagation which was created once it became clear that waves are not transmitted through ether. Perhaps there are force-bearing "particles" that could also explain pure energy, or at least describe it. Calling them "quanta" (Latin for "how much"), Planck had definitely discovered a basic similarity between matter and energy—both exist in units that can theoretically be counted, their position determined.

Planck's discovery led Niels Bohr (1885-1962) to remake the Rutherford model of the atom. Given Einstein's relation of mass and energy, he concluded that if energy is like matter, matter is like energy. In other words, the weightless electron is not an orbiting particle; it is trapped energy. This is the reason that the atom does not run down. When Louis DeBroglie (b.1892) discovered that matter emits a wave however weak, Bohr's theory was apparently proved.

But this was only the beginning. Now that it was clear that matter can be converted into energy, scientists attempted to crack the "sub-atomic particles," and to relate them to the basic unit of energy now called the "photon." As it turned out, electrons are made of photons while protons and neutrons ("nucleons") can be broken down into a number of parts, and parts of parts, including the "Hadons" which carry the so-called weak forces that hold together the atomic nucleus, and the "Zeptons" which carry the strong nuclear forces. Together with electro-magnetism and gravity, the weak and strong nuclear forces are presently considered the *four* forces that make the universe go. Moreover, physicists have even found evidence that the particles now distinguished by their forces are themselves composed of something smaller, and similar. Called "Partons," they are said to occur in six "flavors." There is even evidence of a "Graviton," the source of gravity predicted by Einstein. What is suspected to be the single underlying particle is tentatively called the "Quark." In any case, nucleons are already related to photons in terms of specific, if astronomical, numbers. The lifetime of nucleons is described in terms of the loss of photons over billions of years.

B) Uncertainty, Indeterminism, and Their Supposed Implications

1. Uncertainty and the Denial of the Existence of Matter

When Planck discovered the quantum nature of energy, physicists were faced with a serious conceptual problem. Though a particle of sorts, energy was still to be measured as a wave, something very different. Furthermore, depending upon whether one considered it a particle or a wave, the means of determining its position was different, and so were the results.

Faced with this problem, the physicist Werner Heisenberg (1901-76) devised the so-called "uncertainty relations," a system of equations designed to synthesize the different results of measurement.

Surely inspired by the positivism which dominated the philosophic thought of the day (cf. p.162), Erwin Schrödinger (1887-1961) came to conclude that the uncertainty relations are the only suitable definition of underlying reality. (Followers of Einstein preferred to speak of nature as a sea of distortions in space-time.) Claiming that physics had mathematically discovered realities which have no model in the world of human experience, he declared that the classical idea of matter was obsolete. Only mathematics can accurately describe reality; we should give up our false picture of the little "things" which make up everything else.

2. Indeterminism and the Assertion of Caprice in Nature

Positivism was also responsible for the willingness of many physicists to give up the idea that nature is propelled by forces which cause every motion and determine exactly when and where things go.

With the abandonment of the mini-solar system model of the atom, the electron was no longer pictured as a particle orbiting a nucleus. The equations designed to locate the electron offered only a statistically based prediction of where it "probably" is at any time. The problem was further complicated by the fact that experiments now concerned realities as small as light itself—the means by which information is gathered. Thus, to do an experiment was to affect the reality that one is attempting to study and to remove it from its natural situation. Therefore, its true nature can never be known.

As these facts were viewed under the influence of positivism, Bohr and his followers (later known as the "Copenhagen School") took experimental indeterminism to mean that nature is fundamentally unpredictable, the interaction of the most underlying realities is given to a certain caprice. Statistical studies were the best that science could ever hope to do.

The assertion of caprice in nature was a denial of the causality that would otherwise determine everything with exactness.

Taken over by more macroscopic sciences, "indeterminism" came to mean that science does not offer "explanations," it observes and offers only "correlations." This was a return to "old science" (cf. p.112).

3. An Addendum: The Idea of Spiritual Matter

Old science was not the only idea to be revived thanks to the results of modern physics.

As the philosophical thoughts of certain physicists became known to the wider intellectual community, certain philosophers came to the conclusion that Spinoza and Hegel had been right: reality is not matter but idea. But, accepting the evidence that things are made of smaller things, they concluded that the smallest, most fundamental realities have a mind of their own. The idea that matter has spiritual properties in and of itself was given a Christian articulation by Teilhard, whose idea that "matter becomes self-consciousness in spirit" (cf. p.224) actually involved his theory of "complexity-consciousness"—matter has an inherent consciousness which emerges steadily as matter exists in ever more complex forms.

C) Responses to the Supposed Implications of Uncertainty and Indeterminism

1. The Existence of Matter

The denial of the existence of matter was the result of a mistaken assumption that the word "matter" could refer only to the inert billiard balls of the classical mechanistic system. But, this is not the meaning of the word matter. From the time of Aristotle, the word matter has most often referred to the simplest stuff of which the universe is made. The existence of such a stuff is evident. Visible things are plainly made of something smaller, and simpler. Science has shown that these are made of something smaller and simpler. But science cannot break things down indefinitely. There must be something not made of something smaller and simpler; there must be something not made of something else.

The idea that mathematics must replace models as the description of underlying reality is both mistaken and irrelevant to the question of materialism. It is irrelevant because the intelligibility of materialism requires no more than the fact that everything in the world and of it can be explained in terms of the action of the simplest underlying realities whatever they are, however they are described. Moreover, it is mistaken to suppose that numbers have a meaning apart from what it is they count. It is also mistaken to conclude that since elementary particles or waves or, better, "units" have no model in the realm of the things with which we deal, mathematics is the only way they can be discussed. We have no exact models of anything that has been discovered in the last three hundred years. For example, our model of something such as water, i.e. the water molecule, is far from the actual reality of what one is. Still, this model tells us more than we would know without it. We need models. And we have them. Everything is made up of something else; and the product must bear some relation to the parts.

Plainly, since the product must bear some relation to parts, the "particle" model of matter is preferable to the "wave" model. Matter substantiates things of definite dimensions and locality; a wave presumes something else that definitely exists. Now, it is true that the particle model presently available does not offer a complete view of what the elementary units really are. But the science of sub-atomic physics is in its infancy. A more complete view may involve something presently unconceived. Surely, there is every indication that there is much more to be discovered. This is surely the spirit of science.

2. Caprice in Nature

Scientists betrayed science when they concluded that *their* failure to have discovered exact laws with which to describe the movement of energy in an atom—after so brief a scientific attempt—means that there are no such laws to be discovered. Neither does it mean that there are no causal forces. Although the existence of causal forces is actually a question of philosophy, one which Hume answered negatively on the grounds of epistemology (cf. p.144)—an issue we shall in due course address (q.v. p.265)—to assert the same thing on the grounds of physics is surely the most irresponsible of opinions in no way called for by the facts.

On the contrary, the statistical laws which presently represent the scientist's achievement presume many specific motions which bear explaining. What drives them? What keeps reality dependable? Is not the dependability of nature the central presumption of science? Without it, what would be the value of law or its explanation?[10] As a matter of fact, it was this presumption, and in it, the idea that nature is knowable, that led the first modern scientists to cast aside the strictures of old ideas and penetrate nature for the betterment of man. As another matter of fact, the idea that the 20th century has reached the limits of what can be known is far more provincial than anything that the medieval scientist was willing to insist, and far less forgivable because he had not the benefit of the recent centuries of constant and often surprising discovery. After all, if Dalton had taken Boyle's gas laws as the last word, he would not have been the author of modern atomic theory. Instead, thanks to Dalton (and Avogadro) the essentially statistical gas laws were themselves explained in terms of the predictable aggregate effects of the many interactions of molecules in a container. In like fashion, the statistical electron laws will give way to a more complete explanation of the interactions of energy in the atom.

3. Spiritual Matter; Idealism in General

Since we have almost reached the point where the firm and final case for materialism·is to be stated (q.v. p.237), a response to the postulation of spiritual matter, or any other form of idealism, can here be quite brief.

The materialist finds the notion of spiritual matter easy to reject. Since everything—including consciousness—can be attributed to matter in motion, the idea that matter is in some way spiritual is utterly unnecessary. Indeed, not only is there no persuasive evidence of spiritual matter, but everything we know about matter proves that it is quite dumb, exhibiting a simple capacity for interaction and nothing akin to spiritual activity by any definition.

This is the materialist critique of idealism in any form. Not only is "idea" explicable in terms of matter, but everything we know proves that things are made of something smaller and dumb. Moreover, whenever it is mind against matter, matter wins. The speeding car will still kill the pedestrian even if he is unaware that it has hit him until it is too late.

D) The Contributions of Modern Physics to Materialism

Not only is it clear that modern physics poses no threat to materialism, but the developments in modern physics have made definite contributions to the metaphysic. Most notably, they have offered scientific proof of much that one should expect if everything can indeed be explained in terms of matter.

10. Einstein himself stated that without causality he would rather be a shoemaker. He is also remembered for his oft-quoted insistence that "God does not play at dice."

1. The Unification of Matter and Energy

The most important contribution of modern physics to materialism has been its unification of the concepts of matter and energy. Since the essence of materialism is the possibility of accounting for anything in terms of the interactions of elementary matter, the existence of pure energy as a separate substance fundamentally different from matter would have involved a somewhat mysterious qualification of the utter simplicity of materialism's most compelling appeal. From this we are freed. Matter is no longer "inert"; it is structured energy. In other words, truly elementary matter is the source of its own action. Moreover, in accord with the classical reasoning to the conviction that reality is underlyingly "one" (cf. p. 59), it is also to be expected that each of the four forces—and any that have yet to be discovered—will eventually be explained in terms of the *one* which accounts for all of them through either static or dynamic combinations. The description of this one force was the object of Einstein's search for the unified "field." The idea of a "force-field" leaves open the question of whether matter is to be conceived as a "force-bearing particle," or a "force-center" in which force extends diminishingly outward from a point, not a particle. Depending upon the extent of force, either idea could complement a statistical conception of waves. If the force extends indefinitely, the universe is a "plenum" (cf. p.136) as Hobbes, and Descartes have already concluded.

Either way, regardless of how matter is to be conceived, it remains both possible and necessary to recognize that the underlying stuff of the universe can be quantified and mapped.

2. The Unification of Matter, Space and Time

A second major contribution of modern physics to materialism has been the unification of matter, space and time. Classical physics postulated not only ether—another detraction from the simplicity of materialism—but space *per se,* and also time. Not only does modern physics do away with the need to postulate undetectable ether, but, in its relation of "space measured" to "matter present," it involves an idea of space as nothingness which resolves the conceptual problem of conceiving space as infinite. The relation of time to matter in motion saves us from explaining the passage of time *per se.*

But, nothing said about the so-called relativity of space or time means that the universe involves a mysterious co-existence of many essentially separate worlds. The relativity of measured space presupposes some standard against which its bending can be conceived. Though no one person is its privileged observer, this standard remains an inferably "absolute" space. Furthermore, given the field idea of forces—particularly if it is conceived to mean that the extent of any one field is limited only by others—we can even define an absolute motion. We can also infer the absolute time which makes possible the talk of time's slowing as all processes within a system occur at a slower rate of relative motion. Therefore, relativity can be conceived in terms of the "drag" of increased mass and therefore gravity, or space-time displacement. Of course, energy's evident power to attract other energy—which may also account for mass—has yet to be related to energy's also evident "desire" to move at the speed of light. But this is the future of physics.

3. Precedent For a Positive Shift in World-Views

The last major contribution of modern physics to materialism may be the least obvious but most helpful. Modern physics offers a model with which to illustrate the positive character of a shift in world-views, the fact that such a shift does not so much involve a repudiation of the old view but its extension.

Einstein's theories were a departure from the classical physics of Newton. He proved that certain historical presumptions about space, time, and matter were incorrect; he demonstrated that their measurable value was a variable in relation to energy as described in terms of the speed of light. But, as both the facts and equations also indicated, changes in these variables were all but infinitesimal except for systems moving near this speed. At the velocities of normal experience, they are all but absolute. At such velocities, Newton's theories hold.

Thus, Newton's world-view was not repudiated; its truth was simply placed within the context of a larger explanation of physical phenomena, one which explains more of the now available data. Given the universe as it was perceivable in Newton's day, his theory was the best that could be done. It is still recognized to contain much truth. But, with the wider perceptions made possible by scientific progress, a refined, more comprehensive theory was needed and found.

The same is to be understood of the need for the passage from scholasticism to materialism. Given the state of knowledge during the medieval period, scholasticism was the best that was possible. With the advent of new knowledge, however, the truth of what it did see must be placed within the larger context of materialism. Just as the discovery that matter is organized energy did not mean that there is no matter; the discovery that the mind is organized matter does not mean there is no mind.

Section IV: Creative Materialism

A) The Creative Power of Complex Organization

It is indeed the triumph of science and the essence of a new world-view that the organization of matter accounts for everything in the world and of it. Moreover, since organizations can themselves be organized, the complexity of things can increase by leaps and bounds. It is for this reason that reality can be said to involve various "levels" of organization, if not existence.

1. The Organization of Organizations

Whether they are of one kind or several, static or dynamic organizations of whatever the elementary units really are comprise a variety of sub-atomic particles. This is the "physical" level of organization.

Sub-atomic particles are organized into the atoms of the "chemical" level which includes the organization of atoms into molecules and complex compounds.

Complex compounds are organized into the structures which are themselves organized in the cell. This is the "biological" level of organization.

Millions of cells are involved in the "physiological" organization of tissues, organs and systems which make up plants and animals.

In animals, notably man, the complexity of physiological organization is most manifest in the brain, a physiological structure of the greatest complexity of which we are aware.

Composed of billions of cells (the only cells which do not reproduce), the brain is divided into the "medulla" (the autonomic control center), the two spheres of the "cerebrum" (the main storage area of memory), and the "cerebellum" (the central relay). The brain also contains the "thalamus" (which regulates consciousness), the "hypothalamus" (which is involved in autonomic functions), the "epithalamus" (which is involved in reflexive action) and the "subthalamus" (which is involved in voluntary action). The "hypocampus" is a sorting station of memory. The limbic system produces secretions involved in emotion. There is a distinct "speech-center." Actually, the "lobes" involved in many brain activities have been identified. So have many of the complex chemicals (e.g. hormones) upon which the brain's function is dependent.

The brain works electrically through bio-chemistry. (Thus, it emits "waves" which are now identified with its various states.) Its function is distinctly "global"; in other words, thanks to its fantastic internal interconnectedness, the whole is involved in much of what it does. (Yet, it can do more than one thing at a time.) Its processes are fed by blood—using half the energy of the whole body. It controls the body via millions of miles of cellular wiring. Each "wire" is made up of "nerve" cells, or "neurons." These "fire" one after the other as they transfer an electrical impulse. (It is unclear whether they fire in an "all-or-nothing" or "variable" fashion.) Neurons also transfer impulses, as "data," *to* the brain from the sophisticated structures of the five senses. These complete the nervous system, which itself completes a body of such physiology that it must be considered to manifest a higher level of organization, the "psychological."

2. The Creation of Something Dramatically "New"

Let there be no mistake. Complex organization involves the creation of something dramatically "new." It involves the creation of a whole with characteristics not possessed by its parts. The prediction of its behavior involves laws which do not apply to its parts. It is true: the whole *is* more than the sum of its parts.

Structured energy is "hard"; it comprises sub-atomic particles that can collide and combine in the atoms that make up the compounds that make up the cell. The cell, however, is "alive"; it engages in metabolism, growth, regeneration and reproduction. Chemicals are capable of nothing like this. The laws of chemistry cannot by themselves be used to predict the behavior of cells. One could stare at chemical equations forever and never deduce what the cell will do in given situations. For this, one must study the cell as a whole.

Cells may make up the brain but, as a whole, the brain is conscious. It is capable of sense perception, memory and thought; it is capable of the great profundities of human emotion. Cells know nothing of this; cells know nothing. This is no mystery; it is simply that cells can be organized into something that can know, and can know that it knows.

3. The Cause of What is New
a. The Idea

Let there be no mistake. Complex organization is the cause of what is new.

An atom is an atom because of the complex organization of sub-atomic particles. The organization of a nucleus and its orbitals gives it structure.

A cell is a cell because of the complex organization of chemicals. It is this that gives structure to cell parts. It is the organization of these parts that explains their integrated activity. Metabolism takes place because the cell's specially constructed membranes admit only certain kinds of "food." Thereupon, other cell parts incorporate this food or burn it. The combined result of these and other processes *is* life.

A man is a man because of the complex organization of cells. It is this which gives structure to the eye, explaining its ability to react to light, and send a coded message to the right place in the brain. There, other structures analyze this message, reacting to the various components of which it consists. This *is* sight; the "experience" of sight is simply constitutive of what it is, a complex psychological reaction to incoming data. It may spur the stimulation of other structures; this *is* thought. Thereupon, if structures dictate, the data are sent into a region where the structural changes they may cause *is* memory. The combined effect of these and other processes *is* mental life, i.e. spirituality.

b. A Final Response to the Objection that Man is Not a Machine

At this point, we now have enough in evidence to offer a final response to the objection that man is not a machine.

Just as the complex organization of the cell results in something which is alive—something its chemical parts are not—so it is that the complex organization of the brain results in something which is spiritual—something its cells could never imagine. To say that this means that man is a "machine" is correct only in the sense that his function is the working of material parts. But, the complexity normally conceived of when one speaks of a machine, for example, an automobile engine, is in no way sufficient to explain the spiritual life of the brain, a thing of far greater complexity than any machine in the typical sense.

B) The Superfluousness of Neo-Scholasticism

1. The Error of Neo-Scholasticism

It is now clear that the error of neo-scholasticism was its unnecessary presumption that something other than organized matter is needed to explain things. Its postulation of immaterial principles was superfluous. Ironically, it was a violation of the very principle of economy which led to its initial emergence as the mind-set of the thinking world.

An atom is an atom because its parts are this and that, here and there, interacting as they do. We need nothing else to explain its being and behavior.

A cell is alive because the organization of its parts is so complex that their interaction is metabolism, growth, etc. We need nothing vital to explain its life.

A man is spiritual because the organization of his parts is *so* complex that their interaction is thought, emotion, etc. We need nothing immaterial to explain his spirituality.

2. The Sufficiency of Materialism

The sufficiency of materialism is the fact that organized matter so plausibly accounts for everything. There is no question that things are made of matter, and the creative power of organization is evident in what complexity has created—especially at the lower levels.

Matter and organization answer the question of the one and the many (cf. p. 59).

Should someone argue that "organization" is a euphemism for "form"— that organization is an immaterial reality—we would respond by pointing out that organization is made of matter; it is the arrangement of matter. There is no-thing immaterial about it.

3. The Superiority of Materialism
a. The Idea

The superiority of materialism is the fact that it explains everything in evidence, postulating nothing that is not.

It is superior to dualistic systems because it answers the question of the one and the many not with two things but with one—the one which is in evidence.

It is superior to any system that postulates the ontologically spiritual because it solves the problem of the relation of mind and body (cf. p.141). To deny materialism in favor of one of these systems is to be left with the problem: How does the decision to speak become the neurological command that moves certain muscles in certain ways? How does the light bouncing off this page become the idea of this argument? Moreover, if materialism is not sufficient, we are left with the questions: What is the soul? Where is it? How does it work?

b. A Final Response to the Objection from Consciousness

It would now seem appropriate to offer a final response to the objection to materialism from consciousness: the objection to materialism based upon the human experience that "things" like thoughts and feelings are thought and felt, obviously non-material realities; they cannot be physiological processes.

Prescinding from making an issue of the fact that animals are conscious, it is simply to be reaffirmed that the products of complex organization are much more than anything their parts could ever conceive. But, let it be clear. Thought is not matter; it is the working of the brain. Thought is not a simple physiological process, it is a *psychological* process. Its conscious experience is a characteristic of a process of that complexity. To insist on something more is to mistake the object for its characteristics—the thing which exists in itself and the characteristics which are true of the thing. To claim that consciousness is a characteristic totally different from any other is simply to state the truth of the fact that it is a manifestation of the most complex thing in nature.

At this point, a word should perhaps be said about the possibility that man will one day make a machine, i.e. a computer, which is sufficiently complex for conscious experience. It should first be stated that the state of the art is nowhere near the "active inference" which is truly "thought." It is even further from achieving the global function which enables a person to "feel." And such an achievement may never come. But, if it comes, if technology can reproduce anything like the complexity which makes the brain capable of such functions, it would simply have reproduced a man.

C) Reductionism?

1. The Error of Reductionism

The claim that consciousness is explicable in terms of matter in no way warrants anything like the statement that the human mind is "merely" matter, or that psychology and all the sciences can be "reduced" to physics. A pointless conclusion of the 19th century materialism (cf. p.140), this idea betrays the over-zealous scientific hope to know it all—simply.

The word "merely" is in no way justified by anything that has been said so far. To say that a cell is "merely" chemicals is to miss the fact that a cell is an organization so complex that the product is life.

To say that man is "merely" matter is to miss the fact that he is an organization so complex that the product is spirituality.

Therefore, the word "reduced"—as in the idea "everything has been reduced to matter"—is equally inappropriate.

2. The Importance of All the Sciences, Including Philosophy

The word "reduced—as in the idea that all the sciences have been reduced to physics—is also inappropriate. It is clear that all the sciences are important.

We have already observed that an endless pondering of the laws of physics will never explain why salmon swim upstream in order to spawn. They do so—they are salmon—because of the organization of matter that *is* salmon. Organization is the cause—the integrator—of the many motions that give a thing holistic existence. Therefore, explanation must involve a description of organization, or at least its effect. Simply put, though it is indeed true that physics explains the motion of elementary matter, it is chemistry that explains what these interactions holistically make possible once they have been organized into the stable form of an atom. It is biology that explains how chemicals enable the "life" of the cell. And, it is psychology that explains how cells enable the spiritual life of the mind.

The creative power of complex organization certainly confirms the immemorial idea that the essence of scientific activity is observation. The product of organization must be observed for what it is. (It cannot even be imagined until it exists, except by the creation of a model, a project which virtually involves making the thing so that it can be observed.) Things must be observed for their holistic response to different situations and the data of this observation are studied with an eye for the patterns that become scientific laws either general or specific.

Science goes deeper when it attempts to explain a thing in itself—to explain its holistic existence. Then it looks inside a thing. Directly or by inference, it studies the parts in themselves, as the study of the cell involves chemistry. But, it is also concerned with the ways in which the parts, in this case chemicals, can be organized. Thus, biology is more "comprehensive" than chemistry. (Of course, because of human limitations, most chemists know much more about chemistry than most biologists.) Physiology is even more comprehensive than biology. It is a much more comprehensive study of what matter can do.

The increasing comprehensiveness of scientific study offers the philosopher a way to describe the importance of his own discipline. In its observation of *everything,* philosophy is the most comprehensive of studies. It is therefore to be observed that physics and philosophy are at opposite ends of the scientific spectrum. The former studies the most particular aspect of reality; it asks the question: what is matter, unit for unit? The latter asks the most general of questions: what *is* matter; what *is* reality? Considering all that matter can be, physicists and others must acknowledge the limits of their competence.

3. The Truth of Human Experience
a. The Idea

As we now see, the sciences observe the products of complex organization for what they are as such. This is no less true of psychology. Furthermore, the brain is a thing of such complexity that its holistic existence is "experienced," not just observed. Obviously, the content of this experience is information about reality. Moreover, the content of experience is an important part of any explanation of mental life. Since experience is a manifestation of complexity—a statement of what is fully true of the whole—such a statement best explains the mind's passage from state to state. In other words, the psychologist can rightly say: "He was upset because he understood."

By virtue of the above, it is clear that phenomenology (cf. p. 225) also provides information about reality. Therefore, if the experience of man tells him that he is spiritual (as opposed to unaware), or profoundly "in-the-world" (as opposed to isolated self-consciousness), that is what he is.

b. Responses to Objections from Self-Consciousness, "Para-Psychology" and Faith

An admission of the truth of human experience might seem to provide evidence against materialism on the basis of certain experiences all or some could claim.

The first could be claimed by all—the experience of self-consciousness. According to the argument that might be made on the basis of it: there must be more to man than psycho-physiological processes because there is a "self" who can testify to his experience of his thoughts and feelings, something that is distinct from these processes who is self-consciously aware of them as *his*.

The argument certainly departs from *some* truth. Man is certainly self-conscious; and his self-consciousness is distinct from his specific thoughts and feelings. But, this experience is not distinct from his brain. Just as consciousness is a general characteristic of the inner life of organizations of a certain level of complexity, so too self-consciousness is a general characteristic of the human level of organization. It is consciousness to a greater degree. (This is the reason that self-consciousness exists in degree, differing from moment to moment.) Explicit reflection on self is just that.

The objection from "para-psychology" would actually involve as many objections as there are claimed to be para-psychological phenomena, for example, ESP, teleportation, bilocation or clairvoyance, etc. These supposedly prove that there is a "spiritual" at work apart from the body.

As a matter of fact, they prove nothing of the kind. It is first to be stated that the burden of proof plainly rests with anyone who would claim something so extraordinary as a para-psychological phenomenon. This burden will prove especially heavy because most such phenomena are highly private. They are also problematic because they are not very liable to a plausible natural explanation. With the possible exception of very limited abilities for ESP and teleportation—for which there is some evidence, and a plausible natural explanation in terms of the brain's outpouring of waves (cf. p.238)—there is little evidence and no plausible explanation for much else in the para-psychological realm.[11] Most easily explained in terms of imagination, trickery, or the extraordinary coincidences inevitable in a universe of countless events—there is no such phenomenon for which there is evidence sufficiently compelling to require man to abandon everything else he experiences as true. Therefore, even if some such phenomenon is not easily explained away, we can remain confident that there was some material explanation whether or not it will ever be discovered.

The objection from faith falls to our existing critique of such arguments (cf. p.212). Moreover, let us remember that the underlying truth of faith will only be discovered in the retrospect of its synthesis with knowledge generally (cf. p.213). What this means in terms of materialism is the subject of this whole work and must be considered in the light of its whole presentation. For now, however, let it be observed that the truth of all we have seen

11. The absence of a plausible explanation also critiques those forms of clairvoyance which involve the reading of "signs" such as the stars, i.e. astrology, etc. In fact, such things have no bearing upon the events they propose to predict.

so far has involved not a denial of human experience but its more informed, intelligent interpretation.

Section V: A New Nominalism

A) The Creative Power of Organization *Per Se*

It is time to explain what materialism really means. We begin by correcting what might have been the false impression created by the generalities in which the first principles of materialism needed to be stated.

Despite our attention to the creative power of *complex* organization and the products thereof, there is a wider variety in reality and it is due to the creative power of organization *per se*.

1. *The Variety in Reality*
a. The Variety in Nature

Up to now, our presentation of the creative power of organization only mentioned things in nature (not man-made) and it has identified only the most general of its products—the atom, the cell and man. Of course, "the" atom does not exist; 92 different kinds occur in nature and there are over one hundred if we count those that man has made. These compose thousands of known compounds; an astronomical number is theoretically possible. Carbon compounds comprise a fantastic variety of cells. These are known to make over 500,000 different kinds of plants. There are over 2,000,000 known animal species embracing many kinds of insects, fish, amphibians, reptiles and many kinds of mammals.

Given the distinction between an object and its characteristics—such as color, size and swiftness—it is clear that matter can account for anything in nature we can name.

b. "Artifacts"

Reality is further and more visibly diversified by "artifacts"—things that man has made. Indeed, machines were the original source of our awareness of how parts can be made into a greater whole. Moreover, man-made objects diversify reality whether or not they have visibly moving parts. Matter can be made into things as simple as bricks or houses, or as complex as state of the art computers.

Understanding the distinction between an object and its characteristics, and the fact that humankind "bears" a variety of characteristics such as "stories" or "symbolism," it becomes clear that there is nothing left to explain.

2. A True Variety

The products of organization are a true variety; they are really something new.

Although hydrogen and iron are both atoms, they have distinctly different characteristics. This is especially clear when they are present *en masse*; hydrogen burns; iron conducts electricity. Though the general laws of chemistry explain their existence as chemical substances, these laws cannot accurately predict their reactions to given situations; this requires laws more particular. Practically speaking, this involves the general laws for gases and minerals, and, in the case of the latter, the specific laws for metals. But, in the last analysis, it would most accurately involve the exact laws of hydrogen and iron, whether or not anyone has ever bothered to discover them.

3. The Cause of the Variety

It is clear that organization is the cause of the variety.

Hydrogen is the product of a particular type of organization; so is iron. The same is true of every kind of cell; each is the product of a particular type of organization. The same is also true of every kind of plant or animal; in fact, organization differentiates each member of the species. As is especially obvious in man, organization makes each member something new.

B) The New Nominalism

1. Individuality

a. Only in Individuals Is there Existence

As we can now see, materialism is nominalisitic (cf. p.95). The first critiques of scholasticism were correct. "Kinds" are concepts based upon similarity. Only in individuals is there existence. And, the organization of the individual is at least slightly different from every other and to this degree the characteristics of this thing are unique and so too are the laws that would most accurately describe its response to the world around it.

Organization is nothing magical possessed by a thing. It is the particular arrangement of parts which is the thing. And, this particular arrangement is responsible for a holistic life which is just as particular.

Actually, the organization which is the thing is the exact juxtaposition of a certain number of elementary units at a given moment in time. Thus, things are always changing. And, obviously, every individual thing is unique.

b. The Increase of Individuality with Complexity

Although every individual thing is unique, it does not follow that every individual thing is equally unique. On the contrary, it is to be observed that individuality increases with complexity.

It has already been observed that as complexity increases, what is created is something "new." But, it is also something "more." Atoms are "hard."

Cells are not only hard, they are alive. Man is not only alive, he is conscious. Of course there is much more that could be said. Just as the "life" of cells involves a number of characteristics that are not possessed by chemicals, the mental life of men involves an almost inexhaustible number of characteristics not possessed by cells. Men can be fat, funny or famous; they can be French, firemen or friends. In short, as complexity increases, there is more that can be said about what is created.

Furthermore, with the increase in complexity, there is also an increase in the differences between things of the same kind. Any two hydrogen atoms are all but identical. But, no two cells are alike. The complexity of their organization involves too many variables, and many involve major differences between them. (Plants and animals involve differences so major that their study involves special sciences, i.e. botany and zoology, both of which embrace a number of sub-studies.) By the time we get to men, we can *see* that no two are alike. Their organization involves a fantastic number of variables. Thus, like nothing else, men are individual things.

2. The True Nature of Science

The essential and increasing individuality of things tells us much about the true nature of science.

Plainly, science studies what is similar in similar things. It discovers the organizational requirements of certain characteristics. Moreover, as it does, it discovers what is different in similar things, and how these differences affect the whole. Thus, it studies the "patterns" of what matter does.

Actually, this has always been science. In attempting to describe the response of things to situations, science encountered the fact that no two situations are alike, and there is an infinite number of situations in which a thing might find itself. Therefore, scientific "laws"—or "principles"—have always described the patterns of what matter does. Obviously, to the degree that these patterns are informed by a wider variety of variables, they are capable of predicting what will happen in new situations.

But, as complexity increases, there is a greater variety of situations in which a thing might find itself. Moreover and more importantly, there can be a greater variety among similar things. This means a greater number of variables which would need to inform the principles that permit prediction. Therefore, because of human limitations, as complexity increases, science becomes more general, less exact.

3. "Natures"

Thanks to patterns, we can still speak of "natures"—the patterns observed in similar things—whose "typical" manifestations can still be called "normal." But, ultimately, it is the *nature* of matter, i.e. the fact that it does certain things when organized in certain forms, which is responsible for everything that is. This is materialism.

C) The Full Potential of Organization

1. The Creative Power of Simple Organization

Materialism actually means that any arrangement of matter affects what "is." Indeed, even the simple, unintegrated organization of matter can make a "thing." This is especially obvious when a large amount of matter is involved.

a. "Conglomerates"

The simple organization of many molecules makes a rock (in which their juxtaposition is relatively fixed). Many rocks make a mountain. Many atoms make a star (in which their juxtaposition is relatively fluid). These are "conglomerates."

b. "Societies"

Reality is also enriched by the relationships between things that can perceive each other. Ants form the most structured of colonies. Many fish swim in schools. Many animals move in herds.

Humans live in a variety of "societies." They come in couples, friendships and families. They make up teams (where the members are in relatively constant contact with one another), and companies (where those who work together need not know each other). In the widest view, they make up communities, countries, and society at large.

2. The Nature of the Newness of Conglomerates and Societies

There should be no question that conglomerates and societies are more than the sum of their parts. A star is "bright"; it is born, burns and dies. Its study requires a special science—astronomy. The study of society (sociology) embraces a number of disciplines. Economics has produced the law of "supply and demand." History has produced all sorts of principles. All these disciplines study the effects of people living together, something that could not be observed until people did. All determine principles which describe the predictable effects of the simple, unintegrated organization of matter.

But, neither conglomerates nor societies are to be considered things of a "higher" level than that of their parts. As products of simple, unintegrated organization, they do not bear characteristics that are truly new. Theirs are the collective or combined characteristics of their parts. It is because hydrogen burns that stars are bright. It is because individuals can love that two can be "close"; their "closeness" is defined in terms of their mutual feelings.

The above is particularly true of societies. Not only do they lack the internal integration which produces a true whole, its parts are not connected. Societal relations take place through the medium of the atmosphere; it is not the structure of society that determines the behavior of the parts, it is the self-determined behavior of the parts that gives structure to society. Nonetheless, both societies and conglomerates do add to the richness of reality.

3. The Unity of Material Reality

At this point, it is possible to point out that materialism does not permit absolute distinctions between things. To a great extent, the distinction of individual things involves legitimate but artificial distinctions between bumps on a single log. No mountain exists in isolation; it is part of a continent, itself part of a planet. A planet is part of a solar system. Stars exist in galaxies; the gravitation of their fellow stars affects all their motions. Actually, everything affects everything. Not only are material things constantly inter-relating with their immediate environment, their environment is itself inter-relating with the wider environment of the world—and the universe. Material reality is a unity.

Chapter II: The Anthropology of Creative Materialism

Section I: Introductory Remarks

Now that creative materialism has been presented, we must examine the aspect of this metaphysic which will have the most to say to any theology—its idea of man—its "anthropology."

Materialism involves certain perspectives which will prove indispensable to the understanding of man:

1) Mental life is "one." Based in one brain, mental functions such as thinking and feeling are not to be considered fundamentally distinct. Not only do they concern the same mental states, but their contents are completely inter-related. The so-called intellectual and emotional are two sides of the same coin; mind and "heart" refer to the same organ. Hereafter, we shall call this the "unity" of mental life.

2) Mental life is also "incessant." The brain is a psycho-physiological organization. To remain one, its parts must keep moving. Consciously or not, awake or asleep, it is always at work. It is constantly passing from state to state. Lastly,

3) Mental life is "developmental." Affected by events, the brain has experiences. As each is remembered, the brain is changed structurally. In this it is also complexified and, as it proves, developed. This is how the baby becomes an adult—psychologically. Given the relation between structure and nature (cf. p.247), this means that with regard to man, much of what *is* true *becomes* true.

For the above reason, the study of man is essentially a study of human development. For reasons of practicality, we shall therefore look at the various "stages" of development through which man passes—if he makes it that far. Although the distinction of stages does involve a certain artificial compartmentalization of what actually happens as a continuum, it is both practically necessary and essentially honest to categories of experience that we can distinguish. This said, we can begin with a look at a baby at birth.

Section II: A Baby at Birth

At birth, as before, a baby's brain is uncomplexified by experience. It is no more than the genetic heritage of its autonomic bodily control, ability to receive sense data, and an interest in its bodily well-being (and need for food) which comes with certain totally reflexive[1] responses to changes in its primitive—unconscious—perception of its well-being.

Of course, not only do genetics see that everyone starts "differently," it also distributes a variety of "gifts" (such as the proficiency for music given to Mozart). These consist of qualities of certain structures. But, the degree to which reflexive reactions, such as aggression, are not only genetically based but different from person to person is the object of a field of study that has just begun. In any case, it is clear that the principal source of human individuality is not genetics but "environment." This is most evident in the many particularities only attributable to learning—to experience.

The baby's first experience usually involves a slap. Perception, feeling and response are one; the baby cries.

Section III: The Emergence of Consciousness

Bombarded by light and handled no end, the baby is affected by everything that happens to him. However slightly, each of these events is sensed. However slightly, each is remembered. And, as it is, the baby's brain is changed, complexified and developed.

A) Intellectual Developments

The complexification of the baby's brain leads to the following intellectual developments:

Gradually, he becomes aware of things around him. His capacity for sense perception becomes more acute. The five senses begin to distinguish themselves. He sees; he may see his mother.

As more experiences are remembered, patterns begin to emerge. He is unconsciously beginning to associate experiences. He begins to develop certain expectations with regard to both the control of his body and the working of the environment; he has begun to learn.

All the while, the infant is becoming more and more conscious.

B) Emotional Developments

Intellectual developments involve a corresponding development of the baby's ability to feel—the "emotional"[2] aspect of his mental life. His natal interests now involve the conscious experience of pain and pleasure. He begins to distinguish discomfort and hunger. And, he is coming to "want"

---

1. Human "reflexes" can be distinguished from animal "instincts" in the fact that instincts involve elaborate behaviors never learned, which do not need to be sustained by external stimulus. Evidently, the human propensity for learning requires a mind more facile than the permanent structures of instincts permit.

2. The "emotional" has historically been called the "passionate," the "appetitive," and, lately, the "affective." All refer to essentially the same thing.

something he did not seek previously—security. Thus, if he does not feel secure, he "wills" to cry.

If he feels secure, continuing development will carry him to perceive in things something that gives him a very new interest—curiosity. He has become capable of the experience that there is more to things than the simple fact of their existence, or their existence as something that can give him what he wants. If he sees a shiny object, he will draw on much of what he has learned in order to reach for it.

C) An Excursus: The Physiology of Mental Life

At this point, called for is some description of the physiology involved in the phenomena which have now been mentioned. Not only would such a description be essential to the credibility of materialism, it should also be expected to help us to understand the phenomena. Though the following is but a general look at the relatively simple phenomena which the anthropology has already mentioned, it will hopefully provide us the context in which to understand the origin of more complex phenomena as they are discussed.

There has been much study of the structure and function of the sensory organs. Though there is much to be done, studies have shown that the sense organs are structures which react to external stimulus by the emission of electro-chemical impulses which are neurologically channeled into receiving areas of the brain. Upon their arrival, these impulses are "decoded," i.e. the various components of the emission are structurally channeled to different areas of the brain at large. The affectation of these areas is the perception of its cause. If this perception informs the brain of the body's ill or well-being, it is felt as pain or pleasure. These "states" are characteristic of the whole brain; the whole brain is always to be characterized by some state.

In the beginning, almost every perception produces the structural change which is its memory. After a time, the brain will channel them into the areas which result in short or long-term memory.

Presently, memory is little understood. It probably involves the creation of paths, or "traces," which connect the cells involved in a particular perception. But remember, memory is not only the recording of experiences, it is their recording according to the decoding which first made possible their perception. Loss of memory involves the "de-struction" of these connections.

It is the fact that experiences are broken down, their similar elements sent to the same receiving centers, that makes possible their "association"—the essence of learning. Beginning with the association of events temporarily conjoined, learning eventually involves the creation of a structural connection between similar but temporarily unrelated experiences. (Of course, within the brain, there is some connection between every memory.) Forgetting is the failure of this connection.

Therefore, physiologically speaking, "intelligence" is to be defined in terms of an individual's natal (i.e. genetic) propensity for memory, together with a not necessarily corresponding propensity for association. The former involves the ability to remember without repetition while the latter involves the ability to see subtleties.

Materialistically, it is easy to explain the experienced fact that mental life is "sudden"—the fact that one state succeeds another and each comes as something of a surprise. Simply put, one state produces another. Each state bespeaks the whole which is caused by the existing organization of its parts; thereupon, their organized activity carries the whole from state to state. (Thus does the state affect association and *vice-versa*.) But, be it clear, there is no one thinking or feeling apart from these processes. Mental life is a chain-reaction. Its suddenness is not the caprice or uncontrollability of the brain, but the simple experience that it is working.

Section IV: The Emergence of Self-Consciousness

As the infant becomes a child, he develops not just physically but psychologically. Thanks to the experience which has already brought about consciousness, he sees more—and what he sees means more. This increases the internal activity in which his brain is further complexified.

A) Intellectual Developments

1. Perceptions Becoming Ideas and Thought

The complexification of the brain continues to cause intellectual developments. The senses sharpen and are further defined. Moreover, frequent exposure to the same things or persons now involves their familiarity—and their identification. It is also becoming possible for him to distinguish between things and their parts—between mother's head and hand. He is even becoming capable of distinctions between things and characteristics, and things and actions; he knows his ball is "round"; he knows he can "play" with it, "tomorrow."

He continues to learn. He is growing in his ability for bodily control. There is an increase in the number of his expectations. Moreover, similar expectations give rise to rules which permit the prediction of what will happen in new situations. When associations become conscious, they are called "ideas." When the process which produces them becomes conscious, it is called "thought."

Through it all, the child is becoming self-conscious—conscious of himself. It comes as quite a surprise.

2. The Novelty of Self-Consciousness

Before we move on to consider the emotional aspects of the preceding intellectual developments, we would do well to take a moment to reflect upon what a new thing self-consciousness really is. Self-consciousness is what distinguishes man, who alone knows and knows that he knows. It is the supreme manifestation of fact that individuality increases with complexity. In self-consciousness, man becomes aware of himself, and in so doing, he is the only individual aware that he is just that. His, every individual's, self-consciousness constitutes the basis for an absolute distinction between the individual and his environment. No longer just a thing, he is now a person who knows he exists—and cares.

B) Emotional Developments

1. Feelings Becoming Desires and Emotions

With intellectual development, there is a corresponding development of the emotional aspect of the person's mental life. Increased capacity for perception means increased capacity for pain and pleasure. Furthermore, the increasing distinction of sense data has its emotional parallel in the increasingly distinct experiences which the person can have; he can have fear or fun. His interest in avoiding the one and having the other is now consciously experienced as a "desire." At other times, he experiences an "emotion"; he may be bored.

As a person's desires become more intense, some become "needs" whose frustration is debilitating. If his "need" for security is satisfied, however, his interests become newly diverse. He becomes capable of finding things "interesting"—funny, pretty and exciting.[3] This involves corresponding desires to see, to have and to do. Newly conscious of himself, he also feels the attendant desire for attention. Naturally, each desire also involves the correspondingly developed emotions felt when these desires are or are not met. Also known as "motives," because they motivate action, it is to be observed that a variety of motives may have a combined effect upon the desirability of any one action.

The emergence of new desires does not come without new ways of seeing to their satisfaction. New situations no longer evoke an immediate response; the person can delay his response; he can will to think about it. This involves the "deliberation" and "decision" which make possible "self-direction" (which commands the body to act).

---

3. It is to be stated that sexual desires (or needs) do not initially bespeak a separate interest. Initially, sexuality is simply a source of bodily pleasure. But, eventually, it can become one of many motives of a profound interest in other people (q.v. p.402).

2. An Addendum: The Distinction between "Is" and "About"

Having mentioned a number of the qualities that a person comes to see in things or experiences, be they interest, beauty, humor or excitement, it would surely be wise for us to consider in what sense these qualities can rightfully be said to involve what "is."

Unlike the more intellectual statement that something "is," essentially meaning "is there," the more emotional statement that something is, for example, "pretty," more obviously involves the fact that the thing has had an effect upon the person. Although this is really no less true of the source of the data that informed him that the thing is there, he can still insist that the data has told him something that would be true whether or not he was around to perceive it. Therefore, the question is: can statements "about" things be said to involve an objective quality in the thing?

For reasons that will hopefully be made clear, an answer to this question must wait upon the provision of more data through the course of this discussion. But a response *will* be offered and so the discussion will continue to describe the emergence of such perceptions as they are indeed experienced, a fact which will continue to be attributed to the general mental development which probably takes place at the hands of increasing experience.

C) An Excursus: The Permanence of Personal Existence

We must now discuss the notion of "person" and respond to some of the problems which confront a materialistic understanding of such a thing.

As we have said, mental life is incessant; the brain is constantly passing from state to state (cf. p 253). But this was Hume's reason for the denial of "self" (cf. p. 145); and it has since been taken up by positivism.

In responding to this argument, we must first acknowledge that the human experience is that of a succession of states. No perceptions or feelings, ideas or desires, thoughts or emotions characterize a person permanently. But this is precisely the point; they characterize a person. They pertain to a person, a brain, the same brain which is the seat of all its experiences.

Of course, with each memory the brain changes. Therefore, as might be argued, even though the same brain changes, each change produces a new person. Thus, there is no person who exists long enough to be someone.

This argument would mistake development for destruction. Even though the person does change with every experience, this change does not annihilate but adds to him. Each is an experience of learning in which the same person, the same structure, has become more, and therefore "new," but not different. It is the existing self that becomes the old man with new information. Though changing from moment to moment, at every moment he is the sum of his life. He can reflect on his past and has a reason to plan for his future.

Section V: The Emergence of a Person Who Knows
He Is Part of the World

Physically, the child becomes an adolescent. Meanwhile, events continue to drive the internal activity which complexifies his brain. Of special importance are the products of his thoughts.

A) Intellectual Developments

1. Conceptual Thought

Increasing complexification continues to spur development. Perception improves. There is an increase in the number of things that the person can recognize. Moreover, memory makes him capable of "imagination"; he can call things to mind even if they are not there. Furthermore, he can see what is similar in things; and he can speak of it. This involves "abstraction," the creation of "concepts." (This associates whole areas where decoded parts of memories have been stored.) Thus can the person conceive a category, such as "boy," or a characteristic, such as "strength." He can conceive actions, such as "work." (But, all are conceived in concrete examples; after all, they are characteristics of *things*. This explains the experienced fact that conceptual thought is "symbolic.") Thanks to his encounter with others like himself, he can conceive his "self." He can even conceive things which are larger than life, like his home, neighborhood or even country. Altogether, the person is coming to possess a highly inter-related network of ideas that comprise his "outlook." This decides whether or not he will "understand."

Learning continues. Bodily control reaches the point of skill. (As it further increases, skills become "second nature.") Knowledge of the environment also increases. Similar experiences produce expectations more fundamental; but rules become more precise, and more applicable to new situations. The person learns procedures. Moreover, he begins to take an interest in learning. Initially encouraged by reward and punishment, he begins the study which starts with trial and error.

All the while, the person slowly becomes aware that he is part of a world which is "out there" and has its own ways regardless of what he wants.

2. An Addendum: Language

At this point, it has become possible to make mention of one of man's most important developments—language. Not only is language one of the most important human abilities but, as we have seen (cf. p.163), it has lately been an object of philosophic concern with the specific result of a denial of the meaningfulness of philosophic terms.

Though language is the meaningful use of anything for the purpose of communication, it principally involves words spoken or written. The spoken word normally comes first; it dates to the baby's first successful cry. With time, hearing, correction and encouragement, he learns how to make the specific sounds of many words. As he learns that certain forms of certain words are to be used in certain situations, his grammar takes shape. And he can associate words with ideas. (Actually, ideas are being associated with commands in the speech center.) Eventually, ideas can be associated with the visual symbolism of written language. Once the connection is made, the word will lead to the idea if the person sees or hears it. This is the reason that naming things, and creating "terms," will help a person to remember them, especially if they involve complex concepts.

Nonetheless, thinking is not a word-game. Words having meaning; they refer to elements of an individual's understanding of reality. That many words have no referent is due to the fact that man is capable of abstraction, a rich understanding of reality which should not involve something to which one can point. If this were not so, how could the linguistic philosopher refer to his hometown or, better, the "concept" of "word." (How could he translate from one language to another?) The question "what is time" betrayed the failure to recognize that "time" is a concept, not an object. But, since concepts do not bear exact definition, we must take care to define words well—to maximize the degree to which all who hear them conceive the same thing.

B) Emotional Development

1. Desires for Achievement and Approval

Increasing intellectual development continues to involve a corresponding development of the person's emotional make-up. The increasing capacity for detailed perception again involves the capacity for more intense and specific experiences of pain and pleasure; circumstances may now make one sad or happy.

Not surprisingly, the intensity of existing specific interests also increases. Things become *more* interesting—beautiful, funny or exciting. Naturally, the more he sees, the more he wants. Furthermore, things become interesting in themselves; the person begins to wonder, to wonder "what." In the light of his recognition of the objectivity of the outside world, he comes to desire achievement. In light of his recognition that there are others like him, he comes to desire approval. Founded upon more experience, his desires become more constant. All are inter-related within what is now the general context of his "emotional outlook," the general disposition that evaluates the desirability of anything that comes into his life.

But, the person is already thinking about what he wants and how to get it. And, now, he can have "goals." To achieve them, he can make a "plan" and follow it—even if it requires work and patience.

2. An Addendum: Internal Conflict

One of the most important aspects of self-direction is internal conflict. Desires often conflict. This may involve either "primary" desires (things desired in themselves) or "secondary" ones (things desired for the sake of something else). In all cases, there is conflict to be resolved. In any case, the weighing of options may involve the anticipation of difficulties and consequences.

The resolution of conflict with regard to a secondary desire involves a decision about what is most likely to bring about the truly desired result. The resolution of a conflict with regard to a primary desire involves the fact that not all desires are felt with the same intensity. Intensity involves the degree to which a desire is rooted in the structure of a person's brain. It keeps him pursuing his goal. This may involve what is called "will power." But, will power is not a specific "power"; it is a manifestation of the degree to which a desire is part of a person. (Of course, it also involves the various ways a person can channel his thoughts in certain directions, not to mention the fact that he can avoid "occasions" of conflict.) The failure of will power follows the re-evaluation that always takes place as the person is pursuing his goal.

C) An Excursus: Personality and the So-Called "Essence" of One's "Being"

Nothing said about self-direction was meant to suggest that the entire process takes place consciously. Indeed, even though the anthropology has focused on "phenomena," nothing said was meant to deny the existence of the non-conscious aspects of mental life. Quite the contrary, consciousness has already been explained in terms of the degree to which structures are developed in the individual. It was stated that every experience is remembered to the degree to which it results in a structural change. This obviously involves untold numbers of changes that are to be considered "un"-conscious. Many of these result in the unconscious ideas that are responsible for behavior that would otherwise be inexplicable.

For example, bad surprises often lead to a fear of the "unknown." (This combines with desires for "simplicity" and "someone to blame" in some form of "bigotry.") Other bad experiences may lead to a "phobia" or an "obsession."[4] Not so the desire for "freedom" which is rooted in the essen-

---

4. Actually, mental problems can be either "psychological," involving the emergence of undesirable structures, or "physiological," involving the bio-chemical function of the brain.

tial structure of what it is to be a man (q.v. p.278). Nonetheless, on account of experience, the desire for freedom, or individuality, may take the form of "rebellion." At the same time, other associations—involving everything from learned ways of learning to the desire for approval or belonging— may lead a person to "imitation."[5] In any case, the study of these associations—and the dynamisms which produce them—is the competence of psychologists.

The unconscious is to be distinguished from the "sub"-conscious which involves the brain's ability to "block out" (or "repress") structures that are sure to cause pain. Also manifest in the brain's ability to cause the person to faint in the face of terrible pain, both are manifestations of its self-protective nature.

Non-conscious ideas are part and parcel of the whole brain which is the person. Therefore, to the degree that they are structurally developed, they are part of the "who" the person is, the whole structure which contains his potential response to any situation that comes his way. As we know, this whole structure can—and must—be studied as such. This study should yield the pattern of the person's response to the environment, his so-called "personality." It should also inform a personality "type," the pattern of what can be expected from similar psychological organizations (cf. p.247).

Of course, as the metaphysic also attempted to make clear, everyone is ultimately an individual. And, as a psychological organization, the most complex kind we know, there is more to be known about him than could ever be said. Nonetheless, it is still possible to describe the person in general terms. It is even possible to describe *him,* his whole brain most holistically. This, the so-called "essence" of his "being," is best seen in his dominant desires, especially those which can sustain action on their own. The dominance of desires is best to be seen in his response to matters he would consider important, especially if circumstances allowed him a considered, "reflective" decision, which reflects his whole self, rather than a "reflexive" one which may not.

Section VI: The Emergence of Reason

The adolescent becomes an adult, at least physically. Experience continues to drive the internal activity which complexifies his brain. He is especially complexified in the structures created by conceptual thought.

---

5. Not imitation, the power of "suggestion" is the power of channeling thoughts as it is employed by *another* person.

A) Intellectual Developments

1. Analytic and Creative Thought

Complexity continues to propel intellectual development. Perception continues to improve. So does the person's capacity for conceptual thought. He can conceive larger categories, such as "man," and subtler characteristics, such as "intelligence." He can abstract aspects of action, such as the "velocity" of "motion." Not only can he conceive himself, but he can reflect on aspects of his internal life; he can talk about his "thoughts" and "feelings," even those he may now have with reference to himself. Not only can he conceive of the "world," he can conceive of the "diversity" of its "culture."

Of course, learning continues. Skill becomes talent. Expectations become more fundamental. Rules become more abstract, and more applicable to newer situations. Procedures become approaches. (The person develops ways of "relating" to other people.) Furthermore, the person can take a more active role in learning. Previously, his initiative consisted of trial and error. Now, he is capable of the "analytic" thought in which he articulates and applies principles in the attempt to account for his experiences. Thanks to his improving imagination, he also becomes capable of the "creative" thought in which he synthesizes his memories in the attempt to picture new things.

All the while, there is emerging another development in the person's understanding of reality at large. Now, not only does he realize that the world is out there, and does what it does regardless of his desires, but it does what it does dependably. It is this that makes possible trust in past experience—in evidence. This is the basis of reason.

2. Definitions of Reason, Logic, Mathematics, Common Sense, Intuition, Wisdom, Knowledge, Truth and Certainty

In essence, "reason" is thinking as directed by the idea that "reality is dependable."

"Logic" is the formal description of this dependability.[6]

"Mathematics" (which includes "symbolic logic") is a working out of the most basic implications of reality's dependability. Dealing with quantities presumed stable, it involves procedures which streamline the process. Sometimes, these involve the generation of approximations or other formal results such as $.333...$ or $\sqrt{-1}$. But, these symbolisms do not describe some mysterious realities; they describe relations between things.

Reason also involves much less basic implications of reality's dependabil-

6. It begins with the law of non-contradiction (cf. footnote p.162). It includes the rules of the "syllogism"; these permit the formal analysis of logical arguments according to the form X is Y, Y is Z so X is Z.

ity. If nature is dependable, it is also dependable that fire burns. Where the gravity is sufficient, what goes up must come down. The host of these facts make up what is commonly called "common sense."

If the individual's awareness of dependable patterns is sufficiently subtle, he is said to possess "intuition," uncommon sense. Contrary to popular opinion—and philosophical (cf. footnote p.206)—intuition is not inference apart, or less against, reason. It is an ability to perceive what is less obvious but no less dependable.

Neither is "wisdom" not reason. Wisdom is intuition in the extreme. The product of much experience, of wide experience, it can be distinguished from "technology" which deals with quantities of fact, and their much simpler interpretation—with rules that are not so comprehensive. Wisdom involves greater knowledge.

"Knowledge" is essentially an awareness of what is (or what was). Thus, it is also an awareness of how reality works (and thus, what will be). It is an idea about reality that is understood to be true.

In the beginning, "truth" is presumed. The infant does not evaluate the truth of what he sees. It is only after he realizes that he has been wrong that he develops procedures designed to tell him whether an idea corresponds to reality. The result of these procedures is "judgment."

This judgment involves degrees of "certainty." In the end, it is experience that makes a "belief" (or "opinion") more certain knowledge. In the last analysis, "certainty" reflects the degree to which knowledge is part of the structure of a brain.

B) Emotional Developments

1. Interest in What Is "Good" and "Just"

The emergence of reason also involves emotional developments. There is an increase in the intensity and diversity of emotional experience. Depending on circumstances, a person may feel anxious or depressed, content or enthusiastic. His perceptions about the outside become increasingly rich. Things become gorgeous, hilarious or thrilling. Others become "attractive" and, in his desire to have them in his life, a person may become "infatuated." Indeed, in his deepening perception of all that others are, he comes to desire not only their approval but affection, even companionship. Of course, all his interests have developed. Now he wants to know "how." He desires not only to do, but to "be" something special.

Depending upon his past experience, he will develop a plan for his whole life. He will make "career" choices. He will make a variety of "relationships." The well-being of these relationships, and his career, are constantly considered. In their interest, he can, as the psychologists say, defer the gratification of any other desire, no matter how basic or deep. He can endure setbacks and opposition.

More remarkably, as his emotions have fed his intellectual development, he has come to the idea that things are "good." In the beginning, "good" and "bad" were general terms for things that were good and bad for him. Now, as he comes to the idea of the world out there, he also comes to see and want things that "are" good. Moreover, he begins to feel bound by his emerging idea of what is "bad." Though he may be angry, he comes to understand that he "should" not smash a beautiful vase. This is his first experience of un-self-centeredness; the first time he views things apart from how they serve his interests—only. In his perception that others are others, he recognizes that not only should others not be hurt, they are entitled to what is theirs—even if I want it. This is his recognition of other's "rights." Their violation is "wrong." It also calls for restitution, and punishment. This is "just," the same idea that calls for the reward of those who do what is good.

All these ideas, collectively called "conscience," also involve general rules of right and wrong called "principles." The product of much development, they are a major influence on the conduct of the person's life who possesses them. If he does wrong, he feels guilty. (He may actually be moved to self-punishment.) If he does right, he will feel proud. In any case, principles play some role in his every consideration.

2. An Addendum: The Relation of Knowing and Feeling

At the outset of the anthropology, we discussed the "unity" of mental life (cf. p.250). This has had some important things to say about the relation of knowing and feeling.

Feelings are the emotional aspects of what we know. Feelings are caused by the way a person sees something. This is the reason that reasoning with a person can affect his feelings. It is the reason that he will feel (and desire and do) what he "should" if he is sufficiently certain.

As is also evident, feelings have their influence on knowing. What else causes a person to see what he wants to see, and may actually cause him to see what is not there? Feelings can do this because the brain is self-protective. Its evolutionary ancestor was a simple regulatory organ whose sole concern was the internal well-being of the thing. As this regulatory organ acquired more and more complex capabilities, it remained true to its initial structure; it used its new powers for its own good—to make itself feel good. Thus, feelings have their structural way to influence knowledge which is painful. One could say that the gradual increase of what we have called "reason" manifests the conversion of structures such that the truth is perceived by the person whether or not it is painful. In other words, reason makes the person see the truth whether or not he wants to. Reason makes the truth less subjective.

C) An Excursus: Human Nature and the "Objectivity" of Truth and Goodness

If reason makes the truth less subjective, it makes it more objective. But, the objectivity of truth is not something about which everyone agrees. Indeed, people disagree about almost everything.

It is plain that people see things differently. The reason: Genetically, they begin differently. Subsequently, they have been affected by different events. They have had different experiences.

This is the "contingency" of mental life, the fact that what a person sees, thinks, feels and does depends upon his past experience.

Actually, this is only half the picture. Even apart from the more obvious reasons for disagreement, those which involve the contingency of mental life, there are any number of others which involve the "temporality" of mental life, the fact that a person is affected by circumstances—what is happening to him right now. He is affected by the environment, for example, the weather or the music he may hear. He is affected from within. Tiredness diminishes all his powers. He is subject to bodily cycles and their important chemical effects. These contribute to the ups and downs which everyone experiences to some degree.[7] And every "mood" affects his every perception.

Nonetheless, it is still possible to speak about the patterns of a person's perceptions and define his normal view. This would be *his* nature.

Moreover, despite the contingency of mental life, it is still possible to speak about the pattern of people's perceptions and define a normal human view (cf. p.247). This is "human nature."

The existence of human nature permits us to speak about the "objectivity" of truth. We can predict what a person will perceive given certain experiences. And, if he is more intelligent and "more," especially "more widely" experienced—or more informed by the experience of others—what he perceives is more likely more true.[8]

Human nature also permits us to speak of an objectivity of "goodness." It is the goodness anyone would see if he is sufficiently intelligent and well

---

7. Best described in terms of "tiredness," downs are most troublesome because they affect the very processes which recognize downs as such.

8. Now that it is clear that "truth" is the product of events as they affect human nature, we realize that Aristotle *and* Plato were correct: knowledge comes from experience *and* from ideas latently present in the inexperienced mind (cf. p.57).

experienced. On this basis, it is even possible to speak of an objectivity of "taste."

Actually, objectivity is based upon what anyone would see (and be) if he is sufficiently well *developed*. What else is the product of experience; what else explains improving perception? It is all a matter of "maturity."

Of course, mature persons will still disagree. Most minor disagreements are due to the information, the insights, or the other positive influences of particular experiences. Most major disagreements involve "obstacles"— associations which wrongly condition a person's perception of reality and prevent him from seeing a truth he otherwise would.

Obstacles were prefigured in the "blocks" often attributed to "scaring" experiences that usually take place when a person is young, unformed, and therefore most "impressionable." Especially important are parent figures upon whom the child is totally dependent. Their importance endures; their effect is ever felt.

Section VII; A Half-Stage: The Possibility of a Person Who Knows There Must Be a Reason

As time passes, adulthood will surely become aging. But, given the volume and variety of experiences required of continued psychological development, there is no certainty that the person will pass to a new stage. If he does, however, we can expect the following. It is a "half-stage" because, in the normal course of human development, it passes quite quickly to the one which follows it.

A) Intellectual Developments

1. Causality

Perception still improving, the person is becoming capable of even larger categories and subtler abstraction. He can conceive a "thing" or its "existence." Not only can he conceive man's "reason, " but the "progress" of his "history." He can abstract the "power" at work in any influence of events. Reflecting upon himself, he can come to self-knowledge that gives him greater self-control. He can conceive of "reality." And he can try to describe what it is, and explain how it works—to create a philosophy.

All the while, the person is still growing in his sureness that reality is dependable. Moreover, he comes to the conclusion that it is impossible that things happen dependably due to immense coincidence. Thus it must be that things are caused. This was the causality first described by Aristotle (cf. p. 60). In the light of modern physical science (cf. p.234), it means that there are forces which propel the underlying level of reality—exactly and always and always in the same way.

2. A Defense of "Real" Causality Against Kant and Hume

The existence of causal forces, i.e. "real" causality, is not something about which everyone agrees. As we saw, Hume argued that our experience of "constant conjunction" is no basis for belief in causality (cf. p.145). Moreover, this discussion has not yet dealt with Kant's idea that our experience of the outside world is no basis to believe in anything (cf. p.145).

As we saw, according to Kant, we can have no sure knowledge of what the outside world is really like because its every perception is mediated by the mind whose effect upon every experience is both necessary and unknowable. In other words, reality might not involve anything like the world of shapes and sizes as we perceive it. This might be the creation of our brain or our senses, given their stimulation by something entirely different and unimaginable. Either way, we cannot know.

Kant's observation has its element of truth. We do perceive an object from a distance, through the mediation of our senses, not to mention light. And, it is the brain that converts sense data into experience.

But, this does not mean that our experience of the outside world is not true. Though it *is* true that we do not have immediate contact with objects *per se,* this is simply the fact that the perceiver is not the thing perceived. What does Kant want? Unless the perceiver is the object of his perception, the mediation of information is necessary. And, since the information originates in the objects, for example, in terms of its ability to bounce light, it is "true" whether or not the object would look different if it was sent through a different medium or received by a different kind of brain. Indeed, even though we know that objects give off infrared rays which humans do not see—and would certainly affect their appearance if we did—what we do see locates and describes the object usefully. We know this because we operate in the world successfully using these perceptions. As a matter of fact, when we fail to perceive accurately the world around us, we make many mistakes. The question of what the world "really" looks like fails to accept the fact that, even though human perception does not make use of all the data that might be available to the hypothetically perfect perceiver, what we do see is true—if only in human terms.

Furthermore, since the function of the organs of human perception can be described in terms of what is "normal" (cf. p.248), even secondary qualities (cf. p.144) can be said to have their objectivity.

In Hume's critique of causality, we see the failure to realize that constant conjunction *means* causality. It is inferred in the judgment that dependability cannot be coincidence and requires a cause. To insist upon absolute experimental "proof" is the entirely unreasonable demand to see the stuff that propels light itself; how could such be seen?

More importantly, to insist upon "absolute" proof is also the failure to have understood that human knowing is, like the matter that accounts for it, *creative*. It is the product of much experience—a whole which is greater than the sum of its parts.

Even the simplest perception is the product of much experience—the experience which has complexified a brain making perception possible. An idea is the product of even more experience—the many experiences which gave rise to it. Experience also produces certain "global" ideas (about everything) which are not evident in any one event. These are the products of one's whole experience as it is seen for what it means. Reason is one of these ideas. Reason is the idea that "reality is dependable" which comes from the constant experience that things do what they have done. This idea, this interpretation of what constancy means, is itself the product of experience—the experience which has matured a brain so that it sees what has become evident. This happens gradually. And it is the product of several stages of intellectual development. Just as consciousness had to emerge; just as self-consciousness had to emerge—and when it did it was something utterly new; just as a knowledge of the objectivity of the world had to emerge—and is not evident in the simple fact of self-consciousness as Descartes proved (cf. p.142); just as a knowledge of the dependability of nature had to emerge—the basis of the very idea of proof which is not itself provable;[9] so too must emerge the knowledge that there are forces. It will exist in anyone sufficiently mature if no obstacle prevents, in this case, the mistaken idea that reason demands absolute proof.

B) Emotional Developments

Since emotional developments require the wider scope of experience which produces a perception not only of what "is," but also what is true "about" a thing (cf. p.255), those of this stage are even less sure than their intellectual origins. But, if they do emerge, the following is to be expected:

1. "Caring"

There will be increased depth of emotional experience; now the person is capable of joy or anguish. Of course, his interests continue to deepen. The person's perception of others also deepens; now certain others are not only attractive but admired, even esteemed. His desire for affection becomes an interest in giving affection. His desire for companionship becomes a desire to "share"—at least his thoughts.

Most remarkably, the person has developed an interest "in" others; he is

---

9. The so-called "empirical criterion of truth" (cf. p.162) is not empirically verifiable.

interested in their well-being—for their sake. He cares. (If there is offence, there is forgiveness; despite the demands of justice, there is "mercy.") In his deepening perception that *all* others *are* others, he may even care for others who do, or have done, or can do nothing for him. He may pursue "causes" deemed "worthy."

2. A Defense of Caring Against Egoism

Just as causality has its critics, so does the reality of caring. According to the "egoist," everything an individual does is solely self-centered. Therefore, anything that appears "altruistic" was actually motivated by one of the following four self-centered motives:

1) If the person believes in God, he is trying to avoid an eternal punishment or attain an eternal reward.

2) He wants to achieve a good reputation or to prevent a bad one.

3) He wants to avoid the pain of guilt or seeks the pride of having done a good deed.

4) If nothing else is apparent, he is operating out of unconscious but solely self-centered motives. A person always does what he wants.

In responding to the egoist, it must first be acknowledged that self-centeredness does provide most of man's motives. Moreover, it is often the motive for apparently unselfish acts. People are usually conscious of the benefits that any act will bring *them*. Though rewards are sometimes subtle, they can still be very desirable. In this light, one could plausibly suggest a solely self-centered motive for anything an individual does.

It is not so easy to suggest such a motive for everything that everyone does. In fact, it would seem that some men do care about their fellows. The four selfish motives would not appear to account for everything that everyone does.

Many people do not really believe in God and, as we have already noted, such people often lead exemplary lives, less self-centered than the lives of many religious. Moreover, even where believers are involved, there may not be belief that there are eternal sanctions, or that sanctions are a suitable motive for action. Besides eternal sanctions are vaguely conceived, hard to be sure of, and a lifetime away.

The desire for a good reputation has not prevented any number of people from accepting a bad reputation for doing a good thing, including many cases where a person had reason to believe that his reputation would never be vindicated, even after his death.

Wanting to avoid guilt or enjoy the pride in having done a good deed is not self-centeredness. Self-centeredness is the idea that "only I count"; in other words, "only I am good." Therefore, it is obvious that the very capacity to feel guilt or pride is a manifestation of a person's acknowledgment that there are other, indeed greater "goods," even if it is a primitive form of this development whose more mature manifestations would involve a more articulate awareness of what is good and why.

In the absence of other explanations, the insistence that a person must have been motivated by something unconsciously self-centered betrays the prejudgment that caring is impossible. But, in the absence of evidence to this effect—together with the human experience that caring is possible—such a judgment is wrongly predicted of all humanity. This may be the experience of the egoist, though it is not for someone whose experience is different to judge him.

When all else has failed, the idea that everything a person "wants" is self-centered is a misuse of the word "want." Of course, as an exercise of the will, every human act is something a person did because he wanted to; this is a matter of definition. But, not everything a person wants is self-centered.

Section VIII: The Possibility of Faith

Given sufficient experience, a person will come to an even greater maturity than was evident in his perception of "causality" and capacity for "caring." Using the word which has long meant the host of related developments which this involves, this is the emergence of "faith."

A) Intellectual Developments

Intellectually speaking, faith means that the person has come to a belief in some sort of supreme being however He or It is conceived.

1. Belief in God
a. The Origin of the Belief

Just as reason gave rise to a belief in causality—reason becoming the knowledge that there must be a reason for everything that happens—belief in causality gives rise to the belief that there must be a reason for everything. In other words: the world cannot "just" exist. The world requires its cause. There is a God.

To be sure, belief in God does not normally emerge in a systematically articulate way. Moreover, it does not normally arise out of a reflection upon "reality" as such. It normally arises out of a reflection upon "life," "my" life, taking the form of the idea that I cannot just be, I must have come from somewhere, not to mention the need to believe I must be going somewhere when I die. Nonetheless, however it emerges, it always involves some awareness that the world requires its cause, something which is not of the world and must be greater.

b. The Forms of the Belief

Belief in God has taken a variety of forms. The primitives of yesterday and today postulate a different person-like spirit-god behind every obviously distinct natural phenomenon. Called "Animism," this form of belief also tends to involve belief in a "high" god who rules the others.[10]

Belief in the high god of a "pantheon," i.e. a family of gods, has also characterized the religion of China.[11] But, Chinese belief has been divided between Shang Ti, the fatherly head of the pantheon, and "Tien," a heavenly but impersonal principle that orders all things. Chinese religion has also involved the opposing principles of "Yin" and "Yang," mixtures of which make up everything.

Belief in one, supreme but impersonal principle is clearly characteristic of Hinduism.[12] (True Hindus find it remarkable that others should believe that God is like man.) It is the "One" which enforces "Dharma," the law which determines the result of "reincarnation," the rebirth of the person in a new form, human or not, high or low in the system of "castes." This rewards or punishes the person for the life he has lived as a good, content member of his caste until he makes his way up the ladder and becomes one with the One. Actually, he realizes that he was always one with the One. "Atman (man's soul) is Brahman (the One)." In this, Hinduism reveals its pantheism. Hindus also believe that time is "cyclic," i.e. not only repetitive but non-progressive.

According to Buddhism, an off-shoot of Hinduism founded by Gautama the buddha (c. 6th cent. B.C.), the supreme principle, "Karma," requires reincarnation until the individual can purify himself of all desires—the source of suffering—and enter "nirvana," the bliss of non-existence.

Jews, Christians and Moslems believe in one, personal Creator God. Jews and Moslems tend to accentuate the justice of God while Christians have historically placed more emphasis upon His love. Christian history has also come to speak of God in terms of the divine attributes whose debt to the Greek belief in the Uncaused Cause has also been discussed.

Of course, not all who call themselves Christian share the complex con-

---

10. Animism is often combined with the worship of the spirits of the dead ("ancestor worship") which has an especially prominent place in the "Shintoism" of Japan.
11. Contrary to popular belief, the religion of China is not "Confucianism," after Confucius (cf. p.159), or "Taoism," supposedly founded by Lao-tze, both of which are ethical philosophies. The former calls for life in accord with "Jen," the law of social relationships, while the latter calls for life in accord with "Tao," i.e. "nature." Taoism remind us of Stoicism (cf. p.60), while both ethical philosophies spoke of the "paradigmatic" man who reminds us of Aristotle's "virtuous" man (cf. p.60).
12. The Hindu triad (cf. p.159) are actually three forms of the One.

ception of God which Christian history has developed. Moreover, not all believe on their own. Some believe because they have been told. Those at the level of reason believe in a God who is not the cause of the world but part of it, i.e. somewhere out in space. (This level of belief also involves attempts to manipulate the divine—"magic."[13]) Nonetheless, for the most part, from the beginning, Christian leadership has believed in a God who is the Cause of the world and everything that happens in it.

2. *Faith and Reason, Spirituality, Choice, Trust, and Mystery*
Before we consider the emotional developments that can be expected to accompany the emergence of belief in God, some clarification is needed as to what this belief actually involves, especially as it is experienced by Christians.

First, there must be no doubt as to the relation of faith and reason. Reason is one stage of personal maturity; it is not the first; it is not the last. Faith is a stage of greater maturity. Building upon the truth as it has been perceived previously, it goes further. It does not involve a denial of anything reason truly dictates. Moreover, just as belief in causality supports belief in reason, faith supports belief in causality. This is the truth of the classical idea that faith and reason are mutually supporting. But, be it clear, faith and reason do not say the same thing by two different ways of knowing. They are both moments in the developmental march of human knowing. This was implicitly recognized in what has been the modern theological insistence that faith simply "presupposes" reason.

Spirituality is an extension of faith. The Christian believes in God, the cause of the world. Conceiving the cause in terms of creation, he thinks of God as a person. Reflecting further, he comes to conceive, however inarticulately, at least some of the divine attributes. He realizes that the person he conceives is "listening" to him do so. He says hello. This is the beginning of prayer. Historically, and one could argue naturally, prayer has normally taken four definable forms: 1) "Petition," asking for something. 2) "Reparation," asking forgiveness for some sin. 3) "Thanksgiving" for things perceived to be received. And, with maturity, 4) "praise" of God for who He is in Himself. In the form of meditation, praise becomes "adoration" and the "contemplation" which may generate the thoughts and feelings hitherto known as "mystical" experience.

Since the acceptance of spiritual experience involves judgment, faith can be called a "choice." Since the content of the experience involves a person,

---

13. Particular practices have their specific origin in coincidence as interpreted under the influence of wishful thinking.

its acceptance can be called "trust." But, in any case, belief is still a response to the cumulative weight of experience as it brings about certain ideas and greater and greater sureness. (Conversion is the arrival of a big idea, especially as it is experienced in terms of the suddenness of mental life.) The so-called certainty of faith is simply the arrival of a degree of certainty which is enough to vanquish lingering doubt—faith beyond a "reasonable" doubt. Hope is faith in the future.

Of course, the experience of God almost always involves the realization that He is much greater than anything that anyone could ever conceive. And there will always be more to know. This, properly speaking, is "mystery." Faith must not involve mysteries which contradict reason—particularly those that involve the simultaneous assertions of opposing notions. It must not involve contradictions in terms. Thus to the question: "can God make a square circle," the answer is: "this is not a question."

B) Emotional Developments

We can now consider the emotional effects of the preceding intellectual developments. It is of course to be presumed that with increasingly profound perceptions, there will be increasingly profound emotions. As a matter of fact, at the faith stage of maturity, thoughts and feelings have returned to the oneness they first knew (cf. p.251). Emotions will have religious meaning. Certain desires will involve the necessity of a "call"—a "vocation." In any case, the life of true faith will always involve true "love."

1. Love

As we saw, from a theological point of view, love is a respect for what is true (cf. p.198) and good (cf. p.204). From an anthropological point of view, love is an interest "in" others (cf. p.266). At the stage of faith, this means that another's good is to a real extent *his* happiness; the other's pain is *his* problem. Causes are not just worthy, they are worth his "commitment."

2. The Origin of Love and Its Extent

Love can only be understood with reference to its origins.

As we have seen, at birth, a baby is utterly self-centered, not only emotionally but also intellectually—it thinks it *is* the world. It desires little more than bodily well-being.

With experience, the infant begins to see. This is his first sight of truth. The development produces curiosity, his first "outside" interests.

With more experience, the child sees more and he wants more.

With even more experience, the person develops an interest "in" others.

What has happened? The person has grown in his perception of the truth and what is good, and the good was inherently attractive. It attracted him "outside" and then "out of" himself.

Now, under the increasing influence of the good as he learns to perceive it, as perhaps he is taught to perceive it, as perhaps it presents itself—especially in the example of others (especially if he is the recipient of love), or in experience of love as he may himself practice it (especially if he is truly needed), the person continues to unlearn the exclusive self-centeredness with which he was born.[14] But, the recognition of other goods will help him to recognize the enduring, true good in himself. He may even be freed from the variety of insecurities which always attend an exclusive concern for me, now. These include its supreme manifestation in the "pride" which would otherwise prevent him from acknowledging the good of anything else.[15] Thus freed, he will give of his things, his time, his energy, even his well-being. He will take the risk; he will give of himself.

As he receives another's "self"—and is sufficiently struck by it—he will find himself "in" love. He will desire to share his life—his whole life. If this interest is reciprocated, and experiences are shared, and mutual knowledge grows, the persons will feel that they have become "one." Indeed, their *interests* have merged. But, rather than produce exclusivity, this unity always serves as a mutual source of growth—and security—which increases their love for others.

At this point, it must be stated that, because of human limitedness, love has limits that vary from person to person. It also involves a variety of forms. But, to the degree that love is truly present: It pulls a person out of himself. It involves an interest in others, all others, in the proportion that others make possible. It endures, even through the worst of days. It motivates a person to sacrifice, even when otherwise compelled by the increasing intensity of his other interests. If necessary, he will even sacrifice his life, even if those for whom he would sacrifice were not sure to appreciate the offer, had already rejected the person and/or hurt him.

* * *

Needless to say, even the least critical reader may feel that much of what has now been presented as "human nature"—especially the "maturity" of belief in God—leaves a good bit to be justified. It is so. An apologetic for this belief has not been presented and indeed it must. But, before this is possible—and before we return to the Christianity whose modern formulation is also our concern—we must address the most tumultuous implication of materialism that Christian doctrine must face, the hitherto unexplained but constantly evident fact that materialism means determinism.

14. It is true: "love begets love."
15. But, the person will still find it easier to love those who do not "threaten" him—or cease to however suddenly because of some disaster that befalls them.

Chapter III: Determinism

Section I: An Inevitable Implication of Materialism

The time has come to state plainly what has always been an inevitable implication of materialism. Since materialism means that matter can account for everything in the world and of it, everything that happens is the inevitable result of matter in motion as driven by forces that cause exactly what will happen from one moment to the next. This is determinism.

There must be no mistake; determinism was in no way denied by our observation that the product of organization is something "new" whose behavior cannot be predicted by the laws of physics. After all, the product of organization is still a juxtaposition of parts; and each of its parts is, at a given moment, an exact juxtaposition of elementary matter driven by the force (or forces) which drives their interactions dependably and exactly.

An atom is an atom because its nucleus is here and its orbitals are there. If one atom collides with another, itself a juxtaposition of matter, the result is determined by the exact juxtaposition of all the matter in both atoms—and the forces driving all this matter—at the moment of the collision. Had it been possible to know the speed, trajectory and location of each and every unit—and the fundamental law (or laws) which describes the interaction of matter—the exact result of this collision could have been predicted down to the last detail. The fact that this is practically impossible is irrelevant to determinism.

More complex than an atom, a cell is still a juxtaposition of matter. If a cell is immersed in a solution, a juxtaposition of more matter, its response is determined by all of the interactions which would inevitably follow.

This is no less true of a man's response to his environment. However organized, his brain is still a juxtaposition of matter. So is his environment; but it is best described in terms of the sense data which it causes. This propels the processes which may become perception, reflection and decision to act. In any case, they are completely determined.

Not only is man's response to any event completely determined, but his brain was determined by the lifetime of events which caused the structural changes that they did. In other words, the person is the product of his past experience. (This is what we have already called the "contingency" of mental life, cf. p.263.) Therefore, if his experience could be reproduced, it would reproduce him.

Section II: Already an Implication of Causality

Even apart from the demands of materialism, determinism was already an implication of causality. If everything requires its cause, surely so does every mental event—every thought, desire, every decision to act.

Why does a person do anything—because he decided to. Why did he decide to—because of his deliberation. Why did his deliberation result in the conclusion that it did—because of the net effect of his experiences. How could this not be true? To cite a strictly mental event is to invite the question: but why did he think this, feel this then? Why did he feel it with such intensity? To cite another mental event is to invite *its* explanation.

It is impossible that mental events just happen. Nothing just happens; this is the origin of belief in causality. The credibility of this knowledge was a major finding of the anthropology (cf. p.265).

To deny causality would be to undermine the idea of human knowing which gives credibility to belief in God. Of course, religion has known this for quite some time. As his "five ways" surely make clear, Thomas also knew causality was crucial to belief in God (cf. p. 36). God is quintessentially the uncaused cause and, as such, He is the providential source of everything that is and happens. But, if He is, how is the will free? And, if the will is not free, human action is worthy of neither blame nor praise. In the face of this dilemma, Thomas insisted that the soul, in its spirituality, is, in a limited way, an uncaused cause.[1]

Thomas did not justify this thesis. Materialism does not permit it. Materialism means determinism.

Section III: Responses to Certain Predictable Objections

Determinism must respond to certain predictable objections.

A) Scholastic Objections

1. The Argument from Faith

The argument from faith has already been encountered in the conflicts with evolution and materialism (cf. p.174, 221). In this instance, it involves the notion that a denial of free will is a denial of personal responsibility, a denial which calls into question the very purpose of life on earth. Plainly, faith requires free will; therefore, we must have it.

But, the argument from faith did *not* do away with evolution or materialism. It violates the traditional Catholic confidence that faith and reason cannot contradict. The truth of this tradition is especially clear now that we have seen that faith and reason are two moments in the developmental march

1. See his *Quaestiones Disputatae*, "De Malo," 6,1.

of human knowing, where reason is prior and can never be denied (cf. p.271). Furthermore, on account of what has been demonstrated about the development of doctrine, we are bound to respect the competence of other disciplines, and to accept their findings in order grow in our understanding of the true essence of faith, no matter what needs to be abandoned (cf. p.214).

2. The Argument from Reason

The scholastics also defended free will from the fact that man has use of reason. In the use of reason, man shows that he is not compelled to act mindlessly.

This argument does not hold. We now know that reason is the awareness of the dependability of nature. It is possessed by the individual to the degree that his native intelligence and experiences have fostered this awareness. It is not an independent power of thought, but thought guided by certain principles that must be learned. Man's possession of reason has been determined; each man possesses reason to the degree that circumstances explain.

B) The Objections from Unpredictability

A variety of objections will predictably be grounded in the fact that human behavior has always proven unpredictable.

1. The Argument from the Big Differences between Persons of Similar Backgrounds

It is often observed that two persons of similar backgrounds, even twins, grow up to be two very different persons. In a reaffirmation of the classical assumption, the explanation is freedom.

Apart from the fact that no two persons, even twins, are genetically similar, this argument misses entirely the subtlety of experience. No two persons have the same experience. Experience consists of countless events. Each event is unique, if only in relation to space and time. Each affects a person however slightly. And the slightest difference can affect every succeeding experience. Twins may have a similar experience at home, but if one stays after school one day without the other and meets one new person, the event may catalyze a major change that might have happened in his sibling but did not.

2. The Fact of the Failures of Psychology

Determinism is also disputed by the failures of psychology, both theoretical and clinical.

This argument does not acknowledge that psychology is still in its infancy. Moreover, explicability is no guarantee of explanation. That something can be known is no guarantee that it will be.

Furthermore, with complexity, science becomes less exact (cf. p.247).

And psychology deals with the highest level of complexity.[2] Thus, it is no surprise that psychology has been—and will always be—the science least exact. But, it will continue to make progress and there is no reason to assume that it will not continue to make progress indefinitely.

3. "Emergent Probability"

Departing from the neo-scholastic observation that higher laws cannot be deduced from lower ones, Bernard Lonergan also observed that higher laws admit of more exceptions. He claimed that this "emergent probability" is actually the emergence of freedom(cf. p.225).

It is first to be acknowledged that creative materialism always meant the indeducibility of laws. Since organization integrates the normally unorganized activities of lower level parts, the laws which describe the life of the whole should not be deducible from the laws which would otherwise describe the activities of its parts. Furthermore, since organization increases complexity, it should be more difficult to predict what the new thing will do. But, organization is not some occult reality which casts a spell over the parts; it is their juxtaposition, and the holistic effect of their interaction. And, as we know, each of their interactions is completely determined. Moreover, since they are determined, they are determinable, i.e. completely predictable. The fact that science is practically limited to study their aggregate effect makes no difference to determinism.

C) The Objection from the Experience of Freedom

Lonergan's "emergent probability" also involved his insistence on the supremacy of experience and, what is more, his insistence that the human experience bespeaks spirituality and free will. This was the crux of his answer to materialism and determinism.

As has since been made clear, materialism does not require a denial of the experience of spirituality; this would be nonsensical. Neither does determinism require a denial of the experience of freedom.

There are, however, many senses of the word "freedom." People may possess political or social freedom. Few are bound by compulsive behaviors that rule them regardless of their better judgment. A person can be his own master. And people do what they want. But, determinism means that all our

---

2. Actually, failing to accept this fact, certain psychologists have persisted in simplistic attempts to render a complete explanation of behavior. The most publicized example of such an attempt was B.F. Skinner's *Beyond Freedom and Dignity*. The work contained his claim that any human behavior can be "conditioned" through the manipulation of positive and negative reinforcement. In the tradition of the behaviorists' systematic ignorance of the inner life of the mind, and thus, the complex processes (and motives) through which behavior is determined (cf. p.165), Skinner's theory and its obvious lacunae did much to discredit the idea of determinism in the popular mind.

"wants" have their origin in human nature as affected by the events of our lives, the sum total of which are rightfully to be recognized as their cause. We have no experience of a freedom from the effects of our experiences. We have no freedom from the experiences that explain why we thought this now or felt that then. How could we? There is a reason for every mental act. If somehow there was not, the caprice would certainly not be the responsible exercise of freedom. A "free" will never made sense.

This is perhaps the most opportune time to dispense with the spectre of indeterminism (cf. p.232) once and for all. Let it be stated: indeterminism has nothing to do with the question of human freedom. Caprice at the subatomic level would affect only the most elementary interactions; their aggregate effect would be so far removed from the integrated physiological activities of mental life as to have virtually no effect. Even if it did, the result would not be freedom, it would certainly not be anything for which the person could claim responsibility.

Chapter IV: Personal Responsibility

Section I: The Idea of Personal Responsibility

Clearly, materialism means determinism. To the history of thought, this means the demise of personal responsibility, and with it, doctrine's demand that life be lived one way rather than another. But, the presumption that personal responsibility requires free will has always been mistaken. It is time to replace it.

It is first to be observed that the word "responsibility," like freedom, has many meanings. It can refer to all or part of the cause of a given event. In our discussion of determinism, it referred to the events of a person's life—his past experience.

Of course, these events would not have been "experience" unless they happened to a given brain. Thus, we must also acknowledge that the structure of this brain, which is the person, bears part of the responsibility for what he does.

Now, it is sure to be observed that this notion of responsibility is not something for which a person should claim credit. After all, nothing has been said of his responsibility for the structure of his brain. Indeed, a ball has the same sort of responsibility for what happens when it is thrown against a wall. But, unlike the ball, a person is the product of his past experience. He is the product of the lifetime of events which propelled the developments that they did. And it could not have happened without him.

Section II: The Causes of a Person from the Brain's Point of View

Given a lifetime of events, let us examine the causes of a person from the brain's point of view.

A brain's first encounter with events is but a reaction. Few parts are involved, a complex whole is not bespoken. The uniqueness of its reaction is due solely to the individuality given by genetics. But, as the brain encounters its second event, it is an organ changed by the memory of its first experience—a change which was determined by its own unique structure. Thus, its reaction to this second event is something for which it was slightly more responsible.

Thanks to continuing change, complexification, and development, the brain's reaction to events becomes a complex response of thoughts and emotions.[1] This produces more development—development determined by a brain whose structure was itself determined by the history of its response to past events.

Eventually, the brain becomes capable of an ongoing response to the world around it; it deliberately directs itself apart from specific impetus of any one event. This produces even more development.

With the emergence of self-consciousness, the brain has become, like nothing else, a whole, and an individual (cf. p.253). It has become a person. And the "who" his structure is continues to determine his ongoing response to the world around him and, of course, further development. In this we clearly see his increasingly personal responsibility for who he is. Given the events of his life, the person determines himself. He is the result of a lifetime of self-determination.

Section III: Self-Determining, Not Deciding

Let there be no mistake. The self-determinism in no way means that specific decisions are the uncaused determiners of who the person is. Self-determinism refers to the effect of all the mental activity involved in a person's ongoing response to the events of his life. It is this whole process which causes the formation of desires. It is this whole process which determines the path of deliberations that lead to decisions. As important as they are— and revealing—decisions do not happen apart from the process.

Life is the process. It is a process of becoming, not just something different, not just something more, but something more one's own. This is what personal responsibility is all about.

Section IV: Personally Responsible—But Not Absolutely

Of course, nothing that has been said about personal responsibility in any way means that the person has not been determined by his past—by events for which he was not responsible. Self-determinism means that determinism involves the brain—the ever more personal involvement of the brain.[2] But, the brain's involvement was still determined. It was determined by the events which inevitably affected it as they did. Therefore, no one is *absolutely* responsible for who he is.

1. Plainly, any attempt to describe thoughts and emotions as the "by-product" of behavioral influences (cf. p.221) ignores the fact that they bespeak, indeed they *are,* the complex processes by which behavior is determined.

2. Thus, in answer to the modern polemic, it is not the person *or* society; it is the person *and* society, etc. And, there is no line past which behavioral influences give way to freedom; this line does not exist. The notions of personal responsibility and determinism are "compatible."

* * *

The idea of "absolute" responsibility would appear to be implied—and required—by several Christian doctrines. Be that as it may, it must be abandoned. This is a fact of life from which we cannot hide. Therefore, a truly modern theology must reconcile itself to its abandonment just as early modern theology had to reconcile itself to the abandonment of biblical literalism. If the truth is to be found in Christian tradition, this must be possible. But, as we shall now see, it will not be easy.

Part III: The Conflict

Introduction to Part III

As the case for materialism was being made, its Christian interpretation was also taking place. What else motivated and directed the anthropological explanation of belief in God and love unto self-giving? Therefore, we must now allow materialism to interpret Christianity. As the "Introduction" explained, this must first involve an examination of the conflict between materialism and the present understanding of Christianity and, as well, certain other implications of the presumption that the essences of both ideas are true.

Now more than ever, the patience of the reader is requested as we are about to embark upon a survey of the immediate effects of materialism which will not only be fast-moving but, seemingly, violent to a number of sacred subjects.

Chapter I: The Immediate Conflict between Christianity and Materialism

Section I: The Problem of Sin

A) The Impossibility of Absolute Sin

1. *The Argument from Determinism*

Surely, the most immediate conflict between Christianity and materialism involves the utterly central idea of sin. Since absolute responsibility is impossible, so too is "absolute" sin—the free, deliberate, culpable rejection of God's love, an act of pure evil for which punishment is due. No matter how terrible the act, regardless of the extent to which it does reflect the essence of a person's being, it must still be considered the product of a person's genes and past, the product of events for which he was not responsible. Materialism means determinism and nothing said about the reality of personal responsibility vindicates the historical notion of sin.

2. *The Argument from Human Nature*

In the light of determinism, it is also clear that the deliberate choosing of evil is not human nature. Indeed, it is not nature; it is not something that reality could ever make possible.

This has always been the problem of sin. To the most astute of Christian thinkers, it had always seemed strange that a person would willingly opt for evil. To answer "free will" was no answer; this only spoke of the possibility. What of the motive, the reason? Why would man do such a thing? What is the attraction to someone who is not badly misguided and therefore not culpable? And, if God is all-good and infinitely attractive, why do some reject Him and eternal happiness that life with God affords? Here was a greater mystery than that of free will.

To be sure, this troubled the best of Christian minds. Thomas agreed that man has no motive to choose evil; only the good, which, in the final analysis, is God, is desirable. Thus did he distinguish between the "actual" good, the good in good things, and the "apparent" good, the good in bad things—which is still there because God is the source of all being, even that which has been corrupted.[1] Therefore, a person is actually choosing the good even in bad things. As a matter of necessity, Thomas insisted that the person is still culpable for mistaking the apparent for the actual good.

Thomas did not explain *how* the person is culpable for mistaking the

---

1. *S.Th.* I-II, q.8.

apparent for the actual good. Indeed, this would seem impossible since any choice would have been motivated by some appearance. Instead, as is surely obvious now, such appearances are matters of learning, of experience. The person will choose what he sees as good; but, what he sees as good depends upon his life's experience. This is the reason that persons from bad, i.e. "deprived" backgrounds, will lead bad lives if no other experience intervenes.

B) Sin Reunderstood

1. The Idea

In the light of all we now see, it becomes clear that sins are 1) failures to love, and 2) anything else that adversely affects a person's ability to love. The "sinner" is now to be conceived to be a person who has failed, i.e. not succeeded, to develop to a level of maturity which is commonly agreed upon as good. The serious sinner is someone who has little sense of such ideas; or he is someone whose selfishness is so intense that nothing can weigh against it. (The serious sinner is sometimes "sick"; he sees as good what everyone else sees as bad—very bad.) Let it be clear; the sinner is simply a person who has failed to mature (and may have learned the things that make him "sick"); he is not a person who has actively chosen evil except as a victim of his experiences. This fact was expressed in the historical wisdom that one should hate the sin but not the sinner.[2]

Of course, in view of the all-time perception that no one is "perfect," everyone is to some extent a sinner and to some extent "mature." Moreover, since everyone begins as an utterly self-centered baby, it is also clear that everyone is doing his best—to survive, to be happy, and even to be good. Therefore, it is also clear that any notion of the "depravity" of man (cf. p.103) involves a neglect to appreciate the developmental nature of human nature—a nature whose response to the best of circumstance is inevitably "good." (Thus, a person should be judged in positive terms, in terms of how much he has developed, not how much he has *not* developed measured against some imagined notion of perfection.)

2. The Means of Sin

In essence, sin needs no "means." Motivated by a person's natal self-centeredness, he is simply, uncritically doing what he wants.

As the person matures, however, he normally comes to motivating ideas of what is good, right or loving. These cause a conflict which these ideas may win or lose; the question is one of intensity. But, even when the good loses, the person will rarely decide that his principles had the right to be

---

2. This famous thought was originally Augustine's; see his "Letters," 211.

overruled by his other desires. Instead, he will call the wrong right, or acceptable, by some psychological means. All are linked to the essential self-protectiveness of his brain (cf. p.262). Generally speaking, they are four:

1) Rationalization, the most common: The person convinces himself that what he wants to do is not wrong in this type of situation, for "me," now.

2) Reputation: The person convinces himself that the principle is wrong.

3) Suppression, a form of "repression" (cf. p.259): The person blocks out the principle or forgets the act. And,

4) Surrender, the most "religious" of means: The person accepts "his" or "human" imperfection.

C) Responses to Certain Predictable Objections

1. The Argument from the Experience of Guilt

The abandonment of absolute sin would be sure to elicit certain predictable objections.

It might be argued that the reality of sin is confirmed in the experience of guilt, particularly as reflected in the insistence that "I knew it was wrong but I did it anyway."

The objection from the experience of freedom (cf. p.276) from the other side of action, this argument fails because it does not speak to the true meaning of determinism. Guilt testifies only to the existence of principles and some desire to live by them. It says nothing about the origin or intensity of the desire to do so—or to do what they forbid. It is, in essence, the person's unfavorable judgment of himself in the light of the information of what he did or failed to do, say or think. It is not the person's correct understanding that he is guilty—absolutely.

2. The Argument from the Necessity of Punishment

It might be argued that the absence of absolute guilt would make punishment wrong, and would make impossible the raising of children or the securing of an orderly society.

This argument states its own invalidity. The very necessities of punishment are their own justification. Punishment teaches children and adults; it is sometimes the only thing that works. It is sometimes the only thing that will protect society. These are its justifications; they are its only justifications.

3. The Argument from Faith

It might be argued that the abandonment of absolute sin is *too* near the essence of what has always been Christianity and, therefore, represents a death blow which faith will not allow.

But, the argument from faith cannot be reason to deny the facts (cf. p.271). Furthermore, absolute sin is *not* an "absolutely unsuspendable belief" (cf. p.217). The question of whether it is "almost unsuspendable" (cf. p.218) is entirely dependent upon the understanding of faith—and love—that develops in its absence. Therefore, we must first see what is left of those ideas in which absolute sin has played an essential part.

D) The Necessity of Divine Foregiveness?

Plainly, in the absence of absolute guilt, divine forgiveness was never necessary. Neither men nor man needed to be forgiven before the coming of the kingdom.

Though humans can offend each other, and need to have the offence resolved, it is clear that they cannot offend God. Since God is God, He understands His people and their motives and the reasons for their motives. He fully understands that the sinner is essentially a victim. (Thus, the key to human forgiveness is understanding—the ability to see the good of a person despite the trouble or hurt he may have caused.) Thus we can take the gospel more than literally where Jesus says: "Father, forgive them, for they know not what they do" (Lk.23:34).

But, thinking themselves sinners, the first Christians needed to believe that they had been forgiven in order to be worthy of divine life or, at least, life with God. Therefore, the historical belief in divine forgiveness was a necessary if primitive protective of the belief that divine life is man's destiny. It can also be understood in terms of confidence that God's love is not thwarted by man's sin.

E) The Necessity of Christian Life

Although man can no longer be conceived to lose God's love, he can still be said to have been called to respond to that love in some form of Christian life. i.e. love (cf. p.201). The experiential fact of this call has not been compromised by anything that has been said so far. Neither has the superiority of Christian life. Instead, as we have seen, love is the greatest human development. Though this development can no longer be called a response to God's love in the sense of "choice"—in the sense that the failure to do so is to be considered a rejection of God—it *can* be called a response to God's love given the belief that God, as best described by His love, is the source of all being and the Creator of the world to which man does respond in becoming who he is. Given the rest of what is believed about God, it must be assumed that this process is in some way necessary. After all, a God who can do anything cannot be conceived to make man do anything that is not necessary to the fullest possible sharing of His life that He could have brought about with less effort on everyone's part.

F) The Impossibility of Hell

1. The Fact

Necessary though a Christian life may be, it cannot follow that those who fail to live this life will be punished by an eternity of torment. Since absolute guilt is to be abandoned, so must hell. God's love cannot be imagined to punish anyone for doing what he was determined to. This is not even just.

2. The Fact that Love Surpasses Justice

Actually, even if it were "just" to condemn someone for something for which he was not ultimately responsible, God could not condemn him because *love surpasses justice.* As the anthropology made clear, justice and love are two moments upon the developmental path of human emotional maturing (cf. p.271). The recognition of the "other" which begins with justice becomes differing degrees of love. Justice is not a separate set of rules that must be followed despite love. Justice is an inferior form of love, seeing others having their rights but not worth the gifts that are gladly given when love increases.

3. Historical Problems with the Doctrine of Hell

Surely it was an inarticulate understanding of the fact that love surpasses justice that motivated those of Christian tradition who were troubled by the idea that hell was eternal (cf. p. 88). They asked: how could God's supposedly infinite love allow Him to affect—and know of—the eternal suffering of anyone? He surely did not need to; after all, He is author of justice.

Moreover, how could *man* accept the knowledge that others were enduring eternal torment. How could a compassionate person be happy in heaven knowing that his parents, wife or children were forever frying in hell?

The question of justice is raised by the fact that no one asks to be born. In effect, this forces the person to play God's game and accept the terrible penalty for making a mistake.

4. Implicit Modern Recognition of the Need for a Change

The historical problems with the doctrine of hell were inflamed by the deepending faith which was evident in the reform of the teaching on the salvation of non-Christians (cf. p.211). This, together with the increasing attention to the external causes of human behavior, has brought implicit recognition that the doctrine of hell needs to change. To say that modern theology "down-plays" the idea is putting it mildly.

Despite the traditional doctrinal language, hell is no longer spoken of as a "punishment." It is now spoken of as something the person does to himself—his rejection of God, the source of being, the source of life.

Despite the classical insistence upon the natural immortality of the soul, hell is no longer described as eternal suffering. Instead, it is now described with words plainly chosen to suggest "oblivion," not unlike the imagined fate of other animals.

In remarkable contrast to times past, hell is no longer threatened, less promised. It is now the exception, not the rule, as once it was. Now it is wondered whether anyone is really there—even Hitler. But, the possibility is said to be a necessary corollary of belief in free will.

5. A Possibility as to the Truth Contained in the Doctrine of Hell

Despite the impossibility of hell, there could surely be truth to its implicit insistence that the person's earthly life has an *eternal* importance. Indeed, as we already noted, in the very fact that we are called to Christian life, it is evident that this life is in some way necessary. Hell made this clear to the people of our primitive past. It would not appear that it could have been made clear in any other way.

G) The Emergence of a Major Question(s)

In view of all we have now found, we are left with the question: what *is* the importance, eternal or otherwise, of Christian life? The abandonment of absolute guilt was also the abandonment of absolute merit. Therefore, what does Christian life accomplish? How are we to view the fate of those who do not live this life?

Of course, the latter question has always been complicated by the fact that people are born into a fantastic variety of circumstances: historical, cultural, social, familial, and physiological, all of which delimit what can be expected of them. What of those who never attain the so-called "age of reason?"[3] And what of those "determined" to make no use of every opportunity?

Section II: The Problem of Original Sin

A) Another Implication of the Abandonment of Absolute Sin

1. The Fact

The challenging questions that we have raised are further complicated by another implication of materialism. Given the abandonment of absolute sin, it is impossible that all, or any, of the evil in the world can be explained as the proper punishments for any offence. Therefore, human self-centeredness, fallibility, frailty, suffering and death reflect God's intention. Indeed, the structure of creation—in its materiality—was responsible for all these things long before the original sin.

---

3. Theologically, the "age of reason" is seven.

2. A Response to the Only Possible Objection

Should someone claim that the structure of creation is itself the punishment for an original sin which took place in a totally different kind of world—where a responsibly free will was somehow possible—we should respond that such a world is wholly inconceivable. If someone should then claim that our world was made to make this other world inconceivable, we should respond that our world is not then to be taken seriously about anything else.

B) Historical Problems with the Doctrine of Original Sin

Original sin has been a problem from the beginning.

1. The Perennial Problem of Sin

Original sin was the problem of sin in terms even more plain. As Augustine observed, the original sin was the most mysterious of all. Adam and Eve were free from ignorance, other fallibilities, uncontrollable passions, and other frailties; they enjoyed the sight of God in the garden of Eden; they even knew that the wages of sin is death. These were the pre-requisites of a sin for which God in no way could be blamed. Therefore, given all this, why did they do it? Surely they understood the proper relationship of the creature to the Creator; if not, they were ignorant on God's account. If their pride got the better of them, they must have felt an uncontrollable emotion; after all, it was surely in their interest to resist. For Augustine, this was a mystery admittedly beyond his understanding.[4]

2. The Problems of Love and Justice

Original sin was also a problem because of God's love and justice.

Justice notwithstanding, if God loved Adam, and forgave him for his sin, why did He continue the suffering with which He had punished him? Though suffering might be imagined to satisfy the demands of some idea of justice, it should not have been a demand of love. (It was *not* argued that God needed suffering in order to teach man a lesson because God could surely have accomplished this painlessly.)

Even apart from our new awareness that love surpasses justice, history has still observed that the extension of Adam's punishment to all of his descendants was not even just.[5] Of what were the unborn billions guilty? Why were they not preserved from inheriting whatever was wrong with their father? Surely, they could have been.

---

4. *The City of God*, 13,1.

5. Of course, history did not always observe this. It was once just that God should extend his punishments to the third or fourth generation (cf. Ex.20:5).

3. The Problem of Transmission

If justice did not make the transmission of original sin a problem in itself, the means of its transmission was problem enough. We have already considered the controversy over the idea of God's direct creation of the soul (cf. p.177). By and large, those who believed that the parents passed on the soul could also hold that original sin was passed on "naturally," not by God's deliberate act. Those who disputed this position saw the subtle materialism suggested by the idea that the soul arises out of the physical co-operation of the parents. (They also disputed those who said that the soul was contained in the father's seed. This suggested that there were a specified number within him and, of course, many who were never born.) But, the alternative meant that God was directly, deliberately involved in the creation of something quite flawed.

4. The Problem of Concupiscence

Concupiscence was a major problem (cf. p. 77). Pelagius argued that concupiscence means that man is not responsible for his sins. If the will is completely sinful, how is it also free? Though Augustine called this a mystery, doing so did not solve the problem.

5. The Modern Problems of Science

How is original sin to respond to the uniquely modern problems of science? The attempts to reconcile evolution and creation created as many problems as they solved. Even apart from the acknowledged problem of polygenesis (cf. footnote p.223), it is also to be observed that evolution requires *death* in order to work. Thus, there was certainly death (and pain) long before man could have been blamed for it. Moreover, in its willingness to accept the evidence and move away from the idea that the soul is created by an obvious miracle of (cf. footnote p.224), modern theology would appear to have endorsed some notion of its gradual emergence and, in its graduality, the fallibility and frailty this must have involved. As a matter of fact, since modern science speaks of the evolution of "man" in terms of traits which emerge at an accelerated rate in men today, it is surely to be imagined that man was utterly self-centered centuries before his first act of love.

C) Explicit Modern Recognition of the Need for a Change

1. Modern Theologies of Original Sin

Having accepted evolution, theology was no longer able to picture a sudden and complete creation. Thus, it became ever more difficult to picture a state of original justice free of problems. Indeed, it was now to be acknowledged that the first man was not much different from the brute described by modern physical anthropology.

Naturally, this meant that the human subjugation to certain evils was to be explained.

According to pioneers like Piet Schoonenberg (b.1911), the gifts that freed man from evils were given in "seminal" form.[6] Citing Irenaeus, who—prior and in contrast to Augustine—described Adam as a child meant to grow in his relationship with God,[7] Schoonenberg explained that man was meant to grow into his gifts, a plan for history that was ruptured by sin. Of course, "little" sins were inevitable; after all, man was like a child. But the little sins piled up and man began to distance himself from God. Eventually the gap became too wide and man was lost.

In his attempt to deal with the problem of death, Schoonenberg observed that, in the light of faith, death is not really an evil; it is man's return to God. It is the fear of death that is the evil. This is a product of doubt, the result of the distance between man and God. In a related attempt to explain suffering, Schoonenberg observed that even though physical pain was inevitable—it serves as the bodily warning system—suffering is different. Pain became suffering when it was amplified by fear and confusion about the point of it all.

Making use of the modern attention to the corporate nature of humanity (cf. p.207), Schoonenberg also attempted to provide the new theology of original sin with an idea of transmission which would solve the historical problems we have considered. He argued that every man's sin injures all others. Thus, a baby born into a sinful world is so necessarily injured that the effect can rightfully be called "propagation." It was for this reason that Karl Rahner would suggest the problem of polygenesis was not a problem.[8]

2. The Inadequacy of the New Theologies

It is first to be stated that the new theologies, like most of the modern theological developments, represent a great step forward. But, like modern theology generally, they have not gone far enough. The new theologies of original sin do not deal with the crucial question of God's responsibility for what we call evil.

The so-called "seminal" gifts hardly represent God's protection of his people from evil. They did not prevent the "little" sins that led to big ones. Nor do they represent man's freedom from any of the fallibilities or frailties that still cause him to wonder why God has done this to him. Indeed, in view of human progress, they would not appear to have involved anything that has been lost, and what we do not have now is apparently their limit.

Of special concern would be the admission that our primitive parents did

---

6. See his *Man and Sin.*
7. *Adv. Haer.* 3.
8. See his *Evolution as a Theological Problem.*

sin inevitably. Of what real sense is the claim that the escalation of sinfulness did not need to lead to a decisive break with God? What was to prevent it? What was to prevent it if indeed they were primitives not wholly different from our present scientific conception? In any case, God's ultimate responsibility for all this evil is still clear.

The modern insistence that death does not need to be viewed as an evil does not answer the question of why death is *required* of man—why disintegration should be required of the crowning glory of God's creation.

Prescinding from the question of whether maturity could ever be conceived to endure death or pain without suffering—something highly questionable in view of the fact that maturity is actually experienced to *increase* a person's capacity for suffering—we can still point out that sufficient maturity would surely have been centuries in the making regardless of serious sin. Therefore, the new theologies of original sin admit that God intended that suffering should take place. But freeing God from a responsibility for suffering was the original purpose of the doctrine of original sin.

D) Possibilities as to the Truths Contained in the Doctrine of Original Sin

1. A Primitive Protective of God's Goodness

It is indeed true that the doctrine of original sin had the original purpose of freeing God from a responsibility for suffering and evils of every other kind. As we saw, it was inconceivable that the all-good God was responsible for evil (cf. p. 63). Therefore, since man was the victim of evil, and since man was an evident author of some evil, it made sense to attribute all evil to him.

But, since we have abandoned the idea of absolute sin, and with it original sin, we have been forced to accept the fact that God is responsible for the state of things as they are. Since we cannot but conceive of God as all-good and omnipotent, we must believe that He created as He did for the best possible reason.

Moreover, thanks to the idea of evolution, and with it the idea that things are constantly becoming, becoming something better, the state of the world is to be considered not so much "evil" as "incomplete."

In the absence of such an idea, the early Christians had no way of accepting God's responsibility for the state of the world. Therefore, they had no choice but to free Him from responsibility for it. Thus, the doctrine of original sin was a primitive protective of God's goodness.

2. A Protective of Belief in the Necessity of the "Effect" of Christ and Its Universality

A second truth contained in the doctrine of original sin—one which was later in developing but more important to uniquely *Christian* theology—is surely the insistence that the redemptive life and especially death of Christ was both necessary, i.e. had to happen, and universal, i.e. had to happen on behalf of everyone.

E) The Emergence of More Major Questions

1. The Problem of Evil

Though the idea of "incompleteness" may offer some means by which to explain evil, no such explanation has yet been stated. Therefore, we must ask: Why is creation incomplete? Why is nature so often against man? Why must he develop out of self-centeredness, especially the kind that is capable of motivating the most terrible behavior? Why is he so fallible and frail and given to suffering and death?

The question is indeed a major one. The problem of evil has always been a major source of doubt and disbelief. It became increasingly troublesome once progress began to make clear that things did not need to be the way they are. It has become even more troublesome with the deepening human spirituality that has caused more and more people to view with ever greater horror the most terrible things that life can be. Even beyond the horrors of the Nazi death camps (which remind us of the atrocities men have committed against each other from the beginning), perennial problems such as poverty (and starvation, its most evil manifestation), the natural and other disasters that daily make our evening news, and the tragedies physical and emotional that ruin the lives of so many, man has become only more sensitive to the "necessary" evils that befall everyone's life—the physical pain, the spiritual suffering, the depression, the anxiety, the longings and the losses. Why must man struggle to survive, to be happy, to be better, often to fail, never to be satisfied, only to have the effort end in death—the end of life forever in a world where nothing lasts.

2. The Problem of Mortal Life

Actually, given the abandonment of original sin, not only death but the entire fact of mortal life becomes a question. Thus, the truly major question is not "why death," but "why mortal life?"

The perennial Christian explanation of existence states that God created in order to share His life with others. The doctrine of original sin explained that this sharing was intended to begin in the beginning, naturally. It explained that paradise—life on earth as a paradisiacal place—was lost. Thus, history is the attempt to get it back.

But in the absence of original sin the question emerges: If we were created to share God's life, why are we not sharing it now? Nothing given was lost.

Why were we given a mortal life to live *first?*

The question should have been asked long ago. Though the first Christians can be excused for believing that heaven would be the earth as a paradisiacal place (cf. p. 57), centuries were to pass before Christian thinkers began to come to the conclusion that heaven was something utterly superior to anything they could ever imagine. (It was 1100 before Peter Lombard would become the first to say so.[9]) The very fact that it would involve the familiarity of all the saved finally made plain that it was beyond the realm of what life on earth could ever make possible. It took modern times for thinkers to explicitly realize that if no one had ever died the earth would have filled its paradisiacal capacity long ago.

With this realization, the question of the purpose of earthly existence, fall or no fall, should have become the most considered of questions. Nonetheless, the question is surely put to us now. Why do we need to live a mortal life before we can take up an immortal one? What does this life accomplish? We have reason to insist that it must be for some good purpose. Only after we uncover this purpose can we hope to respond to the question: Why does mortal life involve the suffering that it does?

F) An Excursus: Evil

If we are to address the problem of evil, we must first clarify what exactly we mean by "evil," especially in terms of what needs to be explained. We shall then consider some of what the history of thought has already had to say about this problem. Since it has been a problem for a long, long time, it should not be surprising that much that is already thought about evil will have its eventual place in any attempt to explain it.

1. The Evil to Explain

It is first to be stated that, in the absence of absolute sin, we must abandon what has been the classical distinction between "moral" evil, evil that is willed, and "physical" evil, everything else which is properly undesirable. If we were searching for an "objective" evil, it would simply be that which is found evil by those of the most mature perception.

Given that the most mature perception recognizes that death would not be an evil if it were not for the physical and/or spiritual pain associated with it, clearly, the essential quality that makes something evil is its role in suffering.

Therefore, human "frailty" is "the" evil to explain. If a person could not be physically hurt or spiritually disturbed, he would not suffer. If a person had no vulnerabilities, no desires becoming needs, he would not feel attacks

9. *Sentences,* d.2, a.23.

upon his person or suffer for want of anything he could not have.

But, human frailty is only to be understood within the wider context of human "fallibility." Frailty is essentially the lack of some power. If a person lacked *no* power, all of what he needed—all he wanted—could be obtained.

Human fallibility must be seen within the wider context of human "limitedness"—the general fact that man is less than we can imagine him being. If we accept the idea that "perfection" is the most that there can be, and maintain our claim that man is headed for the sharing of divine life, which is the most that there can be, this limitedness is easily to be considered "imperfection"—the absence of some of what can be. Moreover, noting that the word "imperfection" is from the Latin meaning "less than completely made," we would not only confirm Augustine's classic definition of evil—a "privation," something lacking[10]—we also have an idea of evil which can be related to evolution, i.e. incompleteness (cf. p.292).

Although the idea that suffering is the principle manifestation of evil gives first attention to the evil in man, it is also to be observed that imperfection exists in nature at large. As we have already observed, nature is often against man. To classical thinking, the world was "cursed" by a penchant for accidents and natural disasters. It is still to be observed that even if man was "unlimited," the state of his environment will make his life more or less as good as it could be.

It can be said that the imperfection of nature consists in the fact that it is still developing. But, nature, i.e. material existence is permanently imperfect in the fact that it needs to keep moving in order to be what it is. This we can call the "impermanence" of nature. In its need to move, the imperfection of nature can also be characterized by "circumstantiality"—the fact that the interactions of lower levels can never be perfectly well organized to cooperate fully with what would be *desired* by the higher levels and, until these interactions are organized, they proceed as they do indifferently to the needs of higher levels. (This would support the scholastic habit of calling evil "disorder.") The fact that the machinations of nature often work against man can be called its "impersonality," a sort of metaphysical description of bad luck.

2. An Evaluation of Certain Ideas About Evil

Now that we have identified the evil(s) that needs to be explained, we can examine certain ideas which have already been advanced in order to explain it.

---

10. *Confessions*, 7. A privation, something that is lacking and needed, is to be distinguished from a "negation," something that is simply not there.

a. Christian Ideas

As has been mentioned, ideas about evil are almost as old as religion. By and large, the following have been the *Christian* ideas.

1) Christians have traditionally insisted that God does not "will" evil but "allows" it "in order to make up for what is lacking in the sufferings of Christ" (cf. Col.1:24). This idea presumes an absolute sin we no longer accept. (Determinism also disallows the popular idea that God uses evil in order to "test" us.) Moreover, in the absence of original sin, it is clear that the world *does* exist as God originally intended. If not, He is guilty of a caprice and cruelty we cannot convince.

2) It has sometimes been said that God needs evil in order to teach good. The idea has an appeal from the rather indisputable fact that our perceptions of what is good often (if not always) come from the experience of what is bad (or at least less). But, surely there are better ways of teaching good. Moreover, often evil does not teach; and, instead, it sows the seed of further evil. Besides, God could have created beings that do not need to learn. Lastly,

3) It is most often said that evil is a mystery that cannot be explained. According to the models of Job and Jesus, evil is to be borne with the special faith which is necessary and therefore possible because it is a mystery. This idea involves the legitimacy of the concept of mystery, a question we have yet to address. Nonetheless, it is still to be pointed out that the human need to have some understanding of this mystery was the reason for the doctrine of original sin. Since this need has only become more intense, it would not seem that the abandonment of one explanation should not give way to the search for another.

b. Modern Ideas

Modern ideas about evil are not to be considered "un-Christian." It is simply that they are better described as "modern" because they are based in evolutionary or, at least, scientific thinking.

1) It has already been observed that evil is often the result of the fact that nature works by means of countless events not all of which can be expected to work in man's favor. For some, this idea has the form of the claim that evil is "statistically" necessary.

A true observation of how things happen, this idea involves no explanation of the reason that things were created to happen this way.

At this point, we must admit that we cannot argue that evil is necessary because things are as good as they can be. Even *human* effort has made life better than it was. Surely, divine effort could have done at least as well as we can imagine.

2) It has been observed that evil is not so much something bad or even something lacking, but something good that has its unpleasant aspects. A favorite example is that of pain. Pain is the body's warning system; without it the body would be liable to ever more serious injury.

Although any evil can be described in terms of some good—like the bodily growth which has the "aspect" of aging—what is one to say as this good causes death? Can we not imagine a better way to achieve what is good? Lastly,

3) It is observed that creation is evolving; and evolution is inherently a struggle; and this presupposes failure; and failure can be considered the general category of evil.[11]

Though it is indeed obvious that evolution involves struggle, and struggle involves failure, this is not an *explanation* for evil. First of all, failure does not account for evil *per se;* failure does not account for frailty—or suffering. Neither is it obvious why evolution needs to involve struggle. Finally, and most importantly, the observation that God created evolution does not account for why He did, especially when one considers all the suffering that it involves. Why must creation progress toward eternity? What does this accomplish? And what happens to those who die along the way?

Section III: The Problem of Redemption

Having considered the deaths of billions, we must now consider the death of one, Jesus. We must now face the problem of redemption.

A) An Implication of the Abandonment of Absolute and Original Sin
In the absence of absolute and original sin, neither men nor man owes a debt to God. Jesus did not need to atone for man's sin. Men did not need to be "bought back."

B) Historical Problems with the Doctrine of Redemption
Once again we are dealing with a doctrine which has always presented problems.

1. Problems with the Idea of Blood Sacrifice
As we have seen, it has long seemed strange that the all-good God should demand the blood sacrifice of His beloved Son in order to forgive man the debt of his sin (cf. p.120). Besides, how could the Son's sacrifice—or the sacrifice of any innocent—satisfy the indebtedness of other people? The

11. This was the explanation of evil offered by Pierre Teilhard. It was an object of controversy because his description of moral evil stressed the fact that man is required to learn by trial and error. Nonetheless, Teilhard did accept that man could sin. Sin is the failure to co-operate with the process by which God's love is transforming creation.

demand for blood was a problem in itself. How would blood—how would suffering—satisfy anything?

Pondering these problems, Irenaeus was moved to offer an understanding of redemption that was *not* to become accepted doctrine. Reflecting on Eph. 1:10, which spoke of God "summing up" all things in Christ, he came to explain that Jesus "represented" man before the Father. Thus, His obedience—unto death—was man's obedience. This was Irenaeus' theory of "recapitulation";[12] it did not become accepted doctrine because the "atonement" theory was more straightforward and had precedent in Jewish thinking. (Of course, the theory of "recapitulation" does no more to answer the implications of the abandonment of absolute and original sin.)

2. The Problem of the Need for Redemption

The need for redemption was an even bigger problem. First, there were the old problems with original sin, especially the problems of love and justice (cf. p.289). Then, there was the fact that God is the author of justice. Surely He could have suspended its demands.

Thomas acknowledged it plainly: As the author of justice, God *could* have suspended its demands. He chose to satisfy its demands in order to demonstrate the greatness of His love.[13]

C) Explicit Modern Recognition of the Need for a Change

In view of the historical problems, there has been explicit modern recognition of the need for a change in the doctrine of redemption. There has also been change in the doctrine of incarnation. This followed what was now perceived to be the essential connection between these doctrines. Their combined study came to be called "Christology." It was, at first, a liberal Protestant movement.

1. Liberal Protestant Christology

Troubled by all the historical problems, and attentive to the fact that the death of Jesus did not restore mankind to divine life *en masse* or at once, the liberal Protestants saw the effect of Jesus as His teaching. Therefore, they concluded that this was the extent of His role as our Savior. He was a revealer of God's truth, especially in the self-sacrificial conduct of His life. In the spirit of modern science, this soon led to the denial that Jesus was other than a holy man, a "son" of God, as are we all.

Unwilling to de-divinize Jesus, later liberal Protestantism would attempt to strike a middle ground between complete denials of Christ's divinity and what was still seen as the need to believe that Jesus was absolutely special.

12. *Adv. Haer.* 3, especially 21-22.
13. *S.Th.* III, q.46, a.2.

In what would eventually be called a "functional" ontology, it made explicit the growing identification of what Jesus did (reveal) and who, i.e. what, He *was* (revelation). Speaking of Jesus' Sonship as "the Father in human terms," i.e. Jesus is God as God would appear if He were man, thinkers like Paul Tillich (1886-1965) attempted to retain a reason to insist that Jesus was a truly special revelation in whom common faith is owed today.[14]

2. Developments in Catholic Christology

The developments in liberal Protestant Christology proved to be attractive to increasing numbers who, for all the same reasons, soon came to include some Catholics who sought to link it to tradition.

Simply put, the idea that "redemption is revelation" was now seen to be supported in the biblical insistence that God created by speaking (cf. Gen.1). It was seen to be stated in the Johannine idea that Jesus was the "Word." It was plainly stated in Justin's rather Greek identification of the Word and truth (cf. p.198). Besides, the new theology made sense; the knowledge of God makes it possible for man to become like Him. And this affords the holiness which makes man worthy to share God's life.

Therefore, how better to teach man to become like Him than by becoming man? It was, as Augustine had said: "God became man so that man could become (like) God."[15]

The new theology of redemption was also to affect Catholic thinking on the incarnation. Karl Rahner led the way. He argued that Christology must not involve the idea that God assumed an essentially foreign form in becoming man. Instead, taking seriously the perennial belief that man was already made in the image of God, Rahner insisted that the incarnation was man made fully in the image of God. Therefore, accepting that God did become man "from above," Christology must proceed "from below."[16]

Rahner's thinking resulted in certain statements of the divinity of Christ which must surely be considered a departure from the ontology of the ancient Church councils. He said that Christ was the "enfleshment of God's self-communication"—the embodiment of love. He said that in Christ God "ex-sists," i.e. stands out.[17]

Shortly, the movement away from the ontology of the councils came to involve an even greater reticence to say that Jesus was God. Edward Schillebeeckx (b.1914) called Christ the "sacrament" who made God present to a

---

14. See his *Systematic Theology,* especially Vol. II.
15. See his *De Doctrina Christiana,* 1, 38.
16. See his "Chalcedon—End or Beginning?"
17. See his *Hearers of the Word.* Rahner's Christology was later elaborated in his *Foundations of Christian Faith.*

world that can know Him only through the mediation of created things.[18] And this was only the beginning. Controversy ensued as Piet Schoonenberg denied that the "pre-existence" of Christ needs to mean that His divinity had a life of its own prior to the incarnation.[19] (He also disputed the idea that the "economy of salvation" proves anything about the inner life of the God-head.)

One thing that the new theologies had in common was their abandonment of any distinction between the functions of Jesus' life and death. Naturally, functional ontologies presumed one function for the one person, the one being. Therefore, Jesus' life and teaching, death, and resurrection, were all spoken of as parts of a single "Christ-event" which had to be seen as a whole with essentially one purpose.

D) A Preliminary Evaluation of the New Theologies

Temporarily prescinding from questions of ontology, there are certain observations that can be made about the new theologies at least in terms of the doctrine of redemption.

1. Redemption as Revelation

First, since any theology that involves the payment of a debt is untenable, theologies that speak of redemption as revelation are *de facto* exalted to the fore.

Furthermore, in the unification of Jesus' life, teachings, death and resurrection, the new theologies may also offer us the idea we need in order to make sense of the so-called "universality" of His effect (cf. p.292). The notion of a Christ-"event" bespeaks His effect on history. Therefore, given the corporate nature of humanity and creation (cf. p.207), it might be possible to show that Jesus' effect will extend to each and every person who has ever lived.

2. The Special Purpose of the Passion

Although the idea of a Christ-event does require us to see Jesus' effect (on history) as essentially one, we are not required to view His death, indeed the entire account of His suffering, the "passion," as no more than the end of His earthly life. After all, the "passion" was a particularly brutal end. Furthermore, it has been the constant experience of Christian spirituality that the suffering of Christ on the cross has always been "the" manifestation of God's love for humanity. (Jesus' willingness to give up His life has always been "the" model for Christian living.)

The idea of atonement made this possible. It made sense within the con-

---

18. See especially his *Christ, the Sacrament of Encounter with God.*
19. See especially his *The Christ.*

text of primitive Judaism and it explained Jesus' humiliating death. How *we* shall explain it remains to be seen.

E) The Questions that Remain

Admittedly, our "preliminary" evaluation did not address the questions of ontology upon which any attempt to see special meaning in the life and death of Jesus will stand or fall. Neither did it address the remaining question of redemption—its necessity.

Even if we were to insist that Jesus was teaching man to be like God, we would still be left with the question: why did He need to? Moreover, why would God need to reveal Himself in human terms? We believe that He wants to reveal Himself for all He is; and surely He can do it. Therefore, in the absence of absolute and original sin, there is no obvious reason that He did not. (Surely, Christians have been correct in their contempt for the idea that God was "too" great to reveal Himself, cf. 69.)

Section IV: The Problem of Grace

A) Another Implication of the Abandonment of Absolute and Original Sin

Just as the abandonment of absolute and original sin means that atonement was not necessary, so too it means that the completion of redemption did not need to involve the merit which won the grace needed to avoid sin. Moreover, in the light of what we now know about the nature and origin of sin, it would not appear that supernatural help is necessary, nor in evidence.

B) Another Implication of Materialism

Actually, there is another reason that the idea of grace is a problem. When we concluded to determinism, no mention was made of the possibility that behavior is influenced by grace. This in no way compromised determinism because even if grace were a behavioral influence, it would still be an influence upon a material brain—a determinate one. Therefore, free will could not have been established upon the existence of grace.

Furthermore, since grace must now be imagined as a supernatural intervention in the motion of matter in the brain, it must also be imagined to disrupt the very processes by which a credible notion of personal responsibility has been founded. In the light of the abandonment of original sin—and the attendant emergence of the question of the purpose of mortal life—such an intervention would undo the only possibility of our discovery of a reason for mortal, material existence.

Let it be stated. The above does not require us to abandon any idea of divine intervention. An intervention external to the process of self-determination, and which needed to take place as such—as may well be asserted for the intervention of an incarnation—remains a possibility pending discussion of the point and proof that this was so. But grace presents an insurmountable problem.

C) Historical Problems with the Theology of Grace

1. Grace and Free Will

We have just shown that the intrusion of grace cannot be used to establish the notion of free will. In fact, grace has long appeared to compromise the notion of free will. As we saw, the Christian belief in the absolute gratuity of salvation brought Augustine to insist that no good thought takes place except under the influence of grace (cf. p.77). This made the function of free will quite a mystery.

2. Grace and Predestination

Even more serious was the problem of predestination. Since grace was the inspiration of every salutary thought, salvation appeared to be the result of God's choice. The distinguishing characteristic of Calvinism (cf. p.106), it had also been a problem for Augustine and Thomas, both of whom felt compelled to admit that God had chosen to save some and not others.

But this did not solve the problem of grace and free will.

The centuries following Thomas saw no agreement as to how this problem should be solved. Two schools of thought distinguished themselves. Luis de Molina (1535-1600) advanced the idea that God gave saving grace to those He knew would respond to it best. But, since anyone's response involves the particulars of the present world order, and would have been different in a different world, and God has perfect foreknowledge of how anyone would respond in any world order, His decision to create this world also contained His decision of whom to save. Thus, salvation is still utterly gratuitous. In rebuttal, Domingo Bañez (1528-1604) maintained the classical position that, in any world, God's grace is the initial impulse of any good. Besides, if God could have known the outcomes of other possible creations, why did He create this world knowing that Adam would sin?

Accepting the Calvinist position with the Catholic proviso that grace was given in order to enable both faith *and obedience,* Cornelius Jansen (1585-1638) founded the movement that was later to bear his name—"Jansenism." Considering themselves "elect," its members adopted very severe standards of personal morality and sought to separate themselves from the rest of the immoral world which was already condemned.

In 1653, offended by their elitism, and more by their idea that God wills some men to be damned, Innocent X condemned the Jansenists (DS 2001-07). The condemnation gave doctrinal form to the notion that God gives everyone "sufficient" grace to be saved. Though this is not the "efficacious" grace that would save an individual, it is enough to justify his condemnation even though more grace would have saved him.

D) The Special Problem of Sanctifying Grace

The historical problems with the idea of grace appeared prior to the formal distinction between actual and sanctifying grace and actually concern the former. So does the immediate problem of materialism. This does not mean that materialism has no problem with the latter.

As something that becomes part of a soul, and changes it ontologically, sanctifying grace is supposedly something purely spiritual. (If it is not, it would simply be the effect of actual grace on matter.) But now that we have explained the spiritual in terms of matter, we know that our experience of the spiritual is not pure spirit. Therefore, what is a "purely" spiritual thing? Moreover, how could a spiritual thing become part of a material object and affect it as a "part" and not an intrusion?

E) The "Naturalness" of Christian Life

Actually, there is nothing about a person that betrays an extra something spiritual. As the anthropology has hopefully made clear, there is nothing about Christian life that does not emerge naturally given the proper circumstances. The Christian life is the product of natural causes; it is the product of events affecting human nature.

It would not seem that the "naturalness" of Christian life could be more obvious. Faith was described in terms of its very natural origins; so was love. This explains their essentially predictable presence or absence. It also explains why some Christians have a very un-Christian idea of God, for example, a stern God grounded in the experience of a stern human father. It explains why spiritual exercises work—and why they normally require the "quiet" that permits undistracted thinking. It explains why prayer sometimes produces nothing but frustration. (Spiritual "aridity" is normally to be explained either in terms of fatigue, confusion or fear.) The naturalness of Christian life explains the fact that non-Christians have courageously died as martyrs—some at the hands of Christians. It explains why faith and love sometimes fail. The mysteriousness historically attributed to grace is simply the "suddenness" that mental life always involves (cf. p.253).

F) Implicit Historical Recognition of the Naturalness of Christian Life

1. The Theology of the "Instrumentality" of Natural Causes

The implicit recognition of the naturalness of Christian life can clearly be seen in the classical theology of the so-called "instrumentality" of natural causes (cf. p. 28). Seeing the obvious fact that faith followed certain natural causes—such as preaching or the example of good parents—theologians explained that these were instruments through which invisible grace—which really did the work—was communicated. Of course, grace could be accepted or rejected. This explained the sometime failure of natural causes.

It is now clear that the sum total of the instrumental causes is sufficient to explain what results. Grace is superfluous—and problematic. The principle of economy requires its abandonment.

2. The Modern Theologies of Grace

Implicit recognition of the naturalness of Christian life is also to be seen in the modern theologies of grace. Originating in the increasing awareness of the correlation of natural causes and religious experience—especially non-Christian—these theologies came to describe the end of an absolute distinction between grace and nature.

Accepting the modern scientific contempt for the idea that nature is affected by the invisible interruption of grace, certain thinkers began to insist that there is no such thing as "pure" nature. According to Henri de Lubac (b.1891), nature was created by God to strive toward Him and never exists without the grace needed to do it.[20] This is what makes it possible for a higher to come from a lower.

According to Karl Rahner, nature is "permeated" with grace.[21] Therefore, there is no absolute distinction between natural and supernatural knowledge of virtues. This gave credence to the new theologies of salvation and secularity.

Rahner also held that man was created with the potential to share divine life already built in. Manifest in the fact of man's longing for the "infinite" (or "absolute"), this natural "supernatural" potential (or "existentiell") needs only to be called forth.[22] It is called forth by grace, which, according to Rahner, is Christ Himself, God's self-communication.[23] This was the true foundation of his theology of the anonymous Christian (cf. p.198). This was what made the incarnation God's "definitive" offer of salvation.[24]

---

20. See especially his *Le Surnaturel.*
21. See his *Nature and Grace.*
22. Actually, Thomas wrote of a natural, supernatural potential; but, his "obediential" potential was the capacity to be "elevated" by grace and involved nothing that nature possessed in itself (see his *Quaestiones Disputatae,* "De Veritate," 29, 3). Rahner's idea originates in Justin. According to Justin, if man was to know God, an image of God—and thus the Logos—had to be shown within him (see his *First Apology,* 46). (After all, you cannot know what you are in no way like.)
23. Even *this* idea originated in Justin who explicitly said that it was the Logos who spoke through the prophets, took flesh, and speaks to us now (cf. p.198).
24. See especially his *Foundations of Christian Faith.*

Temporarily prescinding from comment on the more profound aspects of the attempt to relate grace and Christ, it is immediately to be pointed out that the modern theologies identifying grace and nature have actually been denials of the essential character of what was always meant by the idea of "grace"—something utterly gratuitous. In the identification of grace and nature, "grace" has become something whose working is predictable—not something that can be given or not. To argue that, in all its predictability, "nature is grace" is simply to state that nature did not need to be created. To argue that grace gives nature abilities it would not otherwise possess is to violate the principle of economy, and to restate the already failed argument of neo-scholasticism (cf. p.240).

Actually, the stuff not needed to explain Christian life is *sanctifying* grace. To argue that nature still needs to be directed by actual grace is to invite the response to the most startling implication of materialism—divine determinism.

G) The Real Problem of Grace:
An Introduction to Divine Determinism

Materialism means determinism. It also means the unity of material reality (cf. p.249). But, this means that the cause of any event is the juxtaposition of all the matter which is the universe. But the true cause of the juxtaposition of all the matter which is the universe was the juxtaposition of all this matter the moment before. Christianity believes that the universe was created by an all-knowing, all-powerful God. Therefore, since creation necessarily involved an initial moment, and an exact juxtaposition of everything created, God's design of this initial moment contained His determination of everything that has ever happened or ever will.

This we shall now see.

Chapter II: Divine Determinism

Section I: The True Cause of Everything

A) The Inter-relatedness of Immediate Causes

The following is what we have already found:

An event is caused by a juxtaposition of matter. Indeed, all the matter, even the air around the event, is in some way involved. So too is the juxtaposition of matter that makes up the earth, the solar system, the galaxy, indeed, the exact juxtaposition of every unit of matter in the universe the moment before the event occurred. This is the immediate cause of what has happened—the true immediate cause.[1] Thus, the immediate cause of every event is inter-related.

B) The Inter-relatedness of Historical Causes

The inter-relatedness of immediate causes obviously implies the inter-relatedness of historical causes.

Every event has its historical cause—the events which led to it. Of course, each of these was the result of other events, and each of these was itself the result of many others. Therefore, the true historical cause of any event consists of countless events.

Nonetheless, given the inter-relatedness of immediate causes, it is possible to talk about the relatively simple fact that the true historical cause of any event—of every event—was the juxtaposition of all the matter in the universe as long ago as it is possible to imagine.

But Christianity involves the idea that the regression of causes cannot be infinite (cf. p.36). This was not only a matter of apologetics, it was a description of belief in creation. This is a doctrine that Christianity cannot do without.

Section II: Creation

A) The Doctrine of Creation

1. The Essence of the Doctrine

Given the unification of matter, energy, space and time, belief in creation is belief that matter—if only matter—was created. It is belief that matter is not only dependable but dependent—it cannot "just" exist (cf. p.268).

Since the creation of matter would also have been the creation of time, it

---

1. For practical purposes, the "true" cause of any event can be distinguished from its "decisive" cause—whatever was decisively unusual when the event was caused.

is impossible to speak of creation *in* time, as we know it. But, since creation involves the deliberate creative act of a Creator, it is both possible and necessary to speak of its "beginning." Moreover, if matter is dependent, i.e. *not* self-sufficient, it is also necessary to admit that if the Creator did not sustain it, i.e. stopped willing its existence, it would immediately cease to be. There would not be so much as a sound.

2. The Necessity of the Doctrine

The doctrine of creation was a virtual presumption of Christian belief. It was inherited from Jesus' Judaism. It has been one of the last and least contested of all Christian beliefs.

Belief in creation has been all but synonymous with belief in God *per se.* It always will be. In the light of what we have uncovered about the creative power of organization, it is now clear that unless God is necessary to explain matter, He would not be needed to explain anything. Therefore, belief in God would be disallowed by the principle of economy.

B) Models of Creation

If creation was the beginning of nature, a study of the natural origins of the universe can give us some idea of what it must have involved. Just as modern physics informed our metaphysic, a look at modern astronomy can inform our attempt to describe creation.

1. The "Big Bang" Theory

Modern astronomy was born through the telescope of Galileo. It was he who discovered that the Milky Way consists of many stars. Astronomy was again advanced by Charles Messier (1730-1817) who was using the telescope to look for comets. Thus it was by accident that he discovered and catalogued the many nebulae which Kant said are clouds of dust evolving into new stars (cf. p. 152). Messier's findings were incorporated into the star-charts of William Herschel (1738-1822). It was Herschel who produced the first map of the Milky Way, showing the sun's place within it.[2]

Early modern astronomy may have confirmed Kant's theory of the evolution of stars, but it still described the rest of the universe in static terms. The relative juxtaposition of the stars was presumed fixed. Furthermore, the universe was presumed to be what we now call the galaxy.

These were the presumptions Einstein brought to his theories of space and time. But, remarkably, his equations betrayed a fact—unknown even to him—that things were not so static as they seemed. His gravitational equations required a mathematical constant that did not refer to something real.

---

2. He is also remembered for his discovery of the first new planet ever to be known as such—Uranus.

If it were removed, the resulting values would describe a dynamic universe either expanding or contracting.

In 1917, unbeknownst to Einstein, Vesto Slipher had provided proof that the universe was in fact expanding. Engaged in the spectroscopic study of what he believed to be nebulae, he discovered that the spectra had been subject to the "Doppler effect"; a shift to the red side of the spectrum, a sure indication that they were moving away from the observer at speeds proportional to the amount of the shift.[3]

Soon thereafter, in 1923, Edwin Hubble became a modern-day Galileo with his discovery that many nebulae are actually other galaxies. With the development of ever better instruments of observation, a fantastic number of galaxies were discovered. (Today some 100,000,000,000+ galaxies are known to exist. Each consists of an average 100,000,000,000+ stars in various stages of development.) Each galaxy is moving away from us—and from every other—as do dots upon the surface of a balloon as it is inflated. The universe is detectably expanding.

As early as 1927, Georges Lemaître attributed the impetus of this expansion to the explosion of a single mass which once contained all the matter of the universe. The explosion of this "primeval atom," as Lemaître called it, soon resulted in the formation of hydrogen, spectroscopically known to be the principal stuff of the universe. Thereafter, mutual gravitation drew hydrogen into the clouds that would later become the galaxies, stars and planets which populate space. In 1948, George Gamow published a well-documented development of Lemaître's idea calling it the "big bang" theory.

Within two decades, the big bang theory was virtually proved. By 1965, Robert Wilson and Arno Penzias had reasoned that, if there had been a big bang, there should still be an "echo" in the form of the radiation of residue heat. Pointing their radiotelescope[4] into empty space, they detected this radiation almost immediately. Space has a temperature—approximately −457° Fahrenheit, or 3° "Kelvin," i.e. 3° above "absolute zero."[5] This temperature, together with a study of the relative speeds at which the galaxies are receding away from each other, gave rise to the figure of 16-20 billion years as the age of the universe. The diameter of the balloon has been

---

3. The "Doppler effect" is the effect on wave frequency of the motion of the thing giving off waves. If the thing is moving away, its waves spread out; if it is coming closer, they are compressed.
4. A radiotelescope is a device for gathering electromagnetic radiation other than visible light.
5. Absolute zero is the temperature generated by absolutely no motion.

calculated at 10 billion light-years.[6] Today the figures are almost undisputed.

It is their interpretation that is disputed. To some, the big bang is proof of creation. It explains the universe in the postulation of a primeval mass whose existence cannot be explained scientifically. Moreover, even if someone were to insist that it does not need explaining, he would still have the problem of explaining why something that always existed suddenly exploded. After all, how could it have always existed with some internal disorder, be it a big one or something that took half an eternity to develop?

2. The "Oscillating Universe" Theory

In definite opposition to the idea that the big bang theory is proof of creation, certain astronomers were quick to insist that creation is not scientific. They also pointed out that the study of the origin of the universe ("cosmology") was hardly over; it had just begun.

Much was made of the possibility that the laws governing a single mass containing all the matter in the universe were nothing like the physics of today.

Even more was made of the possibility that the outward momentum of the universe will slow, eventually stop, and reverse. Thus, the universe will come crashing in on itself. Thereupon, it could be imagined to explode again, again and again. Perhaps this is only one of what may have been an infinite number of cycles.

Called the "oscillating universe" theory, it offered the scientifically appealing possibility of a closed system that did not appear to need further explanation. But, an honest evaluation of available data did not indicate that there is nearly enough matter in the universe to "close" it, i.e. to stop its forever outward expansion. Scientists have therefore been searching for evidence of more matter than was previously detected. Much was hoped for in the discovery of "quasars"—very strong radio sources which are probably, in most cases, the extremely dense bodies (also called "black holes") that result when big stars burn up their hydrogen (which has become helium) and collapse inward. More hope was vested in the belief that through space there is an untold amount of interstellar "dust," the remainder of what was not used in the formation of stars. Still, studies in these areas have not added enough matter to the universal inventory to make a significant difference. Nonetheless, as what seems to be a point of principle, some scientists are convinced that sufficient matter will be found.

---

6. This is the distance that light travels in one year; approximately 6 trillion miles.

3. The Competence of Astronomy

Even if the scientists trying to close the universe should find enough matter to do so, their point would not be proved. Once the universe did come crashing in on itself, there is no guarantee that it would re-explode. Indeed, certain studies indicate that the momentum of the crash would be so great as to create the ultimate black hole—or perhaps to convert the stuff of the universe into something entirely new. Besides, even if it *were* to re-explode, we are left with the question of where the stuff came from in the first place.

But, even though the big bang theory does present an attractively simple picture of what happened at creation, it offers no proof that creation did happen. Nor can we be sure that the present state of things is not simply one stage in the evolution of a universe that has already been through more stages than we could ever imagine.

All of this makes clear that the issue of creation is not to be settled by astronomy. The issues involve the most global of judgments about reality. They cannot be settled by a study of a particular aspect of reality. They are essentially philosophical. Just as physics informs but is not a metaphysic (cf. p.242), astronomy informs but does not offer a theology of creation. Astronomy simply provides the models by which we can speak in concrete terms about the question. It is this which makes it possible to conceive creation and to understand its implications. It is this which we shall now do.

Section III: The Inevitability of Divine Determinism

A) The Meaning of a Beginning

Regardless of the model that one might favor, creation still involves the fact of a beginning. This involves some very real specifics. Simply stated, it means that all the matter that exists was brought into existence where once there was nothing, no-thing. Now, suddenly, there was.

Given the idea that matter is ultimately "particular," this means a specific number of units of determinate characteristics suddenly came into being with a determinate juxtaposition. Given the idea that the universe is a plenum (cf. p.136), it means that the one thing suddenly appeared as whatever it was. In any case, if the universe was created, there was an initial moment.

B) The Divine Design of the Initial Moment

If the universe was created, there can be no doubt that the initial moment was willed by God in every detail. What can be anything but exactly what it is, or appear anywhere but exactly where it was, apart from the will of the Creator?

And how could God *not* have willed exactly what He wanted? And how could God *not* have known exactly what would follow from anything He willed? Surely, the God who could create is all-powerful and also all-knowing. (And, surely, the God who created wanting man to appear twenty billion years later knew what would happen the next day.) Therefore, we must acknowledge that creation bespoke His plan for everything that has ever happened or ever will. Aristotle and Thomas were right; in the "final" analysis, God is the cause of everything (cf. p.60).

C) Responses to Two Predictable Objections

Divine Determinism is sure to evoke criticism. The best of such criticism would predictably involve one of the following two objections.

1. The Idea of "Continuous Creation"

Neo-scholasticism involves the idea that God is actively involved in the elevation of the lower to the higher. This view also involves the idea that the future is not predetermined by God, but is created by Him continuously—day by day.

But, as we have already seen, neo-scholasticism is superfluous (cf. p.240). Complex organization elevates the lower to the higher. (Moreover, the claim that "God creates as He goes" offers man no more involvement in his destiny than the idea that He determined everything from eternity.)

If "continuous creation" simply means that God must continuously sustain matter—a claim that follows the conviction that matter is not self-sufficient—the fact that matter is creative and predictable renders the word "continuous" irrelevant to the discussion of divine determinism.

2. "Process Theology"

An interesting but ultimately invalid objection would predictably come from exponents of what is called "process theology," a 20th century theological movement for which our sympathy might be presumed on account of its idea that reality is ever in "process"; it is always becoming.

Grounded in the philosophy of Alfred North Whitehead (1861-1949), process theology accepts his idea that, not only are things becoming, things *are* "becoming"—"becoming" has an ontological status. In other words, there are no "things" but a series of states.[7]

Process theology holds that, according to the evidence of what He has created, even God is in a state of becoming. Process theology also holds that becoming is essentially "dialogical," i.e. involving the interplay of at least two realities. Thus, it pictures God and man growing up together. (It is this idea that can be invoked in order to deny divine determinism.) Moreover, to

---

7. See his *Process and Reality*.

the minds of some process theologians, the world *is* God, but not *all* of Him, an idea referred to as "pan-an-theism."

Process theology fails for many reasons. Principally, in giving ontological status to "becoming," it fails to distinguish the thing from what can be said about it (cf. p.241). What becomes? To know "becoming" is to know the thing whose before and after states can be compared. Furthermore, the thing is made of matter, and matter is provably stable. Reason is knowing this.

In the idea that even "God is becoming," we see the failure to understand the very idea upon which belief in God is based—the idea that the world bespeaks the fact that it owes its existence to something else, something different, something which is self-sufficient and, as the source of all that is or can be, cannot be imagined to become anything more. From where would it get this more?

Finally, the idea that becoming is "dialogical" is disallowed by the fact that man's response to anything is determined.

Therefore, if there is a God, materialism means divine determinism.

Chapter III: The Immediate Implications of Divine Determinism

Section I: Confirmations of Conclusions Already Reached

A) The Problems of Sin

The most immediate implications of divine determinism are the confirmations of conclusions already reached on the basis of determinism *per se*.

If God has determined everything that happens, it is obvious that the idea of absolute sin must be abandoned.

It is impossible that the state of the world, evils and all, is a punishment.

Man did not need to be redeemed.

Christian life is not the product of grace.

B) A Possibility as to the Truth Contained in the Doctrine of Grace

Though Christian life is not the product of grace, the classical theology of grace can still be said to have stated the truth that no one should be boastful about who or what he is (cf. p. 76). Divine determinism means that the circumstances which have determined every person were willed by God in every detail. Thus, it is not "grace" but God's "graciousness" to which every particular of a person's life is owed, both good and bad. This surely confirms the perennial wisdom that "there but by the grace of God go I."

C) Providence

The realization that everything that happens is God's will implies an unqualified faith in providence—the belief that everything happens for good.

Given the Christian conception of God, no other idea is possible.

But, let us be clear about what providence does *not* mean. It does not mean that events should be accepted passively as though human action was unimportant. Not only is human action an important source of the events by which God's will is unfolding, but, as we have seen, events do not determine a person apart from his effect on the process (cf. p.278). And, since man is part of the process, it is surely important that his inevitable self-direction—his unavoidable need to make choices—means that some things are better than others. This we shall see.

Moreover, even though everything that happens is God's will, we should not be persuaded that everything that happens is an indication of what God wants for-ever. A divine plan would surely pursue an "end," i.e. a state of things "at the end." Of course, it would also involve the "path" that creation will take to get to this end. And since bad things often lead to good things that no one expected, we can hope that the progress of theology will demonstrate that, even in disasters, God knows best—and victimizes no one.

Section II: The Problem of Sacraments

A) The Problem(s)

1. Another Implication of Divine Determinism
a. The Problem

Obviously, the abandonment of supernatural grace presents a severe problem for any theology of sacraments. Simply stated, if grace is not communicated, what—if anything—do sacraments do?

b. Historical Problems with Sacraments in General

Of course, even before materialism, the idea of sacraments was a problem. To the reformers, they made salvation contingent on an external ritual and the good fortune of someone to perform it—if he could be persuaded to. To scientists, they were magic, attempts to manipulate the divine and to see Him in action. To students of comparative religion, they were the result of a human need for ritual which is present in every culture.

Besides, the sacraments did not seem to work—except in ways much more plausibly explained *via* psychology.

2. Problems with Particular Sacraments

In addition to the general problems, materialism involves problems with particular sacraments. In every case, the issue is further complicated by the results of modern biblical and patristic scholarship.

Baptism is compromised by the abandonment of grace, particularly sanctifying grace (cf. p.303) and, for the same reasons, the idea that it imparts to its recipient a permanent, ontological character. Its purpose is questioned by the abandonment of absolute and original sin. All this gives new importance to the argument that Jesus never instituted any sacraments (cf. p.130).

The exact same critique applies to the sacrament of Confirmation. It is only compounded by the evidence that Confirmation was not a recognized sacrament until the third century. It seems that the spread of Christianity resulted in the Baptism of many people who lived far from the churches of the people who baptized them. The theology of the sacrament was an attempt to justify a practice that had already developed in order to assure that a bishop would administer what was actually the first form of initiation that Christians developed as their own.

The classical theology of Penance is obviously compromised by the abandonment of absolute sin. The problem is compounded by the biblical evidence that Jesus never made the statements upon which this theology is based, not to mention the patristic evidence that the early Christians were solely concerned about the power to impose the punishment that would readmit the serious sinner to communion with the rest of the Church (cf. p. 81).[1] (Obviously, all of this is equally troublesome to the idea of Indulgences.) Of course, the reformers had already rejected the idea that sinners should be required to confess anything to anyone but God.

Although some form of Eucharist can be argued to originate in specific actions on Jesus' part (cf. p.192), we have no such proof as to the meaning of such actions, or Jesus' intention that they be performed in His memory. The classical position is also compromised by the problems with any idea of the union of matter and spirit (cf. p.303). The problem of redemption (cf. p.297) obviously imperils any idea that the Eucharist is a sacrifice. So does the potential problem of the divinity of Christ (q.v. p.369). (Of course, the classical belief that Jesus is God has always involved the problem that God is already everywhere.)

The problems of grace and history also imperil any claim that Matrimony is a sacrament. This is further aggravated by the 20th century innovation of non-traditional (or "alternate") lifestyles. This has raised the question of whether marriage exists according to God's special intention.

The problems of grace and history are especially acute with regard to Extreme Unction. They are aggravated by the fact that this sacrament is supposed to produce empirical results of which there is no good evidence.

With regard to Holy Orders, the problems of grace and history are charged by emotion. The problems of grace center upon the idea that ordination changes a person—ontologically.[2] The historical problems involve the question of whether Jesus intended to ordain anyone—much less found a Church—not to mention the modern historical research which has revealed that ministry in the Church involved the dual development of the so-called "episcopal" and "presbyteral" models. Furthermore, not only is it clear that presbyters were "elders," not "priests," but the study of both models has *not* demonstrated an early or universal concern for sacramental ordination or power.

Neither has historical research revealed an early or universal concern for

---

1. The requirement of frequent, private (or "auricular") confession of all sins did not begin until the 8th century; it was a spiritual exercise innovated by Irish monks.
2. Even before the Reformation, the sacrament of orders was a problem. Was it one sacrament (as the Church taught) or was it three—the episcopate, the priesthood and the diaconate? Did its powers extend to all three of its "degrees?" If they did *not*, it would appear to be more than one sacrament.

apostolic or petrine succession. It appears impossible to prove that the chains have never broken and there is ample reason to assume that they have been.

And the "pope" did not exercise supreme authority until the 5th century.

B) Explicit Modern Recognition of the Need for a Change

1. New Theologies of the Sacraments in General

For most of the reasons that we have just considered, new theologies were both called for and developed. The work of Rahner, Schillebeeckx and many others, these new theologies embrace a variety of positions and approaches. Indeed, it is to be noted that much involved in these new theologies has not (yet) found full acceptance in official Church teaching.

As we have already noted, the problem of Jesus' institution of the sacraments was answered with different forms of Loisy's idea that it was the Holy Spirit working through the Church that had *explicitly* instituted them (cf. p.192). Of course, now that inspiration was conceived to require the mediation of circumstances, care was now taken to demonstrate the circumstances, *particularly ecclesial,* that must have occasioned the development of each of the individual sacraments. The Church became the "universal" sacrament (a phrase was actually used by Vatican II, *Lumen Gentium,* 48).

Taking seriously the idea that God works *through* visible things (cf. p. 85), there was a subtle shift in the classical idea that sacramental signs cause the grace "that" they signify; now it was said that sacraments cause grace "as" they signify. This had the concrete effect of a concern that sacraments be "celebrated" movingly, and not performed as a matter of course. The importance of putting no "obstacle" in their way became a positive need for a proper disposition.

In an implicit recognition of the problem of sanctifying grace (and ontological character), certain sacraments were now said to involve a "relational ontology"—the fact that the sacrament changed the relation between the recipient and the Church.

2. New Theologies of Particular Sacraments

Naturally, the general developments had their effect on the theologies of the particular sacraments. In an implicit recognition of the problem of actual grace, each stressed the "significance" of the sacrament.

Baptism became the "Sacrament of Initiation." And, not only did it initiate a person into the Church, it gave him a share of its mission. Confirmation confirmed his membership; it made him a full member. Holy Orders gave the person an "office" in the Church; this enabled him to act "officially"—

in its name.[3]

Penance became the "Sacrament of Reconciliation"; it also reconciled the person with the Church.

The Eucharist was now said to "re-present"[4] the sacrifice of Christ. Moreover, thanks to a new appreciation for the idea that the Eucharist is a ritual "meal,"[5] it was now seen to bring about the "communion" of those who broke the one bread and shared the one cup. It became the renewable sacrament of initiation. Here was a remarkable change in the legacy of a medieval eucharistic piety which was so severe that receiving communion was a rarity in one's lifetime. Also changed was the ritual of the mass; no longer should the priest "say" mass in Latin with his back to the people; now he led their mutual celebration, in their language, facing them (see Vatican II's *Sacrosanctum Concilium*).

In response to the problems with Real Presence, it was suggested that transubstantiation give way to "transignification," the idea that the actions of the priest (together with the entire believing community) change the "meaning" of the bread, or at least add to it, even if the substance (which we now understand to be chemical) stays the same. This theology was complemented by the notion of "transfinalization," an attempt to give ontology to the new theology with the insistence that, in the final analysis, things *are* what God says they are.[6]

The sacrament of Marriage became a "commitment" properly founded upon "conjugal" love.[7]

In what was billed a rediscovery of the biblical concern for healing, Extreme Unction became the "Sacrament of the Anointing of the Sick." It was no longer a "last" rite in preparation for death.

C) An Evaluation of the New Theologies

Needless to say, the new theologies do not answer either the old or new

3. Though Vatican II did speak of the "priesthood" of all the people (*Lumen Gentium*, Ch.II), this same document still insisted that the distinction between clergy and laity was still a distinction of "kind" not "degree" (Ch.III). It maintained the traditional teaching to the effect that the sacrament did confer "powers" through a permanent change in the person who received them. This was to be distinguished from the "office" which he could lose, making the exercise of power "illicit" but never "invalid."

4. Actually, Tertullian had already spoken in these terms—with a classical-sounding realism— as early as the third century.

5. As a meal, the Eucharist also had its "eschatological" aspect—the fact that the community gathered in anticipation of the return of the Lord.

6. But, Paul VI insisted that the theologies of trans-signification and finalization did not do justice to the substantiality of the Eucharistic change (see his *Mysterium Fidei*).

7. But, marriage remained a "contract" to be kept regardless of what persons might say about the status of their love.

problems with sacraments, at least not completely. What they do *not* say is crucial.

Because of what they do not say, they do not respond to the problems of actual and sanctifying grace. Therefore, in their failure to address the issue, they do not address the question of how or whether the sacramental acts can be considered God's and continue to be "celebrated" as moments somehow essential to the lives of Christians, and to the life of the Church. Ideas of "relational ontology" have not explained the ontological way in which the recipient is changed in his relation to anything.

But, grounding sacraments in the theology of mediation, with special attention to what each of the actions "says," the new theologies do offer a way in which the sacramental acts can be considered God's. If He instituted them, they speak for Him the way the Church does generally—by commission.

Moreover, if a sacramental act causes a major change in a person's self-conception, it can surely be said to involve a change sufficiently profound to be considered "ontological."

Of course, we have yet to see sufficient evidence that God wants to be spoken for in sacramental acts.

Section III: The Problem of Divine Intervention

A) The Problem in General

Now that it is clear that God could have accomplished anything in the act of creating, it is equally clear that frequent divine intervention is not to be expected. Therefore, in the absence of overwhelming evidence to the contrary, the inexplicable is *not* to be considered a miracle. This would confirm the increasing conviction that there is a natural explanation for everything.

Actually, in the implicit recognition that there is a natural explanation for everything, certain theologies have begun to deny that a miracle is, as it has always been understood, a "suspension" of the laws of nature. Instead, they have begun to call it a "surpassing" of nature, according to the idea of the neo-scholastic thought which we have already examined—and rejected (cf. p.240). The word "miracle" needs to mean that matter has *not* done what forces normally, naturally determine.

Once again, it is to be stated that the above does not require us to abandon belief in the incarnation, a related miracle, or another exceptional case in which God can convincingly be said to have spoken *to* creation and not just through it (cf. p.301). The meaning and truth of such a belief involves issues that this work has yet to address. Meanwhile, there are other categories of miracles that can and should be criticized.

B) The Special Problem of Divine Retribution

Belief in divine retribution has long been a problem. The problem is this: Why do bad things happen to good people and *vice-versa?* The fact that is no ascertainable proportion to the good and bad things that happen to good and bad people has been a major source of disillusionment with faith (cf. p.121).

Actually, in view of this increasingly evident fact, there has already been a change. Preachers may say one thing, but theologians now reject the idea that God scrupulously rewards and punishes His people, at least not on earth. Instead, they have become more insistent than ever that providence is at work in everything that happens, regardless of whether whatever has happened seems constructive of anything.

Nonetheless, there could still be truth in what was always involved in the idea of divine retribution. Believing in an all-good God, there was no other way for people to understand the disparity of gifts—or the fact that the punishments for original sin were not distributed equally. Punishment, if only for something "inside" the apparently good person, was the only available explanation that preserved God's goodness. It was all the more plausible because most victims readily confessed the darker side of who they "really" were. But, in view of our new perspectives on human nature (cf. p.283), and the extent of providence (cf. p.313), it is now clear that the idea of divine retribution can be taken to have stated the fundamental truth that nothing happens for nothing.

C) The Special Problem of Prayers of Petition

Any denial of frequent divine intervention is surely a denial that God acts in answers to prayers of petition.

Actually, the supposed efficacy of prayers of petition has always been a problem. Most troublesome has been the question of how the immutable God could ever be persuaded to change His mind (cf. footnote p.121). The argument that "God's love requires Him to be responsive to prayers of His people" ignores the fact that His love is already at work in the divine plan already in action. The argument that His plan anticipates the prayers of His people ignores the fact that prayers are already determined by God's plan, and take place because we believe that they *will* change God's mind. If we continue to pray them, we would effectively be saying that God wants vain prayers.

What happens if two people pray for an opposite outcome, or if the answer of one's prayer is a disaster for another?

What of the evidence that prayers of petition do not work. Prayers have always been offered for a variety of causes good and not. Some are "answered"; some are not. But the results betray a natural pattern. There are no more cures in Catholic hospitals than any others. To some, it may seem that there are, but this is due to the very natural human tendency to remember the times prayer "worked" rather than the times it quite naturally failed. When disappointments occur there is also the tendency to explain it away by an appeal to some unworthiness on the part of the pray-er, or the person or cause prayed for—even though all concerned clearly appear more worthy than those to or for whom God did respond. Though there are cases that defy explanation, there are as many inexplicable disasters. In all cases, we can now accept the modern wisdom that the inexplicable is explicable in principle.

Accepting the modern wisdom, theologians now encourage the faithful to make their prayer "Jesus' prayer"—"thy will be done." In the light of divine determinism, it is clear that this is the only prayer we should expect to be answered. In other words, the Christian is called to an unqualified faith in divine providence.

An unqualified faith in divine providence does not mean that there has been no truth to what has always been a Christian and world-wide religious practice. In essence, it can be said that prayers of petition stated the truth that God is good, that He listens to His people and cares for them. But, it is now clear that faith in providence is a better expression of this truth. (Actually, this truth was already stated in the classical wisdom that, no matter what we pray for, God knows best.)

Section IV: Problems with the Idea of Inspiration

A) The Necessity of Inspiration?

Obviously, the abandonment of belief in frequent divine intervention—and in grace in particular—calls the idea of inspiration into serious question. After all, what is inspiration except a special form of the grace we now no longer see as necessary in order to explain religious experiences? What of the Judeo-Christian tradition—with the possible exception of the incarnation—could not have been caused through nature, and therefore by providence, and does not seem to bear the obvious earmarks of such an origin?

B) A New Perspective on the Old Testament

1. The New Perspective

Of all the sources of revelation, the Old Testament would surely appear the easiest to explain by nature, and therefore by providence. We have already seen that the Old Testament bears the earmarks of all the limitations that one would expect of ancient writings. Indeed, in the light of anthropology as informed by the study of comparative religion, there would not appear to be a single statement in it that could not have been the product of the Hebrew's natural reflections, however unique.[8] This is evident in the fact that most of its ideas have some parallel in the thought of other ancient Near Eastern peoples. Besides, what better explains the fact that the Hebrews developed monotheism slowly, their law was scarcely Christian, and their hope for a messiah was actually political? What of the fact that their hope in heaven was actually the minority opinion?

Clearly, the principle of economy requires that we acknowledge that the religious history of the "chosen" people was indeed a natural development, the product of historical circumstances not unlike the development of any other religious tradition. Unlike all peoples, however, their's was indeed a "chosen" history, chosen by providence to provide what Jesus presumed, its limitations notwithstanding. (Jesus' first followers needed to perceive that He had been foretold by the fathers of what they presumed.) Thus, chosen by providence, the Hebrew tradition was "inspired" in a way that other religious reflections were not. It is "inerrant" inasmuch as providence decided exactly what ideas it would need to provide to later reflection.

But, this does not mean that the Old Testament must be taken literally. As we have already seen, there is little that we understand as the Hebrews did. Therefore, the study of their thought is only secondarily as a source of religious truth. Its unquestioned study as God's word concerns its role in the origin of Christianity.

2. An Addendum: The Inter-religious Dialogue

The new perspective on the Old Testament has some very definite implications for the inter-religious dialogue (cf. p.200). As we have already seen, Vatican II acknowledged the partial truth contained in all the world's religions. Let it be clear, however, by "partial," the council meant partial in relation to Christianity, which is complete, and serves as the criteria of the truth that other faiths contain. The study of other faiths was recommended, but only to understand how others think—for evangelical purposes only. But, now it is clear that even though Christianity can still be called complete—in the sense that Christians can know that the one true religion will not be replaced—its understanding of the truth is far from it. Therefore, given our new sensitivity to the fact that everyone has something to offer, other religions may have much—perhaps quite foreign to Judeo-Christianity—which can inform ongoing Christian reflection as data of the first order, with good ideas that are true, that Christianity did not think of.

---

8. And prophecy is still going on. Now called reading "the signs of the times," it is a function of wisdom.

C) A New Perspective on the New Testament

1. The New Perspective

Now that we have recognized the natural origin of the Old Testament, there is no reason that the ample evidence of the very human authorship of the New Testament should not lead us to the same conclusion. "Inspired" by its subject, the life and teaching of Jesus, it is "inerrant" inasmuch as providence must have made sure that it contains all the information that the history of Christianity will ever need. But, obviously, this does not mean that everything—or anything—it says must be the literal truth.

2. An Addendum: The Canon

The new perspectives on the Old and New Testaments should affect the canon of Sacred Scripture (cf. p.41). Simply put, in the absence of active inspiration, the sacredness of any scripture is solely to be seen in its importance to Christianity.

Thus, the Catholic-Protestant confrontation over the Old Testament canon (cf. footnote p. 103) is rendered null.

Moreover, we are now to recognize the biblical importance of writings which date from New Testament times. There are several. Thanks to modern study, we now know that the "First Letter of Clement" was written before the Johannine writings.[9] All the leters of Ignatius and the *Shepherd of Hermas* were written before the "Second Letter of Peter." Most of the other "apostolic fathers" (cf. footnote p.44) are almost as important—historically.[10] These writings did not receive biblical status because they lacked the credibility attached to the name of an apostle which, as has been shown, was often inputed apart from the facts (cf. p.128). When this was discovered, it was not considered a serious problem for the accepted writings because they were still ancient in origin and did indeed bear the Church's stamp of approval. But, a developmental understanding of Church teaching would surely allow this stamp to be used again. Furthermore, the new perspectives would allow theology to dispense with recently troublesome problems involving the inspiration of potentially discoverable new parts or even whole scriptures bearing apostolic names. After all, the importance of any such work would still depend upon its intrinsic weight as evidence of what Christians thought when. This is their inspiration; their inerrancy remains the fact that providence must have made sure that the early history of Christianity provides us with sufficient data to develop the truth truly.

9. The so-called "Second Letter of Clement" was actually a third century use of Clement's good name.
10. These include the "Letter of Barnabas," the "Letter of Polycarp to the Philippians," and the *Didache*.

D) A New Perspective on Tradition and the Magisterium

1. The New Perspective

Accepting the divine ordination of the Church, providence offers a new perspective on Tradition and the magisterium. Surely the entire "living tradition" (cf. p.195) must be a special case of providence. Therefore, it is to be presumed that the history of tradition betrays the direction truth is traveling, with particular authority in cases of conflict where the Church might have gone one way or the other.

2. An Addendum: Infallibility

With "irreformability" hopelessly discredited (cf. p.215), infallibility must be understood in terms of the simple fact that, like tradition, Church leadership is a special case of providence—whose decisions cannot be involved in the fundamental misdirection of the Church's collective efforts. In terms of truth, the latter point is already the conclusion of theologians like Avery Dulles (b.1918) who says that infallibility means that the organs of the magisterium "cannot commit the Church to error."[11] But, this proviso rightfully refers only to pointless, permanent error that would cause the Church to forfeit its destiny. Therefore, even though doctrinal declarations do propel progress, there is no saying how their truth will be judged in terms of fact (or purpose) as progress continues.

Thus, it should still be clear that nothing that has been said about the truth present in schisms and heresies, and even anti-Christian movements, is being unsaid. Therefore, we can still insist that everyone has something to say, however much or little it may be.

E) Minimalism

1. The Idea

The new perspectives on Scripture, Tradition and the magisterium were effectively restatements of the distinctions between the truth, its expression, and its understanding—and the fact that there is a definite distance between what is written and what is necessarily to be believed (cf. p. 177,179). The new perspective on infallibility was essentially a restatement of the idea that "continuity is confidence in the Church." This was essentially a restatement of the indeducibility of doctrine—the fact that the truth of the future may involve the abandonment of much of what was believed in the past as old truth is synthesized with new as knowledge grows (cf. p.214).

But, the conclusions of "Part III" push us to a new principle.

Formerly, the process of synthesis involved the presumption that the sources of revelation should be taken literally unless there was overwhelm-

---

11. See his *The Survival of Dogma*.

ing reason not to. But, given the new perspective on divine intervention (cf. p.318)—not to mention the abandonment of ideas once so central as absolute sin, etc.—we must admit that no assertion, particularly historical, can be taken for granted. Thus, the simple fact that something is stated by Christian tradition is no longer sufficient evidence it is true. Obviously, the more extraordinary must be supported by more evidence.

Therefore, whenever the historical evidence is inconclusive—as so often it will be—belief should be expected only in those things which are supported by theological evidence, the requirements of Christian or Catholic, faith *per se*. This "minimalism" is a requirement of reason.

2. An Excursus: A New Perspective on the "Sensus Plenior"

Though it may appear that minimalism will require the abandonment of much, it is still to be stated that some purpose must have been served by anything that the Church has taught, especially in cases where a less historically or theologically troublesome way of making a point was available. Therefore, just as the doctrine "Outside the Church No Salvation" saved the Church as an institution, and said that it *is* essential to the salvation of history, so too other beliefs may have had the purpose of protecting one thing while calling our attention to truths we might not have discovered on our own or appreciated fully. This could be the true "sensus plenior" (cf. p.188) of many traditional beliefs.

Chapter IV: The Need for an Apologetic for the Essentials

Section I: The Necessity of Apologetics

At this point, we must face what minimalism really means. It means that not even the essentials can be taken for granted—not even faith.

With the abandonment of grace, we took on the burden of showing that faith, like other knowledge, has its basis in evidence. The fact that faith is beyond reason does not mean that there is no need to give the reason, the sufficient evidence for belief. Quite the contrary, just as reality can be explained so as to demonstrate the essentially unprovable truths of reason and also of causality, so too reality can be explained so as to demonstrate the truth of faith. And it must. Apologetics is necessary.

As the "Introduction" endeavored to explain, nothing else will see to faith's survival and spread.

Section II: Problems with Jesus' Principal Presumptions

A) The Problem of God

Of course, the existence of God must be the principal object of any apologetic. Largely a *presumption* of Jesus—a belief all but universal as He grew up—it was eventually to draw serious criticism. Critiqued on the grounds of a lack of evidence, this is a critique to which we must respond. Materialism makes the question more urgent. After all, if matter is self-sufficient, we do not need God. We could explain the world with something we can see.

B) The Christian Conception of God

The apologetic will also need to support the uniquely Christian idea of God. Partly a presumption of Jesus, partly his teaching, the Christian conception of God involves ideas of His personhood and loving Fatherhood which go beyond belief in God generally. Moreover, His personhood is denied by some of the world's most venerable religious traditions. His loving Fatherhood is challenged by the omnipresent problem of evil.

Section III: Problems with Jesus' Principal Teachings

The problems with Jesus' teachings on salvation are almost entirely new.

A) The Coming of the Kingdom

Even beyond the demands of positive proof, the coming of the kingdom is a problem because it is *coming*. As we have seen, the belief that God would share His life is called into question by the fact that we are not sharing it now (cf. p.293). The solution to this problem must be an answer to the question of the purpose of mortal, material life.

B) The Call of Love

An answer to the question of the purpose of mortal, material life must also be a solution to the problem of the call of love. Even though Christian life can be described in terms of man's greatest development, its importance in terms of eternity has not been explained. The explanation will need to deal with the diversity of developments that persons attain, a problem which is aggravated by determinism, and more so by divine determinism.

Section IV: The Problem of the Divine Sonship of Jesus

There are a multitude of problems old and new with belief in the divine sonship of Jesus.

A) The Problems of the Incarnation

The oldest problems with the incarnation stem from the "mystery," the apparent contradiction in terms, involved in the insistence that Jesus was both God and man. The cause of numerous heresies (cf. p. 50, 69), the problems were later compounded by the scriptural and comparative religious studies that speak about the human origin of this idea (cf. p.129,159).

Minimalism only makes this worse. Moreover, materialism not only makes it more difficult to imagine "God made man," but it encourages a severe skepticism about divine interventions of any kind. Furthermore, since the necessity of redemption has been abandoned, we are bound to ask: what could the incarnation have accomplished that could not have been accomplished otherwise?

B) The Problems of the Trinity

Almost as old as the problems with the incarnation are the problems with the Trinity. An even bigger mystery than the incarnation, the Trinity also appears a contradiction in terms (cf. p.53). The scriptural, theological problems with the doctrine have only been aggravated by the problems of the incarnation.

Minimalism makes them worse.

Section V: The Problem of the Church

Of the essentials of *Catholic* Christianity, belief in the divine ordination of the Church is the one which is distinctively Catholic.

The old problems have been mentioned (cf. p.122,130). There is reason to question Jesus' intention to found a Church, especially a Church as institutional as the one which now claims uniquely divine origin. The not always noble history of the Church also raises the question of divine origin.

In requiring the abandonment of absolute sin, etc., materialism aggravates the question of divine origin. Minimalism aggravates the question of Jesus' intention.

Part IV: The Synthesis

Introduction to Part IV

Christianity has been presented; so has materialism. The immediate conflict between the two has been exposed. Therefore, we are finally ready for the synthesis which was the stated aim of this work.

As we have just seen, this synthesis must begin with an apologetic for the essentials of Christian belief. Materialism demands proper proof. Therefore, since we have discredited the proofs of times past, a new apologetic must be provided. Only then can we see what does or does not make sense in the light of the rest of what materialism demands.

As always, disclaimers are made with regard to the concise character of the arguments to follow, for all the reasons that have previously been stated.

Chapter I: An Apologetic for the Existence of God

Section I: The Idea of an Apologetic

The apologetic begins with a statement of what is to be expected from it. After all, if the creative nature of human knowing means anything, it means that absolute proof is neither possible nor rightfully to be demanded. As we saw, the principles that guide reason are not absolutely provable; reason is not "reasonable" according to the uncritical, modern usage of the word (cf. p.266).

But, reason still obliges us to show the "intelligence" of our beliefs—the evidence and good reasons to accept our interpretation of it.

Thus, in light of the creative nature of human knowledge, an "apologetic" is just that, an "explanation" of what anyone with a sufficiently wide and unobstructed experience should see.

Section II: The Question of a Cause

The apologetic for Christianity begins with an apologetic for the belief which it shares with all the world's religions—the idea that the world requires its cause (cf. p.268).

As we have already seen, this is essentially of the self-sufficiency of matter (cf. p.306). The question is, is it intelligent to believe that matter "just" exists, always has and always will? Is this what reality is all about—the fact that matter "is."?

In considering this question, it is important to remember that it is not solely to be answered by picturing a single unit of matter and asking the question: does *this* just exist? Rather, it requires imagining the whole universe of matter and asking the question of all that matter can do. In other words, the question is: does matter just exist; does the matter that can and does comprise atoms, cells and the thinking, feeling self-consciousness of man just exist? Can it just be this matter which is responsible for human nature in all the richness of its experience? Is it intelligent to imagine that history just happened, that matter just happened to evolve into the universe and all it contains?

Let it be clear. The above is not the evolutionary argument for the existence of God (cf. p.173). No statement of the evolutionary odds is insinuated here. The question is: can the universe of matter—with all its inherent abilities—just exist?

The "believer" says "no." He claims to know that the universe of matter cannot just exist. To him, matter and all it can do bespeaks more than it can ultimately account for. It—the world—requires its cause.

Section III: The Intelligence of Belief that the World is Caused

For the sake of clear argument, the intelligence of belief that the world is caused must first be expressed in positive terms—the explanation of evidence. The crux of the argument will involve its response to predictable objections.

A) Positive Proof

1. The Primary Evidence

The primary evidence that the world is caused is the matter which accounts for all that it can be.

This evidence is so interpreted because the experience of matter also imparts the idea that matter is insufficient to explain its own existence.

This interpretation of evidence is self-evident to the person who reflects upon it.

Its self-evidence is consistent with the creative nature of human knowing (cf. p.266). As we also saw, knowing involves several "global" ideas which are evident in no one event.

These are self-evident to anyone sufficiently "mature" intellectually, who is not prevented by some obstacle.

And, such a person will always have some idea that the world requires its cause.

This has been the all but universal experience of mankind.

2. The Supporting Evidence

We have already seen the supporting evidence (cf. p.268). Though "supporting" in the sense that it presumes the truth of the primary existence, the following is usually the first thing that people think of as they realize that the world must have its cause.

Reflecting not only upon his life, but also upon "life," particularly the fact the world affords only death, and in death, the ultimate "trivialization" of everything that life involves, the person, the intelligent person finds himself forced to admit that there is no true good, no real "value" to anything man does or is. But, there must be more to life than this. The world cannot just be a place in which man exists to struggle and suffer all for nothing. Therefore, the world must have its purpose. And this is something only God can give.

B) Responses to Predictable Objections
1. Objections to the Primary Evidence
a. The Objection to the Idea that Human Knowledge is Creative

Actually, we have already responded to the objection to the idea that human knowledge is creative and involves the emergence of ideas whose truth is not to be seen in any one shred of evidence (see again p.266).

As we saw, conscience emerges only slowly, the result of much experience. Self-consciousness comes as a surprise; it was not evident in consciousness itself. Nothing about self-consciousness proves that the world is really "out there"; and nothing provides absolute proof that it is. Nothing provides absolute proof of the basis of proof—the dependability of the world—reason. No number of specific experiences can prove that reason is reasonable. It is "just" known, the result of one's whole experience as it has matured a mind. This is also the origin of the knowledge that there "just" must be something behind the dependability. In principle untestable, this too is the result of intellectual maturity, when no obstacle intervenes.

It is also the origin of the knowledge that the world cannot "just" be—that the world is dependent. Though this idea is necessarily less certain than those upon which it is built, it is no less a fact of experience. It will be evident to anyone of sufficient intellectual maturity. Therefore, it will be most evident when one's brain is working best (the reason a person will be particularly sure of the existence of God on a "good" day), especially through an experience of all that life can really be (the reason that good news will often be greeted by the exclamation "there is a God!"). Nonetheless, given sufficient experience, it will always come about as long as some obstacle—such as a misunderstanding of reason, or the emotional obstacle of a lack of confidence in one's own conclusions—does not prevent what would otherwise take place.

To the objection that the knowledge of "the world cannot just be" also means "God cannot just be," we respond that this knowledge is based upon the evidence of the world and is in essence a statement that the world makes about itself. The world says it is not self-sufficient; that matter "is" is not the bottom line. Therefore, it says that the world—and only the world—requires its cause; in other words, the fundamental fact of reality is: "God is."

b. The Objection to the Results of Creativity

To a restatement of the Kantian objection that we have no way of knowing if our minds are equipped for an accurate reading of reality, we would re-offer the evidence of our successful dealing with reality (cf. p.265). Let us also notice that the various stages of human knowing fit into a pattern which could well be characterized as the increasing awareness of truth as such. Notice, we begin with consciousness, awareness itself. Then, we become aware of ourselves. Then, we become aware of the world out there. Then, we become aware "that" it works. Then, we become aware of "how" it works. And, finally, we become aware of "why" it works, the reason for reason, the force behind forces—God—the whole truth, the truth in Himself. Without God, there is no truth.

c. The Truth of the Traditional Arguments from a Study of Nature at Large

In view of what we now know, we can see the truth of the traditional arguments from a study of nature at large (cf. p.36). Thomas was correct in his basic perception of the need for a "first" cause, the essence of all the five ways. These were indeed "demonstrations" of the existence of God and not "proofs" except in light of the creative nature of human knowing. In this light, it *is* true that an infinite regression of finite causes is impossible.

Now, we can also see that a higher *cannot* come from a lower; from nothing nothing can come. The apparent contradiction of this argument at the hands of evolution (cf. p.174) and materialism (cf. p.221) was only possible because it did not acknowledge the inherent capacities of matter as actualized by complex organization. In fact, the argument did well to ask how mindless matter could give rise to the mind that would one day study it. The evolutionary argument did well to ask how matter just happened to evolve into the fantastically complex beings who have come to understand it.

2. Objections to the Supporting Evidence
a. The Objection to the Idea

One objection to the supporting evidence would surely involve the critique of religiosity which claims that the believer is someone who cannot accept death or the challenge to make his own values in a world which offers none (cf. p.149). It might also be objected that there "just" are values worthy to pursue, God or no God. All the critics could argue that there are a number of people, and an increasing number, who are in no way positive about God, accept death, and still claim a purpose for their lives.

In the face of such objections, it is first to be pointed out that, in the absence of belief in He who "just" is, the insistence that there "just" are objective values is utterly without basis. Moreover, in view of everyone's certain death, not to mention the possible extinction of the race, nothing a man can be or do for himself or others makes an enduring difference. Thus, nothing is of ultimate importance. And, therefore, nothing is intrinsically good or even better. Finally, in the absence of anything greater than the person to give them value—to provide the reason they are of value—values are a matter of opinion certainly not binding on anyone but he who has proclaimed them. But, despite the "existential" willingness to accept this very fact (cf. p.227), it is impossible to proclaim values of one's own. To proclaim one's "personal" values is to deny the very objectivity that makes them worth the striving. Without God there is no value, and no purpose for life.

Therefore, life is an essentially pointless, unjust, cruel struggle which ends without a trace in the "outrage" of utter nothingness. But, since there must be more to life than this, there must be a God.

Of course, it is to be acknowledged that not everyone sees things this way. This, however, does not disprove the point. Since this perception requires sufficient maturity, it is not to be expected in everyone. What is important is the fact that those who attain a sufficient maturity do see things this way provided they are not prevented by an obstacle such as pride—the perception that one's own value is diminished by the existence of something superior[1]—or, on the other side of the same emotional coin, a lack of the self-confidence needed in order to affirm something unpopular. In other words, men may not see, but nature knows. This is obvious from the fact that today's world is filled with persons who either 1) attribute to their doings an uncritical importance, 2) live "vicariously" in the doings of others, 3) cynically critique everything, or 4) seek constant and complete "distraction" from life—or maybe all four.

b. The Objection to the Idea that the Feeling is Informative

At this point, we must address the predictable objection to the idea that the feeling (that life must have its purpose) is informative. It is plainly a judgment "about" which we are taking as a statement of what "is" (cf. p.255). In other words, upon what basis is the desire that life have a purpose, or even what is essentially the feeling that things are of value, to be taken as information of what is true of things objectively? After all, we spoke of the objectivity of values (of "goodness") only in terms of what could be expected from human nature (cf. p.264).

Actually, this is evidence enough. Since human nature has a need for purpose and value, if there is none, human life is necessarily unsatisfying. At best, the human spirit is restrained in what it can reach for, in the hopes it

---

1. Ironically, in his refusal to acknowledge the existence of God, the person denies the very being that gives him being, and the only thing that gives him worth.

can have, in the joys it can know. Therefore, the reality that gives man this spirit must be judged a senseless thing. Even worse, it should be judged a great paradox—something that should not be but is. Thus, the true bottom line of belief in God is: "reality makes sense."

c. The Truth of the Traditional Arguments from a Study of the Soul

We can now see the truth of the traditional arguments from a study of the soul (cf. p.35). Since the sensibility of reality requires something that can satisfy man's necessary longings, which certainly include immortality, the reality of this longing is a sure sign that its object already exists. Moreover, what else but the perfection of a share in God's life could ever satisfy the human spirit that always wants more—a human spirit that must have been made to want all that it can have?

The truth of the moral argument for the existence of God (cf. p.146) is to be seen in the outrageousness of its denial. Without God, there is no *reason* to respect another's rights, and less for self-sacrifice. Without the Fatherhood of God, the brotherhood of man is not to be imposed upon the opinions of anyone else.

* * *

In closing the apologetic for God *per se,* let us point out that all the arguments state what is self-evident to the person of sufficient and *superior* maturity. This is evident in the wider expanse of what he can explain. He is the man highest up the mountain slope who, looking behind him, sees in the distance a lake his companions cannot see. If he tells them about it and they deny that it is there, all he can do is to help them to get where he is so they will see it too.

Section IV: The Christian Conception of God

Having stated the case for belief in God *per se,* we can move on to an apologetic for the God in whom Christians believe.

A) Belief in a Creator

The apologetic for the Christian God begins with proper proof that He is the Creator.

To a great extent, the case for God the Creator has already been made. When we examined the essence and necessity of the doctrine of creation (cf. p.307), we saw that materialism means that if God exists, He is the Creator—the Creator of matter. If matter was self-sufficient, God would be superfluous. Therefore, it is clear that the Cause of the world is its Creator.

B) Knowledge of God

Having made the case for the Christian idea that God is the Creator, it is next for us to examine the equally Christian idea that He can be known in the things He has made. As we have seen, this involves the *via negativa* and the analogy of being (cf. .49).

But, these ideas have surely had a difficult history. Even before Kant critiqued the idea that we can learn about something outside the world by reflecting upon something in it (cf. p.146), certain medieval thinkers had already rejected the idea that God can be described scientifically (cf. p. 98). Lately, linguistic philosophy has denied that the word "God" has meaning on the grounds it has no referent (cf. 163).

It is first to be stated that God, the Cause of the world and its Creator is, for us, a concept. And no concepts have referents (cf. .256). This does not mean that they "mean" nothing; indeed, concepts provide knowledge as nothing else can.

Besides, nowadays, many "things" that science describes have no referents. Indeed, as we have seen, reflection on the facts has already led scientists to infer the existence of things which are nothing like anything we can see. These defy exact definition to an even greater degree than many concepts. Moreover, since belief in God is based upon reflection on the whole of one's experience, of the whole world, the idea of God should be more complex than any other that man can conceive. This hardly makes it meaningless; though it may defy exact definition to a degree that far surpasses other concepts, it remains possible to say what it is, especially in terms of what it is not.

This is the *via negativa*. It is the simplest expression of what is actually a positive conception of God. It presumes a certain similarity between the created and the Creator. It does so safely. Since God is the source of all that is and can be, in order to create, He had to draw upon Himself. Therefore, everything resembles God to some extent—to the extent that it is good. And, any truth tells us "about" God.

But, we cannot know God as He is. In the essential fact that God is self-sufficient, it is clear that God and the world are essentially different.

This, however, does not dispute the analogy of being. Since it amounts to imagining what can be, it tells us what God already is—at least.[2] And, as our ability to imagine improves, so does our ability to conceive God.

---

2. For the record, it should be stated that Duns Scotus' critique of analogy (cf. footnote p.49) was largely a problem of language. If there is a similarity between created and Creator, they do share "something," but not the same thing.

C) The Divine Attributes

Having described the origins of the knowledge of God, we can move to a look at some of what it is that we can know.

1. The Personhood of God

a. The Assumed Attribute

The first fact that we must consider was not only assumed in the first listings of divine attributes[3] but it was implicitly stated in our every mention of a Creator. Plainly, the idea of a Creator implies a deliberate act of the kind characteristic only of persons. Nonetheless, an assumption will no longer suffice. Not only is the personhood of God questioned by some of the most venerable religious traditions, it is questioned for a good reason: God is beyond anything in the world.

"Beyond" though He may be, God is at least as great as anything of which His creation is capable. But, is not the greatest thing in the world a person? Indeed, nothing tells us more about what God must be like as a person whose characteristics are invoked in explaining the very fact of creation—a divine decision and plan. To the objection that personhood involves matter, we are surely entitled to respond that there is more than one way to do things. Therefore, even though God is surely beyond a "person" as we are "persons," He is more like us than rocks or un-self-conscious animals. He is at least a person.

b. The "Fatherhood" of God

The question of the "Fatherhood" of God is not so simple. God is more than a person—and surely more than what is normally identified in any one sex. After all, the characteristic of motherhood, not to mention those of femininity, also originate in God. (God is not like specific things; they are like Him in so much as they are good.[4]) But, concepts of God's personhood require some concretization. Therefore, since God is first conceived as ruler and provider, characteristics normally identified with paternity, it should not be surprising that Christianity came to call God "Father." The question of whether it will continue to depends largely upon the future of the traditional sexual roles. This is not a question to be settled on the grounds of Christian doctrine solely.

---

3. For the sake of completeness, it should be stated that, in modern times, God has also come to be described in terms of "antinomies"—apparent opposites simultaneously affirmed, e.g. God is "transcendent," i.e. infinitely far from our experience, yet "immanent," utterly close. In fact, it is to be noticed that spirituality often involves antinomes, or "dichotomies," especially those which describe sin and providence.

4. In other words, He does not so much contain the perfect tree (cf. p.60), but the imaginably perfect tree tells us something about Him.

2. *The General Attributes*
a. Another Assumed Attribute

Before we move on to consider the general attributes, we must surely say something about the attribute that was even more assumed than God's personhood—His "oneness," the fact that there is only one God. The testimony of the more developed faiths, belief in one God originates in the knowledge that reality is one. (It is also the testimony of mature spiritual experience; there is only one God experienced in prayer.) This, together with the principle of economy, leaves no reason to believe that there is more than one God.

b. The Other General Attributes

All the other general attributes follow from the insufficiency of matter and, therefore, the self-sufficiency of its Maker—its uncreated Creator (cf. p. 49).

Obviously, God is eternal and immortal. Moreover, it is clear that He does not experience time as we do. Our experience of time is based on matter in motion, involving a definite succession of events, only one of which can happen at once. God is not so limited. Instead, it is to be imagined that God experiences everything at once.[5]

God is obviously immaterial. Historically, this involved the notion that God is "pure spirit." We must still conceive Him without the limitations inherent in matter.

For all the historical reasons, God's self-sufficiency is His simplicity. Notably, His creation resembles Him by means of complexity.

As the source of all that is or can be, God is indeed perfect. What could we even imagine that He is not? Indeed, the very possibility that it could have been imagined must have come from somewhere. In this, even the ontolgoical argument has its truth (cf. p. 35).

As perfect, God is obviously all-good. Who (What) could be more desirable?

Since we can always imagine more of any finite quality, this inexhaustible more is God's infinity. The inexhaustible more of any finite "quantity" is His immensity.

As perfect and infinite, God is immutable. How could He improve; where would He get it? But, let it be clear; God's immutability does not mean (and has never meant) that His life is somehow "static," without activity. Man's life is greater when there is a variety of activities, when life is "dynamic." Therefore, God's life is, in human terms, more dynamic than static. Proof is

---

5. Thus, He sees all things at once. He views the parade from the top of a tall building; unlike the people on the street, He sees the beginning, middle and end at the same time.

present in the fact that creation implies some action on God's part.

3. The Particular Perfections
a. God's Knowledge and Power

Although God is beyond specifics, it remains true that ideas of His particular perfections do offer data as to what He is—at least. Not coincidentally, the two that have historically attracted the most attention are essential to our understanding of God as a person—and as God.

Obviously, ideas of God's knowledge and power should begin with a look of human knowing (and thinking) and doing (and willing) if they were perfect (cf. p.21).

But, this does not mean that God's powers are like man's.

As we have seen, man knows creation through experience. This is not how God knows. In creating, He has drawn on Himself. Thus, God knows creation as He knows Himself—immediately.[6]

God's will is also "immediate." His will is action. Man must put his will into action; and there is much he cannot do.

God can do anything *that can be done*. This stipulation refers to the logically possible (and therefore excludes the creation of a square circle), and also what is positive, what *can* be done. Thus, to the question: "can God make a rock too big for Him to move," the answer is: "no, neither can he make a mistake."

b. The Truth of Spiritual Experience

It is clear that spirituality is faith extended (cf. p.270).

If God knows everything, He surely knows the thoughts of every person. He can therefore be addressed.

He can be petitioned for favors. In the light of materialism, this would primarily be the natural expression of oneself to God as part of His ongoing address which would rightfully conclude with a statement of faith in providence.[7]

He can hear statements of repentance. Materialism notwithstanding, this would be a statement of regret, and resolve, as part of one's ongoing address of Him to whom one cannot lie.

He can receive thanksgiving. Essentially, this would be giving thanks for the gift of life and, with it, the promise of eternal life. What would better be

---

6. This was the thinking of Thomas; see his *S. Th.* I, q.14. It was a response to the problem of what he saw as the repugnance of the idea that God would allow Himself to be affected by an outside fact.

7. Obviously, the historical practice of the recitation of formal prayers as a form of petitioning is no longer recommended. Nonetheless, to the extent that prayers formal or repeated serve to articulate or encourage certain spiritual thoughts, such prayers retain their value.

man's first prayer and last? Of course, thanksgiving will and should involve anything, however specific, that we are thankful for. Nonetheless, as a point of faith, God should also be thanked for any good that can be found in any situation that occasions prayer.

But what would be better than that He receive praise? Like thanksgiving, however, praise states our true relationship to God and thus contributes to our spiritual growth. Thanks to divine determinism, we are spared from considering what was always the wrong idea that God requires or, less, needs either praise or thanksgiving.

God is most profoundly the object of adoration and contemplation. Such meditation generates the ideas upon which become a person's spirituality. More often, it simply results in the "experience" of God.

Historically, this experience has been considered the result of a miracle. (It has even been described as the hearing of voices or the seeing of visions.) Now imagining such an intervention is no longer necessary, nor less in evidence. But, prayer is not a "monolog"; it is dialogical in view of the fact that everything that happens is an expression of God's will and bespeaks Him to the extent it is understood. Indeed, this is one of the principal truths whose knowledge is properly understood as the goal and definition of spirituality. A more complete definition would involve the idea that spirituality is the knowledge to think the right thing at the right time. A more complete goal would be an acute awareness of God, His love, and His care for "me" at every moment. The truths of spirituality give a person "peace"; as circumstances permit, they give him "joy."

3) "The" Special Characteristic of God's Goodness
a. The Motive of Creation

Surpassing justice, love is "the" special characteristic of God's goodness. Just as persons are the greatest of created things—meaning that God is at least a person—the greatest thing about persons is love and this means that God is at least a person of the greatest love we can imagine. (Let us note that this was not always obvious. In times past, power, especially the power to destroy one's enemies, was what made a person great. But, in time, in Jesus, love, especially as manifest in a love of one's enemies, was finally recognized to be the greatest thing about a person.) Indeed, love is our explanation of creation—God's love as manifest in His desire to share His divine life with others.

At this point, mention is owed to the classical idea that God actually created in order to demonstrate His greatness, or "glory," at least in part. We can now admit that the ancients believed that God created *solely* for this reason. But, time marched on and now we know that "showing-off," or less seeking worship, is hardly a manifestation of spirit at its best. Nor is self-sufficiency compatible with the notion that God has any sort of "need." Instead, since God is responsible for all that we are and ever will be, it is clear that He gets absolutely nothing from us and never will. Thus, creation bespeaks a love we can only begin to imagine. And what better bespeaks God's greatness, or glory?

b. The Means of Creation

Having spoken of the motive of creation, we can now describe the means.

First, let us admit: creation *ex nihilo* (cf. p.56) is difficult to conceive (cf. p.143). It is certainly nothing man can do.

It is something only God can do. But, God, the self-sufficient source of all other being must still sustain creation. (Otherwise, He created another self-sufficient being. But this is a contradiction in terms. God cannot make another God.) Therefore, in the final analysis, the stuff of creation is God's power. And where His power is, He is. Things exist because God has given of His own stuff—He has given of Himself. (We have already seen that there can be no distinction between God and the divine substance, cf. p. 49). Thus, the fundamental truth (cf. p.334) is the whole truth: "God is." Not only does He know all things "as" He knows Himself, He knows all things because they "are" Himself. His will is action because "it" is the stuff which is affected.

This is not pantheism. Pantheism asserts that God is the world. Neither is it pan-an-theism which asserts that world is God but not all of Him (cf. p. 312).This is not what is suggested. Although creation is made of God's stuff, it is not God as He is in Himself. Matter manifests only some of what God is, though more and more of Him through the creative power of organization. Thus, there is a definite distinction between God and the world; the world is some of God manifesting some of what He is.

Chapter II: An Apologetic for Jesus' Principal Teachings

Section I: The Idea of Salvation

Now that we have considered an apologetic for the existence of God, and also an apologetic for His Christian conception, we must move on to an apologetic for Jesus' principal teachings: the coming of the kingdom and the call of love—the idea of salvation. Said to be "almost unsuspendable" (cf. p.218), we must now consider whether these ideas *do* follow from faith generally. But, as should be expected, their apologetic will also depend upon the sense that can be made of them in the light of materialism.

A) The Coming of the Kingdom

The Christian hope has always been immortal life with God. Initially conceived a "kingdom" where God was king, the Christian expectation was classically discussed in terms of the beatific vision (cf. p. 87), and a sharing of—or participation in—divine life.

It is clear that nothing else can be man's intended destiny. Not created for nothing—and not for nothingness—he was created such that nothing else could ever satisfy. Human nature always wants more; it will only be satisfied by all that there can be, i.e. God. Not able to be God, the "sharing" of His life is the best that we can do.

It is also clear that the sharing of God's life was well considered the "beatific vision." Sight is the most informative of the senses; to see is to know. And knowledge gives a greater life. To know is to see, and to enjoy, what is good.

Therefore, to enjoy God's life we will need to see Him.

But, we cannot see what we are not ontologically like. Thus, to see God, we will need to be like Him; we will need to be remade out of God's own stuff as it is in itself. But, let it be clear; this will not be the making of another God—which God cannot do—it is simply the gift of *some* of what He is in Himself. It is, however, a true *sharing* of divine life. Not just a "participation," it makes man "part" of God. Moreover, since the seer is now made of the same thing which is seen, human destiny is "union" with God. A conclusion of Christian mysticism (cf. p.203)—and an insight of Hindu thought (cf. p.269)—this had always been an implication of the fact that God is the source of all being.

It should now be clear that immortality is in no way natural. The natural immortality of the purely spiritual soul has already been disproved. In its place, we have the will of God to recast the person in a new form, one not limited by the capacities of matter. God remembers the "pattern" which is the essence of who the person was in matter. He reproduces this pattern in the stuff of Himself. Immediately, the person sees God; in a moment, he learns more than all the experience in the world could ever have taught him. He becomes all that he can be; in God, he gains the greatest life that he can have.

B) The Call of Love

Just as it is clear that man was made for eternal life, it is also clear that earthly life must serve some eternal purpose. God does nothing for nothing. For this same reason, earthly life must involve something that could not have been accomplished by divine fiat—something that must involve man. That this involves love is evident in its self-evident superiority. Clearly, love, and the maturity it bespeaks, is the greatest human development.

Here, perhaps, is the importance of love. Since love is man's greatest development, it also describes his similarity to the God whose life he hopes to share. Thus, love describes his ability to see, to know, the God who is love. And, the better you can see, the more you know, and the more you know, the more you get—the richer will be your experience of God.

There is no reason that the eternal experiences could not differ. Even though the person will be unlimited (in terms of matter) so that he can see God as he is, he will not be infinite in the sense that he can see all that God is; this would mean that he *is* all that God is. Therefore, it is surely to be expected that different persons will see God differently—from different angles. And, for this same reason, the quality of perceptions could also differ.

If the above is indeed a possibility for the purpose of mortal, material life, the classical Catholic belief in the "ontological" character of salvation is clearly vindicated (cf. p.103). Eternity *is* contingent upon the being a being becomes.

Section II: The Problem of Determinism

A) The Problem

Salvation may be contingent upon the being a being becomes, but we are still faced with the serious problem of determinism. Despite the reality of personal responsibility, a person is still the product of events for which he was not responsible. Thus, what could be the purpose of earthly life?

B) The "Effect" of Earthly Life

1. The "Effect"

Plainly, any attempt to determine the purpose of earthly life would most profitably begin with a look at what it accomplishes—its "effect."

Clearly, the effect of earthly life is the creation of a person whose degree of maturity becomes his capacity to see God. The involvement of man is self-determination—his personal responsibility for who he becomes.

2. The Value of the Effect

Perhaps we have found the answer to the problem of mortal, material life. We believe that God created in order to share His divine life with others. In order for these others to be truly "other," i.e. something distinct from Him, they could not be the simple expressions of His will. If they were, they would not share any semblance of the self-sufficiency which is the essence of divine life. Therefore, unable to create another God, God created others in such a way that they would participate in their own creation. Drawing on divine life as it is given in human nature, self-determination gives men a personal responsibility for who they are. With maturity—the ability of eternal life—the result of their self-determination, they simultaneously attain the form of self-sufficiency available to creatures. The importance of self-sufficiency is to be seen in the powerful human desire to be my own man, to do it myself.

3. The "Context" of the Effort

a. The Idea

It is clear that the "effort" requires its "context"; in other words, the self-determination of creatures could not begin with nothing. God needed to make creatures whose bodies would bear the potential of becoming something more.

Also, He had to place them within a world of which they were part. Life in the world is the surrogate for the life "in," i.e. "in union with" God for which man is destined.

The world needed to be the product of evolution because nature needed to be imbued with "becoming."

b. A Tentative, Partial Solution to the Problem of Evil

The requirement of a context provides us the beginning of a solution to the problem of evil. Upon reflection, it becomes clear that all of the basic evils (cf. p.294) are in some way required by the effort of becoming.

Imperfection is obviously required by the simple fact that perfection leaves no space for becoming. Imperfection makes life a struggle; and it is struggle that makes man give himself to the project of his life. This is experienced in the pride which is felt when effort has been expended, when adversity has been overcome.

Becoming requires impermanence because it requires change. It requires circumstantiality because if everything that happens in the world were co-ordinated to co-operate with the highest levels of what matter can do, the "perfection" of matter would already have been reached. (Of course, this would not be perfection *per se*. No existence dependent upon a lower could ever attain such a state; the very fact that the creations of matter are sustained by motion makes clear that they are mutable—and vulnerable.) Circumstantiality makes nature impersonal. After all, if not all can go right, some must go wrong. Therefore, the idea of statistical evil has its validity (cf. p.296).

In man, imperfection means limitedness—the limitation of all his powers. What else reveals human imperfection? Limitedness means fallibility. What else but the failure of some power reveals its limitation?

Fallibility means frailty. What is frailty but the failure of some power? Frailty involves death because material life is meant to end. And death requires a man to take his life seriously. It involves aging because becoming involves growing—the growth of the whole person. And, when aging becomes dying, it presents man with his death while he is still alive.[1]

Frailty involves suffering because life in the world is God's surrogate. When it reflects God well, it is experienced as good. But, when it reflects God poorly, it must be experienced as bad. In other words, life in the world must reflect God "really." Therefore, as it does so poorly, it will be experienced as the opposite of what He really is. Thus, immense sufferings bespeak the immense happiness awaiting us with God.

Attractive though it may seem, the above solution to the problem of evil was indeed tentative and partial. It did not speak to the disparity of experiences that people have. After all, some suffer so much more than others with little or no positive effect on their lives. Lives are ruined (or made) by unforeseeable, uncontrollable circumstances of all sorts. This is the real problem of evil. In view of divine determinism, it has only gotten worse.

---

1. It is possible that progress in modern physiology may one day allow man to manipulate the rate of his aging. A good thing within the limited context of what earthly life can offer, the essential imperfection of matter would not appear to permit progress to halt aging completely. If this should happen, however, it is to be expected that progress would also involve the maturity to let aging take its course—a choice for true immortality. (Of course, the above will not be the first moral issue—nor the last—to be created by progress scientific or otherwise.)

Section III: The Problem of Divine Determinism

A) The Problem that Remains

Only confirmed by the apologetic, divine determinism is still a problem. Not only does it aggravate the problem of evil, but it complexifies the question of the purpose of mortal, material life. After all, if God has determined the whole course of history, what are we to think of the fact that He has determined a disparity of maturities?

B) "Universal Salvation"

1. A Look at the Alternatives

Our attempt to resolve the problem of divine determinism should surely begin with a look at the alternatives immediately available.

1) It might be suggested that God's plan called for the creation of only so many people, and not all those who were ever born. Therefore, since the abandonment of the natural immortality of the soul allows us to speak about a painless oblivion, might it be that those who do not attain a certain minimum maturity just die?

Surely the answer is no. We have no basis to speak about, much less determine, a minimum maturity. Moreover, the idea ignores the fact that billions who did not make it still suffered, wanted immortality, and were in essence victims of their circumstances. What of our primitive ancestors? What of those who were loved by others who did make it? No, it is plainly unthinkable that God would have brought persons into the world in order to be fodder for others.

2) In view of the classical idea that eternity is experienced in different degrees (cf. p. 87), might it be that everyone will experience God according to the degree permitted by the sight made possible by their love?

Again the answer would clearly seem to be no. It would scarcely seem possible that God would stratify eternity—for eternity. The argument that everyone would be perfectly happy in their state does not change the fact that there would be no reason for the disparity—not even a just one. Moreover, a stratified society is hardly what humanity is working toward in this world; it is less to be considered man's destiny. Lastly,

3) Appealing to a classical idea, might it be that some sort of a purgatory will transform everyone, equalizing them before they take up the sight of God?

No, not even this will do. Although a transformation is indeed ahead, it is impossible that such a transformation will accomplish what the world did not. If such a process had always been available, it would trivialize life in this world. This is impossible because life in the world must exist for some essential purpose.

2. The Idea of Universal Salvation
a. Taking Seriously the Corporate Nature of Humanity

What have we? We have the need to find some essential purpose for life in the world. Yet, we would also appear to require some way to assert the ultimate equality of all humanity. Perhaps the time has come to take seriously the corporate nature of humanity (cf. p.207). After all, humanity *is* in some sense "one," where the life of every one is owed to the existence of others.

Plainly, man is the product of people who came before him. Not only is he descendant from others, he is the product of what they have done—and learned. For example, were it not for the struggles of the most brutish cavemen, language would not have developed and men could not have shared a single idea. Were it not for others alive today, man could not be all that he is. For example, the life of modern man requires countless people to do their jobs. He is profoundly affected by those he knows. Moreover, love requires someone to love. And man is more when he loves. He would be all that he can be if love made everyone desirous to share what they have, can do and are, if all people were truly one.

In God, this is exactly how it will be. Unlimited in their interest and ability to share themselves with one another, God's people will truly be one, one family where every member shares everything he has with every other as families do—as families are meant to. Humanity will be what it was meant to be, a family working together for the eternity of all. Thus, salvation is universal.

b. The Working of Universal Salvation
Let us take a closer look.

Christianity has always held that all persons are made in God's "image." Unlike things which resemble God partially, and only in His absence, persons resemble Him wholly. In other words, in persons, the essential who of what God is is present in finite form. Persons know they exist. This is what gives them value themselves. And, this is what makes them "others." Moreover, as others, persons are also unique; in other words, every person is a unique image of God, unlike any other.

In eternity, each person will see the unique image of God that each of them is. Thus, they will love each other, sharing with each other what each one sees of God. In other words, just as the person's experience of life in *this* world is greater because of what he gets from many others, his experience of life in the world to come will be greater because of what the person will get from everyone else. Like the sharing of knowledge now, the sharing of what everyone sees of God—their very selves—will diminish no one.

Indeed, since everyone will be unlimited in his ability to give and to receive, everyone will have all that is available and, mutually enriched, they (we) will go on from there together to explore the infinity of who God is.

c. The "Why" of Universal Salvation

In attempting to determine "why" universal salvation is the structure of our destiny, let us consider what it accomplishes.

Not only does it give everyone an equal share of God's life—while retaining an eternal importance for the life we live now—it does so through a giving of self which we have already come to consider the greatest fact of God's life. Thus, just as determinism is God's way of creating beings that share His self-sufficiency (the essence of His life), the determined creation of *many* beings is His way of sharing the self-giving which is the greatest aspect of this essence.

Universal salvation also has something new to say about God as He is in essence. Must it not be that God is something more than one person could even begin to experience? Actually, we have already discussed the fact that reality is enriched by "societies" (cf. p.248). Surely, it was not to be thought that these were entirely new to existence when first they existed in matter. Indeed, as the possible products of matter, they already existed in God (cf. p.337). In other words, the God who is the source of persons is also the source of the "romance" and "teamwork" and everything else that can exist because there is more than one person. This means that God is more than "a" person. Thus, to share His life most fully, He had to make something else that is more than a person. Not able to make another God, He made a family of finite persons. Our eventual union will know His "super-personality."

But, the super-personality of God does *not* mean that eternity will somehow involve the individual's assimilation into a super-personal humanity in which individual identity is lost. Though this is a feature of Hinduism and Buddhism (cf. p 269)—which is even suggested by Teilhard's idea of the "ultra-man" (cf. p.207)—societies do not have a higher ontological status than their parts. If this were not obvious philosophically, it would still be evident in the fact that if the individual could not expect to survive his death—and know it—he would have no motive to work for eternity and creation would not work.

3. The Rightness of the Idea

Universal salvation is the right idea. It offers an essentiality for earthly life while making sure that divine determinism does no injustice to any of God's people. It saves us from saying that the infinity of His love could allow the unequal distribution of gifts—eternally.

To those who would object that universal salvation does not do justice to those who will contribute "more" to the making of eternity, let them be reminded that not only does love surpass justice, but love is not love if it was done for the sake of the reward. And, a "faith" that stops at justice exists at the level of belief in God as "another" cause (cf. p.269); its attendant spirituality is called "self-righteousness." (It would also betray the failure to experience the "better" as "richer.")

Moreover, since everyone has something special to contribute—and just what they were created to contribute—justice is done. Indeed, in the special-ness of every individual's contribution to the eternal exploration of God, we find the ultimate (if not only) truth to the insistence that all men are created equal, and good. It is the reason for man's interest "in" others (cf. p.266). Thus, the psychologists were correct, maturity *is* the ability to pursue the greatest, most long-term goods (cf. p.261). It is also to be noted that love, man's call, produces his greatest happiness both in heaven and on earth.

To those who would argue that this means that love is essentially selfish, let it be clear that interest in others is still founded in their goodness as an object of interest. This states the essential truth that a man's fulfillment is union with the family of which he was meant to be part. (That a man's love does not involve absolute giving—without receiving—is a simple implica-tion of the fact that only God is absolutely self-sufficient.) Other "outside" interests (cf. p.271) state the essential truth that man's fulfillment is union with God—the source of all that is.

In sum, universal salvation responds to the great question: why did God make the world? Why didn't He just make heaven? We now understand that, from His point of view, this is just what He did. Of course, from man's point of view, the kingdom is still coming; it is coming as humanity contrib-utes to its own creation as the family that we will be.

C) The Divine Plan

1. The Specifics of the Plan

a. The Idea

Now that we know why we are here, it should be possible to deduce some of the specifics of the plan by which the creation of the human family is actually taking place.

Attentive to the fact that the plan involved not only a purpose, but also an end and the path by which this end is to be reached (cf. p.313), it is first for us to speak somewhat more specifically about its purpose, and then to infer its end and the path it must be taking. Let it be stated that this is what *we* must do; God surely conceived of the entire idea from eternity in a single instant.

We begin with God's decision to share His life. Thereupon, He conceived the family best suited to do so.[2] Then, He decided the best way to create this family, a way which would involve its greatest participation in the process. This was the design of matter. But, since He had already conceived the family best suited to share His life—and therefore the greatest maturity anyone and everyone would attain—the design of matter also involved His determination of universal history, and therein the design of the initial moment.[3] This was creation. From our point of view, it is now in process. God and we are creating the family He conceived from all-eternity. This is the object of providence.

b. Final Reflections on Evil

It is clear that providence is no guarantee that everyone—or anyone—will come to a happy earthly end. And, it is a fact of life that this does not happen. Nonetheless, even in the face of the most terrible tragedies, we can still insist upon the wisdom of God's will. As they affect history, tragedies are part of the plan by which He is bringing about the family best suited to share His life. And the make-up of this family will wonderfully and equally enrich every member of it. Moreover, suffering does have its special way of making a man who he becomes. And this will provide a diversity to the human family which will ultimately work for the benefit of all.

Thus, to the question: "why me," the answer is: God chose you for this role in the creation of eternity; it was the best way to create the "you" and "us" He wanted us to be. If it seems unfair that others were required to contribute less of what is borne through suffering, let us remember that suffering will be richly redeemed in eternity—where it will be completely healed and understood. Let us also remember that creation was conceived to involve the least suffering that would still attain the eternity which awaits us.

2. The Human Role in the Divine Plan
a. The Variety of Roles

In speaking of divine determinism, and what is certainly the sure success of the divine plan, it may have seemed that a certain complacency is somehow recommended. After all, if the best possible sharing of God's life is already man's destiny, why does he need to do anything?

---

2. The obviously large number of persons that this has already involved (billions) is simply testimony to the greatness of God. Of course, God's greatness was already evident in serious reflection upon any of His attributes.

3. Thus, history would be describable as the mathematical result of what matter would do given an infinite number of trials.

The answer is simple: Just as determinism does not work except *through* self-determinism (cf. p.279), divine determinism does not work except *through* human action. Therefore, man must know that he is in the position of making his destiny richer or poorer. From God's point of view, the best is inevitably on its way; from man's, what the best is is still to be decided—by him.

In view of the working of universal salvation, it is clear that—initially—the more loving, more mature person has more to contribute to a greater human ability to share God's life. This is a greater "direct" role in the building-up of eternity.

In view of this, it is obvious that anyone who plays a greater part in bringing about more maturity in the lives of more others has a greater "instrumental" role.

Of course, everyone's role is essential to God's grand plan. Given the inter-relation of causes, the slightest causes contribute to the most weighty effects.

Moreover, short, painful, apparently useless or even destructive lives serve the purpose of substantiating the human struggle.

Nonetheless, if a person desires a greater role—the natural outcome of the love of self and others which is itself the love of God—his love is his guiding principle. He should ask: what is love—at least by advancing it? The basis of Christian morality always,[4] it is now to be stated that there is no reason for an absolute distinction between moral and other actions. ("Moral" is a matter of degree.) Therefore, love is the proper first principle of all decisions.

b. The Basis of Christian Action

As the proper first principle of all decisions, the principle of love is absolute; it is the only one that is. But, since different courses of action will bring about different results—regardless of our good intentions—actions prove themselves right or wrong. So much for "relativism" (cf. p.131). Moreover, since actions lend themselves to generalization, principles of action can and should be articulated.

Though man must love himself, the love of self is not doing whatever one wants. Not everything a person wants is good for him—good for his

---

4. The basis of Christian morality has also been called doing God's "will." Although the idea of divine determinism can surely be understood to have complexified this once simple notion, it would remain true that Christian action is doing God's will as long as it were understood that God's "will" is an inference of what He would do, hypothetically, in any given situation.

growth.[5] Thus, there is no saying that the love of self legitimizes anything that 1) does *not* involve others (such as the use of consciousness altering drugs—an "escapism" that defeats the purpose of earthly life[6]), or 2) involves their "consenting" participation (such as the abuse of sexuality—which is destructive of goods meant to be used for greater purposes, q.v. p.402).[7] Such ideas ignore the fact that maturity has definite characteristics which are almost always helped or hurt by certain practices or experiences. This is human nature. It involves a limited validity of "natural law" (cf. p. 75). But, the specific dictates of natural law must be judged according to their actual, dependable effect on man's maturity.

Though man must love others, the love of others is not giving them everything they want. Not everything others want is good for them. Therefore, the "golden rule" would better read: "do unto others as you should want them to do unto you."

If the above principles can be said to "regulate" the first principle of love, the following is surely the first principle of its "qualification."

Though love knows no bounds—and involves many specific "ideals"—the person is limited in what he can do; he has only so much to give. And he has needs of his own. Furthermore, he is first responsible for himself—the one person whose life and growth he can affect immediately. If he does not address this responsibility he will destroy himself and add to the problems which his fellows must address. Therefore, even though he is called to grow—which always involves struggle—the person is called to do all he can "joyfully."

The person must also recognize that he is a product of his century with the increased needs that this does involve. The increase of needs has been the principal stimulus of human progress—a good thing—and new needs are not to be denied just because our fathers did not have them.

Because of human limitedness, charity understandably begins at home, with the specific causes closest to the heart of him who has only so much to give. This is the principle of "proximity." It combines with the principle of "effectiveness" in justifying the person's concern for his family, community

5. For this same reason, it is clear that thoughts and feelings (such as hatred, envy or jealousy, etc.) are not amoral. Thoughts and feelings reflect a person, though they do so to a lesser degree than do his actions. Those that reflect a person least are those occasioned by the human need to react and do not linger.

6. Of course, the use of consciousness altering drugs is also a problem because they put the person "out of control," are normally habit-forming and/or critically injurious to the person's health.

7. The abuse of sexuality is also a problem because of its effect on society, the likelihood of emotional injury, and the possible involvement of an innocent unborn other.

and problems right in front of his face. But, the principle of proximity is qualified by the relative importance of other causes far from home.

Of course, the demands of justice will "normally" serve as the lower limit of what a person should consider his obligations to everyone. But, as has long been acknowledged, especially in the case of the starving man who steals some bread, even justice is a "norm" that can be qualified.

Another implication of human limitedness is the fact that no one can pursue all the goods worth pursuing. Therefore, a person must choose some and forgo others. But, circumstances and his particular abilities considered, he should normally strive to balance his pursuits. And, any idea that he should pursue only those goods that directly serve the basic needs of others ignores that fact that human growth needs to involve the whole man. It is also short-sighted. After all, science has made so much available to so many. The arts have inspired so many in so many ways. A "variety" of goods is worth pursuing.

The fact that there is a variety of goods, some of which compete, proves that Aristotle was right: the "mean," "moderation" is normally best (cf. p. 60). Naturally, the mean will differ from person to person and it will change as persons and society mature.

Of course, this is not to say that the mean should be supreme. A helpful guide to what is good for a day-to-day approach to human problems, the fact remains that situations sometimes call for extremism.

Still another aspect of human limitedness is the fact that man cannot know with certainty what is best. Trying to decide involves more principles.

The first was constantly implied by any attempt to decide what is best, actually, what is better: do what will bring about the "greatest good" (cf. p.133). This also involves the pragmatic principle: "do what works" (cf. p.163). Where nothing will work: "do what can be done."

The greatest good principle does away with the classical conflict between "legalism" (which resolves doubt in favor of law) and "laxism" (which sides with human freedom).

The greatest good principle also eliminates the need to justify action by the principle of "double effect"—the idea that one can never do anything in any way bad for a good end *unless* it can be argued that one was really doing something good whose "side-effect" achieved the end. An informed analysis of the true end of any act would clearly save a person from this casuistry.[8] Implicitly affirmed is the principle that "the end justifies the

---

8. Nonetheless, the principle of double effect remains a principle of practical value. So does the principle of "proportionality"; in other words, the severity of the response should normally be proportionate to the seriousness of the situation.

means." It is affirmed provided that the effect of the means is included in an evaluation of the true end of any act.

It is clear; consequences do determine right and wrong (cf. p.134). And, in evaluating consequences, those of the longest run have the most weight.

Any evaluation of the consequences must include the weight of the principle of "legitimization." Following Kant, we must acknowledge that if a person insists upon his right to act in a certain way, to declare himself an exception to a certain rule—on the basis of nothing other than his own judgment of himself—he must acknowledge that everyone else has this right. Therefore, if he sees that "if everyone did it" the world would be worse, he should not do it. This has been the good motive of many people who honored a rule they did not believe applied to them personally, on this occasion.[9] The obvious basis of traffic laws, the principle of legitimization is profoundly seen in the importance of telling the truth.[10]

Nonetheless, as any society matures, and more people become better able to make good decisions on their own, its leaders should review its law with a mind to generalize or reduce specific precepts. Already a principle of the discipline of children—who grow in their ability to see shades of gray—it should not be surprising that it would also apply to society at large.

3. Reflections on What We Can Expect

Since the divine plan does involve a definite path and end, a knowledge of its purpose should inform a reflection of what we can expect from it.

a. Reflections on History and Its Future

What can be expected from the future is surely to be informed by a look at the past. It is here that we see the pattern of progress which is all but certain to continue.

As a prolog of sorts, we must first address the question of whether history has really involved progress. Convinced that this is a "sick society" about to blow itself up, some might argue that the history of man bespeaks not progress but ruin.

Tempting though the above may be, especially in view of the more terrible things that modern man has done, this objection does not reveal a sufficient appreciation for what history has actually accomplished. As we noted, we are descendant from the most un-Christian of brutes (cf. p.348). As we saw, slowly there succeeded the several historical "ages" which describe the emergence of civilization (cf. p.170).

---

9. This necessity is a microcosm of the individual's sometime need to forbid himself certain things for fear of "habit."

10. Still, it should be said: the principle of truth is not absolute. For example, withholding the truth is often a justified act of compassion.

Progress can also be dated from more recent times. Though some see decline since the Golden Age of Greece or the Renaissance, it is to be remembered that during these periods, life, for the vast majority of people, was an almost mindless struggle for survival. Most people were little more than the brutes of our most ancient ancestry. The world is hardly perfect now, but more people are more developed than ever before. More are more thoughtful, and more feeling. More are more loving. More people have more "rights" that are respected by more others. Of course, human nature being what it is, to get one thing is to want another, and to be more developed is to need more. Therefore, popular patience with the state of things may never have been less. But this has been a result of progress. and it will help to make sure that progress will continue.

Now, this does not mean that serious problems do not remain, problems potentially more serious because of the power that progress has put in human hands. Nonetheless, it is to be expected that with more power will come the increased ability to deal with it, a process that would naturally lag somewhat behind the original achievement. (Indeed, it is to be understood that the modern-day disaffection with faith is the result of a lag between achievements, achievements in technology—and philosophy—having run ahead of the more global growth which is faith.[11]) This dynamic is surely part and parcel of the circumstantiality for which creation has already been excused. After all, if progress were utterly constant—if there was no "pendulum" that needed to swing—man's life would not be the struggle it needs to be.

Now, we do not know what the struggle for progress will require. Indeed, we do not know whether circumstantiality will not require that we learn how to live with atomic power only after the trial and *error* of nuclear war.[12] But, we do know that whatever happens is God's will for our good. And, just as the Moslem conquest of Christian North Africa ultimately proved to bring Christianity into contact with the Aristotelianism that saved it from the eventual failure of hellenism, whatever happens will bring about progress.

Thus, with a mind to what has already happened, it is possible to predict the following:

Maturity will increase among all people. And, with the accumulation of knowledge, and the creation of structures which will propel progress and

11. As a matter of fact, if there was nothing wrong with the faith, the crisis would not be upon us. Therefore, the modern-day disaffection with faith can be considered a sign of progress.
12. Though we also know that biblical talk of "Armageddon" (Rev. 16:16) is no sort of divine warning.

protect it, maturity will increase at an increasing rate.[13] This will undoubtedly involve advances in all categories of human achievement. (In this, man
magnifies himself drawing upon creation. It amounts the increasing "union" of man with creation. Affected by knowledge, it is a prelude to the
union of man with God.) The increase of maturity will also involve increasing human unity and all forms of equality. Though this will diminish the
"differences" between persons, it will increase their "distinction." After
all, individuality increases with complexity (cf. p.247). This will require
increasing personal freedom. (Besides, increasing freedom is a pre-requisite
of increasing self-determination.) Therefore, increasing human unity will
not be accomplished by regulation. Rather, increasing maturity will mini-
mize the need for regulation as it also provides each individual with something to contribute to the direction of the whole.

Progress will continue, but it will not continue indefinitely. Matter cannot be perfect; "utopia" is not the world's destiny. The world is the place for
the struggle of becoming and this struggle will continue until all the people
called for by God's plan have been created. When all have become who they
were meant to be, the world will come to an end.

b. The End of the World

The world will come to an end. God's plan calls for the family best suited to
share His life (cf. p.350). But, if new members will forever be produced,
heaven is something essentially incomplete. What is worse, it would make
the eternal dependent upon the temporal. This cannot be; the world will
come to an end.

Our look at the state of modern astronomy has already offered two models
of the end—naturally speaking (cf. p.307). The in-rush of all the matter in
the universe would obviously involve the implosion that would wipe out
everything. The infinite expansion of space would eventually involve the
diffusion of matter called "entropy." Neither of these models is particularly
attractive. Entropy is problematic because human progress could conceivably create a self-sustaining system that would thwart the disorder that
would otherwise leave the universe dead. Though an implosion would be the
scenario of sure death, it does not seem likely that the progress of humanity
will end with its destruction. What is perhaps most likely is that once
creation has satisfied its purpose, God will simply cease to will its existence.
At that time, God will give His life to mankind immediately, to both the
living and the dead. This is the truth of the so-called "second coming."

---

13. Of course, the increased faith and love of increasing numbers will itself propel the increasing rate of progress.

As to when this can be expected, it is first to be acknowledged that we do not know. We have not been told and there is only *one* thing upon which to base a prediction. It would seem likely that human progress will at least be permitted to achieve the lion's share of those things of which creation is capable. Thus it would appear that the end is a long way off.

c. "Eschatology": A Guide for the Imagination

When the end does come, all humanity will be recast in the divine stuff. Recast in the divine stuff, we will retain our "identity" (with who we were on earth), and our "individuality" (accomplished by physical bodies now, there will still be an ontological distinction between you and me). Recast in the divine stuff, and unlimited therein, we will immediately see God and become the human family who most fully shares God's life.

Reflection upon what precisely this means has traditionally been called "eschatology"—reflection upon the "last" things. Grounded upon the facts of the most mature human aspirations, it will certainly involve life immortal, utterly satisfying, and presently unimaginable. It will involve the understanding of much that is presently unknowable. It will also mean that everyone who has ever lived will know and love each other intimately.[14] (This is particularly unimaginable—but no reason not to believe what the facts indicate. In this, it is not unlike any number of scientific concepts whose truth we still accept. For example, few would deny but who can imagine the full reality of the idea that there are 6×10^{24} molecules of H_2O in the average glass of water?) Universal imtimacy will not be threatening to any relationship because everyone will be perfectly secure, and every relationship will still be special. This will especially be true of the relationships which have been the occasions of love in the world. Since love is what survives the person's death, the special causes of the particularities of a person's love will always have a privileged place in him. But, this will involve no exclusiveness which is only necessary now because of human limitedness. Instead, mankind will indeed be the unity that can best experience the fullness of what God is.

The question "what will this be like" is, of course, a good one and, remarkably, not a difficult question to answer.[15] It is first to be stated that full knowledge of life in God is as beyond man as is knowledge of God Himself. Nonetheless, since the world is God's surrogate (cf. p.345), the experience of life in the world is a bonafide source of knowledge about life in God.

---

14. Though this means that everyone will know all the details of everyone's life, understanding will defuse any reason for resentment or embarrassment.

15. Neither is the question "where will this be?" God is already everywhere. Thus, the answer is: here.

Therefore, the best experiences of life in the world give us the best idea about what heaven will be like. (This is particularly true of "peak" experiences; such experiences give a corresponding "peek" at what is coming.) For more information, we must imagine. We must try to imagine the best possible life, not just life as it can be, but life as it could be if anything—anything good—were possible. But, we must not imagine the perfection of particular things in isolation; after all, eternity involves the perfection of everything. It is also important to remember that this is a "temporal" world in which everything has a "time-value." This is the reason that the enjoyment of something is related to the frequency of its experience. (This is the reason that variety is the spice of life.) Imagining eternity must take this into account. But, such imagining remains but a glimpse of life in God, and the infinitely attractive good that this involves. For this reason, people will never tire of heaven. Besides, heaven will ever be new as the human family eternally explores the infinite God.

d. An Addendum: The State of the Dead

As we conclude our survey of these most crucial topics, it would be wise to state plainly what has been implicit in so much that we have concluded.

Involving as it does the union of God and all mankind, the idea of universal salvation does not involve the one-by-one entry of persons into heaven. The eternal cannot be dependent upon the temporal and, therefore, no one is presently enjoying heaven without us, waiting.

When we discussed the survival of death, we saw that the person's new life is totally dependent upon God, who remembers the person perfectly and recasts him in a new form (cf. p.343). God can do this anytime He wants; He will not forget. Besides, from God's perspective, the conception and completion of creation is one act. From our perspective, persons who have died are with God even though they do not know it.

Chapter III: An Apologetic for the Divine Sonship of Jesus

Section I: Chrisitanity?

A) Facing the Problem of Divine Intervention

Having argued to a development of Christianity which would not have been recognized in Jesus' day, the problem of divine intervention re-emerges—regarding *Jesus*.

This discussion has documented the decline of reason for belief in divine intervention. First, grace was critiqued (cf. p.301). Then, so was frequent divine intervention in general (cf. p.319). Still, the critique of frequent divine intervention did not exclude the possibility of extraordinary miracles—those that took place principally to demonstrate God's power. But, in every mentionable case, the burdens of proof properly prevent them from having this effect. Therefore, since they are more economically explained in terms of nature, we must admit their day has passed.[1]

Let it be clear. This critique also applies to biblical miracles. Given the new perspective on the Old Testament (cf. p.320), it surely applies to all the miracle stories told therein. Given the criterion of minimalism (cf. p. 323), it applies to most if not all the New Testament miracles—even those of Jesus.

This raises the question of whether there is reason to affirm any intervention—even the incarnation. Let there be no mistake; the incarnation was an intervention if it was anything at all. Given the naturalness of Christian life (cf. p.303), it would not seem necessary to insist that Jesus was the product of a miracle. Indeed, if He was the product of a miracle, why did He endorse, if not teach, so many ideas that we have now abandoned? A man ahead of His time no doubt, but so are the founders of every movement. Might it be that Jesus was simply a great moment in the history of man?

The question could not be more important. As we have already noted, the belief that Jesus was from God—in some unique sense—is an unsuspendable whose denial defeats the purpose of "Christian" doctrinal development. In view of all the developments that we have seen since, have we actually recommended the abandonment of Christianity?

---

1. Included in this critique are extraordinary miracles such as the sun's supposed dance at Fatima or the ongoing miracle cures of Lourdes which are more economically explained by the presumption of natural, if unknown, causes.

B) Religion without Revelation

1. The Question

Given the criterion of minimalism, we begin with the questions: Is supernatural revelation necessary? What would religion be without it?

2. Problems with Religion without Revelation

There are problems with a religion without revelation. These stem from the very nature of man—especially the developmental nature of human knowing.

As ideas become more complex, they become less certain (cf. p. 333), and less certain to be possessed by everyone (cf. p. 264). This means that if and when a person gets to faith—the knowledge that most demands action, and most demands that the person affect his fellows—his idea most depends on him.

As ideas become more complex, they also become more individual (cf. p. 247). This means that if and when a person gets to faith—the knowledge that most demands united action—his idea is utterly his own. And it exists at its own level. Furthermore, it is bound to deepen, if not change, throughout his life. And faith will continue to deepen, among more and more people, throughout the history of man.

Therefore, without some "external" truth, no one's opinion, a timeless truth, something for all to affirm or deny, "common" faith would be impossible. (Common worship would be utterly impossible.) Though there might be agreement, to whatever degree, there could not be unity, people bound together by the most important of their beliefs. (Whose opinion would bind; what would bind the would-be reformer?) In fact, there would be no "religion," from the Latin "to bind," or more rightly "to bind together." In essence, every man is his own religion.

3. The Necessity of Revelation

It is not possible that everyone is his own religion. Man is called to be one; this is the making of his destiny. Therefore, man must be one in faith; he must share the fruit of his greatest development.

Therefore, God had to reveal the external truth which makes this possible.

It is clear that this external truth had to be revealed; it had to be made known supernaturally. Nothing of the world speaks for God until it is interpreted by man. Therefore, God had to speak to the world Himself. The world needed "word" from God.

C) Was Christ the Word?

1. The Question

We must now examine the question of whether Christ was indeed the "word" which the world needs.

Once again, we begin with a look at the alternatives. From there it will proceed to a look at the basis of Christian faith *per se*.

But, first, it is important to point out the privileged position of faith in Christ. Faith in Christ directed—and motivated—the reflections which gave birth to Christian Materialism. Moreover, *Christian* Materialism does stand in the line of Christian tradition.

2. Has Word Necessarily Arrived?

The first alternative is likely the least obvious. Are we correct to presume that word has already arrived? After all, it is only recently that man became capable of the technology that would make a recording of revelation all but infallible.

But, now that we know we need revelation, we have a good reason *not* to believe that we must wait for it. God would not want man to be ready but not able to have religion. Furthermore, a modern recording of revelation is not what we would want. If sufficiently convincing to modern eyes, such an event would prevent the world from coming to faith on its own—the purpose of earthly existence.

3. Christianity and the Other World Religions

Next on the list of alternatives are the other world religions (cf. p. 269). But, what of the possibility that revelation has given rise to a faith that has not yet achieved this status? On the other hand, what faith would this be? If it is unknown, the possibility is undiscussable and it would be as though revelation had not arrived. Therefore, it is clear; we are to look among those faiths that providence has already selected for success.

Christianity is immediately favored over Hinduism and Buddhism. Both involve the absolutely central concept of reincarnation, an all but senseless notion in view of the materialistic fact that the body and spirit are one. Simply put, there is no soul to transmigrate from body to body.[2] Moreover, Hinduism conceives reincarnation in terms of a "caste" system which contradicts work for human equality. Hinduism also lacks an historical basis. Neither religion features love. Neither believes in a personal God. (Indeed, Buddhism denies the concept of God *per se*.) Both involve a "cyclic" concept of time which contradicts the idea of creation, not to mention the idea of progress in providence. Both have a negative concept of eternity— non-personal existence.

Chinese religion lacks an historical basis and it has seen a remarkable lack of development.

---

2. This same argument makes clear that so-called "out-of-body" experiences are indeed some sort of hallucination due to the lack of oxygen that reaches the brain of a dying person.

The historical basis of Judaism has already been discussed with respect to the idea of divine intervention in the Old Testament (cf. p. 320). It is also to be observed that Judaism is not a "missionary" religion. This, together with the fact of Judaism's accent on justice, already brought about its reform at the hands of Christianity. The accent on justice is also characteristic of Islam, which also suffers from the fact that it post-dates Christianity but does not represent an improvement. Indeed, the founder is quoted in favor of holy war. Furthermore, though there is a founder, Mohammed, and a story of an event that one could consider an historical revelation—Mohammed's encounter with the angel Gabriel under a tree—the story pales in view of what we have already disallowed in Christianity. Clearly, as an event of revelation, it is implausible—if not to say impossible (q.v. p. 409)—and plainly without sufficient evidence.

4. Christianity Considered in Itself
a. Signs of Credibility

Considered in itself, even apart from its instrumental role in the creation of Christian Materialism, Christianity displays definite signs of credibility. It puts the personal God in personal terms. It proclaims His love and plan. It portrays His love in the sacrifice of the cross.

The historical basis of Christianity is likewise superior. Jesus is the religious founder about whom the most—and most credible—information is available. The evidence of the text makes clear that those who have provided this information believed most of it.

Moreover, the first Christians were so zealous that they spread their faith to an estimated 100,000 people by the year 100. Though this was less than one percent of the Roman world of that time, it was not a time of easy travel or mass communications.[3] And, Christians *were* persecuted.

Nonetheless, Christianity is the world's largest religion today.

b. Christianity as a Cult

At this point, we must address the question of whether Christianity can be explained by the same things that account for "cults"—those small groups of fanatics and "fringe" people which have existed throughout the centuries and still do.

We must first observe that almost any movement starts small with people willing to act—to give all to the cause—and such persons are rarely members of the establishment.

The test of a movement is the reason it appeals, how it sustains itself, and

---

3. Christianity's relative lack of success in Palestine was initially due to Jewish piety, and later the Roman suppression of a Jewish revolt in 70 A.D. This saw to the destruction of the temple and, more importantly, the dispersion of the Jews to all parts of the Empire.

what it becomes.

It is here that Christianity fares well. In its essential teachings, it answered the highest aspirations of the human spirit. It called its adherents to love.

Unlike most cults, it survived the founder and his charismatic successors. It did so without anything like the mind-control techniques which today's cults employ. Instead, it sustained itself on faith—on truth.

It has been supremely instrumental in the spiritual development, and civilization, of the world.

And, today, it is the inspiration of the greatest number of people working for a better world for all.

5. The Resurrection

Of course, the resurrection has always been considered "the" sign of Christianity's credibility.

a. The Evidence of Tradition

The evidence of Tradition is the historical importance of belief in the resurrection. The vindication of everything that Jesus taught and, at the same time, a preview of the resurrection that awaits us all, it has always been the central element of the Christian apologetic. It is still crucial to the minds of almost all Christians. Indeed, most of those who deny all the other miracles in the New Testament still insist that the resurrection must be considered in a class by itself.

b. An Evaluation of the Evidence of Scripture

An evaluation of the evidence of Scripture properly begins with a look at the most primitive pertinent text, in this case, 1 Cor. 15. Actually, *in this case,* this is where the evaluation can end. Not only is this the most primitive text we possess *by far,* but the gospel accounts of the resurrection disagree and bear other signs of embellishment (cf. p. 78). In contrast, 1 Cor 15 is a plain statement:

"For I delivered to you as of first importance what I also received, that Christ died for our sins in accordance with the scriptures, that he was buried, that he was raised on the third day in accordance with the scriptures, and that he appeared to Cephas, then to the twelve. Then he appeared to more than five hundred brethren at one time, though some have fallen asleep. Then he appeared to James, then to all the apostles. Last of all, as to one untimely born, he appeared to me" (vv. 3-8).

Four verses later, Paul goes on to say:

"Now if Christ is preached as raised from the dead, how can some of you say that there is no resurrection from the dead? But if there is no resurrection from the dead, then Christ has not been raised; if Christ has not been raised, then our preaching is in vain and your faith is in vain" (vv. 12-14).

Written in the mid-50's, Paul also says that he is handing on what he "received." As a matter of fact, his is a sequence of statements that bears the unmistakable character of a formula which he was repeating. Undoubtedly, this formula is older than 1 Cor., and it states a faith in the resurrection that Paul first expressed as early as the late 40's (1 Thess. 1:10). The centrality of this faith is confirmed by Paul's insistence that it is of "first" importance, as he goes on to say that "if Christ has not been raised . . . your faith is in vain."

Paul does not say that Jesus raised Himself; it was the Father who raised Him. Nor does Paul claim that anyone had actually witnessed the resurrection. (The Gospel of Matthew mentions only the guards who were also reported to have claimed that the disciples stole the body.) Paul does say that Jesus "appeared"; it was He; there was no doubt. Furthermore, it was He who did the appearing; the witnesses did not see Him by any power of their own. The content of their experience was not described; no words were recorded.

Though the most primitive and, clearly, the most weighty text does bespeak the early Christian faith in a very real resurrection, it does not preclude the very real possibility that the resurrection was imagined or made-up. Therefore, given our critique of divine intervention in any form (cf. p.319), consistency requires that we admit the evidence of Scripture is not conclusive. If we are to affirm the resurrection, minimalism (cf. p.323) requires that we appeal to faith.

c. The Theological Evidence

As has become our procedure, we begin with methodological doubt about the resurrection. Let us suppose that it did not happen. Let us suppose that Jesus' disciples imagined it or made it up.

Immediately we have a serious blow to the credibility of Christianity. Belief in the resurrection was central to the faith of the first Christians. Therefore, if it did not happen, Christianity was founded upon a fantasy or fabrication.

Furthermore, without the resurrection, we have no direct evidence that Jesus was anything more than an important moment in human history.

Therefore, for the same reason that supernatural revelation was necessary (cf. p.361), any claim that Christ was the "word" required supernatural confirmation. Thus, we need to affirm the resurrection—a real resurrection. It is required by faith.

d. What Actually Happened?

Though the theological evidence requires a real resurrection, it does not tell us what actually happened.

Something supernatural is required; but the content of the experience is not required to involve a bodily apparition.

Had it been a concrete bodily apparition—in which Jesus spoke—it is to be expected that every detail would have been rememberd and reported. Paul reports none; the gospels disagree. Therefore, in the absence of a credible description of a concrete bodily apparition, together with the recent realization that eternal life is something entirely unbodily in the earthly sense— something we on earth cannot comprehend—we are left with an experience much more "spiritual" than history has hitherto imagined. This is not to say less vivid, or less sure. Minimally, the Father made known that Jesus was alive. This confirmed that Jesus taught the truth. (The content of the experience confirmed the content of His teachings.)

The absence of a credible description of the experience is also evidence that it was something that happened to the apostles while each was alone. If the apostolic group had been together, the exact circumstances of the event would surely have become "the" story of Christian tradition. The absence of such a story is also evidence that the apostles *did* disperse out of disillusionment over Jesus' death.

All the above is evidence that the experiences took place in Galilee. This is the testimony of Mark, the earliest gospel. Though the other gospels say that Jesus first appeared in Jerusalem, these stories had apologetic import; they did not separate the appearances from the place of Jesus' death. Moreover, the other gospels agree that Jesus eventually appeared in Galilee. But, why did the apostles go there if Jesus had already appeared in Jerusalem— the supposed scene of His ascension? We should also note that the reported time between the Friday of Jesus' crucifixion to the Sunday of His first appearance is more or less the time that it would have taken the apostles to walk from Jerusalem to Galilee.

Actually, the question of time is a matter of separate discussion. But, we have little reason to dispute the universal testimony that the experiences began to take place on Sunday—the first day of the week. Sunday does not have apologetic import. Neither does the Friday of Jesus' crucifixion which is also the universal testimony. The passage of this much time is supported by the most ancient insistence that Jesus rose "on the third day according to the Scriptures." The Scriptures that this supposedly fulfilled are obscure at best, and never mentioned. Neither of the two that scholars normally suggest: 1) the three days Jonah spent in the belly of the fish or 2) Hos.6:2[4]—

---

4. Some scholars also point to the Hebrew idea that the soul leaves the body four days after death.

were pre-existing expectations which would have conditioned the resurrection accounts. And, it is to be assumed that the experiences began to take place soon after Jesus' death.

The experiences probably came one to an apostle. God would not have needed more than one. For the sake of the apostles' credibility, all the experiences—with the possible exception of Paul's[5]—probably took place in close temporal proximity, within a few hours or even simultaneously. Of course, the experiences immediately called them together to share what had happened. (In this, the resurrection experience prefigures the effect it was to have upon humanity—it calls us together in common faith.)

Moreover, it now becomes clear that the twelve, if indeed there were twelve (cf. p.188), were witnesses to the resurrection not because they were chosen beforehand, but because they were chosen by the experiences. Though the gospels mention that Jesus had many followers (e.g. the "seventy," Lk.10:1), God chose to speak only to those whose subsequent lives would complement His plan.

The economy of experiences obviously indicates that there was no separate "ascension." The testimony only of Luke, his unique interest in describing early Church history required some accounting of the end of Jesus' earthly appearances. The period of forty days is reminiscent of a flood that never happened. Moreover, the ascension is inconsistent with the spiritual conception of the resurrection to which we have concluded. But, most critically, the ascension is an extraordinary which is not necessary.

Neither is the empty tomb. Not mentioned by Paul, the accounts in the gospels are not only different, but, since there *was* a need to account for the body, they are far too easily explained in terms of apologetics. Apologetics is the obvious intent of the unlikely story of the guards (reported only by Matthew). The other arguments in favor of the empty tomb (cf. p.191) are as easily explicable. The argument that an apologetically motivated story would not have featured women—because the testimony of women was not permitted in Jewish court—gives far too much weight to this consideration. Besides, who else would have returned to the tomb? (Remember, the apostles probably *did* flee.) The argument that an empty tomb would have disproved the resurrection is really evidence that the resurrection *did* take place in Galilee. The apostles surely remained there awhile. If and when

5. But, since Paul did not know Jesus, he could not have had the same sort of experience as the other apostles. Therefore, the scriptural claim that he was "one untimely born" (1 Cor. 15:8) is obviously to be viewed with a certain skepticism. Perhaps it was added to the Pauline text for apologetic reasons. After all, Paul never again mentions what should have been the dominant experience of his life. The *Acts* account of his encounter on the road to Damascus was written long after the events; it is obviously a myth.

they returned to Jerusalem, they were undoubtedly a small sect that did not attract much attention for quite some time. The fact that the tomb did not become a shrine is simply evidence that the fleeing disciples did not know where the tomb was; if they had, it would have become a shrine, empty or not. (Though it is reported that the apostles went to the temple to pray, e.g. Acts. 3:1, it is never said that they visited the tomb of Jesus.) Finally, given our new idea of the survival of death (cf. p.343), the empty tomb would have meant the needless annihilation of matter for the sake of show.

e. The Changing Role of the Resurrection

In view of all that we have now concluded, something must be said of the place of the resurrection in Christian faith; is it still the primary object, is it a proof, or is it something extra to believe?

Certainly not the primary object, nor a proof, it is clear that belief in the resurrection presumes Christian faith. It is faith that provides the decisive evidence—the realization that human destiny requires the common faith which requires the supernatural confirmation of someone's teaching. Therefore, belief in the resurrection is an "implication" of faith. It is an implication of the knowledge which already accepts that Jesus told the truth.

Actually, it was not so different for the apostles. If they had not known Jesus, and believed His teachings, they could not have believed that He had risen. For them, however, it also served as additional evidence that Jesus told the truth. This was needed—then. Man had not come to accept his own judgment as a source of religious truth. But, with the passage of time, as the weight of this evidence was bound to decrease, there was a corresponding increase in man's confidence in his own ability to know. There was also an increase in man's need to know on his own. Thus, the role of the resurrection changed.

It still confirms the fact that Jesus told the truth, but it does so in a different way, for a different reason.

Section II: Facing the Problem of the Incarnation

A) The Problem

We now come to what will surely be the most challenging test of our willingness to follow the truth wherever it leads; we must finally face the problem of the incarnation.

Minimalism may affirm the resurrection but, inasmuch as the resurrection provides what is required of faith, there would not appear to be sufficient evidence to insist upon the intervention of the incarnation.

In view of this critique, the old and new problems with the incarnation become critical. How *are* we to deal with the apparent contradiction involved in the insistence that Jesus was true God and true man at the same time? How are we to deal with the apparent impossibility involved in the idea that a material body can have a spiritual divinity? What about the abandonment of belief that we needed a redeemer who was God made man? What of the fact that anything that Jesus taught can be explained by natural processes, processes which can also explain the divinization of the founder of any faith—especially one who was resurrected? What of the fact that the modern understanding of the meaning of Jesus' teachings differs so dramatically from those He probably taught—especially with respect to the ideas of sin and hell?

B) Facing the Facts

1. Faith in Christ

Facing the facts, we must acknowledge that we have sufficient evidence to insist upon the intervention of no more than the resurrection.

Jesus was a man, the product of natural causes like any other. In him, however, the history of the human struggle to understand its origin and destiny finally achieved the essential truth of God's love. Proclaiming this truth in word and deed unto death, Jesus was chosen by providence for this mission.

Providence also chose and prepared those involved in the intervention of the resurrection. Therefore, it surely involved the most subtle intervention that could have accomplished its essential purpose. But, an intervention indeed, the resurrection should not be considered to have "disturbed" creation or "changed" the course of its history.

History was conceived with it in mind; thus, it "completed" creation.

It occurred at the moment that man achieved the truth on his own; thus, it "endorsed" creation.

The resurrection cured creation of the "solipsism" (cf. p.142) within which it would have been trapped if God had not spoken to it, calling it out of itself.

Moreover, since *human* history required certain preparations—the billions of years before the emergence of life, the millions of years before the emergence of man—the resurrection can be said to have occurred at its effective beginning, the moment that man needed to hear from God. Thus did God answer with the "word" which both promised him glory and called him to pursue it, making his success both possible and certain.

2. The Divinity of Christ

Obviously, facing the facts will require dramatic changes in the traditional belief in the divinity of Christ. Much must be abandoned, but much can be affirmed.

Jesus was indeed the "Christ," the "anointed one," even if he was not the "Lord" whose divinity was once required of his authority.[6]

Though he was not the "Son" of god, he was certainly "the" son of God. Though we are all God's children, it was he whose sonship made this known.

Of course, he was God's "word." It was he who taught the faith to which all of us are called. In word and in deed, he embodied this faith and God's love which it proclaims.[7] Though he did not pre-exist, he was pre-conceived to have this "saving" role in history.

3. The Essential Truth of the Incarnation—and Redemption

Although we have concluded to a functional ontology (cf. p.299), an abandonment of major proportions, we have not declared that the classical ontology was completely mistaken. Given the divine determinism—particularly as it provides the new perspective on the sensus plenior (cf. p.324)—we can know that the doctrine of the incarnation must have had its purpose. Therefore, since Jesus' *authority* could have been maintained without the extraordinary assertions we have now abandoned—as some of the heretics actually argued—it is clear that there is an essential truth to belief in his divinity.

Plainly, this truth involves one of our most recent findings—the fact that creation is made of God's own stuff (cf. p.342). Here is an idea that the ancients could never have accepted. But, they could accept the idea that God humbled Himself to take the form of man. This is exactly what He did. God became man—mankind.[8] This is the essential truth of the incarnation.

The doctrine of the redemption says that God gave His life—His self—for our salvation. This is exactly what He has done.

The doctrine of redemption also says that God suffered on our behalf. He did; He still does. God knows our thoughts better than we do. He knows our feelings for all they are. Therefore, since He loves us, He suffers with us. Such is the price He pays to share His life with us.

The doctrines of the incarnation and redemption expressed all of this in the only terms understandable—until now.

---

6. In this view, the word "Christian" would well apply to anything that he endorsed, or would have.

7. Karl Rahner is right to consider him the "definitive" word of salvation in a universe of grace (cf. p.304).

8. Note the parallel in Rahner's Christology (cf. p.299). Creation *is* God's self-communication. This fact is uniquely present in the person of Jesus. But, he was not prior to or distinct from creation in any way.

C) Jesus

1. The Life of Jesus

Obviously, our new perspective on the divinity of Christ will require a new account of the life of Jesus. It will be an important project. Jesus' life remains a model for our own. And, it portrays in concrete terms the conceptual truths of faith as best they can be celebrated, if not to say understood.

We have no reason to question the universal testimony that Jesus was from Galilee. We do have reason to be skeptical about the evidence that he was born far to the south in Bethlehem (cf. p.187). Mary was surely his mother. Moreover, her presence in Christian tradition surely indicates that she was with him throughout his life. The lack of facts about Joseph probably means he did die early in Jesus' life.

It is likely that it did take Jesus thirty years to come to the ideas and courage that resulted in his mission. His baptism by John would never have been told if it had not happened. (Thus the obvious attempts to christianize John.)

It is sure that Jesus spent the better part of his public life as an itinerant preacher in Galilee. (He did not write.) His views should have aroused the animosity of the established religious order. His eventual execution proves he did attract a following.

Jesus must have made at least one trip to Jerusalem. Where else could he have been executed? In view of its apologetic unattractiveness, the story of his betrayal is almost certainly true. His crucifixion is indisputable. Even apart from the historical evidence, it is an all but essential element of every resurrection account. He died a human death and did not descend into hell.

2. Jesus' Knowledge and Will

"The" son of God or not, Jesus was still human and subject to all the limitations that this necessarily involves.

There was much he did not know. Naturally, he labored under many of the misconceptions common during his day. Of course, this is already the testimony of Scripture (cf. p.176).[9] But, it is equally obvious that he was granted the greatest spirituality of his time.

Jesus' spirituality must have involved an actue awareness of the loving Fatherhood of God. This is also evident in the scriptural testimony to his sonship. But, it is not clear to what extent he considered himself "the" son. Still, his knowledge of the loving Fatherhood of God must have begun in the personal experience that God was *his* Father, who loved *him*. Moreover, in

---

9. What of his literal sounding statements about Adam, Moses, Noah, and Jonah? What would be better, to admit him his share or to claim a faulty reporting that would further compromise the credibility of the texts?

the call to proclaim this truth, Jesus must have had some sense that he was a special son. Nonetheless, it is not to be imagined that he believed his death would be a sacrifice meant to redeem the world. This would have been a mistake—and an unnecessary one—much more respectably imagined of the disciples he left behind who, as we have seen, surely needed some way to understand the humiliating death of the resurrected Jesus (cf. p.191).

The questions of what Jesus actually thought of the coming of the kingdom or the call of love—not to mention sin or hell—are much more difficult, if not impossible, to answer. It is only clear that he understood as much as "the" mature person of his time could have.

This brings us to the issue of Jesus' will.

Since maturity involves both the intellectual and emotional aspects of a person's life, it is naturally to be understood that the wisdom of Jesus' ideas had its effect upon the holiness of his life. Thus, it cannot be doubted that Jesus was a remarkably loving man. Nothing else so easily explains his devoted following or the lives his followers led after his death. The extent of his love was evident in his acceptance of death; this is itself evident in the Eucharist (q.v. p.397).

But, it is not to be imagined that Jesus did not begin life as a totally selfish baby who had to learn to love. Still, it is to be presumed that he was spared the psychological problems and major mistakes that would have handicapped his spirituality and mission. Other specifics of Jesus' spirituality are to be inferred. Actually, they always have been. *Despite* the testimony of Scripture—which often paints Jesus as a somewhat harsh, incompassionate person, especially in terms of his damnation-talk of which there is so much[10]—Christian spirituality has always imagined Jesus to be a man of every virtue. From now on, attempts to infer Jesus' spirituality must be tempered by reason and, specifically, reflection on the limitations of any man at any time.

3. Jesus' Miracles

As we have already concluded, minimalism requires no miracles other than the resurrection (cf. p.369). Extraordinary, easily explicable in terms of faith-healing[11] or exaggeration, Jesus' miracles can still be seen as evidence in favor of the resurrection. They represent the conviction that he could have done anything by his divine power.

---

10. Realism requires attention to the fact that the earliest Christian tradition tells the "afflicted" to take heart in the "vengeance" God was to bring down upon "those who afflict them" (2 Thess.1:6-10).

11. Faith-healing, practiced by all sorts of persons, has given rise to the study of the effect of mental on bodily health and, specifically, the phenomenon of "psychosomatic" illnesses.

The other New Testament miracles also bespeak this faith. But, they do not represent much evidence. After all, though the book of *Acts* credits Paul with miracles (e.g. Acts 19:10), he himself mentions none. Though he spoke often of the Spirit, he never mentions the descent of the Spirit on Pentecost.[12] He makes no mention of such dramatic happenings as the descent of the Spirit at Jesus' baptism or the miracles that supposedly followed his crucifixion, none of which made it into the Jewish or Roman histories of the period. He does not even attribute miracles to Jesus—except the resurrection.

It is therefore with confidence that we conclude that the resurrection was "the" miracle—after creation.

Section III: The Problem of the Trinity

A) Facing the Facts

Obviously, the new perspective on the divinity of Christ means the abandonment of the classical idea of the Trinity. Always a problem (cf. p.326), it is now clear that the doctrine was formulated as a response to the problem of the incarnation which also freed the Father from countless acts of directing, inspiring and sanctifying. His freedom was provided by the specific doctrine of the holy spirit.

B) The Holy Spirit

There was much truth to the specific doctrine of the holy spirit. The doctrine said that the spirit was the presence of God "in" the world. This was a presence that did not require the Father to step down from heaven. Thus, it stated the truth that God *is* present in the world, and in the believer, but not all of Him. This is already our conclusion on the relation of matter to its Maker (cf. p.342). It also reflects our new perspective on the incarnation (cf. p.370).[13]

---

12. Reported only by Luke, this story was an attempt to Christianize the Jewish feast of "Weeks" (cf. Deut.16:9) which came to commemorate God's giving the Law to Moses. The several accounts of the apostles and others speaking in "tongues," (or "glossolalia"), actually describe the murmurings not uncommon to the religious experience of the hellenic world. The result of emotional excitement, there is indeed evidence that the early Christians expressed their faith in this way (cf. 1 Cor.14). But, now that the natural origin of this excitement is to be recognized, it is not to be expected that future Christians will express their faith in this way. This, however, does not mean that the spontaneous personal prayer of today's "charismatic" groups should not be a fulfilling form of spirituality for persons so disposed.

13. Note the parallel in Rahner's idea that history is God's self-communication—the Spirit making its home in matter (cf. p.224).

C) The Essential Truth of the Trinity

There is also an essential truth to the general doctrine of the Trinity. The doctrine said that there is more than "one" person in God. Thus, it stated the truth that God is more than "a" person. This is our explanation for the fact that God created a family and not just one other (cf. p. 349). Moreover, in its explanation of God's self-sufficient creativity and community (cf. p. 56), the doctrine stated the truth that nothing is new to God. In its idea that self-giving is a source of unity, trinitarian theology explained the working of universal salvation (cf. p. 53). In its idea that God extended His substance, the doctrine of the Trinity explained creation. The doctrine of the Trinity did all of this in the only terms that man could understand—until today.

Chapter IV: Catholic Materialism

Section I: Introductory Remarks

Plainly, Christian Materialism has been constructed out of the presumption that Church teachings have something essential to say. Plainly, this presumption involves the belief that the Church is of uniquely divine origin. Therefore, as promised, this belief will be tested. And we shall show that certain aspects of materialism argue forcefully on its behalf.

Thereupon, we shall see what materialism has to say about the nature of the Church—its proper self-conception, structure, and scope of concerns.

Finally, for the sake of completeness, we shall see what materialism has to say about certain other issues which could not have been dealt with until this point.

Section II: The Church

A) The Need For Christians, Christian Community and Christian Unity

Given the necessity of revelation—the fact that men are called to be one in faith (cf. p.361)—if Christ was the "word," men are called to be "Christians."

But, what of the argument that Jesus did not intend to found a church, much less a religion, but was interested only in a reform of Judaism (cf. p.130)? Given the facts that we have now uncovered—our new view of Jesus' divinity and his knowledge, not to mention minimalism—we must admit that this is possible. But, it is not decisive. Jesus did not recognize a Judaic authority from which he and his followers broke away. The resurrection established *his* authority. *It* created a new religion. Therefore, even apart from the fact that providence led Jesus' followers to break away early and permanently (cf. p.192), it is clear that "Christianity" exists according to God's special intention.

For all the reasons that revelation was necessary, it is also clear that Christians were meant to be a community. How else are Christians one in faith? How else should Christians live out a faith that calls them to love one another—particularly as must involve "pastoral" work for their mutual growth in the maturity of faith? How else are they to work together for the spread of that maturity—particularly as must involve "evangelization" and work for progress generally. Therefore, even apart from the historical fact that Christians did think of themselves as an "assembly" from the moment that they considered themselves Christians, it is clear that their existence as such, as a Church, is still what God wants.

Obviously, if Christians are called to community, they are called to unity. How else are Christians really one in faith? How else should Christians really live out a faith that calls them to love one another? How can they more effectively work together?

Of course, even though anyone will acknowledge the importance of unity, they can still question the means by which unity is to be achieved.

But, before we address this question, we must first address the question of whether a community can be considered to include people who do not know each other. A Protestant issue, qualms about this notion have even found their way into Catholic thinking which speaks of the priority of the local community over the universal on the grounds that the local community is more "real" because its members live together.

But all people do live together. If this was not always obvious, it has become obvious thanks to recent advances in communication and transportation. Besides, what is human destiny but the unity of all people? How does man pursue it except by working for unity in this world?

Still, Christians who know each other do have a special relationship that is to be recognized. But, the varying degrees to which people can know (about) each other is already recognized in the organization of the Church into various levels—the parish, diocese, etc.[1] Nonetheless, any idea that the smallest units, presently parishes, are the "real" communities is essentially arbitrary. After all, the mutual knowledge of persons, even at that level, is limited and often results in the formation of sub-groups where faith is shared more personally. What would represent the level of greatest relation—the family, the couple? The real community should embrace all the people who share the common faith.

Plainly, other communities embrace people with less in common than faith. How can Christians consider themselves less a community than the citizens of a country? Indeed, only the Church can be the world-wide community that will be the only force capable of dealing with national and

1. It is clear that the structure of the Church should continue to be based upon "territorial" organizations; people have an unavoidable relation to those with whom they live. This is not to say that there is no place for Church associations based upon ethnic origin, occupation or spirituality. And there is definitely a need for organizations which are dedicated to special services, specific causes or politics in general.

global problems, acting sometimes in opposition to other powers[2] that have no problem existing as organizations wider than individual families.

B) The Need for Leadership and Authority;
The Hierarchical Structure of the Church

Now that we have seen the need for universal community, we can address the question of the means by which unity is to be achieved. We begin with an accounting of what unity requires.

1. The Requirements of Reality

Unity requires leadership. The very structure of reality makes this so. Communities cannot depend upon a grand coincidence of co-operation. The activities of nature's most individual actors must be organized. They require an organizer, a leader. What more need be said? If everyone does his own "thing," there is no community. Thus, the Church requires leadership.[3]

If there is to be leadership, the leaders must be followed—i.e. obeyed—especially with regard to those things that most plainly pertain to the community's common life and mission. What more need be said? If Church members follow only those directives that suit them, Church leaders cannot make plans or carry them out.

Of course, no one need follow a leader without "authority"—the right to lead. As we saw, historically, this right was based upon "truth" (cf. p. 46). But, the truth of what to do is rarely obvious. Therefore, someone must decide. And, without authority, no one can presume the co-operation of individuals most of whom have their own ideas.

The requirements of reality were recognized by the early Church (cf. p. 47). Despite its insistence that all authority was ultimately from God, it was obvious that anyone could claim "God told me." Therefore, if God had not established earthly authority, He would have no Church. Thus did He conceive Jesus. The resurrection was the establishment of his authority. It, the resurrection experience, passed his authority to the apostles (cf. p. 191). But, when they died—and were not resurrected—where did it go?

Two options are at our disposal: 1) the "hierarchical" idea in which

---

2. Here specific reference is being made to "totalitarian" powers whose suppression of freedom is not to be tolerated as a permanent condition of a large part of the world's population. What else but the internal conversion of a large majority of a nation's citizens, policemen, or political leaders could ever bring about peaceful and permanent change? What else but the internal conversion of nations could defuse mankind of the fear that the already public, unforgettable technologies of warfare will one day be used? True world peace will never be reached by political arrangement.

3. The Church also requires rules and structures such as those embodied in "Canon Law." Though this makes the community an "institution," a big community cannot be anything else.

authority is passed on from leader to chosen successor, and includes the notion that authority can be delegated in degrees (and repealed), and 2) the democratic idea which gives persons the power to choose their leader.[4]

Of the two, the hierarchical model is clearly recommended. It is recommended by the developmental nature of man—and mankind.

The Church is an institution whose basis is faith. Therefore, it is best led by persons of more mature faith—and greater religious knowledge.[5] But who picks these? Plainly, persons of more mature faith and greater religious knowledge. The people's choice is almost never superior to the wisdom of the most mature persons. The people did not conceive Jesus' teachings; Jesus did; he then taught the people; and the people have learned only slowly.

For this reason—if inarticulately—the first fifteen centuries of Church history saw the all but universal acceptance of the hierarchical model. It saved the founding fathers from the impossible tension of the fact that accepting a simple and/or untested person into the Church would be to give him authority, not only over community life, but also over doctrine, i.e. truth. It allowed the founding fathers to entrust the Church to those of proved qualifications.

Of course, the system shows its imperfection every time a bishop or his delegate picks the wrong person. But, the choosing of leaders is always a difficult business. The hierarchical model of authority leaves this task in the hands of persons who are presumably the best qualified to make the decision. In its implicit acknowledgment of a supreme authority, it settles conflicts among the faithful—including the membership of any leadership body—which would be sure to divide the Church. The democratic model of Church authority implies the right of any group to get together and proclaim that *theirs* is the only authority they acknowledge. In the fact that there are already over 20,000 independent Protestant groups, we can see that this is exactly what happens.

The hierarchical model also prevents the would-be visionary from claiming the authority of his self-proclaimed superior knowledge. Divisive and deadly have been the teachings of self-proclaimed prophets like Marcion and Mani of ancient times, or, of more modern times, Joseph Smith (1805-44), founder of the Mormons, and Jim Jones whose "Jonestown" was the

4. The "presbyteral" model would appear to fall somewhere between the two depending upon the way it is practiced.

5. Let it be clear. In speaking of the person of greater knowledge, the hierarchical model does *not* envision rule by theologians. Maturity bespeaks the whole person, and his "wisdom" (cf. p.261) in a vast majority of matters. And leadership calls for leaders, not scholars.

scene of the 1978 mass suicide which was such powerful evidence of the power that cult leaders can have over their following. Although the hierarchical model does involve the sometimes stifling conservatism that is to be expected when people choose people like them to succeed them, in so doing, it encourages a caution that would normally save the Church from being swept away by the tide of the latest untested idea. Indeed, the conservatism of the Church kept alive beliefs it needed, beliefs which have now become the stuff of Christian Materialism.

All in all, despite the inevitable tension between conservative and progressive forces—or because of it—the Church should be a hierarchy. Required by reality, no other model is recommended by the developmental nature of man. Therefore, it is clear; in the resurrection, God ordained a hierarchy in order to see to the coming of His "kingdom."

2. Shared Authority in an Evolving Institution

Although the developmental nature of humanity recommends the hierarchical structure of the Church, it also involves the increasing maturity of increasing numbers. This involves increasing individuality and an increasing need for the personal freedom which is the pre-requisite of continued development. Therefore, as the Church matures, the regulation of its individual members should decrease, particularly with respect to the conduct of their lives in normal circumstances. Moreover, as the Church matures, more of its members should contribute more to its direction—the increasing application of the principle of "collaboration."

Actually, collaboration has always been in evidence. There were many ministries (cf. 1 Cor.12:5), the Spirit gave many charisms (cf. Eph.4:12). By medieval times, Church leaders had learned to seek competent advice. In modern times, they have even discussed the sharing of authority (cf. p.201). Clearly discussed in terms of the principle of "collegiality": the bishops' collective responsibility for the universal Church,[6] Vatican II also involved the following movements which should continue:

1) Increasing application of the principle of "subsidiarity": normally, a higher authority should not make decisions which can better be made by a lower one, closer to the people affected by the decision.

2) Increasing application of the allied principle of "consultation": normally, the authorities should obtain the opinion of those to be affected by a decision. Ideally, consultation becomes the sharing of ideas in an attempt to achieve the greatest possible "consensus." The principle has the additional good effect of motivating leaders to lead by honest forms of persuasion, i.e.

---

6. Priests became "collaborators" with their bishops; they became "associates" of their pastors.

teaching and personal example.

3) The principle of consultation should also involve the principle of "constitutionality": the delimitation of "powers" and the delineation of "rights" which, under normal circumstances, pertain to persons of various positions in the Church—or even out of it. This latter should involve the publication of policies and procedures. With the maturing of the community, and training, it should even include the creation of representative bodies.

But, be it clear, policies and procedures are suspendable; representative bodies remain "consultative." Their authority was delegated and it can be withdrawn. The Church is a hierarchy and this its leaders cannot change; they cannot change the requirements of reality.

This, however, is not the legitimization of tyranny. The Church is a voluntary organization out of which one can opt. Therefore, if a person is truly in conscience convinced that the principles of Christian action (cf. p.352) recommend disobedience—with respect to a specific directive to which the authorities require obedience—he can resign. Given the doctrine of universal salvation, this does not damn him. Instead, it will serve as the proper "check" on the mis-use of authority. It involves the automatic curtailment of the power authority meant.

C) Is the Catholic Church "The" Church?

1. The Question

At this point, finally, we can and must address the question: Is the Catholic Church "the" Church?

In answering this question, we must remember that the Catholic Church has the first claim to such status because it was reflection on *Catholic* doctrine—under the presumption that Church teachings contain the essence of the truth—which brought about the creation of Christian Materialism. This was the same reason that Christ had the first claim to be considered "revelation" (cf. p.361). But, the question remains: does the Church have the *best* claim to have inherited the authority of his resurrection? And, if not, who does?

2. Apostolic Succession and the Papacy

Actually, the question of whether the Catholic Church is "the" Church is rhetorical. Who else maintains the apostolic succession which also maintains the unity found only in the papacy? Since no one else has ever even claimed universal authority, it would not appear that much more need be said.[7]

The above does not mean that all bishops can trace their ordination to an apostle. Indeed, it is impossible to prove that *any* can. But, effectively, the succession was extended whenever the bishops came to accept someone as a member of their group.[8] If the bishops disputed each other, the issue was decided by the pope.

It is clear. Without a common adherence to one authority, disagreements between bishops would have divided the Church to death long ago. There-fore, for all the reasons that have always been given (cf. p. 46), the effi-ciency of leadership *not* by committee, and the spiritual-symbolic value of allegiance to one person, the Church requires one supreme authority.

In a hierarchy, this means spiritual descendancy from the Church's first supreme head, someone who was selected, if not by the resurrection, by Jesus.

This was supposedly Peter—no one else was ever mentioned (cf. p.192). Therefore, in view of the requirements of reality, minimalism recommends that we accept the evidence that Jesus chose Peter to lead his disciples in the event of his death. (Since he probably *did* know that his death was immi-nent, q.v. p.399, such an action is easily explained.)

The above does not need to mean that Peter or his immediate successors (as what but bishop of Rome) exercised supreme authority. But, we can know that the petrine office was meant to emerge. Its gradual development followed the increasing demands on the leadership of an ever bigger Church in an ever smaller world.

Peter became the head of an apostolic *group* because a group provides natural protection against the possibility that the leader will die without designating a successor, or lose the ability to function. (Of course, it also spared the Church from the credibility problems with a resurrection re-ported by one person.) And, a group broadens authority's base; and this will normally make it more open to progress.

3. The "Essence" of Catholic Faith
a. The Idea

We can now explain the underlying judgment that constitutes Catholic faith.

---

7. Actually, the absence of competing claims is an apologetic for Christianity itself. The leader of no other religion has a credible claim to divinely ordained universal authority—not the Chief Rabbis of Judaism (who do not claim to be the inheritors of the High Priesthood), nor the Shi'ite Imams whose claim to the Caliphate supposedly left by Mohammed is disputed by the far more numerous Sunnis.

8. Of course, "acceptance" normally meant ordination. This demonstrated the hierarchical structure of the Church even in those documented cases where the man to be ordained had been chosen by popular election.

Given faith in God, i.e. the judgment that the world cannot "just" exist, and faith in Christ, i.e. agreement with Jesus' principal presumptions and teachings, Catholic faith is faith in the Church, the understanding that humanity is called to be one—one family in faith.[9] (Thus, it is understanding the corporate nature and destiny of humanity.) It is understanding that membership in the Church is an essential element of the call of love. Moreover, in view of the fact that there are no other specifically Christian acts required of a loving person, membership in the Church should normally be considered the stuff of a distinctively Christian life *per se.*

2. Ecumenism and the Future of the Church

Of course, just as the truth of Christian belief does not mean that Christians are necessarily better persons, the truth of Catholic belief does not mean that Catholics are necessarily better Christians. It may not even mean that Catholics are better theologians. Indeed, Christian Materialism has identified the truth of many Protestant ideas. Their "protests," however, must be viewed in context. First of all, reform movements can easily critique a Church that cannot repudiate its history. But, for this reason, the Church retains its claim to the history of conversion. Besides, the Church must be judged in the context of its times. (And just prior to Luther's time, most people could not read.) If the Church sometimes seemed un-Christian, so did almost everyone else. (Luther's suppression of the "Anabaptists" was almost as brutal as the suppression of Protestants in Catholic lands.) And, when the Church was simply wrong, it reflected its humanity.

(Because of its humanity, the Church will continue to make mistakes.)

All the above notwithstanding, ecumenical activities aimed at reducing unfamiliarity, suspicion and animosity should continue. Joint efforts at good work for the world should also continue as long as the ultimate aim of Christian unity is not compromised.

The Church must work to re-establish a unity that may never have existed. And it must not lose hope that unity will be achieved. Divinely ordained, the Church bears the special protection of providence. In fact, the Church will be the principal instrument of the world's maturity and the home of its unity. Here is the truth of the Doctrine "Outside the Church No Salvation."

Section III: Special Questions in "Ecclesiology"

Having discussed the necessity of the Church, we now can turn to certain special questions concerning its nature—"ecclesiology."

---

9. Therefore, there is no reason for an absolute distinction between "schismatics" and "heretics." (Thus, ironically, the "Orthodox" are "heretics.")

A) The Need for a Magisterium

1. An Unmistakable Implication of Materialism

The first question that we shall consider concerns the first duty of Church leadership—teaching the truth. What is the faith but truth? What else determines Christian and ecclesial action? (Thus, there is no basis for an absolute distinction between "doctrine" and "morals.")

Plainly, truth is the basis of unity. (If this were not obvious for practical reasons, it would still be evident in the fact that knowledge is the basis of "union," cf. p.343).

Therefore, since agreement about the essence is the minimum that unity demands, someone—someone with authority—must declare what the essence is.

Of course, as we have already seen, there are unsuspendable and almost unsuspendable beliefs (cf. p.217). These, however, cannot be considered the extent of the essential minimum that demands agreement. After all, anyone can interpret this minimum to mean anything. Therefore, the authorities must continually decide what is "Catholic" and what is not.

This was the reason that there has always been a need for a magisterium (cf. p. 46). Further confirmed in the need for doctrine to develop, the highly dramatic developments required by materialism leave no doubt. How else will these developments ever become the official faith? And what of future developments? Indeed, from now on, the magisterium should lead the pursuit of truth.

Obviously, the work of the magisterium will be, and has been, a special case of providence. Herein lies its infallibility (cf. p.323). Here is the reason that Church teaching is to be presumed true unless there is sufficient reason to think differently.

2. Orthodoxy and Dissent

When there is sufficient reason to think differently, to disagree with what is taught, the person cannot but disagree. Though obedience can take place against one's better judgment, belief cannot. Of course, in times past, when belief in infallibility meant irreformability, a ruling from Rome was in itself sufficient reason to conclude that one's own idea was faulty. But, now, given our new view of the development of doctrine, it becomes clear that another new view, however condemned, could well represent progress. And the person who has this view is obligated to share it. Nonetheless, as he does, he must be sure to acknowledge the essential truth in the teaching with which he disagrees.

This, however, does not make him "orthodox." Orthodoxy cannot be something the person declares for himself. But, he can believe that his ideas will become orthodox and, for this reason, "dissent" from Church teaching does not need to mean that the person has separated himself from the Church. This decision belongs to the authorities.[10] They must decide the line between what is essential and what is secondary. This is the proper distinction between acts of the ordinary and extraordinary magisterium (cf. p.196). A distinction based upon infallibility is no longer necessary, nor possible.

B) Social Action

1. The Idea

"Social action" is work for a better world generally. Normally conceived in terms of the attempt to obtain a "Christian" distribution of economic wealth—the misnamed fight for social "justice" (cf. p.147) which is actually based upon what can only be called a love for the least of his brothers (cf. Mt.25)—it is explicitly tied to the Christian mandate according to the proponents of "Liberation Theology." An umbrella term covering a number of approaches, Liberation Theology departs from a vital concern for the world which has only been encouraged by universal salvation. After all, the spread of maturity must involve all people, and all areas of human progress. And, obviously, love does call the Church into conflict with other bodies if the future is at stake. But, the principles of Christian action never recommend violence except as a last resort. Even though violence has been required in self-defense, and still may be, the Church should normally pursue change through internal conversion—the conversion of owners, workers and consumers.

2. Church and State

The topic of social action immediately involves the proper relation of Church and state and, particularly, the degree to which the state should be expected to further the Church's ends.

When first posed, the question involved the Church's claim to have granted the state the power of civil government (cf. footnote p. 91). Then, in the controversies which spilled the blood of Thomas à Becket (d.1170) and Thomas More (d.1535), it involved the idea that a national church was subject to the head of state. It later involved the idea of a "state religion" (cf. p.199). It now involves what some call the attempt to "legislate morality."

Any dealing with these ideas must involve the following clarifications:

It was an historical accident that the Church existed prior to the modern

---

10. Still, some such decisions should await open debate. Debate can be a most effective way to expose and explore the truth.

national states of the West. Other forms of civil government existed prior to the Church.

States exist by necessity, and therefore by right. Since societal life requires people to respect each other's rights, societies require governments to protect these rights. According to John Locke, the basic rights are life, liberty and property (cf. footnote p.143). To protect these rights, states may take life, liberty or property. Thus, in essence, states infringe upon the freedom of individuals for the sake of everyone's freedom to live the best life he can make.[11]

Everyone's freedom is also seen to involve those things (such as public works and money) required of the "order" without which a modern society could not function. It is seen to involve those things (such as public health and education and the acquisition, maintenance and beautification of public space) which constitute the so-called "common good."[12] Lately, it is even seen to include the attempt to improve the lot of individuals who contribute little to the common good themselves. But, even this may be required by freedom—freedom from the disease or ignorance which eventually penalizes all of society.

Certain things are immediately to be observed:

The state, the civil government, is not society. It is an institution within society—the maker and enforcer of its "laws." Since these infringe upon the people's freedom for their sake, they should reflect the people's will, in other words, "democracy." Practicality almost always requires "representative" democracy, and government governed by a constitution.

It is also to be observed that there is nothing that the state does that does not involve some judgment about what is good or bad—right or wrong.

But, the state imposes its judgment. It infringes upon personal freedom—an infringement which most definitely involves the taxing of otherwise disposable funds. Therefore, its acts are legitimate to the degree that the freedom of persons is ultimately advanced. This proviso offers *limited* agreement with the notion that the common good is a major contributor to the "freedom" of individuals in the widest sense. Still, the degree to which

---

11. States may also impose limitations which protect people from the "indirect" loss of their freedom. Such is the jurisdiction of "zoning," etc.

12. But, the health and education of persons is best the Church's business. To whom should Christians entrust the care of their lives—and life? To whom should they entrust the education of their children? Faith is knowledge. It provides the true, complete interpretation of all reality. At the same time, faith is taught (or contradicted) through the interpretation of reality. Thus, the Church was wise in its historic insistence upon the need for Catholic schools. The future will only increase the need.

the state can legitimately infringe upon personal freedom depends upon importance of the good which is pursued—and cannot be secured otherwise with any measure of efficiency.

But, the state is not like the Church whose rule pursues the good of a variety of values. This is not the role of the state. Values are not to be pursued by force—the force of the potential loss of life, liberty or property. (Though individuals may approve of what the state is doing here or there— particularly when it is being done for them—their insistence that others, who may not approve of it, pay for it, is not right.) The pursuit of values remains the province of the Church, a voluntary organization out of which one can opt without any other penalty.[13] Unfortunately, in the wake of the effective collapse of the Church as the principal structure in societal life, some in the Church have fallen into the mistaken belief that it was meant to be the "conscience of the state"—and no more. In fact, the Church must strive to re-assume the direct leadership of co-operative efforts to build a better world.

Of course, since Christians remain members of the state, bound by its laws—giving to Caesar what is Caesar's (Mt.22:21)—they have both the right and obligation to use political or, if need be, extraordinary means to see that it does its rightful job well and effectively—and no more. Christian efforts at social change are best directed at influencing society to voluntary action, the kind that requires the spiritual maturity whose increase is the world's true goal. Indeed, it should be the task of the Church to reduce enforced regulation, and taxation—something that cannot be done until the Church is ready to take up the slack. As a general rule, the Church should not solicit from the state, nor accept, anything that it would not want given to another faith in another land. Finally, though Christians remain members of the state, and must work "in" it[14]—and, when need be, "for" it—they

---

13. Plainly, the Communist management of an economy, and therefore society, is far too great an infringement upon the freedom of persons. It also involves the error of attempting to force what are essentially "Christian" behaviors upon people who have not been converted internally. Finally, it attempts to have direct human control over something far too complex to be controlled directly. Therefore, an economy—a "market"—needs to be free. (Adam Smith was right.) This is not to say that moderate forms of "socialism" involving public ownership of those things essential to society—particularly where competition would be impossible—could not be recommended. Otherwise, a society could be liable to the impossible tension of enslavement by its own laws. Indeed, in certain situations, it may even be recommended that the state would take from the rich to give to the poor; preventing a revolution may require it. Nonetheless, the greatest reticence must be observed in the judgment of what is really recommended.
14. Since the Church *must* exist within the context of the state, it has done well to have utilized the existing civil law in order to protect its essential structures.

retain the right to civil disobedience when they are truly in conscience convinced.[15]

C) Worship

1. The Idea

Having discussed the rules which would well guide the Church's relationship to the outside world, we shall discuss those that should guide its most internal concern, worship.

The Church exists so that faith can be shared (cf. p.375). Since faith is most plainly shared through prayer, the Church must assemble if only to pray. Since this should only involve the kinds of prayer which can be presumed of everyone present, i.e. thanksgiving and praise, it is rightly called "worship." And it is rightly considered an "obligation" in the custody of the Church.[16]

Worship should be both inspirational and instructional. These are man's basic religious needs. And they are intrinsic to worship. The latter follows from the very fact that worship is happening. The former follows from the fact that public prayer—public attention to God—has always moved Christians to be more aware of the presence of God who is always around them. It is true: "where two or three are gathered in my name, there I am in the midst of them" (Mt.18:20).

2. Ritual

Worship requires ritual. Required by the need for order, making possible the efficient and credible use of time, ritual is also meaningful. Utilizing gesture—which is most important because of the symbolic nature of conceptual thought (cf. p.256)—it portrays the truth. It also involves the deliberateness of action, or "solemnity," needed in order to make clear that the matter at hand is important.

Immemorially present in all cultures at all times, ritual is actually required by man's need for structure. This has been discovered by those groups who, in reaction to what has sometimes been a "magical" use of ritual, tried to do away with it only to discover that they had replaced the old rituals with new ones. Therefore, rather than do away with ritual, it must be designed in order to convey its meanings most effectively, with the least "ritualism"

---

15. Here is the wisdom of Pope John Paul II's insistence that clerics should not put themselves in positions of "civil accountability."

16. Thus, those who do not "go to Church" may still be good persons—who pray elsewhere—but they cannot be good Catholics.

which is necessary.[17]

Naturally, the design of "Catholic" ritual is the prerogative of the proper authorities.[18] This should surely involve weighing the value of "tradition" (which appreciates the fact that special meaning is attached to something that is known to have been done for a long, long time) against the value of "modernization" which responds to the realities of an ever changing world. It should involve weighing the value of "uniformity" (for the purpose of unity) against the value of an "adaptability" which would allow different cultures to do what is uniquely meaningful to them. Adaptability would also involve the provision of options by which the "liturgy" can be adapted to changing intra-cultural circumstances or other local considerations, not to mention the community's or minister's own strengths or weaknesses.

Section IV: The Sacraments

A) The Idea

We can now affirm the truth of the doctrine of sacraments. Already we have heard the idea that sacraments are divine acts by commission (cf. p.318). At that time, we were still waiting for evidence that it was God's intention to speak in this way. This evidence is the simple fact that ritual is necessary. But, the extent to which a specific ritual can be said to speak for God depends upon the extent to which it flows from the natural necessities of the Church's mission and/or follows an action of Jesus which was meant to be repeated. Thus, the divine institution of individual sacraments must be decided on a case by case basis. It is on this basis that we shall also determine their effects.

B) Holy Orders

1. The Need for Ordination

The first sacrament that we shall consider is the one whose divine ordination has already been established: Holy Orders.

In establishing the necessity of the hierarchical structure of the Church (cf. p.377), we also established the necessity of the "delegation" of author-

---

17. Actually, it has long been a point of Catholic pride that the Church would appear to stand about midway between the extremes of Orthodox and Protestant worship.

18. Obviously, the authority to redesign ritual includes the right to rewrite the so-called "liturgical year." The singular exception would be the Passover-based placement of "Easter" which was actually named for the goddess of spring. Christmas was a totally arbitrary christianization of the Roman Feast of Light.

The Church's prerogatives also include the creation of official symbolism. The singular exception would be the sign of the "cross," an immemorial Christian symbol of obvious historical origin and great meaning.

ity. How else does a hierarchy exist?

From the very beginning, the Church understood the delegation of authority to require the solemnity, and certainty, of a rite of ordination; it chose the
laying on of hands (cf. p. 84). As definite degrees of authority were widely
delegated, "offices" in the Church were created.[19] The exercise of their
authority *is* power (cf. p.316). Nonetheless, ordination can still be said to
"change" the person. It changes his relation to the Church and, as it does, it
calls for the commitment of his whole self. Since the rite really speaks for
God, it is He who makes the person "sacred" in the original sense of the
Latin word for "consecration," i.e. "set apart" for especially holy
purposes.

Consecreation notwithstanding, the above is clearly a "relational ontology" (cf. p.316); it is departure from the traditional ontology involving as it
did a metaphysical and, therefore, permanent change. An idea appropriate
to times past when power meant powers and required a metaphysical
base, it was also appropriate to the fact that, with so little communication
between churches, some way was needed to see how local churchmen—and
missionaries—could carry the power of the Church with them. But, now that
times have changed, this idea is no longer needed. And, it is no longer
helpful. The Church can no longer afford to be at the mercy of ordinations
which may have been mistaken or became so. A relationship ontology will
allow the Church to "repeal" ordinations which would otherwise harm its
health or unity.

As times change, the structure of authority can also change. Clearly, we
have no reason to insist that the three-fold structure of ministry—bishops,
priests, and deacons (cf. p. 84)—exists according to God's special intention.

Actually, the traditional structure is already a problem. It speaks of deacons but does not delegate to them the true authority of official power. Of
course, the authority given to deacons reflects the degree to which they are
normally at the disposal of the Church specifically in terms of time and
mobility. This, perhaps, offers us a clue as to a "new" diaconate. Ordained
to perform all the Church's sacramental acts—given proper delegation[20]—
the deacon becomes an officer in the community of which he is a permanent
member, but not necessarily full time. He might be one of many associates

---

19. Here is the limited legitimacy of "clerical" clothes. A uniform which helpfully identifies
the officer who wears them—they are something of special importance to an institution whose
members may not know each other. They also have sign value.

20. This concept of ordination would spare the Church from useless quibbling about whether
orders is one sacrament or three (cf. footnote p.315).

of a priest. The priest is the head of the community who serves full time and moves within a diocese at the direction of the bishop. The bishop is already committed to the needs of the Church universal.

But, this does *not* mean that the Church is best organized with the bishop as the head of what must be considered the basic unit of the Church local, the diocese. Not only do Christians exist in smaller units, i.e. parishes, which are more basic, but they exist in larger groups, which exist ineffectively because they lack unifying leadership. They comprise a nation which should be headed by a "primate" who has real authority over archbishops—who head provincial realities—with real authority over local bishops. In any case, we can still say that there is nothing about what is presently considered a diocese that requires its head to share the universal authority of the apostolic group which is actually shared only by the "cardinals" who elect the pope.[21] Regardless of what is done, and the words that are used, the organization of the Church should correspond to the societal realities that either exist—or should. Of course, not only would these be changeable, they would not need to involve precisely the same structures in all places.

2. An Addendum: Questions of Ministerial Life; Religious Life
Christian Materialism should surely be expected to have something to say to the emotional issues of ministerial life, specifically, celibacy, women's ordination and the possibility of a limited term of ordained service. After considering these, we shall take a look at the future of "religious" life.

It is first to be stated that minimalism has already relieved the binding force of Tradition. Thus, decisions of ministerial life are the prerogative of the Church, informed but not bound by the past as changing circumstances or progress may require different things at different times. Any such decision is to be made on the basis of the principles that govern Christian action generally (cf. p.352). Therefore:

The requirement of celibacy must be understood with regard to the pros and cons of whether the full-time ministry is better or worse because of it. An issue with many aspects, the following facts are pertinent:

Though Jesus may have favored celibacy, his favor is neither proved, nor should it be binding on us today. Nor was it binding on the early Church. In the beginning, most of the Church's officers were married (cf. 1 Tim.3). They were married for the first thousand years of Church history. Celibacy came to be required (in the West only) in an attempt to reform the clergy. This involved the idea that such a sacrifice would select only the most

---

21. Therefore, it would no longer be necessary to view the bishop as the true "pastor" of every soul in his region, or to deny the direct responsibility of his superiors.

sincere candidates. It also involved attention to the ancient (Greek) idea that he who offers the sacrifice should not be engaged in an active sexual life. These would not appear good reasons to maintain the discipline. The argument that the priest is emotionally freer for the love of his people must be weighed against his greater ability to identify with them. The notion that he is "freer" must also be weighed against the emotional work that a healthy celibacy requires. It is also to be acknowledged that the experience of intimacy in marriage is often a source of maturity and security that may not be attained otherwise. Most of the arguments on the basis of practical concerns must be recognized to have their "flip-side." For example, though married clergy would be less mobile, they would be more likely to become part of their community. It is by no means clear (or decisive) that a married clergy would be more costly, or less prone to cause scandal. Therefore, since celibacy is not—and is not claimed to be—intrinsic to Christian leadership, and marriage addresses several important human needs, and celibacy restricts, and will continue to restrict ever more severely, the numbers of ordained ministers, both before and after ordination, it would seem that the rule of celibacy has seen its day.

So has the rule which prohibits the ordination of women. Historically, this rule was recommended by the male dominance of a species in which females bear the children. This fact of biology gave males the role of provider and evolutionarily suited them to this role. But it has not produced a great difference between male and female psychologically, and women have proved themselves capable of leadership. The argument that Jesus did not ordain women—not even his mother—is immediately invalid on the grounds that Jesus did not ordain anyone. (Besides, as we have seen, Jesus' culture would not have allowed women a leadership role, cf. p.180.) Neither is valid the modern argument from "sacramental anthropology"—the idea that since the ordained administers the sacraments *in persona Christi* (cf. p. 86) and Christ was a man, the ordained must be men. Clearly, women continue Christ's mission of making God's love known *at least* as well as men in other circumstances. Therefore, once a particular culture was taught to accept the change as an instance of progress, there would seem no other reason that qualified women should not be ordained.

Instituting a limited term of ordained service is not recommended. Christian leadership is only to become more demanding, and demanding of more maturity. (Thus, the cleric should still be considered a Christian model.) Leadership training is only to become more extensive. Therefore, it will only become less likely that suitable candidates would not want to commit their lives to this great work. And the Church should not want candidates who do not feel "called" to do so. This is especially obvious when we consider the trust—not to mention the stewardship and secrecy—vested in Church leaders.

But, excepting the papacy—which cannot be subject to statute—the Church has been wise to expect the resignation of persons with administrative authority once they reach a certain age. At the same time, like the papacy, such positions can profit from the stability (and personality) offered by open-ended terms of service.

We can now take our look at the future of "religious" life—the vowed life of poverty, chastity and obedience in community. Let be it clear; nothing that has been said of the possible changes in ministerial life were meant to critique the lives of religious. Religious life offers special incentives to spiritual growth; and it responds to special needs. Not for everyone, and not necessarily better, religious life remains a path to God which is not to be critiqued by those who do not take it. Thus, the future of religious life is to be determined by just that, the future, as progress determines the degree to which it will have a prominent place in the Church and in the lives of mature people.[22]

C) Baptism

1. The Sacrament of Initiation

If the need for ordination was obvious, so is the need for initiation—some formal way for people to be accepted into the Church. Since the Church is a hierarchy—and membership means the delegation of some authority—it is clear that a person must be received; he does not declare himself a member.

It is also clear that this necessary, formal act of initiation is indeed God speaking—by commission—as He receives the person into His Church. By this "rite," the person is not only changed in his relation to the Church but also in himself to the extent that this knowledge affects him.

From the beginning, initiation has involved a Baptism of water, a ritual taken over from more primitive times which symbolized the cleansing from sin. In view of our new perspectives on sin and salvation, it would seem that a change in the rite of Baptism is in order. After all, a sacrament is supposed to symbolize what it affects (cf. p. 85). The imposition of hands much more clearly demonstrates that a person is being given a share of the Church's mission. Moreover, the imposition of hands was the first rite of the Church's choosing (cf. p.314). It would be a better rite of what would better be called "initiation."

---

22. The future of "societies of apostolic life"—societies of mutually committed people "in the world"—is to be viewed with a similar perspective. But, it is possible that the increasing maturity of all Christians (in parishes) will eventually render them obsolete.

A change in the so-called "matter and form" (cf. p.85) of a sacramental act is possible because it was the Church's decision to adopt the old ones. Furthermore, as acts of the Church, it is clear that the sacraments do work *ex opere operato*. In other words, as official acts, they affect what the Church says they affect regardless of the holiness of the minister who is delegated the authority to "celebrate" them—if all the conditions specified to make them "valid" are met. Of course, their spiritual effectiveness does depend upon the way they are celebrated.

2. An Addendum: Questions of Infant and Re-Baptism

The new theology of Baptism has something to say to the principal historical controversies over Baptism, namely the questions of infant and re-Baptism.

There is no reason that infants should not be received into their parent's Church. After all, infants are totally dependent members of their parent's family. Moreover, since the faith of adult Church membership involves the most complex—and most global—knowledge of which man is capable, the formation of this faith should begin as soon as possible. Indeed, we have only become more aware that the earliest years are the most formative.

The importance of upbringing is not the only reason to require faith on the part of the parents. Since an infant cannot speak for himself, it is his parent's faith that validates his reception. To receive him regardless is to involve God in a dishonest (and pointless) act that serves only to diminish His Church's credibility. This is "sacrilege."

Unlike the question of infant Baptism, the question of re-Baptism is *not* one which so clearly bespeaks the wisdom of the past.

The Church has constantly confirmed its decision not to re-baptize those baptized by heretics (cf. p.80). Since Baptism is a reception into the Church, this is no longer recommended. But, what of the fact that re-Baptism was not only available but proposed by Cyprian?

The fact that this was not the Church's decision is in itself reason to search for a good explanation. One is available. In view of what was then the whole faith—and the place of Baptism within it—the decision showed the Church's desire not to be legalistic about salvation, and to maximize it. The decision bespoke the importance of repentance and the belief that God created a new person in its wake. Thus, the Baptism of heretics was valid though "illicit," the right to use this power supplied by the Church.

The idea that "the Church supplies" ("Ecclesia supplit") was the Church's attempt to protect its faith in both sacraments and salvation. But, this idea is no longer needed. The distinction between illicit and invalid sacramental acts should be maintained as degrees of what is required of proper matter, form and even minister.

D) Confirmation

1. A Requirement of Infant Baptism

Obviously, when infants are received into the Church, they must later be given some way to speak for themselves. The Church must have some way to confirm their membership.

Though the sacrament may have developed for different reasons (cf. p.314), it always served as the completion of initiation. It should now become the person's commitment to the Church—and the Church's acceptance of him as an adult member. Naturally, this commitment must wait until the individual is an adult who can mean what he is saying. Obviously, it would not be necessary to confirm a baptized adult; this would be the same rite.

2. An Addendum: The Rightful Requirements of Church Membership

The question of Confirmation brings up a question that could as easily have been mentioned in conjunction with the faith required of parents seeking Baptism for their children. What is the minimum that is to be expected—to be required.

Rigorous requirements have characterized the many "elitist" movements that attempted to make the Church an exclusive assembly of only the best Christians. Instead, by and large, the Church as accepted almost anyone who was baptized and willing to call himself Catholic. This decision was consistent with what we now call the developmental nature of man and, specifically, the fact that human progress only takes place as maturity is given time to make its way through society. Indeed, in its willingness to accommodate persons at a variety of maturity levels, the Church christianized the West and dragged it out of barbarism.

Because of the Church's success, however, society is now capable of "faith" and critical of hypocrisy. Therefore, now that we no longer believe "outside the Church no salvation," the Church can and must establish and enforce requirements which follow truly from what it is to be a Catholic. The present casual and cowardly approach to requirements does little or nothing for nominal members—except to confirm them as such—as it injures the credibility of the Church and saps its energy.

Though the rightful requirements of Church membership should be a special study, it would be difficult to imagine that they could involve less than the following:

A Catholic must be willing to profess faith in God, in Christ, and in the Church, in terms of the essence the Church has established. Naturally, this would include assent to the principle of obedience to Church leadership. (He should also be willing to state: "The Catholic faith is the most important

thing in my life.") Of course, there is no faith if it is not practiced. Therefore, if a person has Catholic faith, he wants to be a Church member. If
accepted, he must do at least the minimum which the Church considers
essential to being a member. And the Church cannot ask less than that its
members assemble, not only to pray, but to learn, to support each other, and
to participate in the life of the community. This they must do faithfully, i.e.
regularly. This means weekly, in tune with the cycle that governs almost
everything else we do.[23] If they will not accede to these minimal, rightful
requirements of Church membership, they have effectively declared that
they are not "Catholic." And the Church must accept this decision, remov-
ing them from the rolls of those in communion.[24] Though this will result in a
big drop in the number of nominal members, IT WILL RESULT IN A BIG
DROP IN THE NUMBER OF NOMINAL MEMBERS.[25] It will restore
credibility and a proper pride to the Church and spare its energy and morale.
It will challenge. And, it will make the Church attractive and effective. In
time, this Church will re-evangelize the West.

E) Penance

1. The Necessity of Reconciliation

The very idea of rightful requirements of Church membership and, the fact
that membership is a privilege not a right, includes within it the understanding that the Church has the right to excommunicate members who fail to
fulfill these requirements. For the sake of the Church's health and credibility, these should also include certain moral standards.

A recognized need from the beginning (cf. p. 80), it was also recognized
that love also requires some way for the repentant person to be reconciled to
the Church. But, in view of the obvious requirements of reality, the Church
retains the right to refuse the person and, if necessary, to determine what
will be required to rectify the wrong. Therefore, it would naturally fall to
the Church's officers to make these decisions, and to restore the person to
communion. Of course, in doing so, the officer speaks for God and this
should involve some rite of "reconciliation."

Naturally, not every offence can cost a person his membership in the
Church. All people commit countless failures to love. But, there are serious
sins that people do not need to commit—sins not expected of Christians.
Though the Church's conception of what is serious has changed, and will

---

23. Obviously, the necessity of "coming to Church" presumes there is a Church to come to. It
also presumes a person is able to come to Church.
24. Obviously, this will require the Church to become even more serious about record-keeping
than it actually is. (And it will make sense of the record-keeping which is already required.)
25. This should be accepted according to the principle: "What have you lost?" Besides: "If
you could so easily lose 'em, you never had 'em."

continue to, and may need to involve some specific law, or some specific directive, it remains the Church's right to make such decisions.

2. An Addendum: Reflections on the Historical Value of Confession
No discussion of the essential validity of the sacrament of reconciliation should ignore the variety of values which the historical development of the practice of frequent confession has definitely represented. Even beyond the value of hearing a human voice speak words of forgiveness—words we do not "hear" from God—confession provided the objectivity of requiring a person to formulate and speak his sin (out loud) to another person. It also offered an utterly secret forum for counseling. It fulfilled the function now more explicitly served in ongoing "spiritual direction." Though the spiritual direction is not explicitly "confessional," it need not be. There is an obvious value in the objectivity of discussing one's life with another who is hopefully wiser.

F) The Eucharist

1. The Problem

Plainly, the Eucharist presents a special problem. Though it may express, and thereby bring about, the communion of those who receive it, a relational ontology would not appear to justify the immemorial faith that the Eucharist is, in some real sense, the body and blood of Christ.

The problem involves the need to supply sufficient evidence that Jesus' identification with bread and wine was both his intention and God's. Then, the meaning of this identification must be re-thought in the light of our new understanding of Jesus' divinity.

2. The Evidence of Tradition

The evidence of Tradition is the historical importance of the Eucharist in the life of the Church. Though there may be doubt about the meaning of the New Testament texts, there is no doubt that, by New Testament times, the eucharistic celebration was the central act of Christian worship. Though it did express the communion of Church members, it was perceived to have this effect because it was *first* perceived to involve communion with Christ. Within a century, it definitely involved belief in the real presence of Christ in the eucharistic species (cf. p.82).

With time, attention to the real presence only increased. It culminated in the doctrine of transubstantiation. This was the official reason the Eucharist was "pre-eminent" among the sacraments. It still is—to Catholics. What is more, even in the most non-Catholic denominations, a eucharistic service is still the central act of worship.

3. An Evaluation of the Evidence of Scripture

The evidence of Tradition definitely recommends an evaluation of the evidence of Scripture.

Naturally, our evaluation will begin with a look at the most primitive text that we possess, namely 1 Cor. 11:23-25:

"For I received from the Lord what I also delivered to you, that the Lord Jesus on the night when he was betrayed took bread, and when he had given thanks, he broke it, and said, 'This is my body which is for you. Do this in remembrance of me.' In the same way also the cup, after supper, saying 'This cup is the new covenant in my blood. Do this, as often as you drink it, in remembrance of me.'"

Once again, Paul claims to be passing on a tradition he "received" (cf. p.365). Obviously, he is repeating a formula that gives evidence of its antiquity.

But, it may not be the most ancient tradition of which we have evidence. Some scholars insist that Mark's account (14:22-25) sounds more semitic and may be based upon a more ancient tradition. It reads:

"And as they were eating, he took bread, and blessed, and broke it, and gave it to them, and said 'Take; this is my body.' And he took a cup, and when he had given thanks he gave it to them, and they all drank of it. And he said to them, 'This is my blood of the covenant which is poured out for many. Truly, I say to you, I shall not drink again of the fruit of the vine until that day when I drink it new in the kingdom of God.'"

Mark's account is plainly the model for Matthew's (26:26-29), while Luke's (22:15-20) appears to be dependent upon Paul.

In any case, the two distinct accounts bespeak the antiquity of the common tradition that underlies them. The following common elements are to be observed: the setting is pointedly a meal, a "supper," and it was Jesus'

Mark's account is plainly the model for Matthew's (26:26-29), while Luke's (22:15-20) appears to be dependent upon Paul.

In any case, the two distinct accounts bespeak the antiquity of the common tradition that underlies them. The following common elements are to be observed: the setting is pointedly a meal, a "supper," and it was Jesus' last taken with his disciples; it took place the night he was betrayed. All the synoptics say that it was Passover and, by and large, they describe a Passover meal. But the breaking and blessing of bread, and the blessing of the cup, did take place at other meals. Nonetheless, if the last supper was a Passover meal, it would explain the Johannine omission of a last supper account. Since John's Jesus was the "lamb of God" (Jn.1:29)—whose sacrifice on Passover was pre-figured in the "paschal" lamb sacrificed at Passover—his Jesus could not celebrate the traditional ritual. Still, John does speak of the necessity of eating Jesus' body and drinking His blood. He speaks explicitly of Jesus' identification with bread (6:51-58).

Mark and Paul agree on Jesus' use of the phrases "this is my body; this is my blood." Since Jesus spoke Aramaic—which lacks the present tense of the verb "to be"—he would have said "this my body; this my blood." The sense is *not* evident in the words themselves or their immediate context. Neither is it evident in Paul's claim that consuming the species is a "participation" in the body and blood of Christ (1 Cor. 9:16-17).

It is also to be noted that blood is further identified with the "new covenant." The accounts also share the idea that either the body or the blood is "for" someone. Paul says this of the body—which is for "you"; Mark says that the blood is for "many." Neither speaks of an explicit sacrifice for the forgiveness of sins.

The accounts do not agree that the action is to be repeated as a memorial; the instruction is missing from Mark.

Though reported by Paul, the phrase "do this in memory of me" is too helpful to be accepted as Jesus' own. Moreover, it would mean that Jesus meant to establish himself as the center of Christian worship, an act totally out of character for the founder of what we now understand as Christianity. Jesus' inferable self-conception—and our theology of redemption—also argue against the idea that he offered his body in terms of sacrifice. Neither does it encourage the idea that he believed that his blood established a new covenant.

Surely, the references to body *and* blood reflect the semitic idea that both are constitutive of the person; blood was believed to be the "life-source." The abandonment of this anthropology is reflected in the classical doctrine of "concomitance" (DS 1199)—the insistence that each species contains the whole Jesus.

But, we have yet to determine in what sense Jesus meant to identify himself with bread, wine, or both. Neither have we shown that the eucharistic action was meant to be repeated. Furthermore, since we are unsure, and an alternate explanation of the eucharistic accounts has been suggested—the idea arose out the disciples' sense that Jesus was still with them, especially at mealtime (cf. p.130)—we must ask: is there sufficient evidence that Jesus meant anything? Did the last supper take place? Does minimalism allow the Eucharist?

3. The Theological Evidence, A New Theology of the Eucharist
Even though the alternate explanation of the eucharistic accounts is plainly implausible, the evidence of Scripture and Tradition remains inconclusive.

Therefore, theological evidence must decide the question. To obtain it, let us suppose that the eucharistic accounts were made up or imagined.

Plainly, the denial of something so ancient and so central would compromise the credibility of Christianity so seriously that the necessity of revelation would not be satisfied. Therefore, for essentially the same reasons that we affirmed the resurrection (cf. p.365), we can affirm that Jesus must have identified himself with bread and wine.

Therefore, there must have been a reason. If it was not the representation of his sacrifice in a representable form, what is left?

Let us consider the situation. Accepting the evidence that this was Jesus' last supper with his disciples—the most plausible setting for such an extraordinary action—it is also to be accepted that Jesus *did* know his end was imminent. Hardly supernatural knowledge, there were surely indications that the establishment was out to get him, not to mention the definite possibility that he was warned. In the face of this grim fact, a person who surely had a great sense of "mission"—the mission to proclaim God's love—would certainly have wanted to see that his work would continue. Identifying himself with his mission—as all such people do—it is easily imaginable that he desired to give "himself" to his disciples, commissioning them, through the rich symbolism in the giving (and receiving) of sustenance.

Since there are no viable alternatives, this is what we have left. It is present in the immemorial idea that the species affect communion with Jesus, and also the modern idea that the common reception of the species brings about the communion of the recipients (cf. p.317).

Given this understanding of what Jesus must have meant, it is also clear that the Eucharist would have been repeated whether or not Jesus explicitly intended that it should.

That this is what God intended can be seen through the essential truth of the incarnation (cf. p.370) through which we can derive the essential truth of the Eucharist:

Jesus was "the" manifestation of God's love, His gift of self, Him. "The" manifestation of Jesus' love was his acceptance of death—his own gift of self. Therefore, in the Eucharist, we see *God's* gift of self; we see Him. Of course, we can already "see" God in everything. But we cannot pay attention to "everything"; after all, God is present in the light, the eyes, and the brain of our every perception. Therefore, through Jesus' action, he has ordained one place for us to pay attention to Him, and to see Him pay attention to us. In the bread, we are presented with the body of Christ, God's gift of self—the essential truth of the incarnation. The blood of Christ more specifically presents the essential truth of the redemption—the fact that God has given His life for us. In this repeatable presentation of His gift of self, He is continually inspiring His Church to do the same. And, according to Jesus' explicit intention, He is re-commissioning its members. Thus, it is still true: the Church receives the body of Christ to become the body of Christ.

In partaking of the *one* bread and cup, the Church is reminded that it is called to be one.

As the Christian community assembled, it is most appropriate that the Eucharist is a meal. At no other time is a family more a family. (A meal is the best form of celebration because it involves the mutual enjoyment of something that everyone already needs.) It is properly presided over by the head of the family.

As the central act of Christian worship, it is entirely appropriate that the "Eucharist"—Greek for "thanksgiving"—should be just that. Of all the forms of prayer, thanks come first (cf. p.341).

As "grace" before the meal, it involves thanking God at the time when we are normally most conscious of our dependence on Him—at the time when we feel our needs and know that they will soon be satisfied.[26] Moreover, food and drink are visible, tangible, and can be tasted. Therefore, what would better represent everything we have to thank God for? And, as we do so, God responds presenting all we have to thank Him for.

5. The Idea of Sacrifice

From all that has been said, hopefully it is clear that the Eucharist is not just a "representation" of God's self-giving—an act of our own contrivance—it is a "re-presentation" of this giving, something that God intends to mean what it does. Thus does it re-present the self-giving most fully presented in the sacrifice of the cross. Moreover, as we commemorate this event, it is *our* sacrifice in terms of worship.

As worship, offering sacrifice has always seemed the most sincere thing that man could do for God. In doing something that served no other purpose—and actually involved the destruction of goods man could use—man showed God deference. When Christianity was establishing itself, the Eucharist seemed the perfect sacrifice. Naturally, as a good work, merit was obtained.

But, now that these ideas have given way to the realization that the merit of worship is the inspirational effects of its doing—not to mention our new view of prayers of petition (cf. p.320)—it is clear that the Eucharist is not an

---

26. It is the latter fact that most clearly involves the so-called "eschatological" aspect of the Eucharistic celebration—the gathering of the community as one to receive God's gift of Himself—a sure anticipation of what is indeed our destiny.

efficacious sacrifice in the historical sense.

But the Eucharist remains the thanksgiving of the community, the God-given way to offer Him the worship He wants for our good.

Thus, from the beginning, Christian tradition has called the community together every Sunday, the "Lord's Day," in order to worship, and to commemorate not only the cross but also the resurrection.[27] This has undoubtedly been a good thing. What has not been so good is the frequent celebration of community life when the community is not there, the idea that the Eucharist needs to be celebrated every day, and as a part of every other Christian assembly. This confuses the purpose of the Eucharist and makes it less effective.

6. An Addendum: Questions of Inter-Communion and Reservation

As a matter of cleaning up the loose ends, this discussion of the Eucharist would well conclude with statements about certain issues that should also prove to clarify the theology that has been struck.

The new theology surely has something to say to the idea of inter-communion, the idea that there is some good in giving communion to members of different churches not actually in communion. Here is the key. The Eucharist is "the" sign of Catholic unity. Therefore, it is difficult to imagine what is good about giving communion to those who, essentially speaking, do not want it. Thus, the Church is right to have declared that "communion is not a means but a goal of unity (*Unitatis Redintegratio,* 8). Since this hardly constitutes the withholding of salvation, the perennial wisdom of giving communion only to those in communion (cf. p. 82) is clearly to be seen. How else is the effectiveness, and sacredness, of communion to be maintained?

The idea that the sacredness of communion depends on how we treat it also recommends the historical practice of the reservation of the sacrament. Not only a practical necessity, the question hinges upon the simple fact that nothing special to *us* will continue to be unless *we* give it special treatment.[28] A phenomenological fact of life also manifest in the defense of the flag, it is obvious that something consecrated by God should not be treated as garbage. Since consecration could hardly be said to "wear off"—and, for phenomenological reasons, should not be declared to "be" off—respect for the Eucharist species should continue to be commensurate with the specific content of the belief in what they are. Although this would not necessarily recommend Eucharistic "adoration," this practice should be allowed to seek

---

27. Indeed, changing the Sabbath from Saturday was the first, great unwritten act of Church Tradition. Plainly, the most ancient wisdom of a "Lord's Day" of rest, and reflection, is only more true today.

its own level.

G) Matrimony

1. How Is Marriage a Sacrament?

The question of how, indeed, whether marriage is a sacrament rests upon the question of whether marriage exists according to God's special intention.

a. The Question of Monogamy

The question of whether marriage exists according to God's special intention rests upon the question of monogamy—the question of whether He intends one man and one woman to live together for life. The question raises itself in the discovery of non-monogamous cultures and the innovation of "alternate" lifestyles which involve persons in either non-permanent or non-exclusive relationships whose viability cannot be dismissed out of hand.

A question which would actually require much more study than is here appropriate, it can still be stated that the perennial Christian tradition of monogamy clearly reflects God's special intention:

Biologically, the complementarity of one man and one woman is responsible for every new member of the human family. And who should be responsible for the continuing care thereof? Moreover, the overwhelming evidence indicates that the nurturing of children cries out for the stable, parental influence of both kinds of human person.

More importantly, especially in cases of relationships that do not expect children (or no longer expect them), marriage is the lifetime commitment which concretizes the "union" which is the goal of the one such relationship that human limitations still make possible.

This confirms much of the truth of the traditional wisdom with regard to marriage.

Because sexual expression is best what it can be, an expression of the union of persons—which involves the "vulnerability" which once caused it to be viewed as an evil thing[29]—it is honestly appropriate only to those who have made the commitment which concretizes this union. Indeed, not only does it express this commitment but, in doing so, it continually remakes and helps to sustain it. This is the "unitive" function of sexuality. (It is an anticipation of the union of persons in eternity.) And, let it be clear: by "commitment" is meant the sincerity which, normally, is not demonstrated

---

28. Here surely is the reason for reverential treatment for any number of "sacred" things, especially those used in services, not to mention the importance of the symbolism involved in the normal requirement of wearing "vestments."

29. Actually, the Western distaste for sexuality is also rooted in the Greek contempt for the "irrationality" to which it was perceived to drive its participants.

except in the formal public promise which is marriage.[30]

Because sexual expression is the means by which others most directly share in God's creation of others, all of whom will share His life, married couples possess an opportunity so great that it constitutes a "call" to which they must in some way respond. This is the "procreative" function of sexuality; it is the call to give life as life has been given to you. A proper response should follow from the principles of Christian action generally (cf. p.352). One point is particular to this issue: in the light of divine determinism, it is clear there is no storehouse of unborn persons some of whom might not come to the life for which they were meant. Moreover, man's cumulative sight of God involves both quantity (in terms of perceivers) as well as quality (in terms of love)—in proportions not directly determinable. But, surely, the proportions relate to what will work for man in the world. Surely, God would not "normally" ask man to ruin his life or world in order to do the best thing. Therefore, decisions of family planning should balance quantity and quality and, thus, are matters of individual and/or global circumstances.[31]

30. The possibility of homosexual "marriage" has *not* been established by the above. An exceedingly complex issue, it also involves questions of what is "normal" and "natural"—and what is "sick." Therefore, the resolution of this issue would require much more discussion than can here follow. When discussion takes place, however, the following should be kept in mind. The question of "naturalness" involves the obvious evolutionary intent of sexual organs and desires. The question of "normalness" involves the predictable product of "typical" genes and experience. But the question of whether homosexuality is a sickness is more complex, involving as it does a judgment of what has resulted. Nonetheless, facing the facts of what is natural and normal, productive of families and less problematic to persons and society, a homosexual orientation must be considered an unfortunate development. (All things being equal, it is nothing anyone would choose.) Therefore, even apart from someone's objection to the judgment that such an orientation is caused by bio-chemical "imbalances" (which originate genetically) or an "imbalanced" experience of personality models, it is clear that homosexuality does mean that something has gone wrong. This, however, does not mean that homosexuality means that something has gone so wrong that personal commitments are impossible—or cannot be good for the persons who would make them. But the public sanction of such a commitment may not be something so good for society as a whole. Like almost everything else, homosexuality exists in terms of degrees with any person subject to the influence of any number of models and the cultural climate at large. Therefore, a solution to this problem could well involve a private form of sanction presently unheard of. Needless to say, no decision in an individual case could be made without a serious attempt to determine the true status of the persons' homosexuality, not to mention other services designed to help them cope with the problems that their situation usually involves.

31. In view of the validity of family planning, and the fact that natural law involves no absolutes (cf. p.353)—a fact also evident in the approval of pain-killers which thwart natural processes meant for our good—the question of natural vs. artificial contraception is to be decided on a case by case basis after weighing the factors which argue for and against either. These should certainly include the potential risks of tampering with the natural rhythms of a body whose function is still quite mysterious.

b. The "Sacramentality" of Marriage

Surely, the importance of the Church's past and future involvement in marriage is already clear.

As a commitment that involves one's whole life and that of another person, marriage obviously involves God to a degree that other promises do not. Therefore, it must involve the Church. Sacramentally, the Church speaks for God accepting the couple's mutual promises. Thus, the marriage is not a "deal" that they have struck—a promise to which they must hold each other; it is their mutual promise to God to care for one another.[32]

The Church's administration of the couple's promises also establishes their union as something to be respected and supported by the Church at large. Moreover, the marriage becomes a "sacrament," a sacred sign of the love that God has for us all (cf. p.83). This makes the marriage a moral good to which the couple is committed even if they should conclude that they would both be happier elsewhere.

As the administrator of the promises and, thus, the true minister of the sacrament, the Church requires the competence to regulate marriage—particularly to decide the proper pre-requisites. Furthermore, since it is speaking for God, the Church must not participate in any promises that would not be meant or cannot be kept—if indeed there is outstanding reason to think so. This presumes a serious pre-marital interview. Given the fact that marriage involves so much the world has learned the hard way, the Church should normally require serious pre-marital preparation.

As a "sacrament," Catholic marriage presumes true and practiced faith. It also presumes that both persons are Catholic.[33] But, human realities being what they are, it would be impossible to expect that Catholics will marry only Catholics. Therefore, the Church has been wise to sanction the union of a Catholic to someone outside the Church.[34]

---

32. Let it be clear. In the realization that he is called to self-giving that ideally extends to everyone, the Christian also realizes that he cannot commit himself to everyone. But, perhaps, he can commit himself to someone. Thus, if he finds someone who inspires him to make this commitment, he (she) asks that person into his life—so that he (she) may be the object of his love.

33. It always has. The so-called "Pauline" privilege (cf. 1 Cor.7:6-16) permitted the re-marriage of a convert whose pagan spouse was a danger to his or her faith. The "Petrine" privilege permitted the same to someone who had always been a Catholic.

34. The Church has also been wise to "encourage" its members to marry someone of their own faith. Since faith should be the most important thing in a person's life, the inability to share faith should present a good marriage a real problem. At the same time, "mixed" marriages have been the source of many conversions. Nonetheless, they should not be sanctioned without some agreement about the raising of children which allows the Catholic person to be true to his (or her) faith.

2. *Indissolubility*

Marriage is a lifetime commitment. This is what the couple promises. This is what they promise God. Speaking for God, the Church must insist they keep this promise.

Historically, by insisting on the "indissolubility" of marriage, the Church has saved marriages and kept the institution sacred.

But, given the imperfection of persons, the Church has long acknowledged the right of separation, without the right to remarry. The Church has also acknowledged that marriage has certain pre-requisites—such as freedom to marry—which, if lacking, make it possible to declare an "annulment," a declaration that no real marriage ever existed.

Lately, the Church has acknowledged that marriage involves certain spiritual pre-requisites whose lack might not have been apparent at the time of the ceremony. (For example, the persons were not mature enough to know what they were doing.) Therefore, on the evidence of the circumstances of the subsequent—usually quick—breakup, the Church has come to declare that such a marriage never really existed.

Needless to say, this attempt to be compassionate to tragic situations is not without its problems. First of all, in determining the status of persons' promises *after* the fact, on the basis of their response to problems that have successfully been faced by every couple that never broke up, the modern practice of annulment is effectively ecclesiastical divorce. But, as such, it discriminates. The idea does not serve persons who, in honesty, are unwilling to deny that they had made a real marriage, which still failed. This leaves them to live alone regardless of the hardship this may involve.

Unable to permit the remarriage of the victims of such situations because of Jesus' injunctions on indissolubility (cf. Mt.19), the ontological change which the sacrament was thought to involve, and the perceived needs of the sacredness of marriage, the Church has had no way to address such situations which cause persons to suffer for their adherence to Church teaching. This is especially problematic because, often, despite the scars, a failed marriage will teach the persons more about loving than they might ever have learned otherwise.

In response to this problem, the Eastern Orthodox Churches have long offered a compromise solution. Called *economia,* it involves forgiveness for the failure of a marriage with permission for one non-sacramental re-marriage. This compromise accepts the fact that marriage presents a special problem for forgiveness because, as long as both parties are alive, there remains the possibility of reconciliation. Forgiveness puts an end to this possibility. Nonetheless, given the modern recognition that "conjugal" love is constitutive of marriage (cf. p.317), it is to be recognized that even though both parties are alive, their marriage can be dead. Though, ideally, true love never dies, not everyone can live up to this ideal. Moreover, even if love remains, the parties might not be able to live as husband and wife. For example, one might have been abandoned. Therefore, in such circumstances, if a person is *unable* to keep his (or her) promise, and not just *unwilling,* the Church can and should forgive a failed marriage. (Of course, in order to maintain the integrity of the institution, no such forgiveness should be granted without sufficient evidence that the marriage is irreparable.) This is not to say that the Church should reconcile itself to divorce; however, the war against divorce should be fought on the field of marriage preparation, marriage counseling and, most of all, in the general encouragement of people to love.

H) Extreme Unction

1. The Problem of the Anointing of the Sick

Coming to the last of the classical seven sacraments, Extreme Unction, the anointing of the sick, we come also to the most serious problem we have with regard to the sacraments. Already a problem for a variety of reasons (cf. p.315) decisively compounded by the problem of prayers of petition (cf. p.320), we must now admit: the anointing of the sick does not make people better except inasmuch as they believe it does, something that would not work if they were told the truth of what they should expect.

Therefore, now that we know that the sacramental system was a product of the development of doctrine, the continuing development of doctrine ought to abandon the anointing of the sick. An outgrowth of the Church's need to show the sick some sign of God's care, the pastoral care of the sick would better involve the explanation of providence—something that will never disappoint.

2. The Adaptability of the Sacramental System

Naturally, if the Church can take one away, it can add one.

One idea presents itself immediately. The Church has always had rites of burial, the obvious result of the extremely religious dimension of death. In the past, these were "sacramentals," rites which did not (could not) result in an ontological change but did inspire *ex opere operantis* (cf. p. 86). But, now that we say that sacraments result in a relational change—and we notice that the other sacraments "cover" the major moments of a person's life—it would appear that the Church should consider a sacramental Christian funeral which would state the person's final relation to the Church.[35]

Of course, a change in the status of Christian funerals does not mean that other sacramentals should not be retained. A useful distinction of degree, the blessing of persons and even objects—setting them aside for sacred purposes—might well be continued with the stipulation that this rite does not establish a permanent or demanding relationship between the Church and that which was blessed.

Section V: Mary and the Saints

A) Mary

1. The Marian Doctrines

Needless to say, Christian Materialism has much to say to the classical Marian doctrines. Since these doctrines have been so divisive of Christianity, it must be allowed to have its say.

Given the absence of original sin (cf. p.288), in a certain sense everyone is an immaculate conception (cf. p. 67). But, an immaculate conception which involves a freedom from sin, properly conceived, is impossible. Human nature is developmental and not perfectible in any respect. Furthermore, the theology of the incarnation no longer requires such a state for Jesus' mother. Since this requirement gave rise to the doctrine, the immaculate conception can be viewed as a primitive protective of the divinity of Christ.

The same thing can be said of belief in Mary's virginity (cf. p. 67).

The principal doctrine, the virginal conception was clearly a protective of the divinity of Christ—which also exonerated Mary from sexuality. But, it is no longer necessary. Actually, such a miracle would have provided Mary, and then Jesus, with information which would have prevented the world from coming to faith on its own.

Naturally, if the virginal conception is not necessary, there is no reason to insist that Mary remained a virgin for the rest of her life. Indeed, she and Joseph might have had other children. As a matter of fact, the New Testament mentions Jesus' brothers and sisters (e.g. Mt.13:55-56, Mk.6:3); some are even named, especially James. Though the aramaic word for "brother" is the same as the word for "cousin," this does not explain why the New Testament, written in Greek, used the word for brothers ("adelphoi") when a word for cousins ("anepsoi") was available. Since it would have been apologetically preferable to picture Jesus as an only child, the evidence to the contrary gains weight.

---

35. A "final confirmation" would allow the person to speak for himself. It would respond to the opportunity in the fact that modern medicine is only becoming more capable of predicting death—not to mention the progress that may one day offer almost everyone a "death day."

At this point, it is surely clear that we need a new way to understand the assumption (cf. p. 67). Always the doctrine supported by the least evidence, it is hopelessly qualified by all we have concluded about the soul, salvation, and state of the dead. Clearly, the assumption is another of those doctrines whose truth is to be seen in the service it provided the whole faith. It followed all that was already believed about Mary, not only on account of Jesus, but because the early Church remembered *her*.

2. The Future of Devotion to Mary

Let there be no mistake. Mary somehow gave impetus to most of what would eventually be believed about her. Though the Marian doctrines bespeak faith in Jesus, they could not have been formulated without the corroboration of Mary's real life.

According to the Scriptures, Mary was present throughout Jesus' life and she was always described in glowing terms. That she was present—and important—is evident in the fact that if she was not, she would not have been invented. That she was a person of great love is evident in the results of what must have been her major role in Jesus' upbringing. Indeed, considering that she must have had "the" influence upon Jesus, her singular role in the history of salvation is only to be affirmed. Considering the many reasons we have to picture her as a very simple woman,[36] this is especially noteworthy.

Actually, this is the essence of what has always been the value of "devotion" to Mary. Though motivated by belief in intercessory prayer (cf. p. 86)—and, therein, by the need for an approachable person to address the unapproachable God who was not to be bothered, especially by women—devotion to Mary also involved the inspirational value of reflecting upon her willingness to accept God's will. Although belief in intercessory prayer is no longer necessary, Mary still makes known that great things can be affected by simple people who simply love. This is the value of devotions; they teach us what is possible, and good.

B) Devotion to the Saints

Not unlike Mary—and not unlike Jesus—the saints reveal what is possible and good in a diversity of circumstances. Therefore, in the "canonization" of saints, the official endorsement of extraordinary lives, the Church teaches. But, the future of this practice will depend upon a scrutiny of its past.

The doctrine of the "communion" of the saints (cf. p. 86) was a prefig-

---

36. She was probably about fourteen when Jesus was born.

urement of the corporate nature of salvation (cf. p.348).

The "veneration" of the relics and other religious objects has the limited legitimacy of providing focal points for worship or other religious gesture.

The creation of religious objects—artistically—has the legitimacy of their inspirational value. Valuable on account of the symbolic nature of conceptual thought, the future of faith will determine what continues to inspire.

Section VI: Demons and Angels

Now, wanting the Church to teach the truth—and nothing but the truth—we turn to a consideration of the existence of demons and angels. We consider them in this order because the existence of demons presumes the possibility of angels.

A) Demons

Demons died with absolute sin. This puts to rest the always perplexing question of why God would allow evil beings to have the run of the earth, often preventing His people from using the freedom for which they were here.

Based in the need to explain 1) evil itself, 2) the "voice" that tempts one to sin (which is now understood in terms of the predictable struggle of conflicting desires), or 3) psychological illnesses which were not recognized as such, the idea of evil spirits was common to all primitive cultures.

But, the most obvious reason to abandon belief in demons is the fact that we must also abandon belief in angels.

B) Angels

Easily explained in the primitive idea that God was far too great to dirty His hands in a direct involvement in human affairs—an idea which is evident in the very word "angel" which means "messenger," belief in angels is not supported by sufficient evidence.

Actually, there is positive evidence that there are no angels. We have found that mortal, material life prepares us for life with God as true "others." If this was not necessary, if angels were spared this process, the question of the purpose of mortal, material life is hopelessly re-opened.

Section VII: Miscellaneous Questions

What remains are certain questions not conveniently answered during the course of the discussion.

A) The "Suffering" of Animals

Having insisted that creation involves no suffering that will not be redeemed (cf. p.351), what are we to think of the suffering of animals?

That animals exist is no mystery. They are products of what needed to be an evolutionary creation (cf. p.345). They substantiate the increasing complexity of which man is the product.

But, the suffering of animals will not be redeemed. Animals cannot look forward to eternity. They "cannot"; they are not self-conscious and they do not "want." It is self-consciousness that distinguishes man (cf. p.254). It is self-consciousness that makes him truly "other." It enables the self-determination which makes him capable of the eternity that only he desires. Therefore, we should expect that only man suffers. It is so. True suffering—a person's awareness that he is in pain—requires self-consciousness. Thus, animals do not suffer.

Though we should be cautious in describing the content of another's experience, we do know that the richness of any experience is contingent upon the complexity of the brain in which it takes place. Though insects may writhe when you step on them, making motions which—in humans— would mean agony, they feel no pain. Their writhe is all but mindless; it is caused by the self-protective nature of any brain. Other creatures may feel pain—the motivation to alleviate some problem—but still they do not suffer. Only creatures of self-conscious complexity can suffer. Indeed, even though *human* babies may utter a scream which—coming from an adult—would mean agony, they are not suffering. The ability to suffer accompanies the emergence of self-consciousness.

B) The Beginning of Personal Life

The answer to the question of the suffering of animals calls our attention to a much more important question: the beginning of personal life. The criterion of self-consciousness may appear to legitimize abortion, an issue which is commonly perceived to hinge upon the beginning of human life, itself an issue which is commonly perceived to hinge upon the arrival of the human soul.

Two things are immediately to be observed. First, any idea that human life begins at any moment other than conception is to play a word game. When else does a member of any species begin to exist? When else would a member of the human species begin to exist? The argument that an acorn is not an oak tree is invalid because, in the case of the acorn, the process of growth has not yet begun, and may never. But, there is no soul that makes a member of the human species a person. Described and distinguishable *only* in terms of self-consciousness, is it to be declared that there is no person until this point in human development?

The answer is not so simple. Self-consciousness emerges only gradually as the aggregate result of complexity. This graduality suggests that the entire pre-self-conscious life of an infant (or fetus) may involve the primitive form of a person that *can* be empowered to see God. The truth is, we do not know.[37] Therefore, it would be irresponsible to declare when a person exists.

Plainly, this does *not* stand in favor of abortion. Uncertainty rules in favor of life. The woodsman should not shoot into the rustling bush until he knows for sure that it is not a fellow hunter. So, too, our ignorance about the personhood of the unborn stands in favor of the greatest esteem that might be owed them.[38] Moreover, even apart from the issue of ignorance, it remains a long established principle that potential is always to be respected for what it is already becoming. Finally, the criterion of self-consciousness would not forbid the killing of infants up to the age of two.[39] After all, nothing of greater importance distinguishes the born from the unborn.[40] To insist that infanticide is not wrong is to establish a principle of disrespect for life which would surely be detrimental to humanity in the long run.

It is here to be noted that in the name of principle, there are times when the principle of respect for life still permits its taking. This could well be a consequence of the just war which may even require the taking of innocent lives. It could also permit a truly "therapeutic" abortion. In situations where carrying a child would "almost certainly"[41] kill the mother, the stalemate of life against life can be decided in favor of the "surely real" versus "possibly potential."[42] Historically, this conflict was resolved by

37. Actually, given the confusion caused by the ancient and medieval idea that the "seed" of the male contains the whole infant which is implanted in the woman, the Church has never declared a date by which the soul is infused.

38. This same principle stands in favor of a similar respect for the severely retarded.

39. This is normally the age of speech and first memories.

40. Plainly, the so-called "viability" argument—based upon the fact that the unborn depends upon the mother and cannot survive on its own—is invalid for the same reasons that we would protect the helpless infant after birth. This argument has also been compromised by developments in modern medicine which will soon make possible the extra-uterine survival of the baby from the moment of conception.

41. By "almost certainly" we are actually speaking of a "moral" degree of certainty that is arguably commensurate with the consequences of a given act.

42. Plainly, this would not warrant the death penalty, even in cases of murder. Indeed, everything we have discussed would normally mitigate against it.

taking steps to save the life of the mother even though these same steps would "indirectly" kill the child. This invoked the principle of "double effect" (cf. p.354). But, from now on, act and intent are better reconciled in favor of the "greatest good."

C) The End of Personal Life

The conflict of principles concerning the respect for life is also encountered in dealing with the preservation of life at the other end, life's end.

A new issue, it has been created by the progress of modern medicine and its ability to prolong life—even after brain death has taken place. It arises 1) when someone in great pain wishes to have his life ended, or 2) when concerned others, for whatever reasons, wish to end the life of someone perceived to be permanently unconscious. In both cases, what is desired is called "mercy killing," or "euthanasia."

Regardless of the motive, euthanasia is not justified. Even apart from the principle of respect for life, Christian Materialism makes clear that life is for living. It is given us by providence to prepare us forever. The person is called to co-operate by accepting life's struggle and grow through it. (This is what makes suicide wrong.) Therefore, as long as God gives life, the person is called to accept it. Surely no one should take it from him.

Still, certain clarifications should be made:

Brain death is death. If this were not obvious before materialism, it is certainly obvious now.

Moreover, since death is birth to eternal life, its avoidance at all costs is a denial of faith. Therefore, allowing a person to die when spiritual growth has become impossible—the so-called "death with dignity" policy already endorsed by the Church[43]—is justified.

* * *

We have finally reached the proper place to deal with one last question which follows from the fact that materialism means that there is no soul separate from the body. As we have already seen, this means that the survival of death is not natural; a person is beholden to God to remember him (cf. p.343). But, how are we to view the fact that a person may "decline" during his life, if only because of the natural processes that make a certain senility all but unavoidable? Does this mean that he goes to God with less than he once had?

Of course not. Decline involves not the person's pattern but his parts. And

---

43. The "death with dignity" policy also involves the distinction between ordinary and extraordinary means of life support. Embracing not just necessities like food—whose withholding is killing—ordinary means also involve anything that would be done for a person whether or not he was dying.

God knows the effect of worn out parts. Therefore, when He re-creates the person, He corrects for said effect; and this reveals the personal progress that never ceased.

As to the decline that seems to take place when a good man goes bad, this simply reveals the limit of what goodness there was—and deep-down remains.

D) Extra-Terrestrial Life

The last question to be considered is surely the least urgent—the theological implications of the possibility of extra-terrestrial life.

To keep a proper perspective on this question, let us note the following:

The question is a real one. There are more than a million billion stars (cf. p.308); there are at least that many planets.[44] A certain percentage must be like earth—or otherwise suitable to support some form of life. Therefore, it would be scientifically irresponsible to insist that intelligent life did not emerge elsewhere, is not emerging now, or will not later.

But, this is not evidence that life did emerge elsewhere. We do not know whether the emergence of life required fantastically rare circumstances. As we saw, some scientists contend that the development of amino acids occurred against odds of billions or more to one (cf. p.173). What were odds against the development of the brain? We do not know. We do not know whether creation was designed to make the one universe home for one species of beings destined to share God's life.

But, any other self-conscious beings are God's children. Moreover, as creatures of the same creation, we will all be part of the one family in God. It is unthinkable that creatures we might see in the world, we would not see in heaven. No matter how different they may be, they too are made in God's image and they will see Him in their way. Therefore, they would complement what we see, and *vice-versa.*

The above does not mean that one revelation (ours) was meant to unify the universe. Indeed, we have no reason to be sure that all species will have discovered each other before the end of time. Moreover, by the time of space travel, they would long since have required the confirmation which revelation involves. Therefore, it is to be presumed that the revelation best suited to particular species would have been provided.

In conclusion, it is to be noted that if there are many species in the one family of God's children, the worldly success of each need not be the design of providence. Perhaps the failure of one world has been (or will be)

---

44. Distance has precluded the observation of planets of other stars. Nonetheless, we have no reason to doubt that they evolved as ours did. This does not mean that all stars have planets but, undoubtedly, some have many.

required by the nature of the design that best achieves God's over-all purposes. Though this would not seem necessary—especially since the histories of the various worlds might never or only briefly meet—we do not know. We do know that in the end creation will have produced exactly that family of beings best suited to share God's life for all eternity.

Chapter V: A Summary of the Synthesis

The time has come to take stock of what we have seen.

We saw how evolution caused Christianity to understand that it has always been an interpretation of reality, not its description. This allowed us to follow the progress of Christian thought through its semitic, hellenic and scholastic periods. We then examined the progress of problems as a new but unrecognized period began. This was eventually described as the rise of materialism, the only metaphysic in which evolution ever made sense. Thereupon, we saw the real but inadequate progress that was made as Christianity—Catholic Christianity—attempted to deal with evolution and modernity generally. This made it possible to identify the essence of Christianity and Catholicism.

The essence of Christianity in tow, we explored a true but creative materialism.

After pointing out the conflict of Christianity and materialism, we saw what could, and should, be maintained if the essence of Christianity were true.

Thus were we freed to see that materialism offers evidence that the essence of Christianity is true. Following the lead of this evidence, we offered solutions to the problems new and old.

These solutions reveal a breath-taking historical pattern. As we can now see, human history has been the progress of reason—belief only with good reason. This culminated in materialism—and the realization that reality is one. But, human history has also been the progress of faith—a knowledge of God and His love. This has culminated in universal salvation—and the realization that humanity is one.

Founded upon evidence that could no longer be ignored, Christian Materialism leaves the nature of God Himself the rightful, sole, true mystery. It reconciles the dual demands of faith and reason, grace and nature, free will and determinism. It proves providence but leaves an essential role for man's mortal life. (It offers man the opportunity to make an eternal difference but it absolves him of the possibility that he will make an eternal mistake.)

Though Christian Materialism involves the abandonment of much that was once considered essential, it replaces what is abandoned with appealing ideas which embrace the truth in what everyone has seen—the "sensus fidelium" (cf. footnote p. 177) of the whole world. It offers a way to Christian unity at a time when such would otherwise be unthinkable. It has an apologetic strength which will evangelize the world even as it assures the world that, in the end, all will be well.

Conclusion

The State of the Faith

Though Part IV concluded to the assurance that, in the end, all will be well, it also involved the insistence that God's will requires human effort. And human effort is especially needed now. Let it be said. Things are bad and unless courageous steps are taken, they will only get worse—much worse.

Things *are* bad. Christianity is currently in the midst of an almost five hundred year decline, the end of which is nowhere in sight. Even before evolution brought so much to the fore, the faith in all its forms had already lost the esteem of most of the intellectual leadership of the West. This was sure to lead to what has happened since. With prosperity and the advent of mass communication and education, the ideas of the leadership are being communicated to the public at large. With the explosion of progress through and after the Second World War, an entire generation has lost faith and is raising another without it.

Though statistics will always be disputed, it is still safe to say that the practice of faith has declined dramatically in recent decades. Fewer than fifty percent of baptized Catholics attend Mass faithfully. Among young adults, the figure is closer to ten percent. (Vocations have declined more than dramatically.) Plainly, the Church is becoming a geriatric society and it is getting older every day.

And it is bound to get older faster. The disaffection of today's young adults has taken place despite the faith and example of their parents. What is to be expected of their children, who, in ever smaller numbers, attend Catholic school or receive the equivalent in religious instruction? Plainly, the decline is bound to accelerate at a geometric rate. (This will only be aggravated by the effect of declining vocations.)

Declining numbers, particularly declining numbers of credible spokespeople, will only add to the increasingly a-Christian climate of what will surely become an ever more modern society. Beyond the effects of what is called "peer pressure," this situation will be an increasingly effective teacher of the idea that the Church has nothing to say. (It will further decimate the ranks of potential candidates for the ecclesial leadership that will be needed in order to turn the situation around.)

Let there be no mistake. The problem *is* one of faith. Although the typical person will not admit he has no faith—or has lost it—his is almost invincible agnosticism that he had to learn somewhere. In short, he has learned what the intellectual leaders of society have indirectly taught him in school and on television. He has not learned the faith of his fathers. He does not believe it with sufficient certainty to motivate action, not in a world that allows and encourages him to gratify desires that presume less maturity and require less work.

The crisis of faith has been aggravated by the explosion of progress, and especially prosperity, that followed World War II. What happened was tragically well-intentioned. The explosion of prosperity brought leisure and a surplus of energy. And, with nothing better to do, a whole generation of new parents decided to live for, or at least through, their children—their fewer children. Thus did they teach their children that each is the center of his own little universe. This idea has proved an obstacle to the growth that would inevitably contradict it.

Even where there has been growth, and some have found that the relentless gratification of immature needs is a fundamentally dissatisfying "bore"—with the most sensitive of persons enduring the "anguish" of life without meaning or hope—very few have found their way to traditional faith. Indeed, excepting those who sacrifice themselves intellectually and emotionally for membership in cults, the otherwise sensitive and sensible person has found that he has nowhere to go.

Of course, the Church has not always appeared the place to go. Too often has it caused, or simply allowed, itself to appear hypocritical or cold. Its clergy have driven people away—about half as often as people claim. Poor Sunday services served only to diminish faith. Of course, during times past, the most unintelligible of the services, conducted by the most notorious of characters, were still well attended by those who *knew* they had to be there.

Indeed, though much has been done to renovate the life of the community, the clergy, and the liturgy, the decline has only accelerated. Though some see this as reason to return to the past, a return to the past is neither possible nor wise. It is not possible because you can never go back. It is not wise because the past has already failed. The reform must continue.

But, the reform will not succeed until credibility is re-established. And this will not happen without major developments in doctrine—the creation of a Christian Materialism.

Let it here be stated. Even though love is the most powerful teacher of Christian faith—and an essential sign of its credibility—love itself needs credibility. Love needs reason, good reason, and this only Christian Materialism can provide.

The Need to Complete the Work Begun By Vatican II

The Church needs to complete the work begun by Vatican II—the christianization of evolution. What should this involve?

First, the Church must accept Christian Materialism. This must extend to the reformulation of its positions on the most important "moral" matters.

Then, the entire package must be apologetically stated within a universal "catechism."

The Church must also undertake those changes in government, organization and ministerial life which human progress has already required. (The changes in ministerial life will serve to attract more, and more qualified persons to full-time ministry. In time, the inherent importance of this work will begin to re-attract the upper-most qualified persons that society can produce.) A surplus of ministers will address the abundance of worthwhile things that will need to be done. And it will see that Church policies are carried out.

The liturgical reform should continue; but the principle *Legam credendi lex statuat supplicandi* should be reversed; it should be "Let the law of belief determine the law of prayer."

It is only partly for this reason that the modern Church must do what the ancient Church felt free to—to write its own sacred texts. We have now come so far from the literal truth of scriptural texts that the attempt to teach through them would surely be inefficient to a degree approaching impossible. New sacred texts would not only offer a more straightforward, systematic treatment of the faith *per se,* they would employ the examples and imagery to which we can better relate. And a new "lectionary"—for use on Sunday—would surely be open to cultural adaptation.

Sunday must be the center of efforts to re-educate the faithful—to get our house in order—the first part of any plan to rebuild the Western Church and evangelize the world.

But, nothing done at the local level will succeed without a change in the cultural climate which can only be affected through the mass media. In ways that reflect the dignity of Him for whom it speaks, the Church must get His truth to the alienated, the unchurched and everyone else. Particular efforts must be directed at the intellectual leadership of society because it is here that the battle for everyone else's ideas is to be won. (The use of mass media will serve to put the Church's best foot forward, partly compensating for lacunae at local levels.)

First, the Church must obtain attention. It must explain that it has something to offer—the good news of man's origin and destiny. Though this knowledge is naturally appealing, it must be presented in terms of a critique of the alternative and a call to greatness. It must be presented apologetically, beginning with the truth that people already see.

Obviously, all of this would require the approbation of an Ecumenical Council. Only in the debate of a council will the whole truth emerge. Only in the agreement of a council will there be confidence that the right thing has been done. Such an event would capture the attention of the entire world. It would herald a new era, making it possible for everyone to make a new start. A Vatican III, the christianization of materialism, must complete the work of Vatican II, the christianization of evolution.

The Need to Act

Dramatic an act as Vatican III would be, dramatic has been the decline it is meant to reverse.

Let it be clear. A third Vatican Council is not only necessary, it is needed now. With each passing day, the decline deepens further, draining the Church's resources across the board. Moreover, diminishing is the place in society that the blood of the martyrs gave the Christian West. This must not be squandered.

The Church must not give away what it took centuries to build up. Contrary to what some would say, it must not throw in the towel of defeatism and accept the role of persecuted "remnant" in a world that it created. It must not reconcile itself to a move to the so-called third world which is striving tc become just like the first and will eventually succeed. It must not retreat from the places where people have progressed. It must instead go aggressively into modernity and assume its rightful place of leadership.

Though this will involve the abandonment of much that was believed on faith, the Church's leaders must trust their faith and act in accord with the truth they have always believed—that God is the author of all truth, they are His spokesmen, and nothing will derail His plans.

The time for reform is *never* now. Therefore, the truth must make it now. Inaction cost the Reformation. Action will prepare the Church to respond to the existential crisis that society is just beginning to experience. Inaction will cost centuries of progress. Action will reap rewards of infinite value.

Granted, great change will still take time. Of course, the pace of change is itself changing, so who knows? In any case, being on course makes possible a patience we should not pursue otherwise.

Either way, we can still know that no matter what happens, God's will is still being done. He is preparing us to share His life. And we shall share His life forever.

Fin

Acknowledgments

Contrary to custom, these acknowledgments occur at the end of work, not the beginning. Perhaps the reason is obvious. Many to whom this author owes so much would not have appreciated his public gratitude. Nonetheless, they know who they are, and their interest, questions and criticism leave me forever in their debt.

I can and must mention my family and friends. Their support sustained me for the ten years it took to bring this work from thought to print.

I owe particular thanks to Mrs. Camille Cormier, my mother, who deciphered and typed the original manuscript, Mr. John Britton, Jr. who proofread each of the many drafts, Miss Christine Spernal who put the final draft into the form of pages, and Mr. Michael LaForge, my business advisor.